AF361503

NISHIDA KITARŌ'S CHIASMATIC CHOROLOGY

NISHIDA KITARŌ'S CHIASMATIC CHOROLOGY

Place of Dialectic, Dialectic of Place

John W. M. Krummel

Indiana University Press

Bloomington and Indianapolis

This book is a publication of

Indiana University Press
Office of Scholarly Publishing
Herman B Wells Library 350
1320 East 10th Street
Bloomington, Indiana 47405 USA

iupress.indiana.edu

♾ The paper used in this publication meets the minimum
requirements of the American National Standard for Information
Sciences—Permanence of Paper for Printed Library Materials,
ANSI Z39.48-1992.

Cataloging information is available from the Library of Congress.

ISBN 978-0-253-01753-6 (cloth)
ISBN 978-0-253-01786-4 (ebook)

Manufactured in the United States of America

1 2 3 4 5 20 19 18 17 16 15

To Reiner Schürmann

Contents

Acknowledgments

I WOULD LIKE to thank Professors Shigenori Nagatomo, J. N. Mohanty, and Mahmoud Ayoub for intellectual help, advice, support, and encouragement during the composition of this project. I would like to express special gratitude to Professor Nagatomo for helping me get started in reading and translating Japanese philosophical texts. I also want to thank Professors Kazashi Nobuo and Inaga Shigemi, who were helpful in pointing me toward some useful sources. I would like to express my appreciation to Professors Agnes Heller, Richard Bernstein, John Maraldo, Fred Dallmayr, Graham Parkes, and the late Joan Stambaugh, who helped me along the way with words of encouragement throughout this project. Special thanks are due to Bret Davis, an editor of this book series, for showing interest in and supporting my work. I express my gratitude also to Professors Robert Carter and Jason Wirth for reviewing and commenting on my manuscript. And I thank the production team at Indiana University Press, especially Dee Mortensen and Sarah Jacobi, for their work, enthusiasm, and helpfulness. I am also very much in debt to Hobart and William Smith Colleges for providing me with a grant from the Faculty Research Fund during 2011–2012, which helped me complete this book. I cannot thank enough my parents, Fusako and the late John William Krummel, who provided me with support and understanding during the many years of my studies and research leading up to and through this project.

NISHIDA KITARŌ'S CHIASMATIC
CHOROLOGY

Introduction

Many who have read the writings of the seminal philosopher of the Japanese Kyoto School, Nishida Kitarō (西田幾多郎) (1870–1945), have been mystified by his enigmatic assertions regarding "contradictory self-identity," "inverse correspondence," "continuity of discontinuity," and "self-negation," which seem to shamelessly defy any allegiance to the logical law of non-contradiction. All these ideas pertain to his "dialectic" (*benshōhō* 弁証法) and his philosophy of "place" (*basho* 場所), which together characterize what has come to be called "Nishidian philosophy" (Nishida *tetsugaku* 西田哲学), belonging to the later half of his oeuvre. In this work I propose to explicate Nishida's dialectic of place—a dialectic of mutual "self-negation" (*jiko hitei* 自己否定) that results in his notion of "absolutely contradictory self-identity" (*zettai mujunteki jikodōitsu* 絶対矛盾的自己同一)—vis-à-vis Mahāyāna Buddhist thought and Hegelian dialectical philosophy and in terms of what I will call a "chiasmatic chorology." What I mean by the latter phrase, in brief, is that Nishida's so-called dialectic seeks to express the concretely real in its complexity that proves to be both a *chiasma* of (over-)inter-determinations and an undeterminable field or *chōra* that makes room for these determinations. Nishida as a philosopher was concerned with the perennial questions of metaphysics, questions concerning the one and the many, identity and difference, being and non-being, and so on, in the determination of things, including the world, the cosmos, the human self, and their interrelations. These concerns inform his epistemological interests, for example, the relationship between the epistemological subject and its object or the determining act of knowledge and its determined content. I find that the metaphysical and the epistemological in Nishida's thought are inseparable: they mirror each other as self-expressions of the real. One's self-awareness mirrors the self-awareness of reality predicated on a self-determining place. What is mirrored or expressed precisely is what Nishida regards as the "contradictory" or "dialectical" nature of reality, wherein all that is is implaced. Nishida's interest in the interrelationality between opposites and among distinct elements becomes most pronounced and most developed dialectically under the rubric of "contradictory identity" in his later years, from the 1930s to his death. (Commentators differ in exactly how his oeuvre is to be segmented. I shall adopt a fourfold periodization for heuristic purposes.)[1] It is during this period that Nishida develops his conception of "contradictory self-identity" in a "dialectical" fashion to encompass not only the internal self-reflective experience of consciousness—the concern of his earlier works—but also, beyond that, the historical unfolding of reality in man's relationship to his environment.

Throughout his works we notice Nishida's employment of the terminology of Hegelian dialectics, not only in the later works but even in the earlier ones. Yet Nishida's conceptions of "contradictory identity" and "self-negation," along with his related conception of "absolute nothing" (*zettai mu* 絶対無), seem to owe much to the Mahāyāna Buddhist tradition with its "dialectic of emptiness," that is, the line of thought that can be traced back to the non-dualistic notions concerning inter-dependence (e.g., between form and emptiness or *saṃsāra* and *nirvāṇa*) and the lack of ontological independence (*svabhāva;* "own-being" or "self-nature") in the *Prajñāpāramitā sūtras* and Nāgārjuna's Mādhyamika philosophy, via their subsequent East Asian appropriations in Tiantai (天台), Huayan (華厳), and Chan/Zen (禅) thought. Although Nishida's formulations of the issue make ample usage of Western philosophical concepts in general and Hegelian dialectics in particular, the core content of his conception of dialectic of place appears Mahāyānistic. One of my purposes is to clarify Nishida's dialectical thinking of "contradictory identity" in relation to that line of thinking in the Mahāyāna traditions and to the dialectics of Hegel, that is, to clarify in what regard it owes allegiance to them and wherein it diverges from them. Wherein lies the Hegelian influence and wherein the Mahāyāna influence? In seeking the answer to these questions, we cannot ignore how Nishida viewed his dialectic of contradictory self-identity vis-à-vis Buddhism and Hegelianism. And what are the merits or demerits of this appropriation of Hegel's language, especially in light of further developments of his ideas by some of his pupils?[2]

While attempting to answer these questions dealing with the relationship of Nishida's thought to its forebears, this work will underscore that aspect of his dialectical thinking wherein lies its unique and distinct creativity. I shall characterize (especially in the concluding chapters) Nishida's dialectic of contradictory identity and place as a "chiasmology" or "chiasmatic chorology" to emphasize the inter-dimensional and placial complexity involved in his so-called dialectic. What I mean is a dialectic of place (basho) as encompassing both the vertical interrelations between whole and part, indeterminate and determined, absolute and finite, and nothing and beings, on the one hand, and the horizontal interrelations among finite determinate individual beings, on the other; and furthermore in both the temporal and the spatial dimensions, that is, the diachrony of the unfolding of history, collectively or individually, and the synchrony among correlative individuals, as well as between individual and environment. The interrelations are inter-determinations, while the field or place itself remains undetermined. "Chiasmatic" and "chiasmology" refer to the chiasma of those vertical and horizontal, spatiotemporal as well as ontological and meontological, cross-dimensional interrelationalities that come into play in Nishida's dialectical thinking of "contradictory identity." In addition, I call Nishida's dialectics a "chorology" in reference both to his general characterization of his thinking—already during his middle period but expanded and developed in his final period—as a "logic of place" (*basho no ronri* 場所の論理, *bashoteki ronri* 場所的論理) and to his explicit characterization of this "place" (basho) in Greek (Plato's) terms as chōra (χώρα). This notion of chōra in its chiasmatic self-formations (via self-negation) provides us with a unique standpoint from which to view Nishida's dialectic vis-à-vis Hegel's dialectic of the idea along with the Mahāyāna motif of self-emptying emptiness. In reading Nishida, I shall thus argue for a "chiasmology" against the ousiology of a substance-oriented metaphysics, and for a "chorology"—a term borrowed from John Sallis—against the "ideology" (idea-logy) of an idea/concept-governed metaphysics. The use of the terms "chōra" and "chiasma" in discussing Nishida allows me to bring him into dialogue with some major figures of contemporary Continental philosophy, who have appropriated these terms in different ways.

In summary, the work will thus be guided by two overarching concerns: (1) the relation of Nishida's dialectic of contradictory identity and self-negation to its forebears, Mahāyāna Buddhism and Hegelian dialectics; and (2) the distinctness of that dialectic as a "chiasmatic chorology." It will be an analysis of Nishida's dialectics vis-à-vis Mahāyāna non-dualism and Hegelian dialectics and its explication in terms of a "chiasmology" or "chiasmatic chorology."

The Problem and Its Significance

Nishida's dialectical thought involving his notions of contradictory self-identity and self-negation owe much to certain intellectual predecessors, especially Mahāyāna Buddhism and Hegelian philosophy, from which he inherited a set of concerns, concepts, and terms. Juxtaposing Buddhist and Hegelian concepts in a preliminary discussion of Nishida's forebears will enable us to see that their synthesis in Nishida was not necessarily ready-made. Awareness of their essential differences will safeguard us from the temptation to uncover through their comparison some sort of naïvely assumed perennial truth. Such awareness in a look at his inheritance also provides a foundational background from which to view Nishida's unique contribution. We will see what aspects of each tradition he inherits and wherein he develops their ideas and diverges from them. There is a temptation to argue that what Nishida took from Hegel in his dialectical thinking was mainly the terminology, while much of the content of his dialectical thinking in regard to self-contradiction and self-negation and related ideas may be traceable to Buddhism's Mahāyānistic thinking of emptiness. Especially in his conception of the "absolute nothing" (zettai mu), an idea inseparable from his dialectic, his kinship with Buddhism (as well as Daoism) may be undeniable.

Nishida's development of the interrelationality inherent in "contradictory identity" and "absolute nothing" is reminiscent of ideas traceable to the *Prajñāpāramitā sūtras* and furthered in East Asian Buddhism. And his notions of "inverse correspondence" (*gyakutaiō* 逆対応) and "mutual self-negation" also point back to the Mahāyāna logic of emptiness and inter-dependence as opposed to the Western metaphysics and epistemologies of synthesis or subsumption under a general concept, traceable to Platonist idealism, of which Hegelian sublation (*Aufhebung*) may be the prime exemplar.

At the same time, however, I do not intend to argue that Nishida's dialectic is entirely, and nothing but, Mahāyānistic or Buddhistic. We cannot ignore the significant concept of the concrete universal (*gutaiteki ippansha* 具体的一般者) that Nishida inherited from Hegelian thought early on in developing his epistemology of basho. We also cannot ignore the various Western philosophical trends—especially Neo-Kantian dualism—to which Nishida was responding and that shaped the development of his thinking toward his basho theory and then his dialectics of interactivity in the world. (Emil Lask would be a huge influence in that regard.) If one looks at Nishida's thinking as a whole, it would be difficult to place it within any one tradition of the East or the West. The eclectic nature of Nishida's philosophical project—that is, its being composed of elements drawn from a variety of sources—precludes it from being confined within traditional and specific boundaries. For this reason I also want to emphasize the truly global stature of Nishida's dialectical philosophy. As a marvelous synthesis of various strands of thought from the Eastern and the Western traditions, it provides a model for a world philosophy in this global age, but in such a way that it also introduces one to a new way of experiencing and seeing the world. For example, Nishida's understanding of the unfolding of history and man's role therein, involving interaction with the environment together with a bodily prāxis (πρᾶξις)—even when it is relatable to the general Buddhist concepts of inter-dependence or emptiness and even Zen prāxis—is a unique and new development when we view it in light of the history of Buddhist thought. And his development of the notion of the basho or place of absolute nothing as a "place" in its utter indeterminacy, a place that permits the "contradictory identity" of and in all things—again while developing the Mahāyāna notions of emptiness and inter-dependence—takes us beyond the traditional Buddhistic modes of expression and into a uniquely Nishidian formulation and mode of thinking. Nishida's conception of self-identity via contradiction involves the self-negation of this place of absolute nothing as the indeterminate groundless ground of the world of individual and correlative beings. It is this vertical relationship of an absolute nothing to finite beings in their horizontal correlativity—as a crisscrossing relation of mutual self-negation—that Nishida designates "inverse correspondence" (gyakutaiō). While seemingly rooted in, or at least commensurable with, certain Mahāyāna notions, Nishida's notion of "contradictory self-identity" as explicated in such a multi-dimensional chiasma, and its "placial" (*bashoteki* 場所的) or "chōratic" nature in conjunction with a bodily prāxis—that is, embodiment as dynamic implacement—encompasses a complexity that extends beyond the previous formulations of Nishida's forebears, Buddhist or Hegelian.[3] If we keep this in mind, we cannot simply reduce the creativity of his dialectical thinking to any of its forbearing traditions.

To sort all of this out, I will first examine the major influences to which Nishida was responding, which led him to develop his enigmatic dialectics. In particular, I will examine the dialectic in Hegel's works and the non-dualistic thinking involving emptiness and inter-dependence in the various Mahāyāna schools of thought. I will then look at Nishida's development of his dialectical ideas in relation to those influences. The resulting picture of his thought will not be simple.

In viewing Nishida's unique contribution vis-à-vis its manifold influences, I want to argue in the end that although the core content of the sense of his dialectical ideas is to a large degree Mahāyānist, and the vocabulary and formulations expressing it in many of his writings sound Hegelian, the cross-dimensional complexity of the dialectic that encompasses bodily prāxis in history and the founding of this dialectic on a notion of "place" (basho) are uniquely Nishidian developments. His dialectic of contradictory identity is a dialectic of place, which we can further understand, if we are permitted the liberty of stepping beyond Nishidian terminology, as a "chiasmatic chorology." It is such a chorology of a place of nothing, allowing for that crisscrossing inter-dimensionality of inter-dependent matter, but as non-substantial—a chiasma of being and non-being—that places Nishida's dialectic not only beyond previous Buddhistic formulations in unfolding their implications but also in stark opposition to Hegel's idealism, which is a dialectic founded on the idea or concept. This brings us to the question of the adequacy or inadequacy of the use of Hegelian terminology or, more generally, the language of nineteenth-century German philosophy—and even of the language of a dialectic in general or of a logic even of place—in capturing Nishida's matter of thought.

Why this look at Nishida's dialectic vis-à-vis Buddhism and Hegel now? It is evident that the world today in its globalization is unfolding its chiasmatic nature as a place of contradictions and oppositions. Because of the technological facilitation of communication and travel, regions and horizons hitherto isolated now must face one another and learn to deal with the manifest multiplicity of— and differences in—ways of thinking, living, and being. Philosophers of the West can no longer pretend to remain isolated within their own tradition. Reflective traditions other than one's own can no longer be ignored as irrelevant. Just as Japanese thinkers have been dealing with the influx of Western ideas since the diplomatic opening of Japan in the mid- to late 1800s, Western philosophers can no longer ignore the influx of non-Western ways of being. A little over a century ago Nishida Kitarō was at the forefront in the intellectual encounter between East and

West in Japan. Our situation today is not completely different. The globalizing trend that commenced in the 1800s, however, proceeds even more extensively and intensively today and with broader ontological impact and greater destructive force. Nishida's thinking, therefore, cannot be totally irrelevant to our contemporary situation. With its cross-cultural inheritances whereby Buddhism meets Hegel and other Western philosophers, Nishida's thought can serve as a paradigm for today's cross-cultural philosophizing.

Comparing texts, ideas, and authors from different periods or cultures is certainly a risky undertaking. We need to be aware of the contextual background of their cultural and historical milieus to see what contributed to their formulations, what are they responding to, what led them to develop their ideas in such a manner, whether positively or negatively. Comparative philosophy is no simple endeavor, especially when the theories and ideas being compared are products of different environments without any direct connections of influence or reference to one another. That indeed is the case with Buddhism and Hegel. However, in this case, the philosophy of Nishida—a world philosopher who incorporated insights from the Eastern traditions, including Buddhism, along with those of Western philosophy, including Hegel—provides a somewhat sturdier bridge on which we may experience the coming together of distinct horizons, Hegel and Buddhism, albeit through the lens of Nishida's eyes. A look at Nishida as the locus wherein such ideas from different traditions and contexts and periods come together, for better or worse, will in turn allow us to see how we—a century later in an increasingly complex, inter-horizonal, globalized world—might be able to engage in a similar sort of philosophical undertaking while emulating his successes and avoiding his mistakes.

I would like to underscore that what I intend here is philosophy rather than simply history or biography. My aim is a thorough explication of Nishida's dialectical philosophy, especially in its mature stages. But in addition to explicating Nishida's thought, I will read him philosophically. Philosophy, as I understand it, is an inquiry into the meaning of being, existence, and life. It can never be reduced to the history of ideas. This is not to say that history is useless or should be ignored. Historical knowledge, as well as biographical knowledge, can contribute to philosophical understanding. But the analysis of Nishida's thought here is intended to be more than a regurgitation of his ideas or their placement within the history of philosophy or within his biography. To be true to Nishida's spirit as a thinker of his time and place while remaining authentic to our context as philosophers, we ought to philosophize with him in a manner befitting our contemporary situation, our existential wherein or basho. That is to say that this work will engage in a critical hermeneutic of Nishida's project that at times will go beyond what Nishida may have intended or could foresee. In reading Nishida, I philosophize with him, and I invite my readers to do the same in reading this text.

Stages in Nishida's Lifework

The purpose of this work is to look into Nishida's so-called dialectic, and my thesis takes as its standpoint his mature thought, wherein we observe the full blossoming of the dialectic. Yet it is still necessary to look at his oeuvre as a whole, for we cannot ignore the development of his thought leading up to that blossoming. We need to see in what way his dialectic emerged and developed over the decades of his writing career. For this purpose, we need to pay attention to the conspicuous differences that emerge in the course of his thinking and warrant the division of that course into stages or periods. Nishida's commentators have divided his lifework in different ways, into two, three, four, five, or even six stages.[4] For example, Sueki Takehiro divides Nishida's lifework into three periods, centering on (1) the thought of "pure experience" (*junsui keiken* 純粋経験) (1911–1915); (2) the thought of "place" (basho) (1917–1933); and (3) the thought of the "absolute dialectic" (*zettai benshōhō* 絶対弁証法) (1934–1946). What unifies them for Sueki is the thought of "self-awareness" or "self-realization" (*jikaku* 自覚), and, briefly put, he takes the three periods to correspond to three stages of self-awareness: self-awareness begins with the immediacy of "pure experience," in its process of unfolding awakens to the structure of "place," and finally comes to recognize the world of the "absolute dialectic." He bases this thesis on what he takes to be a "thorough immanentism" in Nishida's philosophy. My focus, however, is on the emergence of the dialectic that, in my reading, ultimately exceeds in its complexity any dichotomization between immanent and transcendent.

Many commentators writing in English seem to have for the most part followed a comparable threefold division of Nishida's oeuvre, but with differences in where some of the periods begin or end and where the focus lies. We must keep in mind, however, that the division of his oeuvre into distinct stages or periods is, to some extent, an interpretive imposition. At the same time, nonetheless, we can acknowledge that Nishida in retracing his thought process in his 1936 preface to *Zen no kenkyū* (『善の研究』; *Inquiry into the Good*) divided his work into five stages, centered on the ideas of (1) "pure experience"; (2) "absolute will" (*zettai ishi* 絶対意志); (3) "place"; (4) "dialectical universal" (*benshōhōteki ippansha* 弁証法的一般者); and (5) "acting intuition" (*kōiteki chokkan* 行為的直観) (Z1 3).[5] For the sake of comprehending Nishida's work as a whole, it may be helpful to make use of a similar division as a heuristic device. I am more inclined to follow Nishida's fivefold division than Sueki's threefold division. Yet I fail to see a clear division between the fourth and the fifth stages in the fivefold scheme since the concepts of dialectical universal and acting intuition in many of his works of the later period/s are mutually implicative. Hence I would rather treat them as belonging to the same period. In order to account for significant developments in his thinking, I think that we can thus appropriately divide his lifework into four periods instead of three or five, the last two (third and fourth) periods comprising his so-called Nishidian philosophy. This is not to deny, however, that there is also a coherent theme that continues through the different periods of his thinking.

The four stages of Nishida's lifework may be set forth as follows: (1) 1911–1915: the psychologistic period; (2) 1917–1923: the voluntaristic period; (3) 1924–1932: the epistemological period; and (4) 1934–1945: the dialectical (or historical-cultural) period.[6] The first period is represented by the work *Zen no kenkyū* (*An Inquiry into the Good*) (1911). The major theme here is his concept of "pure experience" (junsui keiken). The second period is exemplified by two works, *Jikaku ni okeru chokkan to hansei* (『自覚に於ける直観と反省』; *Intuition and Reflection in Self-Awareness*) (1917),[7] which takes "self-awareness" (jikaku) and "absolute will" (zettai ishi) as its themes; and *Geijutsu to dōtoku* (『芸術と道徳』; *Art and Morality*) (1923),[8] which develops the idea of "absolute will." Three major works make up the third period, inaugurating what came to be called "Nishidian philosophy" (Nishida tetsugaku): *Hatarakumono kara mirumono e* (*From the Working to the Seeing*) (1927), *Ippansha no jikakuteki taikei* (『一般者の自覚的体系』; *The Self-Aware System of Universals*) (1930), and *Mu no jikakuteki gentei* (『無の自覚的限定』; *The Self-Aware Determination of Nothing*) (1932). In these works Nishida develops his theory of basho or place primarily in response to the epistemological dualism of the Neo-Kantians. During the fourth and final period, turning his attention to society and history, Nishida develops the dialectical implications of place, specifically the aspect of its "contradictory unity" (*mujunteki tōitsu* 矛盾的統一) or "contradictory self-identity" (*mujunteki jikodōitsu* 矛盾的自己同一), in the various concepts of the "dialectical universal" (benshōhōteki ippansha), the "historical world" (*rekishiteki sekai* 歴史的世界), and "acting intuition" (kōiteki chokkan). This period is represented by the two-volume *Tetsugaku no konpon mondai* (『哲学の根本問題』; *Fundamental Problems of Philosophy*) (1933–1934)[9] and the series of essays leading up to his death in 1945, including his final essay, "Bashoteki ronri to shūkyōteki sekaikan" (「場所的論理と宗教的世界観」; "The Logic of Place and the Religious Worldview").[10] However, for the purpose of this work, I will treat the first and second periods, when the dialectic is still nascent or only implicit, together in chapter 3. Chapter 4 will deal with the third period, and I will devote three chapters (chapters 5, 6, and 7) to the fourth and final period, when the dialectic has fully blossomed into view. Still developing at the time of Nishida's passing in 1945, the dialectic is most pronounced in its manifold aspects in this period. These three chapters will focus on those different aspects of the dialectic: acting persons, the dialectical universal, and religiosity. We can safely say that all these themes of the four periods are in fact linked as unfoldings of what Nishida was concerned with, and convinced of, throughout his philosophical life: the concrete, non-differentiated but dynamic foundation of everything.[11]

Outline

This work will be divided into three parts. The first part consists of preliminary investigations; the second part consists of an in-depth look into the development of Nishida's dialectic in the various periods of his oeuvre; and the third part is the conclusion of the inquiry. In part 1, the first chapter is a short overview of the development of Nishida's dialectic in response primarily to the philosophical issue of dualism, and the second chapter compares and contrasts the two conspicuous elements in Nishida's dialectic, Mahāyāna Buddhism and Hegel. Part 2, consisting of chapters 3 to 7, provides a more in-depth look at Nishida's dialectic in the various stages of the development of his thought from its inauguration in 1911 to his death in 1945. Part 3 provides conclusions with a close look at the relationship between Nishida and Hegel in chapter 8; a discussion of the relationship between Nishida and Mahāyāna, as well as religion in general, in chapter 9; explications of the concepts of chiasma and chōra in chapter 10; and some final questions and a brief look at the relevance of Nishida's dialectic for today's globalizing world in chapter 11. Parts 1 and 2 are more expository than part 3, and the emphasis is on clarity of presentation. Part 3 is more creative and original in its development of Nishida's ideas, especially in terms of chiasma and chōra and chiasmatic chorology. The reader must thus be forewarned that its style will differ from that of the first two parts, and philosophically it may be more challenging.

The bibliography at the end of this book contains all works that I have read or consulted in the course of researching for this work, including works that are not necessarily cited.

PART I

PRELIMINARY STUDIES

1 From Aristotle's Substance to Hegel's Concrete Universal

The Development of Nishida's Dialectic

CHAPTERS 1 AND 2 consist of preliminary investigations, which I feel are necessary before I embark on a detailed look at the dialectic and its development in Nishida's oeuvre. In this chapter I look at the development of dialectics in Nishida's thinking as a response to the two trends of substantialism and dualism that he noticed in Western philosophy. His search for a non-substantialist and non-dualistic alternative is what led him to the dialectical way of thinking. In this development we see him reacting and responding to the ideas of Aristotle and the Neo-Kantians while also struggling with and appropriating alternative notions presented by thinkers such as Henri Bergson, Johann Gottlieb Fichte, William James, and J. S. Haldane. In his search for a non-substantialist and non-dualistic alternative, Nishida turned initially to Hegel's dialectics and appropriated his concepts and terms. It was through this encounter with Western philosophical theories that Nishida eventually developed his unique theory of basho or "place" in the 1920s. From that notion of place, Nishida then unfolded his dialectical understanding of the world in the 1930s. Nevertheless, in this development of what came to be called "Nishidian philosophy" (Nishida tetsugaku 西田哲学), we also notice insights that suggest, or at least are commensurable with, ideas of Mahāyāna Buddhism traceable to the *Prajñāpāramitā sūtra*s. To what degree, then, was Nishida a Hegelian, and to what degree is his thinking Mahāyānist?

After tracing the general development of Nishida's dialectics as a response to Western philosophy, I will investigate (in chapter 2) Hegel and Mahāyāna Buddhism—both of which seem to provide alternatives to Aristotle's substantialism—and the issue of their commensurability. To what extent are Hegel's dialectical ideas and Mahāyāna's non-dualistic notions compatible? Examining each in its own terms and in relation to each other should prepare us to better understand Nishida's dialectic vis-à-vis Hegel and Buddhism.

A dialectical mode of thinking that deals with the interrelationships between opposing terms is evident from the beginnings of Nishida's oeuvre. It becomes especially pronounced, however, during the 1930s and 1940s. How did Nishida come to formulate his thinking in such terms of benshōhō (弁証法) (dialectics) and,

13

in particular, his enigmatic concept of the unity of opposites or contradictory self-identity (mujunteki jikodōitsu 矛盾的自己同一)? One way to answer this difficult question is to look at the various trends in Western philosophy to which he was responding. Two trends that are especially significant in the development of Nishida's philosophy are substantialism, traceable to Aristotle, and epistemological dualism, which reached its culmination in Neo-Kantianism. One might even assert that Nishida's work as a whole is an attempt to provide a non-substantialist and non-dualistic alternative to those two related ways of viewing the world. This alternative is what eventually takes shape in the dynamic form of a dialectical non-dualism.

The start of Nishida's original thinking, as exemplified in his 1911 *Zen no kenkyū* (『善の研究』; *An Inquiry into the Good*), was also a break with the dominant philosophical trends of Meiji (1868–1912) Japan. His attempt to find a pre-reflective unity of experience and reality in the concrete, however, coincides with a general trend noticeable in European philosophy at the turn of the twentieth century. This was a period when philosophers such as Wilhelm Dilthey, Henri Bergson, William James, and Edmund Husserl, among others, were similarly attempting to surmount the barriers of traditional metaphysics. Although Nishida showed interest in these contemporary trends, he nevertheless found their formulations in the end to be inadequate. Against Henri Bergson's conceptions of the *élan vital* and pure duration, Nishida felt the need to emphasize the primacy of spatiality in terms of a place (basho 場所) wherein things interact not only diachronically but also synchronically. Moving not only beyond naïve materialism or mechanism as well as idealism and the dichotomy between materialism and idealism, Nishida also felt the need to surmount both Husserl's phenomenology of mere consciousness and J. S. Haldane's restriction of a holism between individual and environment to the biological realm. Nishida in the 1930s instead came to emphasize the significance of the sociohistorical world of human interactivity and its self-creative dialectics as providing the standpoint of a concrete reality wherein we find ourselves first and foremost implaced. In his attempts to overcome their difficulties, however, Nishida also borrowed much insight from these thinkers. But the Western thinker most conspicuous in Nishida's formulations of a concrete dialectic is G. W. F. Hegel. This has even led some commentators to claim that Nishida is a sort of Hegelian. On the other hand, many have noted the influence of Buddhist insights, in particular, from the Mahāyāna tradition and its *Prajñāpāramitā* roots. We are thus led to ask the following questions: To what extent is Nishida's thought Hegelian, and to what extent is it Buddhist? And to what degree is Nishida's appropriation of Hegelian concepts and terms adequate for expressing his insights concerning concrete reality?

With these questions and thoughts in mind, I would like to begin my investigation with a look into what initiated Nishida's philosophical voyage in the first place, leading him to develop his theory of place and eventually to unfold it in the dialectical terms of a "contradictory self-identity" or "continuity of discontinuity" (*hirenzoku no renzoku* 非連続の連続). To do this, I will first focus on the two significant trends that I mentioned earlier, and that in the history of Western thinking are linked: Aristotelian substantialism and Neo-Kantian dualism. There is a connection between substantialism and the epistemological issue of the thing-in-itself in Kantian thought. This is also related to the issue of the relationship between the epistemological subject and object, which becomes explicitly expressed in the hylo-morphic terms inherited from the Greeks and developed by the Neo-Kantians. Nishida's reading of the Neo-Kantians contributed to his formulation of the concept of basho or place in terms of a self-forming formlessness in response to their hylo-morphic dualism. But this theory of place also borrows significantly from the terminology of Hegel, for example, in its understanding of place as a self-determining concrete universal (gutaiteki ippansha 具体的一般者). Nishida's view of basho as a place of self-contradiction, a place enveloping the ultimate opposing terms of being and non-being, in its dialectical unfoldings thus takes on the coloring of Hegelian dialectics. I will examine in the ensuing sections how Nishida developed what eventually became his brand of dialectical philosophy as a response to what he viewed as the shortcomings of the various Western philosophers he had encountered and especially to the tendencies of substantialism and dualism, but also with significant borrowings from Hegelian thought. This preliminary look will prepare us for the subsequent examinations of the Hegelian and Buddhist aspects, as well as of the unique distinctness of Nishida's dialectics.

Aristotle's Substantialism

The dualism between epistemological subject and object leads to the question of their relationship. This issue of dualism is also closely related to the question of object-centered thinking, or what Nishida called "object logic" (*taishō ronri* 対象論理), for in posing the question concerning the relationship between the two terms of the epistemological dichotomy, the formulation of the question already assumes that there are two objects, that is, determinate things, to be related. In this way of thinking, the object of cognition that can be made into a grammatical subject of judgment becomes the center of focus. Nishida traces this, as the predominant mode of thinking in Western philosophy, back to Aristotle. In the structure of judgment, the object qua grammatical subject is specified by properties predicated of it, with the assumption that underlying them is its substance. Aristotle takes this "substance" (*ousia* οὐσία) as such to be what serves as the grammatical subject or substratum (*hypokeimenon* ὑποκείμενον) while it itself is never predicated of something else. It cannot be a predicate (Z3 325; Z7 221).[1] Nishida explores this Arstotelian notion of substance in the essays of both *Hatarakumono kara mirumono e* (『働くものから見るものへ』; *From the Working to the Seeing*) of 1927 and *Tetsugaku no konpon mondai* (『哲学の根本問題』; *Fundamental*

Problems of Philosophy) of the 1930s. But before looking into Nishida's assessment of this doctrine and his ensuing response in the form of his theory of place and concrete dialectics, one ought to inquire into what Aristotle meant by "substance." By examining how it relates to knowledge and judgment making, we will begin to understand what led Nishida to his ideas.

Aristotle discusses substance in both ontological terms and logical terms in his *Metaphysics* and his *Categories*. In the *Metaphysics* substance is what is ontologically the most real. The Greek word is *ousia* (οὐσία), a noun formed from the feminine participle form of the verb "to be" (*einai* εἶναι). A strict translation of *ousia* would thus be "beingness."[2] Of the various senses of the word "being," Aristotle takes "substance" to be its most primary sense. Throughout the *Metaphysics* it becomes obvious that by "substance" he means that which is ontologically independent, having its own essential nature, that is, that which necessarily is what it is in virtue of itself and not due to anything else, constituting its individuality and separateness from others. In the *Categories* (ch. 5), however, Aristotle distinguishes substance into primary and secondary meanings. Primary substance (*prote ousia*) is the individual thing, while secondary substance is the species or genus,[3] the kind, to which that individual belongs as a particular. Substance in the latter sense is secondary because it has no existence apart from the individual thing, that is, primary substance. That is, universals are always asserted of an individual as their subject. Substance in the primary sense thus must be individual. Aristotle also takes substance in that primary sense to be the most primary vis-à-vis all the other categories, which must refer to it as its quality or attribute. If primary substance "did not exist, it would be impossible for anything else to exist."[4] The essence or identity of a primary substance is thus absolute, ontologically prior, and everything else is relative to it. The *Metaphysics* thus characterizes substance as the primary subject or substratum (hypokeimenon) for other things. Thus "the many senses in which a thing is said to be . . . all refer to one starting point," and "all that 'is' is related to one central point, one definite kind of thing,"[5] namely, primary substance. And this is the sense of substance that becomes associated with the grammatical significance of subject, that is, as that of which everything else can be asserted but which itself is not asserted of anything. Substance in that sense is what becomes the substratum of assertions, that is, the grammatical subject of predication, while the other categories serve as its predicates.[6] Although those qualities or characteristics asserted of substance may alter in their accidental nature, the substance itself, having its essence in virtue of itself, maintains its identity as what it is. As long as the individual, qua substance, maintains its essence, its identity remains the same even when its qualities undergo change.

This theory of substantial identity was Aristotle's reply to the Heraclitean doctrine of constant flux, whereby "all things are and are not" as if to "make everything true."[7] Parmenides had also earlier set forth an alternative to Heraclitus's theory with his doctrine of being as unchanging and undifferentiated. By means of the logical principle of the excluded middle that "X is or is-not," with the second alternative being inconceivable, Parmenides had extinguished the conceivability of time, motion, or change.[8] Plato, on the other hand, convinced of the truth of Parmenides's conception of being as eternal and unchanging, but also recognizing the reality of change and plurality, had divided the world into two spheres. He thereby relegated the Heraclitean flux to the phenomenal realm and placed Parmenidean being in an intelligible realm, hidden behind the phenomenal while providing structure and order to its flux. Like Plato, Aristotle also believed that there must be something essential that remains unchanged despite apparent change, but he disagreed with Plato's doctrine of the ideas as transcendent to phenomenal reality. His doctrine of the substantiality of individual things was thus set forth in response to both Plato's ontological dualism and the Heraclitean denial of the law of non-contradiction. Aristotle's doctrine of substance, however, as we shall see in the next section, leads to a more modern epistemological form of dualism.

There is also a connection in Aristotle between the unchangeable self-identity of substance and the principle of non-contradiction that is not totally irrelevant to the formation of Nishida's dialectical thinking. In *Metaphysics,* book 4, Aristotle asserts that "A is true when not-A is false" and that "not-A is true when A is false" (ch. 4), the point being that it is not possible to truthfully assert and to deny the same thing, that contradictory assertions cannot be simultaneously true. Aristotle asserts this to be the most indisputable of all beliefs (ch. 6). And if it is not possible for contradictory assertions to be made truthfully of the same thing, it is not possible for mutually opposing characteristics, one of which would negate the thing's essential nature, to belong to that same thing. While essentially remaining what it is, as the locus of contraries, change, and process, a substance can successively take on opposing qualities that are accidental characteristics. But it itself, remaining what it is, cannot take on anything contrary to its essence.[9] Thus Aristotle takes the law of non-contradiction, in its ontological application to substantial self-identity, to be the basic principle of his science of being qua being. The resulting picture is of a world composed of substances with non-self-contradictory essential natures, serving as ontological substrata presupposed by accidental changes.[10] To deny the law of non-contradiction, Aristotle states, would entirely "do away with substance and essence."[11] We thus find, in their ontological applications, not only the principle of self-identity but also the principle of non-contradiction to be inseparable from Aristotle's doctrine of substance. This point proves to be significant when we look into Nishida's non-substantialist turn away from the grammatical subject and toward the predicate in his epistemology of place, as well as into his later expositions of the dialectical implications of place in terms of a contradictory self-identity.

The ontological subject, as undergoing accidental changes, is what underlies the grammatical (or logical) subject. The two senses of "subject" (hypokeimenon), ontological and grammatical, are not exactly the same for Aristotle. The real substratum is the primary substance as the ontological "subject-in-process," the ultimate locus of processes. As the ultimate referent, it is pointed to as the subject of what might be said of it. The primary substance qua ontological subject thus becomes—or is referred to by—the grammatical subject that occupies its place in a sentence while being "neither predicable of another subject nor present in another subject."[12] The two are distinct in meaning since not everything that is a grammatical subject can be hypostatized as ontologically real and treated as a primary substance. The truth of a cognitive statement, a judgment, however, must be founded on that ontological subject, the substance, as the ultimate referent maintaining its self-identity.[13]

Aristotelian substantialism as explained above entails a form of discourse that takes reality in terms of objectifiable entities, substances, that can be spoken of as grammatical subjects. Nishida calls this form of discourse "the logic of the grammatical subject" (*shugo no ronri* 主語の論理) or "object logic" (taishō ronri). That is, it is a logic of the subject of predication based on the definition of substance as the subject that cannot become a predicate. From Nishida's perspective, this discursive logic reifies or hypostatizes reality into substances, that is, determinate things with self-identical essences. It is an ontologization of the principle of noncontradiction, and it is also a view of the world under the limiting lens of the Indo-Aryan linguistic structure with its subject-predicate grammar. The world in this light appears as consisting of substances with properties or attributes about which we can make assertions in the conjoining of subjects and predicates. Taking this form of assertion to be the most fundamental and presupposed by other propositional forms, Aristotle implies that the world, linguistically described, has a structure corresponding to that of language and whose basic elements are substances with properties. Yet, curiously, what at first thus seems to be a straightforward correspondence between language and world is not exactly so, for primary substance as the ontological subject-in-process cannot be exhausted by linguistic assertions. The grammatical subject is not quite the ontological subject; the name is not the thing-in-itself.

The problem that Nishida finds with Aristotle's doctrine is that true primary being qua substance is unknowable, and in his view this is inseparable from the issue of epistemological dualism. As the underlying matter of its predications that is in itself but not for us, primary substance on its own cannot be known. Knowledge of something particular means knowledge of its determinate predicates that render it intelligible. The cognitive content can be only what is predicated of the individual but never the individual in itself without predication.[14] Every cognition is established in the structure of judgment, conjoining the grammatical subject and the predicate, whereby the subject qua individual is subsumed under the predicate qua universal. For example, in the judgment "Man is an animal," "man" is subsumed under "animal." Knowledge, then, is of the universal, for example, the animality of man. But substance in itself that makes something uniquely what it is qua individual, apart from its predications, remains unknown. Alone, the ontological subject refuses subsumption by the universal. And its thoroughly irreducible individuality, transcending all concepts, means that it cannot even be conceptualized. Because it is beyond conception, predication, and hence judgment, it is a transcendent object. Nishida questions this Aristotelian substance that in itself is unknowable and irreducible (*Z3* 294, 325–326, 328, 390). If substance transcends our knowing and judging acts, how does it come to be the object of our knowledge and the subject of our judgments? How can we have knowledge of it and form a judgment about it, especially when it is taken to be the foundation of the truth of cognitive assertions?

In modern philosophy, René Descartes took this Aristotelian notion of substance and applied it to the cognitive subject. So we can ask a related question in regard to this subject of cognition qua substance: Can the epistemological subject be objectified and made into a grammatical subject of the judgment, "I think . . . *X*"? In Nishida's view, Descartes sought the real in what can be reduced to a substance and what becomes the grammatical subject of a judgment. Unable to escape "Aristotelian logic," Descartes thus fell into "dogmatic metaphysics" (*Z10* 125).

The world conceived as consisting of substances, whether as object or subject, is but a reflection of our projection on it of the grammatical structure of our language. The transcendence of substance indicates the limit of that projection. At best, substance metaphysics, then, is but one limited perspective on the world, but alone, it is inadequate for explaining our relationship to the objects of cognition. What must be taken into account is the concrete world of our interactivity in the sociohistorical sphere (*Z6* 139 140). In Nishida's position, Aristotelian substantialism and its "logic of the grammatical subject" thus point beyond themselves as always already contextualized. Cognition involves the process of objectification as an act that in itself is already implaced; that is, the act implicitly refers to a place wherein it makes sense. The logic that Nishida proposes instead is a "logic of place" (basho no ronri 場所の論理).

Neo-Kantian Dualism

Nishida initially formulated his logic of basho in the mid- to late 1920s as an epistemological alternative to the dualisms of the modern epistemologies found in Western philosophy. His immediate target was the German schools of Kantian thought that, inheriting Greek categories, explicated the epistemological relationship between subject and object in hylo-morphic terms. For many philosophers in Europe during the late nineteenth and early twentieth centuries, Neo-Kantianism provided the context that could not be ignored and from which key thinkers struggled to differentiate their emerging positions.[15] The Neo-Kantian influence extended to Japan, and among Japanese intellectuals Nishida was one who partook in that struggle. The Neo-Kantians took cognition to involve the synthesis of its matter in accordance with a priori forms in the epistemological subject's (re-)construction of its object. Their epistemology was a constructivism that took as its point of departure the dichotomy between constructor and constructed. For Nishida, this was already to lose sight of the concrete immediacy wherein the two terms are inextricably intertwined, an abstraction from the holistic situation of their inseparable dynamism.

As I alluded earlier, Kantian dualism inherits from Aristotle's doctrine of substance the issue of its ontological independence, that is, its transcendence of judgment. In hylo-morphic terms the matter of cognitive determination in itself transcends its determination. Hence Nishida, for example in his "Sōda hakushi ni kotau" (「左右博士に答ふ」; "In Reply to Dr. Sōda," 1927), faults Heinrich Rickert's epistemology for failing to clarify the ground of *the given that* would establish objective knowledge ($Z3$ 489). If the objective source of the material of cognition transcends the determining process to begin with, the thing-in-itself remains unknown. Beyond the content of cognition there lies its unknowable source transcending the whole process. What we know is but a projection of our demands imposed on the given material. Reality, then, becomes dichotomized into two realms, the transcendental realm of a priori conditions qua forms of determination, on the one hand, and the transcendent realm of what becomes the matter of determination but is in itself unformed, objectively undetermined, on the other.[16] This gives rise to the question of the extent to which their conjunction in the judicative terms of subject and predicate accurately portrays the world of objects independent of our mental acts. Nishida in "Torinokosaretaru ishiki no mondai" (「取残されたる意識の問題」; "The Stranded Issue of Consciousness," 1927) thus asks: In what way does the transcendent object come to relate to consciousness for its re-constitution as object ($Z7$ 223)?

In epistemological dualism a related and similar sort of issue arises in regard to the other pole of the dichotomy. In reflecting on the cognitive process as involving the dichotomy between the objectifying act on the part of the transcendental subject, on the one hand, and the objectified content referring to the transcendent object, on the other, we have already objectified, in fact, not only the content of that cognitive act but the subject behind the act. Consciousness is thus made into a determinate being, an object of thought, a subject of the judgment "I think . . . X" ($Z7$ 218). Both terms of the duality—subject and object—are thus objectified. Nishida takes this to be the hidden premise behind, or at least the implication resulting from, Kantian epistemology: it conceives of cognition as an act occurring between two objects. Yet, as in the case of the grammatical subject and its underlying transcendent object, an unknowable indeterminacy underlying and transcending that objectified subject must be presupposed.

Of the Neo-Kantians, Emil Lask exerted the most influence on Nishida in his formulation of his theory of basho. Lask was a figure who from within the Neo-Kantian movement attempted a deconstruction of sorts of its dualistic premises with a radically new vision and in turn exerted a profound influence on post–Neo-Kantian thinkers in Europe, most notably Martin Heidegger. Several scholars of Continental philosophy in recent decades have written on Lask's connection to Heidegger, as well as to phenomenology in general.[17] The Lask-Nishida connection likewise ought not to be ignored. What Lask succeeded in doing, from within Neo-Kantianism, was to unveil the premise behind all traditional dualisms, that is, the standpoint that takes each side of the dichotomy entitatively, that is, as a being (*Seiende*), some thing. On this basis the history of philosophy becomes a series of attempts to bridge the gap between the two realms of being (*Sein*).[18] Hermann Lotze, a precursor of the Neo-Kantian movement, however, came up with an utterly different sort of dualism that no longer took both sides as beings. Rather, for Lotze the distinction was between being (*Sein*) and validity (*Geltung*), the ontic and the normative, reality (*Wirklichkeit*) and value (*Wert*), what is or occurs and what counts or holds.[19] Lask inherited from Lotze this restriction of being to the spatiotemporal realm of events and causal connection that, he ironically remarked, Western thinkers of the past, starting with Plato, had dismissed as "non-being" (*mē on; Nichtseiende*).[20]

Lask's contribution here was to collapse the Lotzean dichotomy between being and validity, matter and form, into a primal unity that is pre-theoretically experienced or lived. In other words, being and its value (or meaning), in Lask's view, are already intertwined before their abstraction as separate elements in the act of judgment, for example, as grammatical subject and predicate or as object and subject. The predicate in this regard designates for Lask the domain (a "domain predicate," *Gebietsprädikat,* that is a "domain category," *Gebietskategorie*), which saturates the material with meaning before the judicative act.[21] As Hegel had already remarked, the German word for "judgment," *Urteil,* literally means "primal division" (*Ur-teil*). What profoundly affected both Heidegger and Nishida was this Laskian notion of a primal non-duality of being and sense (*Sinn*) in an "immediate intuitable lived experience" (*unmittelbare anschauliche Erleben*).[22] This provides the clue to Nishida's attempts to overcome Kantian dualism through the development of his notion of place,[23] which, however, would subsequently unfold dialectically to reveal a complexity that even Lask was unable to foresee.[24]

Hegel's Concrete Universal and Nishida's Basho

Nishida thus developed his position in response to the object logic of both Aristotelian substantialism, which accounts for the determination of enduring objects, and Kantian dualism, which in the transcendental direction accounts for the constituting features of subjectivity. Each side—subject and object—presupposes their pre-objectified link. Nishida thus aimed to formulate a new paradigm of the real as concrete that would account for that relationship. He found a clue in Hegel's concept of the concrete universal (gutaiteki ippansha). Nishida had already appropriated this Hegelian concept in his earlier works in a variety of ways, so the formulation of the concrete universal in terms of basho or place was a further development taking off from those earlier appropriations. For an individual thing to become objectified and made into a grammatical subject of a cognitive statement, it must somehow be subsumed under, determined by, a universal that becomes its predicate. But an abstract concept that stands opposed to the individual fails to capture the uniqueness of the transcendent individual, as I noted earlier. So how can Aristotle's individual thematized as substance (ousia) and Plato's universal thematized as idea (*eidos* εἶδος)—or, in grammatical terms, the subject that is never a predicate and the universal predicate characterizing what the subject is—ever be conjoined when the subject qua substance transcends that predication (Z3 325, 405; Z6 186–188)? Borrowing Hegel's terminology, Nishida argued that the universal must instead be a "concrete universal" that already contains the individual within it as its self-determination. Hegel made the distinction between the concrete universal that expresses itself in each individual as its self-determination and the abstract universal formed by extracting what is common from various individuals while excluding what distinguishes them.[25] While Aristotle considered the individual substance as indicated by the grammatical subject the foundation of true judgments, Hegel thus looked to the concrete universal that qua predicate determines itself in the subject. The universal is concrete in that it particularizes or individualizes itself in that grammatical subject. The individual, then, rather than being ontologically independent as substance, is the individualized expression of the concrete universal. But Hegel's concrete universal is still a concept (*Begriff*), an idea (*Idee*) that grasps itself in its self-determining self-conceiving (*sichbegreifen*). So there is still the question whether it is sufficiently concrete to do justice to the pre-objectified status of the individual thing in its relationship with the knowing subject providing its determining predicates.

Nishida, in looking to Hegel's concrete universal, thus re-interpreted it in a more concrete direction. He took it as the holistic situation or context enveloping the terms in relation, serving as their primitive unity to hold their dichotomy in place and thus guaranteeing the possibility of cognition. This line of thinking is what led Nishida to the formulation of his theory of basho (place) in the mid-1920s and then to his concepts of the "dialectical universal" (benshōhōteki ippansha 弁証法的一般者) and "absolutely contradictory self-identity" (zettai mujunteki jiko-dōitsu 絶対矛盾的自己同一) in the 1930s. Rather than focusing on the object, the grammatical subject, Nishida in *Hatarakumono kara mirumono e* of 1927, turned away from it in the direction of that which cannot be stated as a grammatical subject, that which cannot be objectified. The Hegelian concept of the concrete universal took on, for Nishida, this significance of the un-objectifiable indeterminate but presupposed unity: the determining predicate rather than the determined subject of judgment (*Z*3 330). Judgment is established by the self-determination of such a universal, by which Nishida meant the necessarily presupposed concrete contextual whole. To support his point, Nishida also referred to Hegel's etymological explanation of the German meaning of "judgment" (Urteil) as a primordial differentiation or division (*ursprüngliche Teilung*) (*Z*3 331).[26] Judgment is accordingly seen not as the combination of two independent terms—individual qua grammatical subject and universal qua predicate, or matter and form, determined and determining—but rather the self-differentiation of a concrete whole, its segmentation that makes explicit what is implied within it. For Hegel, that differentiation in judgment was of the original concept (Begriff) of the whole. Nishida, however, would disagree with Hegel about the nature of that concrete whole, the self-differentiating concrete universal, and exactly how it is to be descriptively formulated.

In his maiden work of 1911, *Zen no kenkyū*, Nishida formulated that concrete whole in terms of a "pure experience" (junsui keiken 純粋経験) that is prior to the subject-object bifurcation. In *Jikaku ni okeru chokkan to hansei* (『自覚に於ける直観と反省』; *Intuition and Reflection in Self-Awareness*) of 1917, he developed this further in terms of "self-awareness" (or "self-awakening" or "self-realization") (jikaku 自覚), and arrived at the notion of an "absolute will" (zettai ishi 絶対意志) that unfolds in its internally self-mirroring self-awareness. Nishida took objectification, accordingly, to be that process of an internal self-mirroring whereby the resulting objects mirror the self-mirroring whole. But the concepts of experience, will, and self-awareness led his critics to charge him with psychologism. This compelled Nishida to reformulate his ideas, and the result was his theory of basho or "place." Self-awareness, however, still remained the starting point in the development of his theory of basho. This is made clear in his 1926 essay "Basho" (「場所」), wherein he stated that he would like to begin his inquiry not from the assumption of the subject-object relation but from the idea of self-awareness that mirrors itself (*Z*3 420). The point was to regard the formation of unformed matter, its objectification, from a broader perspective that encompasses the dichotomized terms of subject-object or form-matter in a self-forming formlessness. Cognition or judgment is thus seen to occur on the basis of an immanent self-determination or self-differentiation of what in itself in cognitive terms is an un-determined, non-differentiated, transcendent unity. In Hegelian terms this would be the concrete universal, mentioned earlier, that determines itself in primordial differentiation. Yet for Nishida, the self-determining universal cannot be a mere concept or idea but rather is the holistic pre-conceptual situation of our concrete livedness. Seeing the simultaneity of terms in these dichotomies—subject-object, form-matter, predicate-subject—from this concrete standpoint led Nishida to conceive of the dynamic of this process in terms of an empty field wherein determination takes place. This is what Nishida designated, from the mid- to late 1920s on, as "basho" or "place," that which is ultimately not even a universal in its conceptually determinate sense. And the dynamic of its self-determining acts resulting in the dichotomies is what Nishida eventually in the 1930s and 1940s worked out dialectically in the various terms of "absolutely contradictory self-identity" or "inverse correspondence" (gyakutaiō 逆対応).[27]

Nishida's reversal of Aristotle's object logic, the logic of the subject of predication, was thus undertaken with a turn away from the object and toward place or basho, away from the grammatical subject to what he also called the "predicate pole" (or "predicate plane") (*jutsugomen* 述語面). That is, in opposition to the substance that "becomes the grammatical subject but never a predicate," Nishida looked to place as the transcendental predicate pole that determines the grammatical subject but itself remains un-objectifiable, incapable of being spoken of as a subject of judgment. He took its determination of the grammatical subject to be analogous to Hegel's concrete universal that determines the individual. And like Plato's chōra (χώρα), it recedes into the dark to make room for the objects of our attention. The difference from Plato, however, is that while the Platonic chōra is a mere receptacle for the determination of the Platonic ideas—precisely what eventually led to Aristotle's form-matter duality and its Kantian reformulation in epistemological terms—in Nishida, basho as a living creativity is self-forming. The predicate qua place, for Nishida, signifies that presupposed and un-objectifiable environing and backgrounding context wherein things are meaningfully determined, that is, objectified, in our cognitive or judicative acts. "Predicate" (*jutsugo* 述語) here, then, means more than simply its grammatical sense. As a place (basho), it is the concrete field that allows for the foreground abstraction of beings qua objects or qua grammatical subjects. It appears that Nishida is using the word "predicate" as a heuristic device to turn our attention away from the object, the grammatical subject, to the contextual dimension that environs what becomes the grammatical subject.

Nishida developed his theory of place as involving a series of implacements within implacements. In his attempt to overcome dualism, he overlapped the various dichotomies of grammatical subject-predicate, epistemological object-subject, particular-universal, matter-form, *noema-noesis*,[28] content-act, and determined-determining/determiner in general, all in terms of implacement between "the implaced" (*oitearu mono* 於いてあるもの) and its "place of implacement" (*oitearu basho* 於いてある場所). That is, he understood the subsumption of the grammatical subject qua particular in the predicate qua universal to mean that the former is implaced within, enveloped by, the latter (Z3 390, 464–465, 498; Z4 81). And in the reverse direction, Nishida saw this implacement as involving the universal's individuation through self-differentiation, or, in Hegelian terms, the concrete universal's self-determination in judgment (Ur-teil) as primordial differentiation (ursprüngliche Teilung) that I mentioned earlier (Z3 347–348, 391, 400, 402–403, 431, 465, 517). The universal's envelopment of the particular, then, is also its self-particularization. In judgment the grammatical subject is thus cut out from its necessarily presupposed contextual matrix (i.e., the "concrete universal"). That matrix of implacement is therefore a "place," basho.

For terms to interrelate, there must be a place (basho) that establishes their relationship. Physical things relate within a common space or, in terms of physics, a force field. And phenomena and acts of consciousness relate within the field of consciousness (*ishiki no ba* 意識の場). This is why Nishida decided to conceive of that contextual matrix presupposed by judgments in terms of place or basho. It is within that space of basho that we see consciousness and its object co-relating. What exactly, then, is basho? To put it too simply, it is the standpoint vis-à-vis reality, the most concrete entailing the non-distinction between experience and reality, before the dichotomization between subject and object or the distinction between ideal and real. At its most concrete level, presupposed by all other levels, basho envelops and encompasses all a prioris, mental acts, categories, contexts, and perspectival horizons that constitute the world of objects. In his later works, starting from the 1930s, Nishida also unfolded its significance beyond the epistemological framework to speak of place as the contextual whole of a dialectical world (*benshōhōteki sekai* 弁証法的世界) wherein individuals interact, a matrix of interpersonality wherein person and person interrelate as "I and thou" (*watashi to nanji* 私と汝). The physical field of forces, the field of consciousness, and the sociohistorical world, then, all are understood in terms of basho.

In his basho epistemology of 1926 and 1927 (e.g., in his essay "Basho," included within *Hatarakumono kara mirumono e*), the most fundamental and concrete standpoint, mirroring everything else within as its own reflection, is called "the basho of true nothing" (*shin no mu no basho* 真の無の場所). As the broadest and deepest background in its undifferentiated wholeness, it is "absolutely nothing" (*zettai mu* 絶対無) to make possible the foreground emergence of "beings" qua objects of cognition. The nothing thus forms itself into beings in self-differentiation, that is, as a self-forming formlessness. The field of consciousness (ishiki no ba) that envelops the phenomenal world, providing an arena for the appearance of its objects, in contrast, is regarded as nothing only relative to, or in opposition to, its objects—a non-being in relation to being. Nishida thus called this field of consciousness "the place of oppositional nothing" (*tairitsuteki mu no basho* 対立的無の場所) or "of relative nothing" (*sōtai mu no basho* 相対無の場所). The determining predicates that render their subjects of discourse intelligible as objects of cognition refer to what in Kantian terms would be the transcendental or a priori forms and categories. Nishida described their activity in Husserl's terms as the noetic determination of the noema. On the basis of these determining acts, the object appears in the transcendental space, the epistemic field, of consciousness, that is, relative or oppositional nothing.

True nothing, on the other hand, is absolute (*zettai* 絶対) in that it transcends to encompass the oppositions between being and non-being, object and subject. Since consciousness can thus be objectified as a term in relation, that is, the grammatical subject of "I think . . . *X*," it is not yet the un-objectifiable and un-delimitable space that is the "true nothing" enveloping consciousness and its determining acts. Consciousness and its acts must still be contextualized on a further background that in its concreteness is no longer objectifiable. For Nishida, this is yet another way of speaking of that concrete holistic situation, the self-forming formlessness, that serves to root and envelop the subject-object dichotomy and all oppositions, including the most general sort of opposition between being and non-being, whose interactions unfold the self-determination of the concrete universal. By "absolute nothing" (zettai mu) or "true nothing" (*shin no mu* 真の無), then, Nishida does not mean that there is literally nothing at the ground of things; rather, he has in mind the most fundamental concrete (back) ground that allows for the dichotomizing standpoints in our discourse. As that contextual background that is not made into the subject of discourse, the predicate pole as opposed to the grammatical subject pole, in noematic or objective terms it is "nothing" (*mu* 無). Presupposed by the objectifying act, it cannot be formed into an object or noema. In the sense that it cannot even be objectified as the subject of "I think . . . *X*," the place of true nothing reaches beyond the delimitations of consciousness. It is the formless root of the formed.

But this place of true nothing as the deepest and broadest level enveloping all other standpoints, providing the concrete contextual horizon of the knowing self, also becomes developed by Nishida as the site wherein the personal self is immediately implaced in its interactions with the world. This aspect of the personal self's interactivity with other persons and things in the world is one of the major themes in his later works, from the 1930s on, and is worked out in explicitly dialectical terms. Each successive deepening of place—or broadening of implacements within implacements—is also a passage to the more concrete and fundamental ground of reality-cum-experience, moving from judgments about things qua objects of cognition to self-reflection about acts of consciousness and to meaningful encounters in interaction with things and persons in the pre-objectively lived world. In other words, cognition and self-reflection occur within the context of the world. Despite his terminological borrowings from Husserl's phenomenology of consciousness, Nishida thus found fault with its objectification of acts of consciousness that does not look deeper into the broader contextual underpinnings operative behind consciousness and its objectification.[29]

Nishida's Dialectics of the Socio-Historical World

Nishida's theory of basho developed in 1926/1927 as an epistemology presented in opposition to the dualistic epistemology of Neo-Kantianism but also in response to Aristotle's substantialism. It also proved to be a further concretization of Hegel's notion of the concrete universal, the concept's self-determination in the form of a judgment, which simultaneously was a deepening of Nishida's idea of self-awareness. Ever since his maiden work in 1911, Nishida had been dealing with the reifying object-centered starting point of philosophy and its concomitant subject-object dichotomization. The formulation of his theory of place that began in 1926 was its culmination, but he continued to develop variations and implications of its logic in the ensuing years, especially its dialectic. Even though his earlier ideas have dialectical aspects and implications, it was really not until the 1930s that Nishida began to characterize his standpoint as a "dialectic" (ben-shōhō). In the 1930s and 1940s he worked out the dialectic of his so-called logic (*ronri* 論理) in terms of the sociohistorical world (*shakaiteki rekishiteki sekai* 社会的歴史的世界) wherein human beings are implaced and interact with one another and work on their environment.

It is through Nishida's discussions of the dialectics of place extended into the sphere of the world of action that the spatiality of place in connection with its temporal unfolding becomes even more pronounced. Henri Bergson is one target here, for example, in Nishida's *Tetsugaku no konpon mondai* (*Fundamental Problems of Philosophy*) of the 1930s, which extends the meaning of place in this world-dialectical direction. Bergson, like Nishida, had the aim of erecting a philosophy that would counter dualism.[30] But to counter any Platonist or Hegelian postulation of the idea as an absolute standing above the world of experience, Bergson emphasized the flow of time. His notions of "creative evolution" and "pure duration" were conceived, according to Nishida, from the standpoint of the internal flow of time.[31] Although he agreed with much of Bergson's thinking in this matter, Nishida found Bergson's standpoint still to be subjectivist, taking off from the Kantian understanding of time that subsumes the spatial and the environmental within the individual subject's time determinations. Nishida claimed that Bergson's understanding of creativity was still formulated from the standpoint of the self's interiority, and his "pure duration" remained likewise bounded by the subjective interpretation of time in terms of an internal linear process. The environing sociohistorical world was thus de-emphasized. This may seem an unfair criticism of Bergson, especially when, for example, in a later work, *Matter and Memory*, Bergson emphasized the inseparability among mind, body, and environment as opposed to the internal-external dichotomy and distinguished what he called "concrete extension"—involving the continuous flux of environing matter—from mere abstract measured space.[32] But even in that work Bergson substituted a temporal for a spatial distinction in order to explain the mind-body relationship, that is, that the difference is to be understood in terms of a difference in degrees of duration, a difference in the rhythms of time between the rapidity of vibrations in extension or matter and memory's capacity to prolong the past into the present.[33]

In any case, Nishida criticized Bergson's conceptions for lacking a genuinely dialectical character that would seriously take into consideration the interplay between space and time (Z6 114, 121). Rather than conceiving of world creation subjectively from within or from without—the latter would require the postulation of a transcendent God—Nishida argued that true creativity is found at the point where outer and inner meet, where one's creativity is at one with the world's creativity, in the simultaneity of immanence and transcendence (Z6 121–122). Accordingly, he found Bergson's formulation of the *élan vital* to lack genuine spatiality as well (Z6 64; Z7 146). True creative evolution must be a dialectical determination involving individuals and environment. Nishida now conceived the holistic dynamism of the concrete in the direction of the world (*sekai* 世界) at large that spatially encompasses and informs one's situation in one's interactions with other persons, other things, and the environment, involving the dialectic of inner and outer, self and other. Especially on the basis of his conception of a "continuity of discontinuity" (hirenzoku no renzoku)—both in terms of time, whereby each moment, despite its giving way to the next, entails the fullness of a complete world, and in terms of space, whereby each individual element, despite its independence, interacts in simultaneity[34]—Nishida found Bergson's formulation of pure duration to be lacking if it was to be taken beyond the status of a mere thought experiment (Z6 64). Nishida's point is that to understand concrete life, its conception merely in terms of an internal duration is not sufficient. Not only linear time but spatiality, that is, the environment, must also come into play (Z5 339; Z6 102–103; Z8 89, 376). At this point one might also wonder, however, whether his criticisms of Bergson here are in fact a disguised self-critique of his earlier formulations of pure experience, self-awareness, and absolute will, an expression of his self-recognition of their limitations.

Partially under the impact of thinkers like Marx and Leopold von Ranke, as well as his Japanese critics, Nishida in his works from the 1930s thus extended the dialectical implications of his earlier vision of the concrete as involving a "dialectical world" (benshōhōteki sekai) that encompasses both temporal and spatial dimensions, that is, both history and society, as the medium wherein individual persons interact with one another and with their environment. This extension of his concept of basho into the sphere of the sociohistorical world was also a response to J. S. Haldane's philosophy of biological holism.[35] Haldane undertook to understand life in terms of its coordinated maintenance, involving the interrelationship between the individual organism and its environment. Nishida, while finding insight in such holistic views, developed his brand of holism dialectically and in the uniquely human sphere, which, concretely speaking, is where we find ourselves first and foremost, always already, and in relation to which merely biological or materialistic conceptions would be but abstractions.

The resulting conception of the dialectical matrix of the spatiotemporal world also extends Nishida's critique of substantialism. That is, it is not simply a critique of the Aristotelian notion of individual substance but also is an attack on any universal substantialism that would extinguish the individual in monistic absorption (as in Spinoza or Advaita Vedanta). In other words, Nishida retained in his dialectics the creative independence of the individual person while at the same time denying it any absolute sort of substantiality contra Leibnizian monadology. The resulting picture of the concrete world, then, is of a truly dialectical matrix of individuals acting on, and being acted on by, one another; and acting on, and being acted on by, the world. What Nishida here denied was any substantialism that would reify the individual, on the one hand (as in Aristotle or Leibniz), or reify the universal, on the other (as in Spinoza or even Hegel). Nishida's dialectic thus treads a middle path between these two reifications; it takes a middle position embracing both individual and world in dynamic interrelationality. To focus on one or the other, however, would be an abstraction from the concrete dynamism of that dialectical whole. Might this not be comparable to the middle position of Mahāyāna Buddhism and its notion of emptiness qua dependent origination that we find, for example, from the *Prajñāpāramitā sūtras* to Madhyamaka and Huayan?

As we can see, Nishida's path of thinking in pursuit of the concrete that began with his epistemological concerns in regard to dualism and the issue of the transcendent object led him to his epistemology of place and then to the unfolding of its dialectics in the sociohistorical world. Nishida developed his ideas in response to what he felt was lacking in the various thinkers he had encountered: Plato, Aristotle, the Neo-Kantians, Spinoza, Leibniz, Bergson, Haldane, and Husserl, among others. Yet of all those Western philosophers, from whom he drew the impetus to develop his philosophy, it is Hegel whom we find most noticeable in Nishida's dialectical formulations, especially in the 1930s, when his dialectics becomes most pronounced. To what extent, then, may we consider Nishida a Hegelian? Furthermore, we have not yet seriously considered the traces of Mahāyāna insight in Nishida's dialectical thinking. One commentator, for example, has even claimed that Nishida's philosophy is a "synthetic product of Zen and Hegel."[36] To assess such claims, we need to first examine the so-called dialectical aspects of both Hegelian and Buddhist thinking. To what extent are Hegelian dialectics and Mahāyāna non-dualism compatible or incompatible?

2 Hegelian Dialectics and Mahāyāna Non-dualism

İn examining Nishida's dialectical philosophy, we find insights drawn from both Hegel and Mahāyāna Buddhism. Most conspicuous from the Buddhist tradition is the concept of "nothing" (mu 無), and most conspicuous from Hegel is the concrete universal. In the 1950s Ha Tai Kim, for example, took Nishida's work to be "a synthetic product of Zen and Hegel" that treats Hegelian dialectic in light of Zen Buddhism.[1] If Nishida's dialectic was inspired by both Buddhist and Hegelian thought, how close and compatible are these two ways of thinking? Each in its own way attempts to overcome oppositions and dichotomies. As a preliminary to discussing Nishida's dialectics vis-à-vis Hegel and Buddhism, in the present chapter I will examine the major dialectical features noticeable in Hegel's thinking, as well as the non-dualistic notions in the major schools of Mahāyāna Buddhism that may be characterized as "dialectical." At the end of this chapter I will also consider their compatibility or incompatibility and similarities or differences to lay the groundwork for a more in-depth investigation of Nishida's dialectics, which draws insight from both of these sources.

Hegel

As we saw in chapter 1, Nishida develops his dialectics of the sociohistorical world by unfolding dialectical implications from his epistemology of place. In the formation of his dialectics, Nishida was influenced by many Western philosophers, such as Leibniz's monadology and Haldane's holism, but Hegel's influence is the most conspicuous. From his maiden work of 1911 to the beginnings of his epistemology of place in 1926 and throughout the development of his dialectics of the world of interaction during the 1930s, Nishida's appropriation of Hegelian ideas becomes increasingly noticeable. The Hegelian concept of the concrete universal is already implicit in the concepts of pure experience in 1911 (e.g., Z1 22, 52) and the absolute will in the early 1920s (e.g., Z2 13–14, 394–395). In the late 1920s it becomes re-understood in terms of place as the foundation of judgment, and it then becomes developed in the 1930s in light of the sociohistorical world as the dialectical universal that determines itself in the mutual interactions of individuals in the world. Nishida's usage of the word "dialectical" (*benshōhōteki* 弁証法的) to describe both his and Hegel's systems, however, makes it difficult for the reader upon first reading to distinguish Nishida's dialectic from Hegel's. Nishida has even been classified as a "Neo-Hegelian" who was "faithful to Hegelian philosophy."[2] Before we can evaluate such claims about the alleged Hegelianism of Nishida, we must familiarize ourselves with Hegel.

In examining the dialectics of Hegel, I will avoid the mistake made by many of simply reducing it to the triadic terms of thesis-antithesis-synthesis. Although the triadic formula was used by Kant, Fichte, and Friedrich Schelling, it was never used in exactly those terms by Hegel.[3] Hegel uses the term "dialectic" to signify the process that resolves oppositions between conflicting positions through what he calls "sublation" (*Aufhebung, Aufheben*).[4] For this, Hegel makes use of the double meaning of the German word *aufheben*: (1) to clear away or annul and (2) to keep or preserve (*EL* § 96z 142).[5] On the one hand, sublation entails the negation or canceling of the partiality of positions that leads to their opposition, but on the other, it also entails the preservation of their essential truth that overcomes their opposition to elevate them to a more comprehensive truth (*PG* 90/*PS* 68; *WL*1 94/*SL* 107). Hegel also calls such opposition "contradiction." But based on the mechanism of sublation whereby each negation of an opposite raises both opposites to a more comprehensive conception, dialectical contradiction differs from mere formal-logical contradiction. Through the process of sublation, the dialectic works itself out toward a culminating conception (Begriff) of what Hegel calls "the absolute," that is, the most comprehensive standpoint encompassing all opposing terms. The process moves toward the reconciliation of all opposites into that culminating state of the absolute, its all-comprehensive idea (Idee). This culminating comprehension encloses the entire development within its self-conception, realizing its self-identity. What is realized is the self-grasping of the entirety of the process presupposed all along as its driving telos (τέλος): "The movement is the circle that returns into itself, the circle that presupposes its beginning and reaches it only at the end" ("Sie is der in sich zurückgehende Kreis, der seinen Anfang voraussetzt, und ihn nur im Ende erreicht") (*PG* 559/ *PS* 488). The dialectic thus moves toward the closure of its process, closing in on itself in its self-conceiving (sichbegreifen) end.[6] In the following I will examine Hegel's dialectic more carefully by looking into several of his major works.

Hegel's erection of his system of dialectic, similar to Nishida's case, was in response to what he viewed as the inherent dualism he found in the idealisms of Kant and Fichte.[7] According to that dualistic worldview, a set of unknowable things-in-themselves (the "not-I") interacts with the epistemological subject (the "I"), causing sensations or some sort of "impingement" (*Anstoß*). The mind then processes those sense-data according to its a priori set of laws (conceptual categories and forms of intuition) to produce the world of appearances. But beyond that world of appearances there still lies the world of things-in-themselves that we can never know. This means that in knowledge we simply project (*hinauswer-fen*) our categories onto experience (*GW* 309). Hegel opposed treating determinations of thought primarily as forms distinct from its matter (*WL1* 17/*SL* 38) and instead wished to overcome the allegedly unbridgeable gulf between appearance and thing-in-itself. He regarded the whole idea of a realm of unknowable things-in-themselves as empty. Rather than viewing the received sense-data and the a priori conceptual categories as independent elements somehow brought together in synthesis, Hegel, in reading Kant, started from the conception of an underived whole, as an original synthetic unity (*ursprüngliche synthetische Einheit*), of which the elements are moments (*GW* 305). He took this to be "the absolute, primordial identity" (*die absolute, ursprüngliche Identität*) of self-consciousness (*GW* 306). He viewed the "wholes" toward which reason is compelled to move, which Kant noticed, as inferential structures belonging to a particular epoch in history, in terms of which judgments can make sense. And in view of history, the "whole of these wholes" is the unfolding of history itself. This holistic structure, which Hegel called "mind" or "spirit" (*Geist*), unfolding in history, serves as the starting point for the possibility of cognitive judgment making. In this regard Hegel took over from his friend Friedrich Hölderlin the insight concerning the unarticulated unity of subject and object, thought and being, that makes judgment possible, but developed it in terms of an historical unfolding of consciousness or Geist.

In *Phänomenologie des Geistes* (*Phenomenology of Spirit*) of 1807, Hegel traces the development of that holistic structure, spirit, in the journey of self-consciousness that eventually leads to its "resultant simple concept [Begriff] of itself" as the process of its development. The path proceeds through every relationship of consciousness to its object until it reaches the concept of its own movement (*WL1* 29/*SL* 48). Hence "the true is the whole" ("Das Wahre ist das Ganze"), but it is realized only in the result as that which becomes itself: "The true . . . is the process of its own becoming, the circle that presupposes its end as its goal, having its end also as its beginning; and only by being worked out to its end, is it actual" (*PG* 20, 21/*PS* 10, 11). Through this self-enclosing circle of self-reflection, thought becomes pure concept (Begriff) grasping the organic whole of the process of thinking, its history (*PG* 31/*PS* 20; see also *PG* 53/*PS* 40). This circular development of the spirit is also expressed in terms of an inter-subjectivity—in the *Phänomenologie* and earlier in *System der Sittlichkeit* (*System of Ethical Life*, 1803)[8] and *Naturrechts* (*Natural Law*, 1802–1803)[9]—whereby man is led to self-consciously regard himself qua spirit in mutual recognition, thus tying the comprehensive standpoint of the whole to a social space (*NR* 503/*NL* 111).[10]

Recall from chapter 1 that one conspicuous concept that Nishida inherits from Hegel is the concrete universal. In Hegel's system the concrete universal has much to do with how he understands dialectical development. In his system of logic in *Wissenschaft der Logik* (*Science of Logic*) (1812–1816),[11] Hegel explains the concept's immanent development within the self-reflecting movement of spirit also in terms of its self-determination (*WL1* 7/*SL* 28). He articulates this primal unity in terms of the concrete universal that contains its own principle of individuation, through which it develops distinctions within itself while maintaining self-identity, a movement of self-determining self-differentiation (*WL2* 245/*SL* 605–607). In the *Phänomenologie* this movement is said to involve the sublation (Aufhebung) of contradictions, whereby it goes beyond itself, negating itself, in "self-externalization" (*Selbstentäusserung*) to meet its other or not-self. But in doing so, it returns to itself to encompass the whole of the process of negation and sublation within itself, thus maintaining its self-identity. The thing-in-itself that transcends this movement of the concept proves to be but an abstraction for Hegel. Hegel in his *Logic,* therefore, takes the essence of things to be in their concept, the concrete universal expressing itself in the process of thought encountering thing (*WL1* 14–15/*SL* 35–36). Thought qua activity is thus an active universal self-actualizing itself (*EL* § 20 29). Hegel makes the claim in this regard that thought as the universal behind all acts of conception and recollection, in every mental activity, is also the constitutive substance of external things: thought is everywhere present as the substance of the real (*EL* § 20 31, § 24z 37–38). In Aristotle's case, as we saw in chapter 1, the individual qua substance is self-identical in that it has no attribute contradicting its essence. But in Hegel self-identity requires dialectical contradiction and its sublation in the concept comprehending the whole process. Substance thus proves to be that absolute concept.[12] The world that we encounter is thus the dialectical process of that self-development of the absolute concept of the whole, the concrete universal—not this or that specific universal but the universal principle of universality as such—serving as the directive force in everything, ceaselessly developing itself immanently in the world.

In judicative terms this concrete universal proves to be the most subsumptive predicate encompassing everything, including its negations but sublated, within it. Like Nishida after him, Hegel here takes up the issue of the judicative unity of the heterogeneous elements of the grammatical subject denoting the individual substance and the predicate representing the universal concept. Every judgment takes the basic form of the subsumptive judgment, "S is P," meaning that "the individual is the universal," or in terms of grammar that "the (grammatical) subject is the predicate." The self-identity of the individual qua grammatical subject is thus found in what is different from it: the individual is universal and the universal is individual (*EL* § 166 231, § 169 and z 234). Self-identity thus must be constituted dialectically vis-à-vis its other rather than remaining tautological or being founded on the substantiality of the individual.[13] Hegel understands this connection of the two opposing elements in terms of the concrete universal already containing its opposite, the specificity of the grammatical subject. Judgment then makes explicit that implicit dialectic of self-differentiation. Therefore, the individual is a particular of the universal containing it, whereby the universal is individualized. Their connection is a problem only when they are taken abstractly as independent of each other.[14] It is in that sense that judgment (Urteil) for Hegel entails a primordial division or differentiation (ursprüngliche Teilung or *Ur-Teilung*), as mentioned in chapter 1. In the self-differentiation of the concrete universal's originally undifferentiated unity, judgment articulates that self-identity of the concept into elements (*EL* § 166 231). Qua concrete universal the concept is self-specifying, and its immanent differentiation, its movement of self-determination or self-realization, becomes manifest in the judgment (*EL* § 163z 227, § 165–166 230, § 166z 232; see also *WL2* 486/*SL* 826). Hegel thus states that to form the notion of a thing is to recognize its inner essence, and to form a judgment about it is to realize its internal development as the realization of a universal truth, the concept of the totality. In his *Logic* he speaks of that larger whole within which all judicative acts take place as the "idea" (Idee). As an original unity of being and thought, the idea is both the universal substance and the (epistemological) subject as mind or spirit (Geist), active in the spirit's self-development (*EL* § 213 275).[15]

With his notion of a self-unfolding concrete universal, the self-realizing idea, Hegel attempts to overcome the opposition between realism or materialism and idealism. He understands both viewpoints to be connected to either the "objective" or the "subjective" standpoint, both of which, despite their distinction, imply the connection between subjective awareness and the objective world, the pre-dual unity of thought and world. In his earlier work *Differenz des Fichteschen und Schellingschen Systems der Philosophie (The Difference between Fichte's and Schelling's Systems of Philosophy*, 1801), Hegel claims that ideal-real, subject-object, thought-world oppositions, implicit within Kantian philosophy, are to be found within consciousness itself (*DFSg* 62/*DFSe* 127–128). Hegel comes to regard that primal unity underlying all bifurcations between consciousness and the world as the all-comprehending standpoint of the "absolute." In his system of logic, Hegel thus explains the idea as truth in itself and for itself, the absolute unity of the concept and objectivity, the concept's ideal content and its real content exhibited in external existence (*EL* § 213 274–275). And the idea of all such movements, expressed in all of them, grasping itself in them as its own object, is the absolute. Each perspective of the opposition must presuppose the absolute and its self-limiting activity. He identifies that activity with the workings of universal reason as the principle of reality, the "soul of the world," directed onto itself to grasp its own grounding within itself, to recognize itself in the totality of its realization, its ideal pattern manifest in reality, through human thought. Hegel quotes Kant to makes his point: "Reason comes to know itself and deals only with itself so that its whole work and activity are grounded in itself" (Kant, *Kritik der reinen Vernunft* B xiii; *MF* 17; also *EL* § 24 & z 36–37, § 142z 201). The self-differentiation of the concrete universal in judgment, then, is an expression of this self-development of universal reason, the self-limitation of the absolute. Its self-articulation in self-differentiation makes overt that original unity of subjective and objective. Hegel's absolute idea is thus this self-thinking thought articulating itself in all judgments, in the various self-differentiations of the concrete universal, distinguishing itself from itself to contemplate itself as its own content, as a self-identity dialectically maintained in the system of self-differentiation encompassing self and other, subject and object, ideal and real, and so on (*EL* § 236 and z–§ 237 292).

The idea comprehends and realizes itself in all of reality and in its own history. As I noted earlier, identity for Hegel requires dialectical contradiction. We thus see in the movement of Hegel's concept qua concrete universal a negative unity that negates itself to become its other but in turn resolves that contradiction in the idea, comprehending the entire sublational process (*WL2* 62/*SL* 442). The outcome of this system or logic of self-development is the absolute idea as the concept of this circle, returning to and completing itself, recognizing itself in everything as its manifestation, a self-converging recognition of its own process encompassing both knowledge and reality, and ultimately as the concept of the circle of all such circles fulfilled in its all-comprehensive self-grasping (sichbegreifen) concept (Begriff) (see *WL1* 56/*SL* 71; *WL2* 432, 504–505/*SL* 777–778, 842–843; *EL* § 15 20, § 17 23, § 215 and z 278–279). Its end is accomplished as the system of that totality (*WL2* 502/*SL* 840). Hegel speaks of the resulting science or knowledge (*Wissenschaft*) as thus realizing a totality that mirrors the world as a whole, a unified theory of reality that "returns into itself and reaches the point with which it began ... [and] exhibits the appearance of a circle which closes with itself" (*EL* § 17 23). And this is Hegel's holistic or totalizing stance of what he calls absolute cognition as a self-realizing whole, set forth as dialectically overcoming the finitude of Kantian epistemology and its dualism (*EL* § 160 and z 223–224). In this all-encompassing circle of self-recognition Hegel—in his lectures on history (*Lectures on the Philosophy of History*, 1822–1831)—includes human history itself as the history of the spirit's unfolding. Each epoch of history mirrors the idea of the totality of its development in a scattered image (*NR* 522/*NL* 127; *PH* 457). And the culmination of history, resulting in the all-comprehending self-grasping, self-realizing concept, makes explicit its own development (*PH* 457). It is the idea's self-recognition in making rational sense out of its own self-driven history, a recapitulation of its own historical progression culminating in human self-consciousness.[16] Hence world history, Hegel states, presents a rational process, and reason is both its substance and power, its matter and form.

Nothing else is revealed in the world but this rational process (*PH* 9–10). Reason is the substance of both consciousness and nature, structuring the course whereby the absolute spirit unfolds in history (*PH* 10, 439). Both history and philosophy for Hegel, then, are one big rational circle meant to account for everything real in the absolute idea. Nothing outside its circle is meaningfully real. In the end, Hegel admits that this is a form of idealism, but, distinguishing it from the subjective idealism of critical philosophy, he terms it an "absolute idealism" (*EL* § 45z 73). Hegel's reconciliation of the opposition between idealism and realism thus occurs on the basis of an idealism that is the standpoint of the absolute.

Reality as a whole, including the processes of both knowledge and history, is thus enclosed in the circular self-asserting idea of the absolute. We are told that the universal idea is the substantial totality of things (*PH* 26). Can reality in its dynamism of oppositions ever be so affirmed in one all-comprehending idea? Nishida, like Hegel, was also interested in the whole as the concrete and thus made use of Hegel's notion of the concrete universal. We can see why Nishida found insight in Hegel, whom he viewed as the first to attempt to develop a dialectical logic of practice or action, inclusive of both subject and object, as well as intersubjectivity, a logic of social and historical reality as opposed to the Aristotelian logic of the subject of predication as a mere substance. But for Nishida, the holistic standpoint, as a standpoint that cannot be determined as a grammatical subject, is hence empty of any conceptualizable essence, irreducible to any "being." It is in his concept of "nothing" (mu) that we discern in Nishida's thinking an influence from the Buddhist Mahāyāna tradition, with its insight in regard to emptiness and dependent origination. I now turn to the non-dualistic conceptions of Mahāyāna Buddhism.

Mahāyāna Buddhism

What draws direct insight from Mahāyāna thought most conspicuously in Nishida's writings is the concept of "nothing" (mu). In much of the dialectical aspect of his philosophy, we may also discern inspiration from and reference to the basic non-dualistic worldview of Mahāyāna. If we look at his personal life, we find that Nishida was an avid practitioner of Zen meditation for many years, and one of his closest friends from childhood was D. T. Suzuki (Suzuki Daisetsu 鈴木大拙) (1870–1966), who popularized Zen in the West. His mother was a devotee of Pure Land Buddhism. Yet Nishida's texts in general, except for his last few essays, are short on any direct references to traditional Buddhist sources. As David Dilworth has observed, Nishida's career was characterized by a "general reticence in regard to Eastern religious texts."[17] The exception to this is the cardinal concept of "nothing" (mu), mentioned earlier, which appears in the various stages of his oeuvre. What seems uniquely Buddhist in his thinking, although it is deliberately formulated in response to the ideas of Western philosophers and for the most part without any reference to Buddhist scriptural or doctrinal sources, is the concept of absolute nothing (zettai mu 絶対無) or true nothing (shin no mu 真の無). Strictly speaking, these are not real Buddhist terms, although one finds the expression of "nothing" (mu) in both Zen and Daoist writings. But, in addition, the dialectical aspects of his later thinking, formulated mostly in Hegelian terms, show remarkable similarities with Huayan (Jp. Kegon 華厳) Buddhism's development of inter-dependent origination (*engi* 縁起). (I am thinking here of the manifold inter-determinations found in the Huayan conception of the *dharmadhātu* in terms of *li* [Jp. *ri* 理] [patterning] and *shi* [Jp. *ji* 事] [thing-events] and those found in Nishida's conception of the dialectical universal from the 1930s.) In this section I will examine the non-dualistic line of thought in Mahāyāna Buddhism, traces of which we find not only in Nishida's concept of "nothing" but in his dialectical formulations of "self-negation," "absolutely contradictory self-identity," "continuity of discontinuity," and "inverse correspondence."

When we look at the thinking of some of the representative Mahāyāna schools of philosophy, such as Madhyamaka and Yogācāra in India and Tiantai, Huayan, and Chan/Zen (禅) in East Asia, we notice a certain line or strand of non-dualistic thinking that is recognizable in Nishida's thought, especially in its dialectical aspects that become developed in his later works. The manner in which these schools explicate non-duality in terms of emptiness (Skrt. *śūnyatā*; Ch. *kong*; Jp. *kū* 空) has been described by some commentators as "dialectical." Of course, "dialectic" may not be the right term if we are to limit its meaning to what Plato or Hegel meant. But aside from that, there is a certain way of thinking in Nishida's dialectic that we might trace to Buddhism. The source of that strand can be found in the thinking of the *Prajñāpāramitā sūtras*, for example, the *Diamond Sūtra* and the *Heart Sūtra*. Their non-dualistic mode of thinking, starting with the equation of form and emptiness (Skrt. *rūpam śūnyatā śūnyatāiva rūpam,* Jp. *shiki soku zekkū* 色即是空)[18] in the Chinese translation of the *Heart Sūtra*,[19] becomes worked out in a variety of formulations by these schools. In fact, despite his general reticence in most of his works in regard to Buddhist scriptural sources, Nishida in his last essays of the 1940s refers to these sūtras under the inspiration of their readings by his friend D. T. Suzuki. My discussions of Mahāyāna thought here will present a simplified version of what in actuality proves to be much more complex. I will begin west in India with Madhyamaka and Yogācāra and then proceed east to China with Tiantai and Huayan and from there to Chinese Chan and its Japanese version, Zen.[20]

Madhyamaka is traditionally regarded as the first and the major philosophical school of Mahāyāna to emerge in India, under inspiration from the

Prajñāpāramitā sūtras. Its supposed founder, Nāgārjuna (ca. 100/150–200/250 CE),[21] took the *Prajñāpāramitā* idea of emptiness (śūnyatā) to mean the lack of "self-nature" or "own-being" (svabhāva), that is, ontological substance or essence, in anything, whether material or ideal, whether entity, event, process, or thought. Things are empty of substance because, lacking independence, they depend on various factors for their being. Thus he equates emptiness with the Buddhist notion of dependent origination (*pratītya-samutpāda*). This lack of substantiality means that nothing can be asserted about anything without qualification. Any proposition assuming an absolute truth for itself falls into self-contradiction. Nāgārjuna showed this by considering four alternative positions (called "tetralemma," *catuṣkoti*) about any topic: X ("is"), $\sim X$ ("is not"), both X and $\sim X$ ("both is and is not"), and neither X nor $\sim X$ ("neither is nor is not"), to disclose the emptiness behind each assertion. The proposition (whether positive or negative) can stand only if the emptiness of what it asserts is acknowledged, that is, only if its truth is taken provisionally as conditional or as conventional. That is, a truth can be acknowledged only once it has been de-substantialized or de-reified. Nāgārjuna aimed to refute all substantializing, reifying, or hypostatizing assertions, including annihilating negations, to show that reality is irreducible to such mutually exclusive alternatives of is or is-not, yes or no, affirmation or negation, absolutely being or utterly nothing.[22] The soteriological point was to eliminate bondage to such positions that result in clinging and hence, suffering.

A consequence of the tetralemma was the theory of two truths and their non-dualist equation or collapse, which influenced subsequent Mahāyāna thought. We may even find its trace in Nishida's idea of contradictory identity. The two truths are the relative or conventional (*saṃvṛti-satya*) and the ultimate or absolute (*paramārtha-satya*) (*MMK* 24:8, 9). The tetralemma's disclosure of the provisional nature (*saṃvṛti*) of all truth-claims simultaneously refers to an ultimate truth (*paramārtha*) in regard to their emptiness. While provisionally a statement may hold true, ultimately it is empty. Because emptiness means dependent origination, its ultimate truth does not refer to anything ontologically transcending the conventional: "Whatever is dependently arisen, that is emptiness" (*MMK* 24:18). Both truths refer to the same reality that things are conventionally real but substantially unreal. And while things are not substantially real, neither are they utterly unreal. Rather than dichotomizing reality into the two realms of saṃsāra and nirvāṇa, the two truths simply offer alternative perspectives on the reality of empty phenomena.[23] Bondage to saṃsāra thus means becoming attached to dependently arising phenomena as if they were substantial, and genuine nirvāṇa means seeing reality as it is, without reification, without attachment, as empty. With the recognition that neither possesses substantiality (svabhāva), saṃsāra and nirvāṇa, like the two truths, are thus collapsed as designating alternative perspectives, reifying and de-reifying, on the same reality (*MMK* 25:19–20). In terms of

Nishida's later thought, this means the unity of opposites or contradictory identity.

This collapsing of the duality between nirvāṇa and saṃsāra, ultimate and conventional, epitomizes the "middle way" of Mahāyāna between substantial being and utter nothingness, between naïve realism and nihilism, between reification and annihilation, a "middle" that is "neither one nor two," neither monism nor dualism. This non-dualism precludes any unilateral refutation or one-way transcendence of the conventional in favor of the ultimate. The ultimate in its ultimacy vis-à-vis the conventional does not transcend it. Emptiness must also be emptied[24] to prevent any one-dimensional attachment to nothingness, thus showing that reality is irreducible to either alternative of substantial being or utter nothing (*MMK* 13:3). Via this double negation of *śūnyatāyāh śūnyatā* (emptiness of emptiness), the Mādhyamika "middle" of neither/nor escapes reduction to either extreme. This provides the historical background for Nishida's conceptions in his later works of the contradictory identity and of inverse correspondence in mutual self-negation between absolute and relative, nothing and being. This "middle" becomes explicitly developed by the next major school of Mahāyāna philosophy, Yogācāra, as a hinge mediating the opposing aspects of reality.

The Yogācārins are famous for internalizing the Mādhyamika equation of emptiness and dependent origination, taking it as specifically referring to the mind's karma-fueled projections. The founding brothers, Asaṅga and Vasubandhu (fourth century CE),[25] understood this mind-related world in light of three aspects or natures: *parikalpita, paratantra,* and *parinispanna. Parikalpita* refers to the imagined aspects of the world that appear as discrete substantial objects and subjects but in reality are imaginary projections and thus empty of substance. Such projection is based on the activity of the ego differentiating itself qua subject from its objects through linguistic articulation. *Paratantra* designates the universal dependency of such phenomena, both in their inter-dependence and in their collective dependence on the karma-infested mind. *Parinispanna* is reality understood in its "consummated" form, divested of karmic projections, erased of the imaginary substantiality and subject-object dichotomy, that is, reality experienced in its undiscriminated "suchness" (*tathatā*) (*MS* 2:15; *TK* v. 23; *TN* vv. 1–2).

As in Nāgārjuna's collapsing of the two truths, these three natures do not designate three realms but rather all refer to the same reality. The imagined is how reality appears to the unenlightened, defiled by karmic attachments, and the consummated is how reality appears to the enlightened, freed from karmic defilement. They are different aspects of the reality of inter-dependent phenomena. Their hinge or "middle," then, is the dependent (paratantra) nature of phenomena, which provides the locus or basis (*āśraya*) for both the imaginary projections of substance and the de-substantializing consummation of suchness (tathatā). Thus Vasubandhu states that dependent nature devoid of imagination is consummated nature (*TK* v. 21), and Asaṅga also states that the dependent is sometimes the imagined and sometimes the consummated (*MS* 2:17). Accordingly, saṃsāra is the defiled aspect of paratantra, and nirvāṇa is the purified aspect of paratantra (*MS* 9:1). As in Madhyamaka, nirvāṇa and saṃsāra in Yogācāra thus can be regarded as two ways of viewing the same reality, the deluded and defiled or the purified and enlightened. And paratantra serves as the axis on which conversion from saṃsāra to nirvāṇa occurs (*MS* 2:2, 17; 10:3, 5; *TN* vv. 2–3, 18, 20, 21, 23; *TK* v. 21). This motif of the realm of inter-dependence, which is usually reified into discriminated objects but can also be de-reified into undiscriminated emptiness, we see taken over in Nishida's idea of the dialectical world of contradictory identity as a world of inter-determination among individuals and between the individual qua self and the dialectical universal qua world.

The Mahāyāna trend to collapse the dualities of conventional and ultimate, saṃsāra and nirvāṇa, into a middle becomes further pronounced with its Sinicization. Zhiyi (智顗) (538–597), third patriarch and founder of the Tiantai (Jp. Tendai 天台) school in China, inheriting Nāgārjuna's twofold truth, explicates and expands on it in terms of a threefold truth.[26] The three truths are emptiness, conventional being, and the middle. Insight into the first truth prevents one from clinging to the apparent substantiality of things and frees one from naïve realism. Insight into the second truth teaches one that emptiness is not utter nothingness and affirms the reality of things as conventional, conditioned, dependent. And insight into the middle enlightens one about the synonymy of emptiness and conventional being in reference to the same reality while avoiding discriminating attachments to the reductive extremes of either eternal being or utter nothing. Contemplation of the first truth negates substantiality for the sake of emptiness. Contemplation of the second truth negates utter nothingness for the sake of dependent or contingent being. And with the third truth, both substantiality and nihility are negated for the simultaneous cognizance of the validity of both emptiness and conventional being. Not only must being be emptied of substantiality, but emptiness must be emptied of its reification as well. The third truth thus designates the path that treads the middle between the reductive extremes of being in eternalism and nothing in nihilism. Simultaneously it reaffirms the two other truths to indicate the harmonious tension between ultimate emptiness and conventional substantiality. The middle thus integrates emptiness and conventional being while avoiding their reification. In emptiness everything is one, but this also means dependent origination among the many. The two truths are not simply absorbed into a substantialist or monist oneness. Rather, they are reaffirmed without reifying their dichotomy. Being and emptiness, many and one, are non-dualistically identified in that standpoint of the middle. Reality is "one yet many, many yet one." We thus again see here an example of a tendency within Mahāyāna that comes to expression later in Nishida's dialectic of contradictory identity between one and many, universal and individual, and inverse correspondence between absolute and relative.

If Tiantai explicates Mahāyāna non-duality in terms of three truths, Huayan (Jp. Kegon) develops this idea further in light of four realms collapsed into one *dharmadhātu* (Skrt; Ch. *fajie;* Jp. *hokkai* 法界) or "realm of truth/reality."[27] It makes its explication through the employment of the Neo-Daoist terminology of li ("patternment") and shi (fact, thing-event).[28] Dependent origination here becomes further worked out in terms of mutual implication to encompass the sense of non-obstruction (*wuai;* Jp. *muge* 無礙) among elements, allowing for their interpenetration. Inheriting and expanding on the *Prajñāpāramitā* equation of form and emptiness, the first Huayan patriarch, Dushun (杜順) (557/558–640),[29] regarded emptiness and form as different aspects of the dharmadhātu wherein everything is united in emptiness. Taking emptiness as the interconnective and self-differentiating patterning (li) immanent in all thing-events (shi), he developed their relationship in terms of the non-obstruction (wuai) between li and shi, that is, *lishi wuai* (Jp. *riji muge* 理事無礙). While mirroring and implying the boundless entirety of the dharmadhātu, each thing-event (shi; Skrt. *dharma*) remains its unique self without annihilating absorption into universality or whole. In spite of its shared emptiness with others, each individual is regarded as complete, mirroring the whole. And yet precisely because of their emptiness, each is harmonious with all others to establish non-obstruction among themselves, that is, *shishi wuai* (Jp. *jiji muge* 事事無礙). The non-obstruction among thing-events therefore manifests the full "wondrous being" of each individual thing-event and simultaneously their emptiness. This is analogous to the relationship we find in the later Nishida's formulations of the dialectical universal, between the universal qua world and the individual qua persons, which precludes any uni-directional subsumption of the latter under the former.

This dharmadhātu of li and shi was later further explicated by the fourth Huayan patriarch, Chengguan (澄觀) (737/738–820/839/840),[30] in terms of four realms: (1) the realm of phenomenal thing-events (shi) naïvely affirmed; (2) the realm of the "ultimate" or patternment (li) of emptiness; (3) the realm of the non-obstructed interrelationship between phenomena and their immanent patternings (lishi wuai), referring to the non-duality between thing-events and their emptiness; and (4) the realm of the non-obstructed interrelationships among phenomenal thing-events (shishi wuai), referring to their co-dependent origination. The third realm refers to the vertical interrelationship between things and their interconnecting and inter-differentiating patternment among themselves. The fourth realm refers to the horizontal interrelationships among those co-relative, interdependently originating beings. But if one takes Nāgārjuna's equation of emptiness with dependent origination, li would refer to this inter-dependence among shi so that the first three realms as mere explanatory devices are collapsed into the fourth as the only dharmadhātu. While emptiness is regarded as the patterning (li) of interconnections and differentiations permeating the cosmic dharmadhātu, any reifying tendency into a universal principle is eclipsed by its collapse into the mutual non-obstruction among phenomena (shishi wuai). Emptiness is thus de-transcendentalized; any claim to its substantial separateness from samsaric existence is negated. We find an analogous idea in the later Nishida's "inverse correspondence," whereby the "absolute" (or that which is cut off from relativity by encompassing it) is seen as immanent in the world of relative beings via its own self-negation. Just as the conventional and the ultimate for Nāgārjuna are non-dual, the four realms in Huayan are non-quadruple, many and yet one.

We find the same line of thinking, leading to a non-dualist collapse while precluding absorption in a substantialized one, in the Chan or Zen tradition. Chan/Zen inherited much of the previously mentioned Mahāyāna worldview but developed it into a more practical orientation. Take, for example, the famous saying by the Chinese Chan master Qingyuan Weixin (Jp. Seigen Ishin 青原惟信) (660–740) of the Tang dynasty. He states that before he began his study of Chan, "mountains were mountains, rivers were rivers," but after he began his study, "mountains were no longer mountains, rivers were no longer rivers." However, with further Chan practice, he came to realize that "mountains are mountains, rivers are rivers."[31] What we see here is first a move from the naïve realism of the first stage, taken in by the apparent substantiality of shi, to the emptying of all substantiality of beings in the second stage. But to end there would signify bondage to their annihilation. With further practice, one comes to the positive realization that things are precisely what they are because of their emptiness. Put differently, emptiness itself is emptied (of any substantiality or reification) to reaffirm being in its emptiness. Truth here is in the identity of affirmation and negation, going beyond their contradiction. But this is not the self-identity of substance. Rather, it entails a dynamic non-duality via emptiness.

The first three sentences of "Genjōkōan" (「現成公案」) ("The Issue at Hand; or, Manifesting Suchness")[32] by Dōgen Kigen (道元希玄) (1200–1253), Zen master and founder of the Sōtō (曹洞) Zen school in Japan, likewise express the emptying of emptiness to achieve a non-dual middle.[33] The first sentence asserts that when all thing-events (dharmas) are "the Buddha Dharma," that is, reality viewed from an enlightened perspective, there are illusion and enlightenment, birth and death, and enlightened and unenlightened beings. In this stance, opposites are equally affirmed as undiscriminated aspects of reality. The second sentence, however, states that when the many thing-events are without self, that is, viewed as empty of substance, there is neither illusion nor enlightenment, neither birth nor death, neither enlightened nor unenlightened beings. The opposites initially affirmed have now each been negated with the recognition of the emptiness of each. Stopping here would make Dōgen a nihilist, but he continues with a third statement that the Buddha way is originally beyond both fullness (i.e., being, affirmation) and lack (i.e., emptiness, negation), and that for this reason there are birth and death, illusion and enlightenment, and enlightened and unenlightened beings. This signifies the reaffirmation of opposites on the basis of de-reifying their previous affirmation (both/and) and negation (neither/nor). While Qingyuan's saying shows that it is the emptiness, the negation of substantiality, that allows individual beings to be what they are, Dōgen's statements show that this same negation (of substance and utter nothing) allows opposites and even contradictories to be simultaneously affirmed. Thus this de-substantialized, de-reified reality that is "beyond fullness and lack" can simultaneously be affirmed in its "suchness."

Japanese Zen brings us full circle back to the *Prajñāpāramitā sūtras* that inspired the whole Mahāyāna movement with the modern Zen thinker D. T. Suzuki. On the basis of the *Prajñāpāramitā*'s *Diamond Sūtra*, Suzuki formulates what he calls the "logic of *soku-hi*" (or "is/not") (*sokuhi no ronri* 即非の論理). Its basic idea is that "'*A* is *A*' means '*A* is not-*A*,' and therefore '*A* is *A*.'" Or, in short, its logical formulation runs: "'*A* = ~*A*,' therefore '*A* = *A*.'" Suzuki takes this formula to be the foundation of *Prajñāpāramitā* thought expressed in the various paradoxical thought patterns of the *Diamond Sūtra*.[34] Inheriting this as the quintessence of Mahāyāna thought, Suzuki understands the Zen standpoint as transcending the logical dichotomization between being and non-being, yes and no, affirmation and negation. But what does this really mean? Both the principle of identity in formal logic and the logic of soku-hi assert that "*A* = *A*," the self-identity of *A*. But Suzuki's logic of soku-hi affirms *A* only after negating it. It asserts *A*'s self-identity via its self-negation. The point is that self-identity is not to be taken as ontologically (or substantially) independent, that is, without reference to its opposite. In other words, *A* is *A* only via the mediation of self-negation.[35] To be itself, a thing requires its not-being; it is what it is only in relation to what negates its identity. Self-identity cannot naïvely be assumed but is rather affirmed in relation to negation. Suzuki refers to a famous passage from a Zen story in which a Zen master states the following: "Do not call this a staff. If you do, it is an affirmation. If you do not, it is a negation. Apart from affirmation and negation say a word, quick, quick!"[36] Suzuki's understanding of Zen points to the pretheoretical livedness of experience before the bifurcations of subject and object, affirmation and negation. But as Suzuki's formula shows, that experience cannot be reduced to the simple tautology of monistic self-identity. It entails a dynamic movement, a dialectic involving negation, that reverses the dualistic, objectifying, and substantializing view of things. Suzuki also was a close friend of Nishida from their teen years, and it appears that there was a mutual influence in the formulations of their respective logics, Suzuki's logic of soku-hi and Nishida's logic of contradictory self-identity.[37]

What is noticeable in all these versions of Mahāyāna thought that I have examined is the collapsing of the dualities of conventional and ultimate, saṃsāra and nirvāṇa, and thing-event and emptiness, as well as of affirmation and negation, being and non-being, and yes and no, through their de-substantialization and mutual emptiness as aspects of the same reality. This also involves a double negation, the self-negation or emptying of emptiness. Enlightenment (nirvāṇa) is supposed to entail the experiential awareness of emptiness behind our discriminations of inter-dependent phenomena into apparent substances. The apparently substantial is empty of substantiality in virtue of its dependent origination. Apart from its conditions it is nothing, and enlightenment is the awareness of this emptiness or lack of ontological independence. But it is equally significant for the Mahāyāna Buddhist that this does not lead to the utter negation of the phenomenal world or its absorption into some transcendent oneness. The verdict common to Mahāyāna is that not only must we de-substantialize objects in their inter-dependent originations, but emptiness must be emptied as well to prevent any attachment to a world-denying nothingness or to an individual-absorbing universal. The reductive extremes of utter nothing in nihilism (*uccheda*) and substantial being in eternalism (*śāśvata*) are thus avoided by the middle path. The emptiness of emptiness itself thus prevents its one-sided transcendence of samsāra. It frees us from attachment not only to substantial being but also to utter nothingness. This is why emptiness must be emptied and collapsed into non-difference with inter-dependence and the inter-dependent. We see this inversion of emptiness relating it back to the world of things in the *Prajñāpāramitā* equation of emptiness and form; Madhyamaka's relating of emptiness and dependent origination, nirvāṇa and saṃsāra, ultimate and conventional; Yogācāra's notion of paratantra as the axis uniting parikalpita and parinispanna; Tiantai's notion of the middle that unifies conventional existence and emptiness; Huayan's notion of lishi wuai that collapses into shishi wuai; and Chan/Zen's simultaneous negation of substance and affirmation of suchness, and the logic of soku-hi.

Buddhism and Hegel

It is obvious that Nishida's dialectical thinking was influenced by both Hegel's notions of the self-determining concrete universal differentiating itself in judgment as "primordial differentiation," as well as in world history, and Mahāyāna Buddhism's non-dualist thinking that treads the middle path between the reifying extremes of substantial being and utter nothing. In this chapter we have looked at both Hegel's dialectical thought and the non-dualist strain apparent in some Mahāyāna schools. Before we return to Nishida's thinking, we are now in a position to compare and contrast some of the features we have discussed earlier in Mahāyāna Buddhism and Hegel's dialectics. Because we will conduct a more detailed and direct analysis of Nishida's thinking in light of these Hegelian and Buddhist concepts in a later chapter, I will leave till then any conclusion about the extent of Nishida's Hegelianism or Mahayanism. For now, I will conclude this chapter with a statement in regard to the similarity or difference and compatibility or incompatibility between Hegelian dialectics and Mahāyāna non-dualism. This will prepare us to look into the depth and breadth of Nishida's stance.

Both what Suzuki calls the logic of soku-hi in Mahāyāna and Hegel's dialectics point to the conditionality of self-identity on difference, that is, that it is dialectical rather than simply tautological. The meaning of *A* in its self-identity always entails more than its conceptually delimited sense and is always inclusive of, or refers to, its environing conditions that delimit that sense. *A* is self-identical only in reference to its negation encompassed in the whole situation to which it belongs. We find this both in the Mahāyāna logic of soku-hi and in Hegel's notion that "the true is the whole" (*PG* 21/*PS* 11). Nishida's holistic standpoint seems inspired by both. In negating the delimited significance of the propositional subject, we move toward comprehending the holistic situation to which it belongs and that constitutes its identity, which in Nishida's terms is its implacement in the predicate plane or pole (jutsugomen 述語面), place or basho. In Hegel the power that connects the grammatical subject with its predicate or unites opposites is the self-determining universal that cancels and preserves, hence sublates, the difference or opposition in a more comprehensive conception. This comprehension of the whole via negation, making possible the affirmation of the subject of a proposition, is common to Hegel, Zen, and Nishida. One commentator, Ha Tai Kim, for example, considers both Hegel's and Zen's mode of thought as a "logic of life" while contrasting their standpoints in terms of a "universal of universals" on Hegel's part and "nothing" (mu) on the part of Zen.[38] We may add that for Hegel, that unifying power, the concrete universal, is the concept realizing itself as the idea, as an all-encompassing universal. On the part of Mahāyāna, what constitutes the reality of phenomenal thing-events, as opposed to their nihility, is the emptiness of emptiness (śūnyatā), that is, the immanence of emptiness as dependent origination not transcending phenomenal reality. Hegel's view is still constrained by its conceptualism, while Mahāyāna Buddhism is primarily a practice and emphasizes the irreducibility of the holistic experience to any concept. Through prāxis, via the experience of emptiness treading on the "middle," it attempts to go beyond the conceptual dichotomy of being and non-being or, in logical terms, affirmation and negation. They provide very distinct approaches to the dichotomization of the lived whole and how to regain or realize its pre-dichotomized non-duality.

Another commentator, Alfonso Verdú, in his two books on Buddhist dialectics finds many parallels between Buddhism and Hegel, but he makes this discovery by applying Hegelian categories to Buddhist ideas.[39] For example, he interprets Huayan's conception of the dharmadhātu of lishi wuai and shishi wuai as a "positivistic synthesis" that supersedes or sublates the more "negativistic" dialectics of Nāgārjuna, and he finds this to be analogous to the Hegelian principle of the negation of negation that cancels and preserves, that is, sublates, differences and opposites.[40] And he takes the Huayan and the Hegelian understanding of causality as both involving the unity of essence and appearance that is a dialectical interplay of identity and difference. This is quite astounding in light of the very important Mahāyāna notion of emptiness, that is, the lack of own-being or essence in things. Verdú also sees a correspondence between Huayan's concept of "non-impededness" or "non-obstruction" (wuai; Jp. muge) and Hegel's "absolute concept" or "absolute idea" as both involving the previously mentioned sublational synthesis. Accordingly, in the Huayan development of Yogācāra's three natures, Verdú views paratantra that develops from parinispanna's activity of self-permeation as the concrete universal that brings together parinispanna qua true universality and parikalpita qua mere particularity. Although he admits that the correspondence between Hegelian and Huayan categories is loose earlier in his first book, elsewhere, toward the end of that book, he claims that Huayan dialectics finds its closure and completion within a synthesis of which, centuries later, Hegel became the Western formulator and herald. He states that "the all-comprehensive and all-involving identically subjective and objective dynamic impetus" of Huayan dialectics is the "Oriental foreshadowing of the Hegelian absolute idea."[41] Yet to look for such correspondences and to claim that one foreshadows the other or that one finds its closure in the other is misguided and ignores the disparity of their context and the formulation of their aims. In his second book on Buddhist dialectics, as if to reply to his critics, Verdú claims that he is not trying to "hegelianize" Buddhism or to "buddhify" Hegel and admits that there are wide and deep differences between the two.[42] He explains that the similarity he detects is more in the "form" than in the "content." He admits to being inspired by his study of Hegel in his systematization of Huayan doctrines in dialectical "triadic" form and justifies this by appeal to the structures present throughout the Buddhist texts and especially in the *Awakening of Faith*. As is evident, reality in both, in a certain sense, is self-determining. But he rightly points out the lack of the Hegelian starting point of the structures of pure thought in Buddhist tathatā (suchness). While agreeing with this last point, a triadic formula whereby opposites are unified or mediated in a third term is not unusual and may be found in many other sources from around the world. That alone does not justify the application of Hegelian concepts unless the point is to reduce Buddhism to Hegelianism, that is, to "hegelianize Buddhism." It is far more helpful to understand each by taking note of their differences despite the superficial similarities. What I find interesting here in regard to Nishida is that both approaches to the world, despite great differences, can be found somehow intertwined in his dialectical thinking. In fact, even before Verdú, Inoue Enryō (井上円了) (1858–1919), a significant predecessor of Nishida in twentieth-century Japanese philosophy who seems to have influenced Nishida's dialectical thinking, allegedly wrote in 1873 in his *Bukkyō katsuron* (*On the Revitalization of Buddhism*) that "the position of Buddhism, as manifested in Kegon-Tendai, does not differ in the slightest from that of Hegel" because "matter and mind both become the one reason, the Tathagata."[43]

On the basis of my discussions of Hegel and Mahāyāna, despite their common focus on the interrelationality of knowledge, truth, and reality and on the unity of opposites, we may distinguish their approaches in the following manner. The non-dual middle of Mahāyāna, as opposed to Hegel's sublational dialectic, (1) avoids conceptual reduction (to either extremes of being or non-being or affirmation or negation) and (2) involves the simultaneity of opposites as bi-conditionals rather than the resolution of opposition via sublation. Together, this means that the Mahāyāna scheme allows for the simultaneity of affirmation and negation as inter-dependent and without reifying either, while Hegel's scheme is of a teleological process of sublation that works toward the resolution of opposites in a culminating and all-embracing idea of self-recognition. Hegel's method is conceptual, involving the progression of reason that recognizes its self-identity in the oppositions, that is, the self-differentiation of its own concept qua concrete universal. The series of sublations presupposes that unifying concept and realizes it self-consciously in its self-conceiving, all-embracing idea. But Mahāyāna Buddhism precludes grasping the non-duality of opposites conceptually. Its stance is a prāxis of the middle that avoids both extremes as conceptual abstractions. This middle stance allows for the co-determinacy of what logically would be contradictory terms, that is, affirmation and negation, being and non-being, taking them in their emptiness. While for Hegel, sublational dialectics comes to fruition and realization in the retro-cognition of its entire process in self-conception, Mahāyāna practice aims to experience the paradoxical unity outside conception and reasoning by avoiding abstraction. The point for Hegel is to grasp the whole in an all-embracing concept. The point for Mahāyāna Buddhism is to become free from attachment to concepts that lead to reifying extremes. By contrast, for Hegel, it is the self-conceiving of the all-embracing idea (i.e., in philosophy) that will make man free. Their approaches are thus based on distinct premises.

Despite some superficial similarities, we thus find significant differences in how Hegel and Mahāyāna Buddhism approach the world. Yet we find traces of both Mahāyāna non-dualism and Hegelian dialectics in Nishida's dialectical philosophy. Nishida's conceptions of "absolute nothing," "absolutely contradictory self-identity," and "inverse correspondence" seem to be inspired by Mahāyāna non-duality, but his conceptions of "concrete universal" and "dialectical universal" and even the general use of the term "dialectics" in speaking of his mode of thinking are inherited from or influenced by Hegel. And in his use of the moment of negation (*hitei* 否定), Nishida appears to bind both orientations together. To what extent, then, is Nishida Hegelian, and to what extent is he Buddhist in his philosophy? Or is he more or other than either, whether taken alone or together? In the chapters of part 2 I will look at the dialectical features in Nishida's philosophical works.

PART II

DIALECTICS IN NISHIDA

3 Pure Experience, Self-Awareness, and Will

Dialectics in the Early Works (from the 1910s to the 1920s)

Now that we have undertaken a preliminary look at the various influences on Nishida's non-dualism and his dialectics, we are prepared to investigate the dialectical aspects of his thinking in detail. In this and the following chapters, we will examine Nishida's oeuvre roughly chronologically, so that one can discern the evolution or development of his dialectics from its implicit beginnings to its most pronounced and sophisticated formulations.

As mentioned in the introduction, commentators have divided Nishida's work into stages or periods in different ways. Even if we accept that Nishida's fundamental project remained the same throughout his career—to investigate concrete reality before its theoretical bifurcation—we cannot deny that his thinking evolved from work to work as he experimented with different formulations and terminologies. Yet it is not so easy to make clear-cut distinctions of periods in that development because the different formulations and modes of expression that allegedly characterize each stage of his thinking in fact overlap throughout the different stages. Looking at Nishida's works as a whole, we see the general theme of concrete reality formulated and discussed in different ways, beginning with "pure experience" (junsui keiken 純粋経験) in the early to mid-1910s and moving to the voluntarism of "the absolute will" (zettai ishi 絶対意志) and its "self-awareness" (jikaku 自覚) from the late 1910s to the early 1920s, the epistemology of basho or "place" in the mid-to-late 1920s to early 1930s, the concern with the sociohistorical world (shakaiteki rekishiteki sekai 社会的歴史的世界) and the concepts of "absolutely contradictory self-identity" (zettai mujunteki jikodōitsu) and "the dialectical universal" (benshōhōteki ippansha) in the 1930s and 1940s, and finally his interest in "the religious" (shūkyōteki 宗教的) discussed in terms of "inverse correspondence" (gyakutaiō) in the mid-1940s. All these different modes of expression have to do with what Nishida viewed as the concrete basis of the real that, while prior to the subject-object dichotomy, also encompasses such oppositional relations and contains the seed for their dialectical development. They all express in different ways what Nishida was convinced of throughout his philosophical life: the concrete un-differentiated foundation of everything, encompassing the many, including opposites and contradictories.

The dialectic becomes most pronounced and explicit in the 1930s when Nishida begins to refer to what he is describing as "dialectic" (benshōhō 弁証法). What earlier was still an implicit identity between opposites in pure experience becomes in the later works developed more systematically, first in terms of "contradictory unity" (mujunteki tōitsu 矛盾的統一) and then in terms of "contradictory self-identity" (mujunteki jikodōitsu 矛盾的自己同一), as involving a complex dialectic of mutual self-negation between opposing terms. Nishida's initial expressions of the concrete as a one that differentiates itself into the many later evolves into more of an emphasis on the simultaneity or co-existence between the one and the many.[1] And the heuristic focus on the predicate (jutsugo 述語) in the epistemology of place—the intent of which was to turn attention away from the grammatical subject—later recedes in favor of a greater emphasis on "the contradictory self-identity" between the opposing terms and their medium or mediation (*baikai* 媒介) whereby neither takes precedence. One might say that the dialectic, as it becomes more explicit, also becomes more complex and sophisticated in its formulation. The relationship with Hegel's dialectic, however, was always there from the beginning, with Nishida's explicit references to Hegel's ideas, such as the concrete universal (gutaiteki ippansha 具体的一般者) and judgment (*handan* 判断) as the self-differentiation of a pre-judicative whole. And the relationship with Mahāyāna non-dualist thinking, already implicit in his characterization of pure experience, soon becomes apparent in the mid-1920s when he starts making use of the concept of "nothing" (mu 無), which then continues throughout the later stages of his oeuvre.

For my purposes, I will divide my discussion of the development of Nishida's dialectic throughout his works into this and the next four chapters (chapters 3 to 7). This chapter will deal with his early works from the 1910s to the early 1920s, focusing on the concepts of pure experience, self-awareness, and absolute will. Chapter 4 will deal with his epistemology of place, developed from the mid-1920s to the early 1930s. Chapters 5 and 6 will deal with his dialectics of the sociohistorical world, developed throughout the 1930s. And chapter 7 will discuss his dialectical ideas of religion that he worked on in the 1940s before passing away. The purpose of these chapters will be expository, to help prepare the reader for the more ambitious and challenging discussions in part 3.

Nishida does not employ the term "dialectic" (benshōhō) to describe the method or content of his thinking until the 1930s, but we notice the influence of Hegel's dialectics, along with explicit references to Hegel, from the beginning of his career. In his early works, written from 1911 to the mid-1920s, Nishida seems to be under the spell of a variety of philosophical influences he has been digesting, even while he is attempting to develop his own system of thought. He gropes for adequate formulations that will express the pre-bifurcated concreteness that founds our immediate experience and subsequent reflections. Nevertheless, we can still find in these early works the germ that will sprout into his later uniquely and more explicitly dialectical ideas. In *Zen no kenkyū* (『善の研究』; *Inquiry into the Good*) of 1911, the theme is pure experience (junsui keiken); and from *Jikaku ni okeru chokkan to hansei* (『自覚に於ける直観と反省』; *Intuition and Reflection in Self-Awareness*) of 1917 to *Geijutsu to dōtoku* (『芸術と道徳』; *Art and Morality*) of 1923, the themes are self-awareness (jikaku) and absolute will (zettai ishi). In all these formulations we already see dialectical implications.

Pure Experience

I begin my inquiry with Nishida's first original work, *Zen no kenkyū* (*Inquiry into the Good*) of 1911, which established his name among the intellectuals of Japan right after the turn of the century.[2] As I discussed in chapter 1, what led Nishida to dialectics was his concern with overcoming the dualist gap and providing in its place a new, non-dualist paradigm. In his maiden work, this concern is expressed in his concept of "pure experience" (junsui keiken), a term borrowed from William James,[3] whereby the categories of subject and object in cognition are no longer seen as foundational but rather as abstractions derived from a more originary and pre-reflective experience. At the opening of *Zen no kenkyū* Nishida states, "By *pure* [in *pure experience*] I mean the state of experience just as it truly is without any deliberative discrimination . . . when . . . there is not yet a subject or an object" (Z1 9). The terminology is already misleading in that the "experience" here is not something that lies on the subjective side of the subject-object dichotomy but rather concrete reality, encompassing their implicit dichotomy before bifurcation. It can thus be reduced to neither materiality nor ideality. As neither mere experiencer nor mere experienced, the experience here is "pure" (*junsui* 純粋) in that it is unmediated and is prior to its dichotomization into the various dualities of spirit-body, mind-thing, ideal-real, inner-outer, immanence-transcendence, and so on. Constituting the point of subject-object union (*shukyaku gōichi no ten* 主客合一の点), it precedes differentiation into such dichotomies, that is, as subject-object non-differentiation (*shukyaku mibun* 主客未分) (Z1 11). Nevertheless, Nishida at this stage still reveals an idealist tendency in identifying the primordial fact of experience with the phenomenon of consciousness (Z1 44).

Because we find ourselves always already immersed within it, our attempts to objectify pure experience as such perpetually fail. Take the event of a concert pianist playing his or her favorite piece in masterly perfection, or of a music enthusiast simply listening to that beautiful piece. The most concrete occurrence of reality in either example is nothing but the happening and its awareness together as one whole, an event sufficient in itself, before any reflective dichotomization of it into experiencing subject and experienced object (Z1 9). Thinking can analyze that event into components only after the fact. Pure experience is always in the present, and judgment about it happens only later, eradicating that original purity and unity. Yet Nishida also views pure experience as a spontaneously developing reality, a concrete whole encompassing those elements as implicit components. From that initially unsullied concrete whole, judgment emerges to divide its unity grammatically into subject and predicate or epistemologically into knower and known. Pure experience qua concrete reality then provides the non-propositional basis for its abstraction into the propositional form of judgment. On the basis of the concrete event of the concert pianist playing, one can make the judgment "The pianist is playing." Any intellectual analysis or discrimination must assume that prior concrete whole of pure experience. But Nishida takes this further. Ontologically, the entire world of separate objects and the individual knower emerge only as abstractions out of that concrete whole of pure experience. Experience precedes the individual, not vice versa (Z1 6–7). Thus Nishida speaks of the one reality developing itself out of itself, a universality (*ippan* 一般, *ippansei* 一般性) realizing itself in the fact of pure experience (Z1 22, 52). Nishida thus takes pure experience, beyond the normal significance of "experience," to be a self-forming unifying activity (*tōitsu sayō* 統一作用) that is the basis of the world's dynamism.

Nishida characterizes this self-unifying activity of pure experience in terms of the will or volition (*ishi* 意志). This shows influence from some of the German philosophers of the nineteenth century who spoke of the will in cosmological or ontological terms, most notably Arthur Schopenhauer.[4] For Nishida, it is the drive inherent within that concrete whole to realize itself in self-differentiation and development (Z1 12–13). That volitional reality, taken in cosmic proportions, may be understood as God. Creation thus is God's volitional activity of self-expression, and God is the unifier presupposed by all unities of experience (Z1 145). Nishida characterizes this self-unifying drive of concrete reality in a variety of formulations throughout this book, such as "the great system of consciousness," our "true self" that can be equated with God as the grounding unity of both spirit and nature, and cosmic reason or "patterning" (ri 理) (Z1 21, 61, 81–82).[5] So it is not the individual self that possesses pure experience, but the reverse: pure experience, as the non-differentiation of experience-cum-reality, but understood in terms of this cosmic volitional reality, is what unfolds into the self as subject vis-à-vis reality as object. The subjective experience of each individual person, then, is but a state within the dynamic flow of self-differentiation belonging to that self-realizing concrete whole.

Hegel's influence is already conspicuous here. In describing that self-differentiating concrete reality, Nishida appears to make use of the Hegelian notion of a universal that is concrete in its self-determinations. "I" and "thing" in their mutual differentiation become understood as abstractions from the spontaneous self-unfolding of the concrete universal. Taking "the fact of pure experience" as the self-realization of the universal, Nishida states in *Zen no kenkyū* that "since our pure experience is a systematic development, the unifying force [of concrete facts] working at its root must immediately be the universality of the concept" (Z1 22). We can thus also trace this idea to Hegel's understanding of the "concept" (Begriff). As Nishida states, "I have included at the root of the idea of the spontaneous self-unfolding of pure experience, the idea of the development of Hegel's so-called concrete concept" (Z1 163). He also writes that by the "immediacy" (*chokusetsu* 直接) of pure experience, he means an "independent and autonomous concrete whole, something like Hegel's concept" (Z1 147).[6] One year after *Zen no kenkyū*, in an essay (1912) included later in *Shisaku to taiken* (『思索と体験』; *Thinking and Experience*) (1915) Nishida, while referring to Hegel, even makes explicit usage of the dialectical terminology of *an sich* (in-itself), *für sich* (for-itself), and *an und für sich* (in- and for-itself) in order to explain the process of that universal's transition from implicit wholeness to self-differentiation and self-confrontation and finally to its self-clarifying return to the original whole (Z1 211–212). That is, from the concrete whole of pure experience (the moment of in-itself), there arises judgment about the experience. But the sense of judgment is alienated from that initially pure experience, its concreteness, so that it relates to the original experience as an other (the moment of for-itself). Yet in that relationship it is re-integrated into the concrete qua greater whole encompassing both of those moments (in-and-for-itself).[7] This unifying activity of the universal that encompasses distinctions and contradictions is also characterized, with an eye toward Hegel's notion of Geist (*seishin* 精神, "spirit"), as "spirit containing infinite oppositions" (Z1 58, 149). All these appropriations of Hegelian notions, one might say, are but stepping-stones that lead to more mature developments in Nishida's later thinking. In this early stage of his career, despite obvious differences in the way he takes Hegel's ideas from what Hegel might have meant, Nishida appears to be sympathetic toward Hegel and to feel much affinity with him. Nishida, however, will work out the differences between his thinking and Hegel's in his later works.

In any case, we notice a dialectic already implicit within the concept of pure experience, for its development can be said to be self-contradictory. From its primordial wholeness that cannot be uttered, it differentiates itself in the structure of judgment in order to articulate itself. In itself, before self-differentiation, it cannot be objectified; it cannot be made into a subject of a statement; it is unsayable. Yet in its self-differentiation in judgment, the unspeakable is spoken. This idea of the concrete whole's self-differentiation persists throughout all of Nishida's lifework. Its implicit dialectic is operative behind all of Nishida's formulations of concrete reality. Its formulation here in terms of pure experience provides the germ for its later, more explicitly dialectical formulations, such as those in terms of contradictory self-identity.[8] And that dialectic, described in terms of God's volitional self-manifesting act in *Zen no kenkyū*, also provides the germ for the concept of "self-awareness" (jikaku) as an act of self-mirroring, an idea that Nishida develops in the ensuing years, and that in turn will lead him to his concept of basho or "place" as the horizon of self-mirroring.[9]

Self-Awareness and Absolute Will

In the works following *Zen no kenkyū*, during the late 1910s and early 1920s, Nishida develops the volitional aspect of the concrete in his maiden work further in terms of his notion of "self-awareness" (or: "self-awakening" or "self-realization") (jikaku). We see this, for example, in *Jikaku ni okeru chokkan to hansei* (*Intuition and Reflection in Self-Awareness*) (1917),[10] *Ishiki no mondai* (『意識の問題』; *The Issue of Consciousness*) (1920), and *Geijutsu to dōtoku* (*Art and Morality*) (1923).[11] This is the period when he becomes more involved in debating the dualistic theses of the Kantian epistemology of Lotze, Hermann Cohen, and Rickert, leading to more systematic articulations of his idea of non-dualistic concreteness in the sphere of epistemology. We find Nishida responding to the Neo-Kantian view that, on the premise of the subject-object distinction, takes cognition to be a process involving the re-construction of what is given in intuition. But as we saw in his earlier concept of pure experience, Nishida views the dichotomy as part of a dynamic unfolding from a whole already in place. Rather than a moment external to concrete intuition, reflection is its internal development. The need to explain how that dynamic of fission can unfold from a fundamental non-distinction led Nishida in *Jikaku ni okeru chokkan to hansei* to formulate the concept of "self-awareness" (jikaku) as encompassing both pre-dichotomized experience and dichotomizing reflection. He uses this term—which also includes the connotations of "self-awakening" and "self-realization"—to designate the dynamic uniting the "intuition" (*chokkan* 直観) of immediate experience and the subsequent "reflection" (*hansei* 反省) that analyzes that initially non-distinct experience, objectifying it and re-constructing it in the dichotomized terms of epistemological subject and object or grammatical subject and predicate. As intuition leads to reflection, each reflection can in turn serve as the intuited content of further reflection. "Self-awareness" then names that on-going dynamic, uniting the two moments of intuition (experience) and reflection (thought) in an endless process of self-realization (Z2 13–14).

Nishida further conceives of this dynamic process of self-awareness in terms of an internal self-mirroring, a mirroring of its dynamic into elements within itself. This is not only a development of the earlier dynamic of pure experience in *Zen no kenkyū* but also a further appropriation of Hegel's self-determining concrete universal while also reflecting an influence from Josiah Royce's notion of the self-representative system in his *The World and the Individual*.[12] Cognition, understood thus in terms of this dynamic of self-awareness, is in marked contrast with the Kantian view. The determining of its content, unlike in Kantian hylo-morphism that separates the form and the matter of cognition, proves to be an internal occurrence of self-determining or self-differentiation into elements. Although the elements mirror or image the dynamic whole, the whole escapes reduction to any mirror image since objectification falls only within it. The dynamic whole of this process engulfs the self in its lived experience (*Erlebnis*). The constitution of the individual self is only a product of that concrete process of self-awareness. And not only the subject of cognition but also the world of objects emerges as a product of its self-mirroring self-determination. We are told that this prior concrete holism enfolds an infinity of possibilities in its unfolding.

As in his previous work of 1911, Nishida understands the driving force behind this unfolding in terms of the will. But during the 1920s, starting with *Jikaku ni okeru chokkan to hansei,* the ontological aspect of the volitional act, its free creativity, comes further into the light as Nishida discusses it in greater detail, calling it "the absolute will" (zettai ishi), "the a priori underlying all a prioris," "the act of all acts." Here the volitional act becomes seen as constituting the a priori horizon for all modes of intentionality, such as thinking, seeing, and acting, and their respective objects, and hence enfolding and unfolding the structural dualities of subject-object or noesis-noema (Z2 219, 224, 241). Judgment or dichotomizing thought in general is but the will's self-awareness, mirroring itself in dichotomized terms. The dynamism of the will, then, in its self-awareness is the concrete universal reality that grounds human existence vis-à-vis its world of objects, as the originary fusion point from which stem the various oppositional dualities of subject-object, ideality-reality, and inside-outside, all as distinct aspects of its holistic structure (Z2 394–395). A major influence here, aside from Schopenhauer's metaphysics of the will, is Johann Gottlieb Fichte. In his search for the ground that drives the self-differentiating unfolding of pure experience, Nishida was led to Fichte's notion of *Tathandlung* or "fact-act." For Fichte, this designates the originary pre-reflective self-determining act of the I, accompanied by its intellectual intuition, which grounds immediate consciousness.[13] In *Jikaku ni okeru chokkan to hansei* Nishida interprets *Tathandlung*—under Neo-Kantian influence, specifically naming Rickert—in terms of an "ought" (tōi 当為; Germ. *Sollen*) that precedes being (aru ある; "to be"), that is, the products of differentiation. But Nishida also argues that "*is* and *ought* are two aspects of one experience" (Z2 46–47). That is, one intuits simultaneously one's own existence (being) and one's self-identity in the judgment "I = I" as the ought that logically grounds the former in the distinction of thinker and thought (Z2 45–46).[14] Nishida interprets the will as the driving force of this activity of differentiation and identification. It is the moment of pure experience that grounds reflection and defines the limit of thought by exceeding any causal explanation (Z2 204). As such, the will is the absolute and transcendental creative source of being and hence in itself is nothing (mu 無).

In *Geijutsu to dōtoku* (1923) Nishida continues this postulation of the pure transcendental and absolute will (*chōetsuteki ishi* 超越的意志, zettai ishi), unfolding the dichotomies of knower-known, subject-object, self-thing, and so on that constitute the world of concrete reality in its forming (*bilden*) and reproducing (*ab-bilden*) (Z3 13, 188, 234–235). In *Ishiki no mondai* (1920) each contradiction between opposites of a duality provides the positive content, the material for a deeper receding horizon, and the deepest horizon is provided by the will as the act of all acts that can no longer be thematized or objectified. All oppositions are thus traced to the will as constituting the most concrete horizonal standpoint. And in constituting the horizon for all subsequent acts, that pure activity of the will is enveloped ultimately within a dark abyss that makes possible its self-awareness and self-contradiction. This is the idea that Nishida develops further a few years later (1926) in terms of a "place" (basho 場所) delimited by nothing (mu), or "the place of true nothing" (shin no mu no basho 真の無の場所). Referring to Hegel's contention that the knowledge of knowledge (self-reflective cognition) is self-contradictory and that without it there is no truth, Nishida, in *Geijutsu to dōtoku*, takes the transcendental will as thus providing that contradictory unity that encompasses the contradiction of self-reflective cognition along with all oppositions (Z3 151). The will in its dialectical unity already enfolds the contradictory oppositions it unfolds so that in its self-articulating self-mirroring, the "a posteriori returns to a priori . . . , [and] particular returns to universal" (Z3 180).

Authentic selfhood cannot be separated from the dynamism of that holistic process. We are told that one's consciousness is but a manifestation of this greater dialectic of a "trans-individual self," a creative act belonging to the transcendental will (Z3 186). We manifest the absolute will's self-awareness. The individual self is thus a "dialectical unity of infinite acts" (Z3 48). The individual's consciousness appears at the point of divergence where the enveloping broader standpoint of the universal and the enveloped narrower standpoint of the individual, outer and inner, clash and unite in contradiction. Consciousness appears at this point where the universal as concrete is particularized (Z3 56–57). Nishida characterizes this particularization as "the concentration of the meaning of the whole world into a single point," "the transformation of the whole world into one will," "the inclusion of the whole within the particular" (Z3 215). As a chiasmatic locus connecting inner and outer, self and world, the body also comes into play in this focus or concentration (Z3 246). This sort of interrelationship between inner and outer and individual and universal is worked out in the 1930s more explicitly in terms of the dialectic between the individual acting self and the environing world. And in regard to time, the significance of the concrete whole is condensed and mirrored into the present as its focal point (Z2 192–193). From that singular point of the present, the will unfolds the dualities and oppositions it enfolds, extending its circular horizon in wave-like fashion to articulate its holism (Z2 207). So it is not only the oppositional dualities of subject-object, spirit-matter, self-other, and so on but also the temporal differentiation of past-future that mirror in their coincidence the holistic dynamism of absolute volition in its self-differentiating self-awareness. This chiasmatic concentration of the spatial and the temporal will become another important feature of Nishida's dialectic in the 1930s. But already in the 1920s, as we have seen, Nishida takes the individual's consciousness along with the singular moment of the present as focal points that realize the concrete universal's internal development, differentiating itself from within.

Recent commentators have noticed in these early ideas the tendency toward an idealism or a monism. For example, Yoko Arisaka and Andrew Feenberg speak of an apparent "regression into a naïve kind of objective idealism," and Gereon Kopf discusses a possible privileging of "identity over difference" in the emphasis on unity.[15] The later formulations certainly develop the theme of pre-reflective concrete reality in a direction that is less monistic and more explicitly dialectical without necessarily prioritizing or privileging the universal over the individual or sameness over difference. The non-dualism becomes more dynamic and sophisticated, less easily characterized as another version of German absolute idealism. Yet we must also acknowledge that the later formulations are developments taking off from these early attempts at a non-dualistic philosophy. They are products of Nishida's attempts to overcome the shortcomings of these early formulations, to better describe and further clarify what he was trying to express. In his time, it was the ambiguity of meaning in his conception of pure experience, as well as of self-awareness and pure will, that led some of his contemporaries to charge him with psychologism. Nishida's acknowledgment of the inadequacy of these formulations led him to supplant them with other ways of characterizing the concretely real (Z8 255) and to develop his epistemology of basho or place in the mid-1920s. And his desire to articulate the non-duality of the concrete with greater precision led him to further dialectical adventures in the 1930s.

4 Dialectics in the Epistemology of Place (from the Late 1920s to the Early 1930s)

NISHIDA IN THE late 1920s further develops his conceptions of self-differentiation and self-contradiction that we saw under the earlier rubrics of pure experience, self-awareness, and the absolute will. In the essays of the 1920s, compiled in 1927 as *Hatarakumono kara mirumono e* (『働くものから見る物へ』; *From the Working to the Seeing*), we find Nishida breaking through his previous positions in his attempt to develop a theory that overcomes epistemological dualism while precluding any possible psychologistic mistaking of his position. The result is a reformulation of his ideas in terms of what he calls basho (場所) or "place." The implications of this epistemology of place are further worked out in *Ippansha no jikakuteki taikei* (『一般者の自覚的体系』; *The Self-Aware System of Universals*) of 1930 and *Mu no jikakuteki gentei* (『無の自覚的限定』; *The Self-Aware Determination of Nothing*) of 1932. In all three works Nishida further elaborates on the dialectical implications already present in his ideas, moving toward his radical conception of an absolute dialectic (zettai benshōhō 絶対弁証法) of the 1930s.

The root concept of the dialectical implications of his epistemology here is this notion of basho (場所) that at its most concrete level is delimited by absolutely nothing. As the most concrete level of reality-cum-experience, he takes this to be the grounding immediacy that embraces all the contradictory planes involving self and world, whether in terms of the epistemological subject and its object, the grammatical subject and its predicates, or the determining act of consciousness (noesis) and its determined object (noema). Nishida takes all such dichotomizations to be implaced within this place as hence irreducible to the merely ideal or the merely real. As an expansion of his earlier notion of self-awareness (jikaku 自覚), place is seen as enveloping everything within as its own mirroring reflections. So the concrete, now characterized as a "place," thus becomes explicitly seen as the broadest context, not delimited by anything else, not determined by anything opposing it. In its indeterminacy or un-differentiatedness, it is thus an "absolute nothing" (zettai mu 絶対無) that envelops all in its self-differentiating self-determinations. This formulation thus re-poses the thematic of self-awareness more explicitly as a self-determination of the place of its self-mirroring. The judicative act is thus to be understood accordingly as unfolding from that self-delimitation of the enfolding concrete. This unfolding dynamism involves a series of determinate places within determinate places, bashos within bashos, leading from the concrete to the abstract, from the undetermined place of absolute nothing ultimately to the determination of the object of cognition, the grammatical subject of judgment. This obviously is a further re-casting of Hegel's concrete universal, but this time in terms of place rather than in terms of pure experience or absolute will. Of course, I do not want to suggest here that Nishida and Hegel are talking about the same thing. But Nishida was inspired by the notion of a self-determining universal found in Hegel's attempt to overcome Kantian dualism. We will find, however, that basho in its most concrete sense, for Nishida, is not really a "universal" in the sense ordinarily meant in Western metaphysics, for example, Plato's idea or Hegel's Begriff. Nishida's incorporation of absolute nothing, along with his notion of place, will lead his view of the concrete in a direction away from Hegel's understanding of the concrete. Although Nishida refers to the Hegelian notion of the concrete universal throughout the second half of *Hatarakumono kara mirumono e,* he will eventually distinguish his perspective from that of Hegel's. (In the final chapters of this work, I will examine the related question of the adequacy of such terminology.) In the following sections, I will discuss Nishida's various formulations of his ideas from *Hatarakumono kara mirumono e* that lead up the epistemology of place with their dialectical implications. I will then look at the dialectical implications within his basho theory from 1926 while also drawing from his formulations in *Ippansha no jikakuteki taikei* and *Mu no jikakuteki gentei.*

On the Way to Place

The epistemological theory of basho or place is not clearly systematized until the essay "Basho" ("Place") in the second part of *Hatarakumono kara mirumono e.* In the essays included in the first part, we still see Nishida groping toward an adequate reformulation of his ideas. He searches for a way to conceive the underlying unity of cognition that does not succumb to any sort of dualism, as in Kant's theory. In the essay "Naibuchikaku ni tsuite" (「内部知覚について」; "On Internal Perception") (1924) he still refers to the self-awareness of the dynamic will as providing the connection between ideal and real (Z3 312), and in "Butsurigenshō no haigo ni arumono" (「物理現象の背後に有るもの」; "That Which Lies behind Physical Phenomena") (1924) he refers to Fichte's notion of the absolute I that is at the ground of the opposition between I and not-I (Z3 304).[1] But the pre-basho discussions from the first part that stand out in their anticipations of later dialectical development are on the topics of time and the present and on the universal's self-determination in judgment.

We see Nishida grappling with the issue of time in a manner distinct from its linear conceptions. He does this by focusing on the present (*genzai* 現在) in its internal embracing of past and future, for example, in the 1923 essay "Chokusetsu ni ataeraretamono" (「直接に与えられたもの」; "The Immediately Given") (*Z3* 275, 277). This move anticipates his future working out of the dialectics of the present. In "Naibuchikaku ni tsuite" Nishida speaks of the present as the ultimate point of an infinite depth from which world and self, time and space, unfold in a dialectic of subjective and objective unities. It provides the higher unity that embraces the unities of both the object-world and the epistemological subject, that is, both external and internal unities. The present is this concrete unity of subject-object embracing all the transitions within the world of things and the world of mind (*Z3* 322–323). In the 1925 essay "Hyōgen sayō" (「表現作用」; "The Act of Expression") Nishida elaborates on this theme in a manner akin to Dōgen's (道元) notion of time with the explanation that a singular event, in its momentariness, involves a relationship to the whole of the environing conditions that permit its occurrence, that is, the entire world (*Z3* 368). In other words, the "whole" focused on a single moment is not just temporal in terms of the past and the future but spatial in terms of the environment embracing subject and object. This conception of the present as a focal point of space-time anticipates the inter-dimensional, inter-directional— or chiasmatic—complexity that becomes pronounced in his radical dialectics of the 1930s. But more immediately we see Nishida moving closer, in this conception of the present, to his conception of basho that is explicitly formulated a few years later in his "Basho" ("Place") essay of 1926. In relation to the present, Nishida alludes here to the place, or basho, of self-awareness, a place transcending and enveloping the self, as that wherein the self knows itself in its self-mirroring. What we ordinarily call "time" is established from that place in the interconnections between yesterday and tomorrow, past and future (*Z3* 350–351). Nishida will repeatedly come back to this issue of time as flowing from the present in its place-like quality that embraces past and future. In an application of the Hegelian idea of the concrete universal in temporal terms, Nishida will come to speak of this as the "self-determination of the eternal now" (*eien no ima no jikogentei* 永遠の今の自己限定).

Nishida, in part 1 of *Hatarakumono kara mirumono e,* also develops his analysis of judgment in the Hegelian manner that will become more fully worked out in part 2 in the "Basho" essay. He takes judgment as the self-differentiation of the concrete universal,[2] but also in conjunction with his concept of self-awareness in terms of self-mirroring. In other words, the universal as the predicate (jutsugo 述語) determines itself as the grammatical subject (*shugo* 主語), and this means the self-mirroring of the universal in its determined image qua grammatical subject, its object. Hence in judgment, the universal is really its own grammatical subject and a "substance" (*hontai* 本体) (*Z3* 330–331). Nishida adds that a truly concrete universal must encompass not only a positive content but also its other, the negation of that content that determines it vis-à-vis, and as, what it is not. Only in enveloping that contradiction between its finite content and its negation, its being and its non-being, is a universal thoroughly universal and concretely so. For example, the universal "color" must embrace the opposition between "red" and "not-red," the latter meaning all other colors. And at the deepest and most concrete level, that whole that embraces all such oppositions, that is, between being in general and non-being in general, would have to transcend the categories of both being and non-being (*Z*3 332–333). The universal that forms itself into the grammatical subject of a judgment and into the various dichotomies and oppositions, including relations of contradiction, then, Nishida reasons, must be something like a formless and empty space that can determine itself as the various particular forms and embrace them in their interrelations, in their positions and negations, positivities and negativities (*Z*3 340). For this reason, Nishida chooses to designate the deepest level of concrete reality as "nothing" (mu 無) (*Z*3 332–333). Taking the nothing here as what embraces or envelops its own determinations or differentiations into beings, Nishida is eventually led in the second part of the book, starting with the "Basho" essay, to conceive of this "universal" in the more spatial terms of "place" or basho. Hence the reader of Nishida must be careful not to understand what Nishida means by "universal" (*ippansha* 一般者) as a mere concept, especially at its most concrete level, where it is defined as "nothing."

At this point Nishida already sees himself as bridging the gap opened in Kantian hylo-morphism. That is, form and matter, determiner and determined, are seen here in their dynamic unity in the self-forming formlessness of the concrete whole. The unity here is not a substance (in the traditional sense) but a non-substantial or a substratumless act (*substratlose Tätigkeit*) (*Z*3 344–345). In "Hyōgen sayō" of 1925, Nishida adds to this the necessity of the contradictory co-existence of one and many for the universal's self determination as such a self-forming formlessness (*Z*3 359). That is, the formlessness, the nothing, is one and yet simultaneously plural. With the Hegelian concept of the concrete universal in mind, Nishida explains the act of constitution as an act of self-predication. In other words, the self-formation of the formless in judicative terms means self-articulation via auto-predication. As we just saw, the universal is its own grammatical subject. Furthermore, the term *basho* again makes its appearance here before its theoretical elaboration in the "Basho" essay. Identifying the universal with the will as what is operative behind such constitution, Nishida states that the world of reality is the basho, that is, place, for the will's (self-)realization. The basho or place of reflection for the epistemological I is also the basho or place of realization for the volitional I. The world therefore becomes the cross section or chiasma whereupon the I in both aspects—epistemological and volitional—constitutes its objects and realizes itself. And what encompasses both dimensions of the world, the epistemological and the volitional, Nishida states, is the deeper standpoint of intuition (chokkan 直観), on the basis of which the world is a world of expression (*hyōgen* 表現). The world is a basho or place of reflection for cognition, a place of realization for the will, and a place of expression for intuition (*Z3* 382). This understanding of "intuition" will become significantly associated with the most concrete level of place in the development of his system of places (basho) in the following year (1926). All these dimensions of the world are unfoldings of the self-forming formlessness, the self-differentiating holistic context wherein we always find ourselves implaced. This naturally leads Nishida to the necessity of elaborating this concept of place or basho.

The Epistemology of Place and Its Dialectical Implications

In the second part of *Hatarakumono kara mirumono e,* especially beginning with the essay "Basho," and then in the following two volumes, *Ippansha no jikakuteki taikei* and *Mu no jikakuteki gentei,* Nishida develops and elaborates on the concept of place as the concrete ground on which his previous concepts of will, self-awareness, and even pure experience are implaced. He proclaims that it is the "a priori of a prioris" wherein the true self is found and founded, transcending and enveloping the various oppositional dichotomies, such as subject-object. It is here that, while breaking with some of the previous vocabulary, his formulations take on a more Buddhistic color with the notion of "nothing" (mu) in its relation to the concept of place. But at the same time, that Buddhist tint is shaded by the Hegelian terminology that will become even more pronounced in the 1930s.

The Concrete Universal and Place

By the second part of *Hatarakumono kara mirumono e,* Nishida comes to understand the intuitive immediacy of an undifferentiated holistic situation—as in the example used earlier in *Zen no kenkyū* of "a running horse" that precedes the judgment "A horse is running"—in terms of place (*Z3* 393–400). In other words, he visualizes the undifferentiatedness that implicitly includes its distinctions, containing the germ for its unfolding articulation, in light of this notion of a place (basho) enveloping those distinct terms, the wherein of experience, experiencer, and experienced. In contrast to Aristotle's substance that cannot contradict itself, this place must be non-substantial in order for it to enfold and unfold the terms in their mutual oppositions and even contradictions, for example, between subject and object, self and not-self, affirmation and negation, and being and non-being. As delimited by nothing, its empty space refuses positive determination from without. Instead, it is determined only in its self-differentiations from within. Nishida thus now explicates what he previously took to be the self-contradiction in the will's self-mirroring self-awareness in terms of a non-substantial and un-delimited field that implies, but without articulation, the synchronic immediacy of oppositional terms. He associates the self-differentiating concrete universal with that field as a place clearing space for the beings that emerge within it (*Z*3 403, 523), or, in more restricted epistemological terms, for the beings objectified in our cognitive experience. This more restricted opening of place in cognition is the field of consciousness (ishiki no ba 意識の場), which Nishida comes to characterize as the place of oppositional or relative nothing (tairitsuteki mu no basho 対立的無の場所, sōtai mu no basho 相対無の場所). But deeper and broader than the field of consciousness is the concrete field that grounds—and envelops the perimeters for—even the field of consciousness and the dichotomies of subject-object, subject-predicate, particular-universal, and ultimately being–non-being. This is what Nishida characterizes in these works as the place of true nothing (shin no mu no basho 真の無の場所) or place of absolute nothing (*zettai mu no basho* 絶対無の場所).[3]

In the second part of *Hatarakumono kara mirumono e,* Nishida continues to make use of Hegelian motifs, especially the concrete universal that differentiates itself in judgment. He retains his general approach to the dialectical structuring of opposition and conflict by agreeing with Hegel that "the truth is the whole." That is, he takes opposing terms as abstractions from the concrete universal. The concrete universal (*konkrete Allgemeinheit;* gutaiteki ippansha 具体的 一般者) that Hegel opposed to the abstract universal (*abstrakte Allgemeinheit; chūshōteki ippansha* 抽象的 一般者) is what becomes articulated in judgment in various dichotomized terms.[4] In connection to this, Nishida in both parts (*Z*3 331, 409) refers to Hegel's understanding of judgment as the differentiation or division of what in itself is a concrete whole.[5] While an abstract universal subsumes all its individual terms by eliminating their differences and abstracting their common feature, the concrete universal already includes and retains their specific differences. Its self-determination, whereby the universal objectifies itself into what belongs to it, is in judicative terms the articulation that makes explicit its implicit inner division. But by the time of his formulation of his theory of place, Nishida is beginning to obtain a clearer vision of how his understanding of the concrete universal might differ from Hegel's. As opposed to Hegel's conception of the self-differentiation of the concept (Begriff), Nishida's formulation is made in light of the distinctly non-Hegelian notion of basho, place. Furthermore, Nishida's characterization of place in its most concrete standpoint as an un-delimited "nothing" (mu) alludes to Buddhist ideas. In contra-distinction to Hegel, Nishida here takes the concrete universal in its non-delimitation or non-differentiation as grounded in a nothing (mu) that is a place (basho) rather than a concept (Begriff) (*Z*3 523). So rather than subsuming and imposing itself on individuals like a conceptual universal, Nishida's basho envelops them, recedes to clear room for them, and enfolds them to unfold them. In "Sōda hakushi ni kotau" (「左田博士に答ふ」; "In Reply to Dr. Sōda") of 1927, Nishida explains:

> What I mean by place [basho] is not simply the so-called universal concept but the place wherein particulars are implaced, a mirror that mirrors objects within.

> In saying so, it may be thought that mirror and objects are distinct things. However, while establishing the particular within itself as its own determination, the universal in opposition to the particular, remaining thoroughly universal itself, does not become particular. (Z3 502)

Later, in 1930, in the "General Summary" of *Ippansha no jikakuteki taikei*, Nishida, in distinguishing his thought from Hegel's, states that Hegel does not explicate the sense of the universal that determines the individual by enveloping it. Hegel provides no satisfactory support for, and explication of, the transition from the object of determination to the determining act of self-awareness. Nishida thus characterizes Hegel's logic as still an object logic (*taishōteki ronrigaku* 対象的論理学), a logic of the grammatical subject (*shugoteki ronrigaku* 主語的論理学) (Z4 335). For Nishida, by contrast, place is that which cannot be reified into a grammatical subject or object since it is the place of their implacement. Nishida is thus compelled to find a conceptual scheme that can turn us away from the object, in order to de-focus our attention away from the grammatical subject of a judgment.[6] For this purpose, he instead looks to the predicate but conceives it in a new way.

The Predicate

Nishida makes an association between the concrete universal qua place in its relation to the individual, on the one hand, and the predicate in its relation to the grammatical subject, on the other. Through this association Nishida intends to make a heuristic move calculated to de-focus one's attention from the grammatical subject, turning it away from the tendency of thinking in terms of objects, that is, noematizing thought or what he calls "object logic" (*taishō ronri* 対象論理). The point is to open one's awareness to the concrete whole of one's situatedness, providing the meaningfulness or sense that is lived before any judgment making. Taking the predicate beyond its merely grammatical significance, Nishida designates that pre-reflective whole "the transcendental predicate plane or pole" (*chōetsuteki jutsugomen* 超越的述語面) and equates it with our prior "place of implacement" wherein we are situated. In turn, he associates that "transcendental predicate" (*chōetsuteki jutsugo* 超越的述語) with the concrete universal that differentiates itself into objects or grammatical subjects (Z3 347–348, 391, 400, 402, 405, 431, 465, 517, 523). Turning away from the object, away from Aristotle's substance that becomes the grammatical subject but never the predicate, and turning in the direction of the predicate in that significance of a pre-reflectively lived concreteness or implacement, we arrive at the transcendental predicate "that cannot be made into a grammatical subject of judgment," permitting no further objectification as this or that. This is the most concrete level of place as un-determined or un-delimited by anything, what Nishida calls the place of true nothing (shin no mu no basho) or place of absolute nothing (zettai mu no basho) (Z3 467). Extending without end to envelop every thing, as the ever-implicit horizonal[7] "beyond" of every experience, it is no-thing. The grammatical subject is what is cut out through differentiation from the predicate pole—which Nishida associates with what Hegel called "the concrete universal"—within its vast matrix of potential predicates. Of course, ultimately Hegel's concrete universal is not exactly Nishida's basho at its most concrete significance, and Nishida will come to see his place of true nothing as foundational for any conceptual universal even if it is a self-conceiving concept (as in Hegel's absolute idea).[8]

We might also discern a Neo-Kantian theme in this distinction between the predicate as pointing to the lived meaningful whole that in its indeterminateness is ultimately nothing, on the one hand, and the grammatical subject that points to the determinate individual as an ontic entity or object, on the other. Nishida's concern, as I have already mentioned, was to overcome the dualism of Western philosophy. The tradition of Western metaphysics has always divided reality into two realms: the sensible and the intelligible, appearance and reality, matter and form, becoming and being, the temporal and the eternal. Emil Lask pointed out that what characterizes all such dualisms is the thought that each term is a type of being or entity.[9] The history of philosophy, then, has been a series of attempts to bridge the gap between two realms of being. According to Lask, it was Hermann Lotze who overcame that ontic dualism with a different type of dichotomy that involved the distinction between the realm of being (Sein) that is ontic and involves entities (Seiende) and the realm of validity (Geltung) that is normative and involves values (Werte). Lask writes that the predicate "being" belongs exclusively to the former sphere, which coincides with the spatiotemporal sense-world of causal connections.[10] Lotze maintained that while a real thing is, a true proposition is valid. Being and validity are thus distinct.[11] This radical disjunction between being and validity, as found in these Kantian thinkers, provides a source for Nishida's characterization of the predicate pole as a nothing in distinction from its object, the grammatical subject, which is a being. Nishida's elucidation of the predicate pole as a place that envelops objects is also facilitated by Lask's characterization of values or validities as "domain categories" (Gebietskategorien) that are "predicates" (*Prädikate*).[12] The predicate for Nishida thus becomes the manner in which we can grasp things by dint of an environing context, a clearing that is a nothing in relation to those beings grasped and objectified. And that is why in the "Basho" essay Nishida assimilates what he calls the intelligible universal of values to the final place of absolute nothing, for he has in mind the Lotzean and Laskian "realm of values." Nishida's contribution here is to make the abyssal emergence of those values that ground human life, their un-grounding ground—or what in Reiner Schürmann's terms would be the an-archy in the emergence of those *archai,* the a-principial (un)ground of principles[13]—explicit.

Place as Self-Mirroring Nothing

As we saw in the preceding discussion, Nishida conceives of the particular's subsumption in the universal in terms of implacements of places in places or bashos, which he in turn associates, in reverse direction, with the concrete universal's self-determination. In judicative terms this means the predicate determining its grammatical subject that in fact, however, is its own self-determination. Each self-determination of the universal as the individual is also the implacement of the individual in that universal. Nishida also explains this in terms of mirroring, in allusion to his ideas from the late 1910s and early 1920s. Each level of the self-determination of a universal is also a level of its self-mirroring, so that each universal, viewed noematically, is an image mirroring a broader self-mirroring universal, which in turn mirrors a further universal, and so on. Because each universal can be made into the grammatical subject of a judgment, as a particular belonging to a broader universal (predicate), this entails a serial layering of universals within universals, a system of implacements within implacements. And if we proceed away from the grammatical subject, away from the objectified object as the point of determination, in the direction of the predicate, at the most undifferentiated and concrete level, we arrive at the transcendental predicate pole no longer conceptually determinable as a universal. That broadest and most fundamental basho, escaping further subsumption, can no longer be reified or reduced to any image; it cannot be objectified and hence, in opposition to Aristotle's substance, is "the predicate that cannot become a grammatical subject." And as the determining "circle" embracing its points of determination, it is an empty mirror mirroring itself in all its determinations (Z3 502). It has to be treated, then, as the final context serving as the transcendental predicate presupposed in all determining or predicating acts while itself remaining un-determined, that is, no-thing (mu).

The Dialectic of Being and Non-being in the System of Implacements

To recapitulate, between the individual determined as object, defined as grammatical subject, on one end, and the un-defined universal, the transcendental predicate, on the other end, there is a chain of successive implacements within implacements, bashos within bashos, each articulating levels of differentiation, articulation, and reflection. In terms of positivity and negativity, each determinate being as a positivity, a foreground, is surrounded by an environing negativity in its background. But each such negativity is still positive, a being, from the standpoint of the further negativity wherein it is implaced (Z3 422). In this movement from individual being to universal nothing, the system of place thus comprises a whole succession of meontological-ontological levels that may be understood variously in terms of universal and particular, determining act and determined content, form and matter, noesis and noema, predicate and grammatical subject, epistemological subject and object, knower and known, place and implaced, and so on. Encompassing all of them is the transcendental predicate qua place of true nothing, an undifferentiated field delimited by nothing. Nishida thus re-conceives the various dichotomies in terms of the a-symmetrical relationship of implacement involving the self-determination or self-differentiation of place as if it were a concrete universal. He now views the dichotomies as encompassed within an endless series of implacements within implacements, bashos within bashos. This entails a dynamism distinguishable from simple dualism that eventually, in the mid- to late 1930s, Nishida will characterize in terms of a dialectic between one and many. But even before such later developments, we see a dialectic taking shape here in the oppositional relationships involving object and subject understood in terms of being and non-being or affirmation and negation. This dialectic works itself out in three general standpoints of place.

Although Nishida fails to provide consistent presentations in his different works and leaves it up to his students and commentators to fill in the gaps, we can say that in the works immediately following the "Basho" essay of 1926 there continue in general to be three major levels of place, but each with further sub-levels (which I will not touch on here): (1) the place of beings (*yū no basho* 有の場所): the natural world of material objects, individual substances, and their interrelations, which become determined in our judicative acts as grammatical subjects; (2) the place of oppositional (or relative) nothing (tairitsuteki mu no basho, sōtai mu no basho): the field of consciousness encompassing on the one hand the perceived self and its empirical objects, and on the other hand the various determining acts of consciousness involving the subject-object structure (seeing, knowing, judging, willing, and so on); and (3) the place of true (or absolute) nothing (shin no mu no basho, zettai mu no basho) that envelops the pre-theoretically and pre-cognitively lived dimension from which emerge the various norms or standards that guide the determining acts of consciousness. With each movement from one level to the next, the perspectival standpoint shifts from (1) the perception of objects that become grammatical subjects of judgments to (2) the self-reflection of consciousness as the epistemological subject relating to its object and finally to (3) the loss of that noematic self (objectified consciousness) through a meaningfully lived absorption without further delimitation, that is, the standpoint of intuition as a self-mirroring self-awareness. The progression moves from (1) the focus on objects to (2) the focus in self-consciousness on the acts of consciousness and finally to (3) the focus away from the noematic (the ontic: objects, grammatical subjects) in a "de-focusing turn," so to speak, to the predicate plane as the holistic dimension concretely lived.

One significant realm within that serial layering of implacements is the field of a priori conditions of knowledge assumed by every judicative or cognitive act.

In the preceding threefold scheme this is the second or middle domain, which one may thematize in epistemological Kantian terms as "transcendental subjectivity" or "consciousness-in-general." Emphasizing its basho-like nature that cannot be objectified and reduced to the grammatical subject of the statement "I think *X*" and characterizing it more as a "circle" than as a "point," Nishida calls it "the field of consciousness" (ishiki no ba) (Z3 469, 504, 545). He makes the point that in respect to its objects, consciousness as such is no "being." It is no determinate thing qua object but rather the field (*ba* 場) wherein beings qua objects appear. In this respect it is "nothing" (mu) in relation to its objects, which are thus "being" (*u* or *yū* 有) (Z7 222). Subjectivity qua field of consciousness is thus the negative pole vis-à-vis the world of objects as the positive pole it mirrors (Z3 417). Hence Nishida calls it "oppositional nothing" (*tairitsuteki mu* 対立的無) or "relative nothing" (*sōtai mu* 相対無). Several years after the "Basho" essay, in *Mu no jikakuteki gentei,* Nishida develops this dialectical formulation further, explaining that in the self-determination (of place), self-affirmation is in the direction of the thing, that is, the object, and self-negation is in the direction of the I, that is, the subject. The true self, then, is no determined object of affirmation, no noema; instead, it is noesis, the determining act (Z5 178–179). In determining its object, it negates itself. The I in relation to its object is thus a relative nothing vis-à-vis affirmative being (Z5 174). In *Mu no jikakuteki gentei* Nishida considers this a dialectical determination of the self-contradictory (Z5 174).

The I as the field of consciousness, however, does not yet provide us with a complete picture of the concrete whole of place that acts in self-determination. The oppositional relationship here between subject qua non-being and object qua being, between negation and affirmation, requires that which makes their mediation possible. Nishida characterizes this mediation in the dialectical terms of "the negation of negation." Already in the essay "Shirumono" (「知るもの」; "That Which Knows") of 1927, placed at the end of *Hatarakumono kara mirumono e,* Nishida distinguishes the three levels of place dialectically in the judicative terms of affirmation, negation, and the negation of negation, that is, their "contradictory unity" (mujunteki tōitsu 矛盾的統一) (Z3 528–529). The important point here is that consciousness is determined by further determining "acts" traceable beyond the confines of the ego to what is truly "nothing." Each thematization of consciousness as object implies a prior pre-objective consciousness as its field. In the endless regress of such self-reflection, consciousness sinks into the ultimately un-objectifiable self-determining field of nothing. Consciousness in its relationship to objects is thus merely an "oppositional nothing" (tairitsuteki mu) that provides the entryway to an "absolute nothing" (zettai mu) (Z3 432). Consciousness as the field of potential cognitive predicates or conceptual categories thus dissolves into a further environing and self-determining transcendental field. This is where pre-judicatively and pre-cognitively lived values and meanings emerge. But in its non-differentiation it is truly nothing, serving as the anontological (under)ground of beings (*Z3* 482).[14] And this nothing encompasses contradictories.

Ultimately, all the layering of places is founded on, and sinks into, the self-mirroring of the place of true nothing that transcends consciousness in our pre-theoretical experience.[15] "True nothing" as place is what envelops the oppositional relationship between the "non-being" of consciousness in its determining noetic acts and the determined noematic "being," that is, the subject-object dichotomy. It embraces both moments as abstractions from its concretely lived immediacy. And in embracing that opposition between being and non-being, affirmation and negation, true nothing encompasses contradiction (*Z3* 424). This encompassing of contradiction at the most concrete irreducible level is what Nishida character-izes as "the negation of all negations," which in Buddhist terms would translate as "the emptying of emptiness" (*śūnyatāyāh śūnyatā*). In other words, Nishida here reformulates his earlier appropriations of the Hegelian notion of the self-determination of the concrete universal in the more explicitly dialectical terms of a "negation of negation" (*hitei no hitei* 否定の否定) (*Z3* 425), but with added Bud-dhist connotations in its association with the concept of a self-mirroring "noth-ing" (mu). This underscores the non-substantiality of the ground of knowledge and being as an underground or abyss, for what determines itself is also self-negating. In *Mu no jikakuteki gentei* Nishida explains that in its self-negation, place contains endless determinations of objects within it; it determines beings by itself being nothing (*Z5* 72–73, 80). And this is the dialectical dynamic that Nishida by 1932 (in *Mu no jikakuteki gentei*) finds operative ultimately even behind the field of consciousness. That is, the dialectic involves the concrete universal's self-determination that in reverse direction is simultaneously its negation: "a uni-versal that determines itself by itself becoming nothing" (*mu ni shite jikojishin o genteisuru ippansha* 無にして自己自身を限定する 一般者) (*Z5* 122). While itself escap-ing objectification, place thus encompasses the oppositions between object and subject, being and non-being, affirmation and negation (*Z5* 80, 81–82, 122). Place then, even when taken as underlying its many determinations, is no self-identical substance. In that regard, Nishida contrasts his position here with that of Hegel. Hegel's position, Nishida argues, is a dialectic of thought or the idea, a dialectic of being, that objectifies the noetic process into a noema. It is not a dialectic of place or of the un-objectifiable act ultimately delimited by nothing (*Z5* 122–123, 123–124, 130, 138, 234). Hegel's dialectic ignores the self-determination of facticity in the concrete present (*Z5* 138–139). With that irreducible concrete in mind, Nishida in *Mu no jikakuteki gentei* thus begins to call its self-determination that establishes the dialectical process a "self-determination without a determiner" (*genteisurumono nakushite jikojishin o genteisuru* 限定する物無きして自己自身を限定する)—a phrase that continues to appear in later formulations of his dialectic (*Z5* 154, 161).

In fact, it is in *Mu no jikakuteki gentei* that Nishida for the first time uses the phrase "dialectic" (benshōhō 弁証法) to characterize what he has been attempting to describe: the noematic determination of the self-awareness of the nothing. As Fujita Masakatsu argues, Nishida's point in using this phrase may have been to emphasize the negativity in the involvement of both affirmation and negation in this process of determination. This in turn may have been in response to Tanabe Hajime's (田辺元) criticism that Nishida, in starting from the premise of a kind of religious experience, tends toward a Plotinean emanationism. Nishida's reply is that the self-aware determination of absolute nothing is not a mere *emanatio* from the One but rather a dialectical movement through "rupture" (*danzetsu* 断絶). The term "dialectic" is meant to describe this simultaneity of rupture and continuity, negation and affirmation, in this process of the self-determination of the absolute nothing (Z5 121–124). Nishida also states, however, that while the true self determines itself dialectically by becoming nothing (i.e., in self-negation), the originary nothing itself is not exhausted by that dialectical process. That is, the process of self-determination—the dialectic—does not exhaust the nothing, for the latter is what encompasses the entire process.[16] And here we are reminded of its placial (bashoteki) aspect.

Place as Contradictory Unity

At this point in our investigation, we ought to question the exact nature of what Nishida means here by "contradictory unity" (mujunteki tōitsu). For example, the subsumptive judgment, we are told, involves a unity between the grammatical subject and its predicate. This constitutes a contradictory relation in that the terms are ultimately mutually exclusive: Aristotle's substance as indicated by the grammatical subject that can never become a predicate, on the one hand, and the transcendental predicate that in its unsayability can never become a subject, on the other (Z3 468, 471–472). The connection of these mutually exclusive terms is then a "contradictory unity."[17] If substance, as Aristotle proclaimed, has nothing contradictory, what makes a contradictory unity possible would have to be non-substantial. It is the non-substantiality of the transcendental predicate pole, as delimited by nothing, that permits its envelopment of "that which becomes the grammatical subject but not the predicate." Only on the basis of that nothingness can the mutually exclusive contradictories of the transcendent object (which cannot become a predicate) and the transcendental predicate (which cannot be stated as a subject of a proposition) be united in non-distinction and "become one another" (Z3 514–515). Transcending the judicative structure in opposite directions, the two opposing ends are thus united in their mutual non-substantiality. Nishida will later explicate further the dialectics of this contradictory unity in terms of mutual self-negation in the 1930s.

It is precisely the concrete qua self-determining place that, as contradictory unity, is the unifier of transcendent object and its predicate. Regarding this point, one may raise the following questions: Is there a tension here, as Gereon Kopf claims, between the priority of the universal qua "predicate that encompasses the grammatical subject" (Z3 455) and the predicate's need for self-particularization in the grammatical subject?[18] Is the contradictory relationship one of true symmetry between the noematic aspect of the determined subject and the noetic aspect of the determining predicate, thus requiring a third term, such as the negation of negation uniting affirmation and negation, as I noted earlier? The third term, however, is provided by the predicate in its significance as their transcendental and enveloping place. Is the dialectic instead, then, also a-symmetrical, whereby "noesis utterly envelops noema" (Z5 193)?[19] The dialectical structure of place qua such predicate is inherently self-contradictory. It retains its self-identity in its self-contradiction, an idea that Nishida will also develop further in the 1930s in terms of contradictory self-identity. But in the later writings Nishida will also de-emphasize the primacy of the predicate and instead bring the contradictory identity of the opposing terms in light of their mutual self-negation to the fore.[20]

Like the relationship in judgment between grammatical subject and predicate, each level of implacement involves a contradiction that can be seen from the standpoint of the background universal enveloping the terms. Nishida explains in *Ippansha no jikakuteki taikei* that the discovery of a contradiction as apparent on a certain level of place means that one has sunk, in a deepening of self-awareness, to a more concrete sphere of place wherein the contradictory terms are implaced and co-exist.[21] Each deepening, however, entails no resolution of the contradiction but rather an envelopment of that contradictory relationship, holding the terms in tension.[22] Each universal as the background "nothing" for beings implaced in the foreground of its domain makes space for their opposition. It must remain relatively indeterminate so as to make room for opposite determinations. For example, "color" is indeterminate enough to include both "red" and "not-red." The universal as such a field for opposites and contradictories provides the standpoint whereupon one can shift between affirmation and negation and become aware of contradictions (Z3 401–402). Nishida explains this further in 1931 in "Watashi no tachiba kara mita Hēgeru no benshōhō" (「私の立場から見たヘーゲルの弁証法」; "Hegel's Dialectic as Seen from My Standpoint") (included in *Zoku Shisaku to taiken* 『続思索と体験』; *Thought and Experience Continued*, 1937). He states therein that self-contradiction cannot be conceived merely in terms of the grammatical subject of a judgment. The dialectical relationship between opposites cannot be reduced to determination in terms of noema. This goes back to Aristotle's notion of substance as possessing its own self-identity. Contradiction instead becomes apparent when we turn our attention away from the noema and instead to the noesis, the determining act. In that direction we can understand the contradictory in terms of the self-determination of the place of nothing, that is, in light of their implacement within that place (*Z7* 267, 270). And because the self-determination of the place of nothing is always operative behind the determination of a place vis-à-vis beings, that is, the object-world, there is always something dialectical operating behind the judicative determination of the grammatical subject (*Z7* 267–268, 275). The world understood in terms of grammatical subjects presupposes that dialectical movement involving opposites and contradictories (*Z7* 275). Judicative knowledge with its noematic content is thus an abstraction from concrete knowledge that experiences the dialectical dynamism of the concrete (*Z7* 267–268).

There, in that dialectical dynamism, lies the "true self" as self-contradictory (*Z5* 85). Self-awareness that sees the self is self-contradictory in that the self seen, as mirrored image, is not the seeing self. The self's self-determination here as what it sees is its self-negation into what it is not. The seeing self in relation to the seen self is nothing. It cannot be reified as object or stated as grammatical subject. It is a self-negating nothing allowing for its self-contradiction. Thus in *Mu no jika-kuteki gentei* Nishida also makes the point that "philosophy begins in the fact of the self-contradiction of the self," that is, the self-negation of nothing (*Z5* 92).

Away from the noematic pole of substance qua grammatical subject and in the direction of the noetic pole of the predicate, there is thus a place delimited by nothing wherein lies the true self or place determining itself in self-negation as a contradictory unity encompassing opposites. The non-differentiated nothing at the broadest and most concrete level in the series of implacements thus entails a contradictory unity in its inclusion of all types of beings and their negations, hence being-in-general and its negation, non-being-in-general. It would have to be a field that transcends but encompasses both being and non-being in general. Nishida is thus careful in his "Basho" essay to distinguish what he means by "nothing" here in its absolute sense (i.e., "absolute nothing," zettai mu) from the merely relative sense of "non-being" as the negation of being (i.e., "relative nothing," sōtai mu). In giving rise to and encompassing the oppositional relationship between being and its opposite, true nothing (shin no mu 真の無) must transcend the nothing, that is, non-being, that is contrasted with being (tairitsuteki mu; oppositional nothing) (*Z3* 424). This means that the place of absolute nothing, as encompassing contradictory unity, precludes any sort of ontological or meontological reduction to state that it is or is not. To predicate it thus as being or not being would be to objectify it, but place is not an object (*Z3* 503). I call this "an-ontological" to distinguish it from either the ontological or the meontological. Defying positive description, predication, or determination by something beyond, it slips away from any attempt to make it into a subject of judgment. Yet it mirrors itself in all the opposing terms reflected on its empty surface. As a self-negating nothing, it makes room for their positive being. As Nishida remarks, this is somewhat suggested by Plato's concept of the chōra (χώρα) in the *Timaeus* that defies determination

(Z3 415). The difference from Plato's conception of the place of formation, however, is that basho is not a mere receptacle for the ideas' formations but rather a self-forming formlessness. At that most fundamental level of place, as we have been noticing, mutually exclusive contradictories, for example, being and non-being, affirmation and negation, I and not-I, and transcendent object and transcendental predicate, are thus joined together (e.g., Z3 422, 424, 473–474). The dialectic between being and non-being is thus played out in that space of true nothing that envelops them in their contradictory unity. The place of contradictory unity, then, is "neither identity nor difference, neither being nor non-being" (Z3 419). From that contradictory unity delimited by truly nothing there then unfold the sequential bifurcations of various opposites, endless dialectical developments from the self-identity of the place of true nothing. Nishida will contrast this understanding of the self-determination of nothing in terms of self-contradiction with Hegel's notion of the unfolding of reason.

In addition to the horizontal oppositions within each universal domain, we must bear in mind that this dynamism of unity-cum-bifurcation or contradictory unity, viewed vertically, also extends between the successive implacements and ultimately between the transcendent object, "the true individual that becomes the grammatical subject but not the predicate," on one end, and the transcendental predicate, "the true universal that becomes the predicate but not the grammatical subject," on the other end (Z3 468). On each end of the judicative structure is implied that which lies beyond judgment, an indeterminable transcendent(al), which together are unified, as I noted earlier, in their non-differentiation. All propositions or judgments thus can be viewed as explications or amplifications of a fundamental intuition, the self-mirroring of that concrete whole, wherein all oppositional terms and contradictories are implaced in non-distinction. The grammatical subject and predicate are but moments in the articulation of that original (self-)intuition of the undifferentiated place, the transcendental predicate plane non-distinct from the transcendent object in a contradictory unity. It is their contradictory unity as the self-determining concrete whole that encompasses all other contradictory unities. Via this unity of contradiction, formed and forming, determining and determined, and the transcendent and the immanent are dynamically non-dual. Place is the field of concrete immediacy for that contradictory unity, taken not only horizontally at each level or sphere but also vertically to encompass the entire dynamic. The intuition of its all-encompassing contradictory unity will occur from the standpoint of that concrete whole.

The Intuition of Contradictory Unity

Nishida in 1930 (in *Ippansha no jikakuteki taikei*) describes the concrete place enveloping dialectical development as the plane or pole of intuition (*chokkanmen* 直観面) (Z4 367). As I noticed earlier, taking the self-determination of the concrete universal as founded on a self-mirroring of nothing, Nishida characterizes that concrete standpoint of the place of true nothing, in terms of intuition, as a self-seeing of the dynamic whole encompassing contradictories. Nishida takes intuition as such, the seeing of contradictory unity at the most concrete level of lived experience, to be the necessary premise for cognition. But how can we even think this if non-contradiction rules our thoughts? Parallel to the irreducibility of the transcendental predicate pole to any grammatical subject, intuition as the seeing of its contradictory unity lies beyond the logical forms of thought or judgment. As we saw earlier, consciousness as the field of predicates or categories is still an abstract moment within the dynamism of the transcendental predicate plane that concretely envelops it and its object (the grammatical subject) by determining itself in its self-negation. This means that the concrete universal in its self-determination, as rooted in the transcendental predicate pole (*Z3* 523), entails not only non-duality between grammatical subject and predicate and between epistemological object and subject but the triadic stages of affirmation (of the object), negation (in the subject), and the negation of negation in their contradictory unity (*Z3* 528). At each level the dialectic moves away from the abstract and restricted toward the broader but concrete; it moves from the dichotomies toward the immediacy of opposites, from the theoretical toward the lived or experiential. At the most concrete level, the dichotomized or oppositional terms are seen as different aspects of the same self-mirroring nothing. At that deepest level of place, where there is the negation of negation, that is, the unity of contradiction, there is the intuition of the whole dynamic process of place. This provides a holistic view of self-mirrorings of the place of nothing, a non-dualistic (self-)seeing of the workings of concrete reality in its dialectical nature (e.g., *Z3* 445–447, 473, 475–477; *Z5* 76–77). Even if we cannot logically conceive of a contradictory unity, Nishida's point is that it can and must be "seen" from that pre-reflective standpoint (*Z3* 457–458, 485). In existential terms we are aware of a deep contradiction at the bottom of our lives in terms of birth-and-death or generation-and-extinction. Its true intuition (*shin no chokkan* 真の直観) is immediate in the place of true nothing (*Z3* 453, 475). Nishida in the mid- to late 1930s will eventually work out dialectically the connection between intuition as that self-mirroring of the concrete and the will as "the act of acts" operative behind all determining acts in terms of "acting intuition" (kōiteki chokkan 行為的直観). In any case, in the epistemology of place, during the late 1920s to 1930, Nishida takes the most concrete standpoint to be that of intuition, whereby the dynamic and non-dualistic whole is seen in its contradictory unity, a seeing that in non-duality is a self-seeing.

Generation-and-Extinction, Life-and-Death, the Self-Contradiction of Human Existence

The negation that life must face in its contradictory unity translates to death. At the most concrete level of one's living experience, one is aware of this fact of existence that undermines existence. Hence Nishida in his "Basho" essay characterizes that most concrete place of absolute nothing, wherein the intuition of contradictory unity takes place, as also a place of "generation-and-extinction" (*shōmetsu* 生滅) (Z3 423). This points to what one might call the existential dimension of contradictory unity, for if we take "generation-and-extinction" in its specifically human significance of "life-and-death," we may consider its intuition, in its concrete immediacy, an acute awareness of the finitude constituting our being vis-à-vis death. We live this immediacy whereby our existence is constituted or annihilated in the face of its other, non-existence. Here the place of absolute nothing is an abyssal chiasma wherein and whence life and death, self and world, being and nothing, separate while always remaining in contact. Nishida develops this point in his later works, such as "Ronri to seimei" (「論理と生命」; "Logic and Life") of 1936, in terms of the environment as the place of "the concrete reality of life" from which we are born and into which we perish (Z8 19). Although his concern in *Hatarakumono kara mirumono e* is primarily epistemological, we see here an existential side to Nishida's basho theory, that is, his concern with the lived finitude in the facticity of human existence, which in the 1940s becomes fully pronounced in his theory of religiosity. In fact, one might say that this opposition between life and death is the ultimate context that informs our cognitive acts. Self-awareness here at the place where life and death are de-cided, that is, separated out, is what establishes the founding of an epistemological system.

What Nishida calls the "intuitionism" (*chokkanshugi* 直観主義) of his "Basho" essay expresses this existential concern with self-contradiction lying at the bottom of human existence. In the abyssal depths lying beyond the confines of the psyche or ego, we find ourselves implaced vis-à-vis absolutely nothing, where the self-contradiction of our existence is evident, at the place where life meets death. At the bottom of our personhood, he states, there is the deep dialectic, "the tragic" (*higekiteki narumono* 悲劇的なるもの) (Z5 119). True dialectical determination is to be born through absolute death (Z5 293). But such statements become clearer when we also take into consideration what he says about time, that is, that each moment is the rising and falling of the present. So the endless flow of life is conceivable as a dialectical unity of contradiction, involving the births-and-deaths of our momentary selves (Z5 295–296). At each moment, in facing one's past and one's future, one faces birth and death; one is living by dying. The ultimate issue for Nishida, then, underlying the epistemological one of bridging the dualistic gap, is the existential one of self-reification vis-à-vis one's life-and-death to face the fact of self-contradiction underlying one's being, the non-substantiality at the concrete root of one's existence, the place of true nothing where being and non-being, birth and death, are in intimate contact at each moment (*Z*5 153, 159). His intuitionism points to that contradictory unity in its lived facticity.

Place as a Complete System of Incompletion

The place of nothing, as we have seen, is the source of dichotomized positions. Yet in its unreifiable immediacy, it entails a standpoint purified of the positions of both materialism or realism, on the one hand, and of subjectivism or idealism, on the other, as well as of any sort of dualism. Despite the temptation of some commentators to read Nishida's theory of place as an idealism to contrast it with the later evolution of his thinking—where he explicates the basho-horizon in terms of the world of interactivity—Nishida would reject such a classification. The acute self-awareness of life in the face of death that we just saw would preclude the security of an ideal realm. Instead, it would mean that one is ex-posed to the contingencies of the world, the non-substantiality of being. The system of implacements, seen as a dynamic whole, refuses confinement to an ideal sphere when the knowing I is implaced within a wider horizon enveloping both the ideal and the real. In his attempt to overcome epistemological dualism, Nishida has thus constructed a complete system that includes the impossibility of its completion in virtue of its un-reifiable, un-objectifiable concrete source.[23] We can say this because the most encompassing principle in Nishida's system is that self-founding principle referring to no further principle, the an-archic *archē* he characterizes as a self-forming formlessness. As an absolutely un-determinable nothing, it horizons his system as an open system, "a circle without periphery" (*mugendai no en* 無限大 の円)[24] that envelops the endless dialectical process (*Z*5 148). That absolute nothing that mirrors all as their un-delimited place is wherein we find ourselves as always already implaced within its determining and determined contexts. Here we are exposed to the possibilities of life-and-death at each moment. Nishida's challenge, then, was to articulate that ultimate context or horizon without reifying it.

By the beginning of the 1930s, however, Nishida was already expressing dissatisfaction with his discussion of dialectics in terms of noesis-noema, subject-object, and predicate-subject from the period of *Mu no jikakuteki gentei*.[25] His critics who charged him with idealism were noticing Nishida's focus on interiority, consciousness, and the mind. But already in the second half of *Mu no jikakuteki gentei* we see Nishida shifting his interest toward the world at large, in which we are implaced in our interactivities with one another and with the environment. That is the direction that the most explicitly dialectical phase of his oeuvre would take in the mid- to late 1930s.

5 The Dialectic of the World-Matrix Involving Acting Persons (from the 1930s to the 1940s)

In his preface to *Tetsugaku ronbunshū dai san* (『哲学論文集第三』; *Collected Philosophical Essays, Volume 3*) (1939), Nishida states that his philosophical purpose ever since *Zen no kenkyū* has been to see things from the most direct and fundamental standpoint. To overcome the psychologistic coloring of the concept of pure experience, and through contact mainly with the Southwest school of Neo-Kantianism, he was led during the 1920s, as we saw in chapter 4, to the concept of basho or place. Following his formulation of the epistemology of place in that decade, Nishida extends and further develops the dialectical features of his thinking in the 1930s and 1940s. He describes basho, "the most fundamental and concrete universal," as a "dialectical universal" (benshōhōteki ippansha 弁証法的一般者) and an "absolutely contradictory self-identity of many and one" (*ta to ichi to no zettai mujunteki jikodōitsu* 多と一の絶対矛盾的自己同一) (Z8 257). The shift in the 1930s takes us from a look that penetrates through the interior depths of consciousness into its abyssal grounding to a view that in penetrating beyond that interiority lands outside in the world of one's implacement, wherein one acts. The concept of place almost seems to become eclipsed by the notion of "the sociohistorical world" (shakaiteki rekishiteki sekai 社会的歴史的世界), but the latter is really its external manifestation, an extension of its self-determination. And he still occasionally makes use of the term *basho* in this sense as world (sekai 世界). The change here is no theoretical alteration or rejection of his theory of place; rather, it involves a thorough retrieval of the roots of oneself that takes one from the self as knower to the self as actor in the contextual world.

In both *Tetsugaku no konpon mondai* (『哲学の根本問題』; *Fundamental Problems of Philosophy*), which was published in two volumes in 1933 and 1934, and the several volumes of *Tetsugaku ronbunshū* (『哲学論文集』; *Collected Philosophical Essays*), which were published throughout the mid- to late 1930s and 1940s, and even earlier in *Mu no jikakuteki gentei* (『無の自覚的限定』; *The Self-Aware Determination of Nothing*) of 1932, Nishida extends and applies his theory of place to the dynamic features of that sociohistorical world so that the logical structure of the system of place now becomes explicitly identified with that of historical world-constitution. The exhaustive plumbing of the abyssal interiority of the self in his epistemology of the 1920s enabled Nishida to now turn his attention outward to the world that shapes that interiority, hence the shift in his manner of approaching the theme of place, a turn from an internal view of the depths of self-awareness to an external look at the dynamism of the world wherein one is implaced and in which one actively takes part. This is all founded on the non-duality between inner and outer, which Nishida now characterizes in explicitly dialectical terms. Nishida's concern correspondingly shifts from the structure of judgment and cognition to the dialectical structuring of the historical world (rekishiteki sekai 歴史的世界) and our implacement in that world in terms of what he calls "acting intuition" (kōiteki chokkan 行為的直観). But again there is a link between the two in that the former is founded on the latter. The world's dialectical features become the focus of attention in order to bring out the dynamic non-duality of the concrete. For example, he now develops his earlier discussions of the intuition of contradictory unity in the direction of the world, in terms of the dialectical universal or the absolutely contradictory self-identity (zettai mujunteki jikodōitsu 絶対矛盾的自己同一). Nishida shows the dialectic as unfolding not only internally, within the structure of one's inner experiences and cognition, but also externally, to manifest the creative structure of the world's formations and the interactivity between individual selves that contributes to that creativity. The world becomes seen in its placial aspect as a field of inter-determinations.

In this and the following chapters I will examine these dialectical formulations from the 1930s, when Nishida is conceiving of the world as a dialectical matrix wherein we find ourselves always already acting and interacting. In this chapter I will discuss his characterizations of this dialectic as involving our human existence as a being-in-the-world, interacting with other beings (non-human beings) and with one another (other human beings). In chapter 6 I will look into the more seemingly abstract formulations of this dialectic that attempt to depict its logical structuring, for example, in terms of the "dialectical universal," "absolutely contradictory self-identity," and "absolute negation."

Nishida discusses the dialectic of the world at large in a variety of contexts, all of which involve the interactivity of our personal selves as embodied subjects with one another and with the world: the interpersonality of the I-thou relationship, the unfolding of the historical world, the relationship between individual and environment, the "acting intuition" (kōiteki chokkan) of human existence, the body as a dialectical mediator in one's relationship to the environment, and the self as maker and made contributing to the world's self-formations. Place now becomes more explicitly the arena wherein we exist as acting and interacting beings to historically unfold the world.

The Interpersonal Dialectic of "I and Thou"

Mediating Nishida's turn from the interior self to the exterior world is his discussion of interpersonal dialectics in terms of "I and thou" (watashi to nanji 私と汝) in *Mu no jikakuteki gentei* (especially in the essay "Watashi to nanji" 「私と汝」; "I and Thou"). In this respect *Mu no jikakuteki gentei* of 1932 serves as a transitional work that moves from the epistemology of place developed during the late 1920s to his concerns of the later 1930s, the world in its historical unfolding. Nishida came to realize that self-awareness is not merely a self-relation but is mediated by an encounter with that which negates the self, the absolute other (*zettai ta* 絶対他).[1] We cannot deny the insurmountable gap between self and other. In facing its other, the individual self arrives at a wall of separation, an absolute discontinuity of otherness separating them (Z5 342). Self and other are absolutely other with respect to each other, and there is no universal that subsumes them (Z5 297–298), for no one can immediately know the consciousness of a stranger (Z5 307). Yet at bottom there is also a unity between them that envelops that distinction (Z5 252). Rebounding, as it were, on that mutual border of alterity, one (the I) comes to know oneself (Z5 5, 8, 297–298, 303, 305–306, 309, 310, 323, 324). In that interpersonal interactivity where I and thou come into mutual contact, Nishida states that there is recognition of the absolute other in the depths of oneself. In reciprocity with one's other, one's self-awareness becomes enhanced and deepened in light of that other. This means self-awareness in light of one's interactions and responses to others (Z5 305–306). Our sense of self becomes shaped in relation to other people. In that sense the other as a mirror is the medium for one's self-reflection (Z5 311). The essence of the self is thus constituted specifically as a "person" (*jinkaku* 人格) in the "I thou" relationship, wherein the I discovers itself only by recognizing its other, the thou, as a singular person (Z6 99). Self-knowledge is meditated through this dialectic of reciprocal recognition. And this makes the self and self-awareness, as already implying otherness, inherently interpersonal and social. There can be no solitary ego outside such interpersonal relations of mutual recognition (Z6 30; see also Z6 298). It is in this sense that Nishida can cryptically exclaim that the other gives birth to the I or that the self is established in seeing the other within oneself or in seeing the self in the other (e.g., Z5 8, 313). On the basis of that mutual recognition of the absolute other within each of ourselves, interpersonal contact in terms of "I and thou" is made possible. In opening oneself to the otherness that one can never overcome, one thus touches on that other. That is, in opening oneself up to the absolute independence, that is, the personhood, of the other person, one recognizes and accepts the other as other. But that also means the constitution of one's personhood or self so that in their mutual encounter as persons irreducible to material, instrumental, or biological terms, the I and the thou are inter-dependent;

one cannot negate the other without negating oneself. Nishida expands on this interpersonal dialectic in light of love (*ai* 愛) as what occurs not only for the sake of some value or purpose but for the sake of the beloved's personhood, a love whereby one dies to oneself in the face of the otherness of the thou, *agapē* as opposed to *eros* (Z5 214, 250, 328, 331–332). Nishida will later describe the paradoxical relationship of the interpersonal dialectic in the various terms of mutual self-negation, continuity of discontinuity, and contradictory self-identity—concepts that I will examine in greater detail in chapter 6.

The world, according to Nishida, is constituted through these relationships.[2] With the dialectical determination of the self vis-à-vis its other, "I and thou" emerge in that mutual recognition of co-relating persons (Z5 262, 288; Z7 46). Each individual discovers its true self in the face of the other and becomes constituted as a person. The dialectic thus coincides with the establishment of society (*shakai* 社会) as involving these interpersonal relations. The person's self-determination, as a member of society, is his or her self-determination vis-à-vis other persons as "thous" (Z5 352). They work together and relate to one another in responsive reciprocity as persons, "I and thou," belonging to the same world, the same universal (Z5 288). We thus need to keep in mind that what Nishida means primarily by "individual" (*ko* 個) or "individual thing" (*kobutsu* 個物) in his works of the 1930s is the individual person (*kojin* 個人). If one takes the individual as that which truly exists in itself and works by itself to thoroughly determine itself, there is nothing more individual than the human self, that is, the person. But the human individual can never be utterly solitary; it is an individual vis-à-vis other individuals (Z8 307–308). The human self is constituted by its interrelations with other selves. In this way interpersonality turns Nishida's attention from self to world.

The mutual relationship between I and thou occurs at the edge of the world's determination, for the interpersonal relationship occurs in the mutual implacement of individuals in the world as their concrete place or basho (Z5 333). While their mutuality is determined by the world in their implacement, it in turn forms the shape of the world (e.g., Z7 29). Each person, despite his or her implacement in the universal whole, is irreplaceably unique in the context of the whole. Although the individual self is made by society and history, it possesses the creative significance of being a maker who remodels society and shapes history (Z5 278). It does this in its self- and co-determinations with other individual selves. This interactivity and mutual working of human persons coincides with the world's self-determination, which in this case means the establishment of society (or what Nishida calls in German *Gemeinschaft*) (Z6 124; Z7 149; Z8 19, 20). This is why the world as historical, what Nishida comes to call the "historical world" (rekishiteki sekai), as more than merely biological, is also the social world. Nishida claims that when individuals are enabled to mutually recognize one another's free creativity in their interpersonal relationships, to face one another in terms of "I and thou," there is the genesis of society (Z8 19). But he adds that if we also recognize the un-objectifiable alterity of the surrounding world wherein we are implaced, the thou does not have to be confined to other human persons. That is, we can form a "metaphysical society" with the concrete world in an "I-thou" relation "with mountains, rivers, trees, rocks" (Z6 46).

The Historical World and Its Dialectic of Environment-and-Individual

In addition to the self as interpersonal, Nishida in the 1930s furthers his concrete non-dualistic stance with an emphasis on the self as actor or "acting self" (*kōiteki jiko* 行為的自己) in interaction or mutual working (*aihataraki* 相働き) with other beings. He notices that our seeing, knowing, and self-awareness in general are all inextricably intertwined in our activities with one another and with the world (sekai). We are dynamically active in the world. But at the same time he notices the dynamically active nature of the world that environs us. In *Mu no jikakuteki gentei* he says that the world most immediate to us, wherein we dwell, is neither the world of matter or objects nor the world of consciousness or spirit but this world of activity (*kōi* 行為), the world wherein every act is its self-determination, an expression of its foundational nothingness (Z5 209). This world continually creates itself through the creative activities of its individual elements, namely, ourselves. The existence of the self thus cannot be separated from its environmental and historical determination in that world (Z5 326, 351). Each of us is born into that world as historically determined with his or her own destiny (Z5 262–263). Nishida in subsequent works of the 1930s brings out the dialectical nature of this world of interactivity, calling it "the dialectical world" (benshōhōteki sekai 弁証法的世界). The term "dialectic" (benshōhō 弁証法) here is not restricted to the inner self but is applied more broadly to the world, although to the extent that oneself is inseparable from one's being-in-the-world, world and self are non-dual. Extending his earlier notions of the self-determination of the place of absolute nothing in the direction of its worldly manifestations and assimilating place (basho) to world (sekai), he draws out its dialectical complexity in various terms, such as "reverse determination" (*gyaku gentei* 逆限定) or "contradictory self-identity" (mujunteki jikodōitsu 矛盾的自己同一). I will discuss these concepts in more detail in chapter 6, but I can preliminarily say that in all these dialectical formulations he brings out the irreducible complexity of the concrete. We can accordingly understand now what Nishida initially called "pure experience" (junsui keiken 純粋経験) in his maiden work in light of the dialectical structuring of our concrete implacement into the world of interactivity. Our immediate intuitions, our self-awareness, cannot be separated from this world. Nishida thus turns to the world in its social and historical dimensions as the sphere of the concrete wherein we immediately find ourselves.

Nishida, reconceptualizing the concrete in light of our worldly interactivities, reformulates basho accordingly in terms of the world as social and historical. The place of nothing is still the non-objectifiable, irreducible, concrete basis of reality. But as the world of our implacement, Nishida now sees it in the direction of the environment with which we interact, what he calls "the world of historical actuality" (*rekishiteki genjitsu no sekai* 歴史的現実の世界). The system of the self-determination of place is thus now seen as manifest in the unfoldings of that historical world as topological (Z9 210). And the world's formations are in turn taken to involve our concrete interactivities. In other words, place qua world involves a complex dialectic of social and historical determination of which we are significant players (Z6 128, 132–133). On this basis, place or basho, as "historical space" (*rekishiteki kūkan* 歴史的空間), becomes clarified as not simply the interior depths of the individual self but the individual's rooting in a "public place" (*ōyake no basho* 公の場所) (Z9 171). It is not simply the inner world of consciousness but rather the world of manifold individual selves determining one another in their interactions. So in terms of the concrete immediacy prior to the subject-object split, it is our interactivity in and with that world that is most fundamental. We are not first and foremost cognitive subjects in a de-worlded state observing objects from afar. Rather, we are implaced within the world wherein we find ourselves always already in interaction with other actors and with the environment. Cognition is to be understood only on this basis: "Knowing itself is already a sociohistorical fact [*shakaiteki rekishiteki jijitsu* 社会的歴史的事実]" (Z6 141). That is, our knowing is enveloped, implaced, within a broader context, the world of our concrete interaction unfolding in history. In providing that contextual place of our implacement, the world is sociohistorical (*shakaiteki rekishiteki* 社会的歴史的). The *cogito* cannot be separated from its implacement therein.

Nishida, in *Tetsugaku no konpon mondai,* views this world involving the interactivities of individual persons, as stated earlier, as the most concrete realm, that is, the field of our concrete immediacy, wherein we find ourselves first and foremost, always already (Z6 50). In contrast to this, we can also view the world in more abstract ways, such as in purely material terms, whereby things mechanically act on one another as causes and effects, or in biological terms, whereby living things move teleologically for the organism's survival and the reproductive maintenance of the species. But the concrete world wherein we human beings find ourselves taking part, wherein we are born, work, and die, is specifically this historical, or sociohistorical, world (rekishiteki sekai, shakaiteki rekishiteki sekai) (Z6 137–138, 183–184; Z8 16, 42, 51; Z9 492). It is the communal world, involving the sense of the family or the nation and possessing an ethical significance that determines our personal acts. Referring to Hegel's ethics, Nishida conceives this as "objective spirit" (*kyakkanteki seishin* 客観的精神) (Z7, 1978–1980 ed., 142).[3] We cannot objectify this world because we are already working within it (Z6 171). Nevertheless, the dialectical reality of the concrete is most explicit when we look into our immediate situation vis-à-vis this historical world. It is this sort of concrete stance founded on our lived interactivity with the world that Nishida, during this period, finds lacking in Hegel, Kant, and phenomenology (Z6 172).[4]

Nishida defines the historical world (rekishiteki sekai) as the world of interacting persons (*hito to hito to no musubitsuki no sekai* 人と人との結びつきの世界) (Z14, 1966 ed., 247).[5] This shows the significance of our role as persons within that world. The interactivity is with what surrounds us, the environment of things, as well as other individuals. As elements of a whole, our self-determinations are also the self-determinations of the whole (Z6 110). The whole determines itself via its individual elements working on one another. In developing this dialectic, Nishida, for example in "Ronri to seimei" (「論理と生命」; "Logic and Life") of 1936, borrows from J. S. Haldane's theory of biology. Haldane's thesis concerned the holistic coordination and mutual adaptation between the biological organism and its environment (Z8 18–19).[6] For Haldane, "life" meant not simply the individual organism but this interrelationship as a whole. Although Nishida agrees with Haldane that life, in distinction from mere matter, expresses the holistic interrelationship between the living individual and the environment, he adds that it is only with human life that we see the individual reacting to environmental delimitation by intentionally acting to transform and re-create the environment. We are conditioned by our surroundings and influenced by our upbringing, our friends, the books we read, the television programs we watch, and now the internet and other media. Moreover, for Nishida, the natural environment also takes on the significance of "death" in the sense that it resists our advances, our attempts at appropriation, by negating and delimiting our being. But as human beings, we can confront those determinations and alter the conditions that shape who we are: "Environment makes man and man makes environment" ("Kankyō ga ningen o tsukuri, ningen ga kankyō o tsukuru" (環境が人間を作り、人間が環境を作る) (Z8 162, 314, 329). We not only are affected by the environment but also work and act on it and re-create it. For example, while the land nourishes us with food, we in turn alter the land to increase or decrease its productivity, which again affects our well-being. While being determined and created by the environment, we also determine and re-create that environment. Nishida thus distinguishes his conception of "life" (*seimei* 生命), as involving this full dialectic of human creativity, from Haldane's merely biological conception. The real world of life, the dialectical dynamic that he calls "historical life" (*rekishiteki seimei* 歴史的生命), for Nishida is thus not merely biological but sociohistorical (shakaiteki rekishiteki) (Z6 106). In the concrete dynamism of that sociohistorical world, the dialectical nature of the concrete becomes fully manifest in the reciprocity of creativity as man partakes in the world's self-formations. That is, human persons, in their independent capacity to consciously and intentionally make things and re-shape the world, act and interact as "operative elements" (*sagyōteki yōso* 作業的要素) or "creative elements of the creative world" (*sōzōteki sekai no sōzōteki yōso* 創造的世界の創造的要素) (Z8 51, 52). The world continues creating itself not only through the environment's determination of individuals but also through the individuals' determination of the environment (Z6 83–84, 107, 178). Created by the world, man in turn asserts his or her autonomy by re-creating that world. Conversely, while taking part in that creativity, we, the made, are simultaneously re-making ourselves as makers. Yet in doing so, we serve as conduits of historical life, acting as parts of the world's self-creativity. This was Nishida's answer to Karl Marx's materialist determinism. His reply was a holistic inter-determinism that simultaneously retains the individual's autonomy without becoming an outright self-affirmative individualism. Nishida comes to describe this as the "contradictory self-identity" (mujunteki jikodōitsu) between maker and made, environment and individual subject (Z8 241, 332). The world is the basho, place, of this dialectical interrelationship between individual and environment. And human life manifests that dialectic in its mutual dependence on and alterations of the environment (Z8 15). Our creative autonomy is thus the world's creativity.

The Dialectic of Acting Intuition

The true self, the self in its most concrete immediacy, then, is an acting self (kōiteki jiko) partaking in the world's *poiēsis* (production). Instead of being de-worlded subjects observing the world from without, we are radically implaced within the world's dynamism. The subject of cognition is founded on this fact of acting-in-the-world. We always find ourselves in this concrete situation of a dynamic interactivity, reducible to neither terms of subjectivity or objectivity, to spirit or matter, before the polarization in intellectual analysis between subject and object. As we interact with things, we also come to see them and the world around us in light of the context of that interactivity. We are both spectators and actors in the unfolding of the great play of life (Z14 67). We see as we act; cognition implies action. Contra Descartes, Nishida in the first volume of *Tetsugaku no konpon mondai* (1933) thus asserts that it is not that "I exist because I think" but that "I exist because I act." Thinking already means acting (Z6 136). We see things by acting on them, creating them, giving them form (Z8 58, 64–65, 216–217).

To express that inseparability between seeing things and acting on them, Nishida neologizes the term "acting intuition" (kōiteki chokkan), first introducing it in the mid-1930s. In what sense are "acting" and "intuiting" united in the phrase "acting intuition"? Two terms often regarded as opposites, one implying passivity and the other implying activity, are intentionally brought together in this concept to express their inseparability as complementary moments in the concrete immediacy of how we exist in the world (Z8 215). The concept extends the earlier notions of pure experience, intuition, and self-awareness into the worldly arena of concrete action, wherein self, body, and world are dynamically inseparable. Nishida's point is to show that they must not be understood merely as some passive form of static contemplation. Intuition or seeing is never just the passivity of pure reception. Instead, it entails the dynamism of our acting in the world, our active engagement with our surroundings (Z7 94). Seeing things, that is, understanding them in view of what they are, already implies our acting on them, giving them form, within the context of the given historical world. It involves the active structuring of what we see, rendering it into forms. This occurs not only ideally, as in Kant's a priori forms and categories, but also physically as we literally build the world around us, re-shaping the space of our dwelling. The determining act of intentionality is extended into the world at large. For example, when we are driving a car, we see our surroundings in a certain way that is in accord with our act of driving. This is not a theoretical seeing but a bodily seeing inseparable from the act of driving. We have an immediate grasp of the world by acting within it, and in this pre-reflective immediacy there is no separation between inner and outer or between mind and matter, subject and object. We act on things while being acted on by them. We determine the things that are determining us; we shape the things around us as we ourselves are being shaped. So we see by acting and act by seeing; they generate each other. What Nishida described in the late 1920s as the intuition of contradictory unity thus becomes developed vis-à-vis the world, wherein we interact with one another and with the environment, in terms of acting intuition. Nishida in 1935 (in his *Tetsugaku ronbunshū dai ichi* 『哲学論文集第一』; *Collected Philosophical Essays, Volume 1*) also calls this a "dialectical intuition" (*benshōhōteki chokkan* 弁証法的直観) (Z7 209). The dialectic is such that we are both passively determined by the environment and actively working on it. Acting intuition expresses this dialectical nature of human existence as thus simultaneously active and passive, free and determined, as it partakes in the dialectic of world formation. It is our concrete mode of existence in our implacement in the world's dynamism. And as our partaking in the dynamic of the dialectical world, acting intuition provides the non-dual basis for all subsequent dichotomizations, such as the subject-object duality.

In formulating this concept of acting intuition, Nishida is focusing his interest on the concrete non-duality of that process whereby man as acting self is inseparable from the world of interaction. In acting, we objectify our essence, expressing ourselves externally in the things we make, and in turn those things move us and determine our acting so that subject and object are reciprocal in determination (Z6 277–278). This reciprocity is pre-reflective so that the world's poiēsis and man's poiēsis are dynamically one before subject-object bifurcation. Through our acting intuition, the world thus shapes itself qua historical life (Z8 30, 32, 33, 54, 61, 69, 72–73, 77). Since man is a creative element of the creative world, his or her acting intuition is at the same time the world's on-going act of self-expressive self-formation. Via this dialectic of acting intuition, the individual self as actor and the historical world forming itself are non-dual; they are dynamically—but not monistically—one, a dialectical identity that Nishida comes to call "contradictory self-identity" (mujunteki jikodōitsu).[7] Through acting intuition, we alter the world, giving it form, and this simultaneously means the world's self-formation (Z8 39). And in shaping the world, we are in turn shaped by it through its self-shaping. Our seeing in acting intuition thus signifies, for Nishida, the world's self-awareness as it forms itself. Because in acting intuition we are implaced in the world and partake in the world's dynamism, our self-awareness via acting intuition and the world's self-awareness in its self-determination are dialectically identical. Nishida makes this explicit in a statement in 1943. Just as our creative autonomy is the world's creativity, the same goes for our self-awareness: "When the world becomes self-aware, our self becomes self-aware, and when our self becomes self-aware, the world becomes self-aware" (Z9 528).

The Body as Dialectical Mediator

In discussing the dialectic of the world and man's implacement within its dynamic through acting intuition, one issue that cannot be ignored is the body (*shintai* 身体). Our seeing in acting and our interactivity with one another and with things entails our embodiment; we act on things and are acted on by them through the body. Thus the factor of the body as both a thing at work and a thing worked on is introduced into the dialectic of the world. The true self is neither disembodied nor de-worlded qua transcendental consciousness but is implaced via embodiment in the world of history (Z5 210, 212). Through our bodily nature, we act to build our environment (Z5 287). The lived and living body is what extends our creative intentionality beyond mere ideality to the surrounding world. One might then say that the body is the axis of our dialectical engagement with the world.[8] As actor, the body is subject, and as a tool of manipulation, it is an object. As both user and tool, the body is both subject and object (Z7 127; Z8 50). In this dual nature, or what Nishida calls "contradictory self-identity," the body is the medium where mind and environment meet and co-determine. It is the mediating support for the dialectical interrelationship between our acting intuition and the world's self-formation. And as the body acts on the environment, the environment qua tool becomes an extension of the body.[9] Through this mediation of embodiment in our bodily activities, our self- and co-determinations are equal to the world's self-determination.

Nishida regards the body qua subject-body (*shutai* 主体), engaging in acting intuition and taking part in the world's historical formations, therefore, as a "historical body" (*rekishiteki shintai* 歴史的身体) (e.g., Z8 62–63, 70). The term designates our dialectically dual nature of being simultaneously created and creators: while being shaped by the environment, our bodies actively partake in its re-shaping.

And this contributes to the unfolding of our historical world. Nishida distinguishes this body as historical from the merely biological body (*Z7* 139). The historical body, functioning as a creative element of the world's self-formation, is poietic, that is, creative, productive. That is what makes it historical. The merely biological body, incapable of separating itself from its environment, is not yet creative in that sense. It is not yet truly a subject-body, that is, an actor standing on its own. But the historical body, although it is determined by its environment, in turn becomes independent to the extent that it can determine its environment. As the environment conditions and makes the human subject-body, the subject-body in turn re-shapes and makes its environment. Body and environment are thus co-determining in a dialectic that simultaneously constitutes the world's continual self-reformation. We might then say that human existence in its embodied creativity is a microcosmic mirror reflecting, inter-resonating with, the macrocosm's dialectic.[10] In this conception of the body as a dialectical medium, any functional dualism between mind and body, as well as the dichotomy separating the individual self and the world, is collapsed. On this basis, Nishida provides a foundation for his earlier epistemology with its interrelationships between the epistemological subject and the world qua object or, in judicative terms, between grammatical subject and predicate. All of this also underscores the profound significance of the body for self-awareness; in other words, self-awareness is not determined merely through consciousness but rather through the body working on and with the world (*Z5* 247).

The Dialectic of Maker and Made: From the Made to the Making

Nishida characterizes the dialectic of acting intuition and embodied interactivity further in its historical world-formative aspect in terms of the reversible movement between the made and the making. As a historical body, man, through the manipulation of tools, transcends the biological sphere of life by refashioning his or her environment. The merely biological in its dependence on the environment does not yet stand opposed to its maker. But man qua historical body stands independently to counter its conditioning, to function as the creator of the historical world. Environment makes man, and man makes environment (*Z8* 162, 314, 329). But this also means that man is working as a creative element of the creative world (*Z8* 317–318). In other words, the individual, in mirroring and expressing the whole world, also possesses its creativity, whereby the world forms itself. The dialectic is such that made is making and making is made, and on its basis the world continually evolves "from the made to the making" (*tsukura-retamono kara tsukurumono e* 作られたものから作るものへ) (*Z8* 219). That is, the process of the world's self-formation involves a continual evolution from the conditioning of individuals (i.e., human selves) by their environment to their counter-conditioning of the environment and back again. We are born into this world and conditioned by it as made. But, in realizing our human potential, we in turn become creative as maker. Moreover, the things we make, as separate from us, in turn affect us and determine us. What is made by us in turn makes us (Z6 193; Z7 148). The process is both from what has been made by the environment to what makes the environment and from what has been made by the individual self to what makes the individual.[11] To repeat an example already cited, we cultivate the earth and grow food that in turn nourishes us, enabling us to go on growing more food. The food we receive from the environment, our upbringing by our parents, our relationship with friends, the weather, and other conditions all affect our state of being; and we in turn go on to alter those conditions. In these intimate interactions between the I and its environing things, between maker and made, the made makes, the created creates, and hence "persons are *creata et creans*" (Z10 104, 114; Z8 219). Born into the world of poiēsis that is continually forming and being formed, we are continually and simultaneously forming and being formed (Z8 492). Man qua historical body thus possesses a contradictory identity between made and making. Man as embodied subject is formed and forming vis-à-vis his or her environment as an element born out of the world that is also formed and forming in the same formative acts. Nishida is here asserting a dialectical complementarity between subject and object in terms of self and environment, whereby their relationship of determination or making is reversible. The historical world continually constitutes itself in this manner, moving "from the made to the making" (Z8 240).

Nishida accordingly comes to view true self-awareness as involving our partaking in the dialectical process of being made and making, whereby the self qua historical body expresses itself externally as a creative element of the creative world.[12] But this means that the self-awareness of the acting self as it expresses itself externally is conversely also the self-awareness of the self-expressive world, both self and world moving "from the made to the making." And in this self-awareness qua acting intuition, human existence is both free and taking part in the world's formativity. This distinguishes human life both from inanimate matter that moves mechanistically in causal determinism and from biological life that moves teleologically for species preservation and reproduction. The dialectic of made and making, "from the made to the making," is the concrete reality of which the merely material, biological, or mental, dimensions of reality are but abstractions. For Nishida, that dialectic is hence another way of expressing the most concrete sphere of human existence.

6 The Dialectic of the World-Matrix Involving the Dialectical Universal and Contradictory Identity (from the 1930s to the 1940s)

THROUGHOUT THE 1930s Nishida analyzes the overall dialectical structure of the historical world and the interrelationships involved therein in the various terms of absolute negation (or self-negation) (*zettai hitei* 絶対否定, jiko hitei 自己否定), the continuity of discontinuity (hirenzoku no renzoku 非連続の連続), absolutely contradictory self-identity (zettai mujunteki jikodōitsu 絶対矛盾的自己同一), and the self-determination of absolute nothing (zettai mu 絶対無) and of the absolute present (*zettai genzai* 絶対現在). Through these formulations that may, at first sight, seem abstract, Nishida attempts to portray systematically, in a kind of "logic" (ronri 論理), the dialectical complexity of the concretely real, that is, the world as involving the manifold interrelationships between its oneness and manyness, its universality and individuals. This complex inter-dimensionality of the world as a dialectical matrix, moreover, is depicted in its vast cosmic significance as an infinite space-time matrix. In this chapter I will examine these dialectical formulations of what Nishida takes to be the logical structuring of the world, place in its dialectical unfolding qua world.

In the context of the whole of Nishida's philosophical work, the significance of the dialectical formulations developed during this period cannot be understated. Nishida saw himself as achieving a certain maturity in expression with these dialectical formulations (Z6 3). For example, in the preface to *Tetsugaku ronbunshū dai yon* (『哲学論文集第四』; *Collected Philosophical Essays, Volume 4*), written in 1941, he acknowledges his attainment of a certain clarity that he was seeking in his 1939 essay "Zettai mujunteki jikodōitsu" (「絶対矛盾的自己同一」; "Absolutely Contradictory Self-Identity") (Z9 97). We can thus conclude that the direction his thinking took in the 1930s was extremely important in Nishida's self-assessment. Looking at these dialectical formulations from this period will thus help us understand and assess his overall relationship to the dialectics of Hegel and Mahāyāna non-dualism because their articulation, implicitly or explicitly, contains references to both.

The World as Dialectical Universal: The Manifold Dialectic of Universal and Individual

Nishida's turn to the world was accompanied by his turn to individuals. We saw in chapter 5 how the issue of self-awareness led him to the issue of interpersonal recognition and its mediation in the sociohistorical world. This move is paralleled by his shift in focus from the universal as predicate in his epistemology of place to the individual as what constitutes the world. Equating the universal more explicitly now with society, he sees the individual person at the extremity of the universal's determination. As part of the world, the individual is thoroughly determined. But paradoxically, in order to be a true individual, it must be self-determining. As such, the individual in turn determines the universal. Nishida from the early 1930s views the world as consisting of this radical dialectical process of determination obtaining between universal and individuals.[1] And in the 1940s Nishida states that the "logic of place" (bashoteki ronri 場所的論理) means "the self-determination of the whole" (*zentai ga zentaijishin o genteisuru* 全体が全体自身を限定する) (Z10 168), but earlier, in his predicate logic, the whole was the predicate determining itself as a concrete universal (gutaiteki ippansha 具体的一般者). The focus now has shifted, however. Moving from the predicate of a judgment to the middle term of the syllogism, the focus eventually comes to be on the medium in the sense of the world embracing both universal and individuals. The world as such is radically dialectical.

Nishida's stance toward the world in its dialectical structure poses a radical alternative to metaphysical monism or dualism. In virtue of its radical dialectic, Nishida through the mid-1930s, in his *Tetsugaku no konpon mondai* (『哲学の根本問題』; *Fundamental Problems of Philosophy*) and *Tetsugaku ronbunshū* (『哲学論文集』; *Collected Philosophical Essays*), characterizes that dialectical world (benshōhōteki sekai 弁証法的世界) in its logical structuring as a "dialectical universal" (benshōhōteki ippansha 弁証法的一般者). Altering his earlier appropriation of the Hegelian concept of the self-determining concrete universal, he now depicts the self-determining universal explicitly in its dialectical character. The dialectical universal designates the structuring of the world so that the self-determination of the dialectical universal means the self-determination of the world (Z6 159; Z7 136). But it is the logical form not only of the dialectical world but of our acting intuition (kōiteki chokkan 行為的直観) in virtue of the fact that our acting intuition is also the self-determination of the whole (Z7 126–127; Z8 68). It is the logical structure of the world-matrix wherein we are born, act, and die, so that we exist as creative and constitutive elements of the dialectical universal. The dialectic is such that while being autonomous creators, we are also fully implaced in this universal as our place of being. The mutual determination of individuals requires a universal establishing their reciprocity. The dialectic cannot involve just a process but must also involve their mediating place. Their medium, then, is this dialectical universal as their place (Z6 75, 116, 253). Although Nishida still refers to the concrete universal during the 1930s, he thus expresses a subtle distinction between the concrete universal in its self-determination or determination of the individual and the dialectical universal as embracing both the concrete universal's determination of the individual and the individual's autonomous self- and co-determinations and reverse determinations of the universal. Nishida in "Ronri to seimei" (「論理と生命」; "Logic and Life") thus distinguishes the dialectical universal underlying the dialectical process as neither an abstract universal (a mere concept distinct from things) nor a concrete universal (that becomes the particular), but instead as encompassing both. He characterizes it as "the universal of one qua many and many qua one" (*ichi soku ta, ta soku ichi no ippansha* 一即多、多即一の一般者), the dialectical process of which constitutes and consists of the world's historical reality (Z8 82). Therefore, the world is a world of the dialectical universal (*benshōhōteki ippansha no sekai* 弁証法的一般者の世界) (Z6 183). With this notion of the dialectical universal, Nishida has drawn out the dialectical implications of his notion of place so that the self-determination of the dialectical universal, the self-determination of place, and the self-determination of the world are all identical (Z6 159). And in making this distinction from the concrete universal, we also see Nishida distancing his dialectic from that of Hegel in spite of the prominence of a Hegelian-inspired language during this period. At the same time, however, one also notes his nearness to the Buddhist conceptions of inter-dependent origination and the non-obstruction of thing-events.

As I just stated, Nishida now takes the universal of the world as explicitly a dialectical universal. This underscores precisely the fact that the universal in its dialectical capacity is not placed in a metaphysically privileged position in relation to the individual. The dialectical universal as the dynamic structuring of the world is "one qua many, many qua one" (*ichi soku ta, ta soku ichi* 一即多、多即一). That is, in its self-determination, "the one determines the many and the many determines the one, the universal determines the individual and the individual determines the universal" (Z6 207). To metaphysically privilege the universal here would be to objectify it into a grammatical subject, to relativize it into an individual, even if on a grand scale. We cannot grasp the universal's self-determination, that is, the worldly poiēsis, by objectifying it in opposition to ourselves. As in his epistemology of the 1920s, we must turn away from the grammatical subject and toward the predicate pole to treat the universal accordingly as irreducibly unsayable, as the place wherein we find ourselves implaced and taking part in its dynamic. Yet the emphasis is now also on the medium that mediates grammatical subject and predicate, individual and universal. Because we cannot treat the universal or the world as the grammatical subject of a judgment, neither can we regard it monistically as a cosmic substance engulfing everything else, as in Spinoza. The dialectical universal is the structural medium for correlating individuals, enveloping and determining them. The individuals implaced in it determine themselves and one another and in their implacement are determined by it (Z6 247). In that sense the dialectical universal is not the absolute substance of the world. Rather, it is to be regarded as a place, basho. As the concrete field in space and time, the locus and epoch, for our sociohistorical interactions, it is the an-ontological clearing for ontological emergence, permitting the mutual constitutions of the many. Nishida explains that reality in this sense is "being [yū 有] and at the same time nothing [mu 無], it is being qua nothing [yū soku mu 有即無], nothing qua being" (Z6 344). Such opposites are to be thought only from this dynamically dialectical reality. The dialectical universal is thus a further development of Nishida's earlier conception of the self-determination of absolute nothing, but now understood in more explicitly dialectical terms.

The dialectic of this dialectical universal occurs in several concurrent forms: (1) the universal's self-determination, (2) the universal's determination of the individual, (3) the individual's self-determination, (4) the individuals' co-determinations of one another, and (5) the individual's determination of the universal.[2] The self-determination of concrete (universal) reality is the self-, co-, and reciprocal determinations of its individuals (Z8 239). The simultaneity of these various determinations is made possible by the non-substantiality of the dialectical universal as their mediating place. This place, as delimited by absolutely nothing, grounds the many individuals in their self-affirmative being but also un-grounds them in their negations. Implaced within the self-creative world qua dialectical universal, the acting self as an individual possesses its own identity as an independent self-determining being. The world clears room for that individual's positive self-determination. Yet the individual's being is grounded (but also un-grounded) on that world, for the whole of the world actualizes itself by determining itself as those innumerable individuals.

As in Hegel's concrete universal, the universal's self-determination for Nishida still constitutes the individual. The universal determines the individual in that the historical and social situation—including the network of conditions on many different levels, for example, physical, biological, psychological, economic, national, cultural, technological, and epochal—shapes one's identity and self-awareness in one's present situation. Each individual self is a condensed microcosm (shōchū 小宇宙) expressing the macrocosmic whole comprising innumerable other individuals (Z10 305, 340–341). Yet the dialectic between universal and individual is not one-sided to be hierarchically structured on the basis of the primacy of the universal. The individual still retains autonomy. The non-substantiality of the universal qua place or medium allows for that autonomy. Moreover, the universal cannot determine itself without the individual's free self-determinations. The individual's free act constitutes the universal's determining act. The two are in co-respondence: just as the universal is determining itself in the individual, the individual is determining itself within the universal. The individual's self-determination, then, for Nishida, is also the self-determination of the dialectical world (Z5 222–223). The world qua dialectical universal is determining itself as that acting individual self (Z7 78). The two—the individual's self-determination and the universal's self-determination—are in synchrony.

Before Nishida, Leibniz had also viewed the world as comprising individuals or monads, which microcosmically mirror or express the whole macrocosm, each from its own vantage point. Nishida distinguishes his stance, however, by emphasizing that the individual is authentically individual, that is, a self-determining individual, only vis-a-vis other individuals. It determines itself in relation to other individuals (Z6 13–14, 173–174). Individuality is thus founded on the reciprocal determination of innumerable individuals (Z7 43). As in Leibniz's monadology, each individual has its rightful place within the world. But Nishida also emphasizes how each individual cannot be utterly isolated or alone. Otherwise, its status as an individual is undermined. The monad is a monad in opposition to other monads (Z6 23). The individual is individual only in facing other individuals. One is who one is only in relationship to other individuals, with whom one converses, laughs, argues, loves, and so on. We saw this in chapter 5 in the section on the "I-thou" relationship. Our self-identity is constituted vis-à-vis other persons in the dynamic of inter-determination. Yet each individual as such is simultaneously independent. As reciprocally independent, individuals are co-relating, for only the independent can truly relate to one another as such. This also means, in other words, that each individual is both independent from and inter-dependent with others (Z6 42–43). Furthermore, for Nishida, that mutual determination between individuals coincides with the self-determination of the universal wherein they are implaced, for the dialectical universal as the structure of the dialectical world provides the place, basho, for the interactivity of those innumerable individuals. In turn, the many individuals working together constitute the universal. The self-determination of each individual and the mutual determination of individuals are different aspects of a single but manifold reality, the self-determination of the dialectical universal. By this, however, Nishida does not mean to prioritize the universal's self-determination at the expense of individual autonomy, for the self-determination of the universal is composed of the web of mutual determinations among the many individuals. Nishida really wants to maintain the dialectical tension here between individual determination and universal determination, each on its own and in respect to the other.

If we take the mutual determinations and interrelations among individuals as the dialectic in the horizontal direction, we may take the universal's determination of and as those individuals as the dialectic in the vertical direction. The fivefold determination involves a chiasma of the vertical and the horizontal. On the vertical level, each individual creatively expresses the world's self-creation. Thereby the one world disperses itself into a multiplicity of individual focal points, each expressing or mirroring the world from different angles (Z8 350). The two directional planes of vertical and horizontal are part of the same dialectical matrix (the dialectical universal) forming a chiasma: what on the vertical level is the self-determination of the universal means on the horizontal level the inter-determinations among individuals implaced in its world. That reciprocal determination of mutually independent individuals requires a medium, a place, wherein they meet. Their working activity, in turn, may be conceived as the medium's self-determination (Z6 90, 94–95; Z7 171). Hence Nishida states that the medium of individuals expresses itself in the reciprocal determination among its individuals; the innumerable individuals working together are the medium's self-formation (Z7 120–121, 171). Each individual's self-determination vis-à-vis other individuals is simultaneously its determination by the universal, the medium's self-determination (Z6 13–14, 142; Z7 175). In that sense the world of the reciprocal determination of individuals is the world determining itself (Z8 322). Nishida explains that the self-determination of the world qua medium is simultaneously the individuals' self- and co-determinations (Z7 176, 177). The same obtains in the epistemological sphere: the mutual determination and dialectical unity between subject and object or between form and matter simultaneously mean the self-determination of their medium or place that embraces both to establish the dichotomy.

The dynamic interactions of individual elements constitute vertically, in reverse direction to the universal's self-determination, the movement of the dialectical world. So while the vertical self-determination of the universal is non-different from the horizontal inter-determination of individuals, the latter on the vertical level proves to be the "reverse determination" (or counter-determination) (gyaku gentei 逆限定) of the universal by the individuals (Z5 274–275, 289–290). That is, individual selves, determined by the world, interact with one another, and their interaction or inter-determination conversely determines the world, contributing to its dialectic (Z6 239–334). What this means is that, while determined by the universal, the individual at the point that Nishida calls the "extremity" (kyokugen 極限) of the universal's self-determination determines the universal in reverse. At the point where that self-determination of the universal reaches its extremity (kyokugen), the individuals in turn counter-determine that world (Z6 10, 22–23, 26, 148–149).[3] The world's self-determination takes place by way of the inter-determinations of individuals determining the world in reverse. Nishida has in mind the human capacity to determine history and remodel society, the conditions into which one is born. While living under the influence of society, an individual person also has the capacity to determine himself or herself and to conversely remodel his or her social surroundings and move history itself (Z5 233–234, 277, 278). It is in this sense that Nishida takes the human individual to be (at) the extreme limit of the world's self-determination, its sociohistorical determination (Z5 278). I can illustrate this with an example. The sociohistorical milieu of American academia expresses itself in the activities of each academic belonging to that environment. Each academic enters into and partakes in that environment under certain given constraints. But simultaneously the activities of each individual academic also constitute that environment. The two movements, while moving in opposite directions, are one. We are not only determined by the universal but transcend it to determine it in reverse (Z5 248). We are implaced in the world-matrix as simultaneously its individual determinations and its creative determinants. This is another way of speaking of the self's thorough determination by and implacement in the world, on the one hand, and paradoxically its absolute independence and freedom (*zettai no dokuritsu* 絶対の独立, *zettai no jiyū* 絶対の自由), on the other (Z5 352). In this radicalization of dialectic, freedom and determinism thus co-exist: just as the individual, while determined by the past, freely goes on to determine itself in the face of the future, moving from the made to the making, the individual, while determined by the environment, goes on to counter-determine it. At the extreme limit point of determination—both by the past and by the environment—there is its reversal, its reverse determination. At the point where universal and individual meet, there is thus freedom in determination. Nishida claims, on the basis of reverse determination, that contrary to Hegel, we can even conceive of matter as generating what Hegel called the "idea" (Z5 224). But "matter" here as the acting individuals themselves is ultimately "dialectical matter" (*benshōhōteki busshitsu* 弁証法的物質), by which Nishida really means the self-forming formlessness of absolute nothing (Z5 297). In fact, it is that non-substantiality of the universal qua nothing that allows for its reverse determination. On the basis of this radical dialectic founded on that non-substantiality, the individual is determined yet free, simultaneously determined by the environment, self-determining as independent, co-determining with other individuals, and in its self- and co-determinations counter-determining the environment (Z5 259–260, 269–270, 275, 301). This proves to be Nishida's dialectical radicalization of Hegel's statement that the individual is the universal and the grammatical subject is the predicate (Z6 10, 142–143; Z8 82).[4]

As we can see, dialectic for Nishida is no simple matter. The manifold dialectic on the part of each individual at the extremity of universal self-determination means that the individual is simultaneously dependent, independent, and interdependent. The individual is dependent on the world for its being but is also independent in its unique creativity. And simultaneously those individuals on the horizontal plane are co-dependent in their interactions. Their interactivity, in turn, makes the world what it is in reverse determination. As both independent from and inter-dependent with one another, individuals are also independent from and inter-dependent with the universal. And as the inter-determination among individuals is the self-determination of the universal, so is the individual's self-determination. The many individuals' self- and co-determinations are simultaneously the universal's self-determination qua world (Z6 11, 14–15, 39, 83–84; Z8 41, 54). Thereby the individual's acting intuition, both alone and together in interactivity with others, is at the same time the world's self-formation via acting and seeing. Again, quoting Hegel, Nishida states that the universal is the particular in self-determination (Z8 91, 93). But Nishida has radicalized the dialectic beyond what is covered by Hegel's self-determining concrete universal and equation of universal and particular. Instead, Nishida's vision of "absolute dialectics" (zettai benshōhō 絶対弁証法) encompasses a manifold dimensionality that exceeds Hegelian dialectics in complexity. And as we have seen, this distinction of Nishida's absolute dialectic from Hegel's dialectic hinges on Nishida's development of the notion of the dialectical universal.

As I briefly mentioned earlier, in spite of the Hegelian-inspired dialectics, Nishida's radicalization of the dialectic in terms of the dialectical universal is reminiscent of Buddhist conceptions of inter-dependent origination. It almost seems to account for the worldview of the dharmadhatu ("realm of dharmas") (Ch. fajie; Jp. hokkai 法界) developed by the Chinese Huayan (Jp. Kegon 華厳) school with its explicit encompassing of the vertical (Ch. lishi wuai; Jp. riji muge 理事無礙) and the horizontal (Ch. shishi wuai; Jp. jiji muge 事事無礙) directions. In Huayan terms, the individual is a thing-event (Ch. shi; Jp. ji 事) that is inter-dependent with others (Ch. shishi wuai; Jp. jiji muge) and expressive of the whole pattern (Ch. lishi wuai; Jp. riji muge).[5] In the self-determination of the dialectical universal, as the universal determines individuals and individuals determine one another and in turn determine the universal, one determines many and many determine one (Z6 206–207). Each mode of inter- and self-determination is mutually implicative. Such is the radicalized dialectic of the world-matrix as designated by the term "dialectical universal" (also e.g., Z6 236–237, 326–337). The world for Nishida is thoroughly universal and thoroughly of individuals; it is simultaneously both individual determination and universal determination (Z6 159, 234). The world of such a dialectical medium indeed resonates with the world conceptualized by the fifth–sixth-century patriarch of Huayan Buddhism, Fazang (法藏), as a dharma-realm of non-hindrance among thing-events (Ch. *shishi wuai fajie*; Jp. *jijimuge hokkai* 事事無礙法界)—a phrase Nishida refers to in 1940 (Z9 71). (I will return to this possible Buddhist connection in chapter 9.)

Nishida has thus made explicit the radical dialectical implication of what began earlier as an epistemology aiming to counter reification in terms of the grammatical subject. At the same time, however, having focused on the predicate plane in his epistemology, we were at pains to avoid any mistaking of his position that would reify and prioritize in the reverse direction the universal as an absolute substantiality standing over individuals. The real cannot be reduced to any term of the dialectic. Hence what he calls the "universal" (ippansha 一般者) in its dialectical significance is really that dynamic holism of interacting individuals, a whole that in terms of substance is empty. This is an important point to remember. Only thus taken in its non-substantiality is it the "substance" or "substratum" (*kitai* 基体) of the world's dialectical process whereby one is many and many is one (Z8 82). Nishida distinguishes this radical dialectics from Hegelian dialectics, in which the universal (qua concept, Begriff) subsumes or grasps (*begreifen*) the totality of individuals. By contrast, we are to think of the determination of that non-substantiality, the universal's determination of the individual in its radically dialectical matrix that retains the individual's free self-determination, as a "determination of that which is without a determiner" (*genteisurumononakimono no gentei* 限定するものなきものの限定), a determination of and by the universal qua nothing (Z5 269). The determination is without any agent qua substance. Hence in *Mu no jikakuteki gentei* (『無の自覚的限定』; *Self-Aware Determination of Nothing*) Nishida equates that ultimate environment that envelops everything to determine the individual with the absolute nothing (zettai mu) (Z5 286). The dialectic of the world-matrix, then, is a dialectic of place (*bashoteki benshōhō* 場所的弁証法).

The Dialectic of Absolute (or Self-) Negation

Nishida's radical dialectic that precludes monistic or universal subsumption is founded on a non-substantialism involving the act of self-negation. This is the meaning behind what he calls "absolute dialectics" (zettai benshōhō), that is, a dialectic of "absolute negation" (zettai hitei) or "self-negation" (jiko hitei) (Z6 273, 275). Nishida takes dialectical negation seriously to the extent that it escapes any resolution in an affirmative synthesis. The truly real as what is ontologically independent, not requiring anything else for its existence, is what philosophers like Aristotle and Descartes call substance.[6] But Nishida adds that what truly is in itself must be what includes its other within itself in a self-negation; it must envelop absolute or self-negation within itself (Z10 120). He states: "Dialectical movement . . . must be absolute negation-qua-affirmation, absolute nothing-qua-being. . . . From that standpoint, to die is to be born and to be born is to die. There is established an infinite dialectical process of negation-qua-affirmation" (Z6 29). This means that the real is non-substantial, but here that non-substantiality is expressed as a verb in terms of self-negation. What is unique about Nishida's conception of the dialectic is that it occurs through the mediation of self-negation. True dialectic, Nishida states, takes absolute negation as mediation (Z6 29). There is no mutual determination or conjunction between "I and thou" or among individuals without absolute negation (Z6 43, 209). Mutual self-negation by virtue of the non-substantiality of concrete reality is what makes the various inter-determinations possible in the first place. In turn, the universal's self-negation is its self-determination, which qua self-negation allows for its reverse determination by the individual (Z6 14, 199, 201). That the dialectical universal's self-determination is its self-negation in turn means its individualization to become its other, the innumerable individual beings. It becomes the world of individuals reciprocally determining each other in mutual self-negation (Z6 199, 201–202, 224). The entire world of actuality is thus a world of affirmation passing through absolute negation (Z6 323). The one and the many are "one" dialectically, that is, via mutual self-negation (Z8 376). The dialectical world is thus "substantial" or "substrative" (*kitaiteki* 基体的) only in this sense of its self-negation (Z8 99–100).

Such a dialectic that unfolds the interrelations of opposing terms via mutual self-negation may be contrasted with one that would subsume opposites under a positive sublating concept. In acting on one's other, one seeks to negate the other and make the other into oneself, that is, to express oneself at the expense of the other. One aims in this way to become the entire world, to express oneself at the expense of everything or everyone else. But simultaneously this attempt necessitates self-negation: one can act only as a part of the world, and one can be at work only in being worked on (Z8 373, 384). The point is that without self-negation, one cannot negate that which negates oneself (Z8 75). One cannot determine the other, make it into oneself, and affirm oneself without negating oneself (Z7 175; Z8 310). More specifically, in cognition, for example, the external object (i.e., the transcendent object) is internalized, subjectivized qua phenomenon as known, and the internal self (i.e., the transcendental subject) is externalized, objectivized qua knower relating to that object. And this transformation, for Nishida, can happen only in mutual self-negation. Nishida explains subsumptive judgments—Hegel's identification of individual and universal—likewise in terms of the mutual self-negation of grammatical subject and predicate, allowing for their copulative conjunction and identification (e.g., Z6 186–188). We have already seen how, for Nishida, cognition is predicated on acting intuition. But the latter also occurs in self-negation. In our acting intuition, things move us and compel us to act, and for Nishida, this means our self-negation so that we "become those things."[7] In turn, the things working on us affirm themselves through their self-negation, allowing us to be conscious of them (Z7 104). That is, in both directions, there is activity under negating conditions. Or, put differently, the two opposing moments of activity and passivity in acting intuition are mediated in mutual self-negation. In the dialectic of life, for example, organism and environment, each, in their mutual encounter, is altered, that is, negated for the sake of the other's self-affirmation (Z8 58). Each, in working on its other, must be worked on. Each cannot affirm itself without allowing itself to be negated vis-à-vis the other. The same sort of mediation via mutual self-negation obtains in the co-relative determination of individuals as well (Z8 19, 202). Otherwise they would remain utterly independent, having nothing to do with each other. Mutual self-negation inverts ontological independence into inter-dependence and correlativity. It is the foundation of any sort of self-determination and hence self-affirmation in the dialectical world.

In contrast to any notion of a subsuming absolute concept, the universal in Nishida's system engages in absolute negation in the affirmation of individuals (Z6 243). Absolute negation is the movement of the absolute nothing. Delimited by nothing, the universal must ultimately be nothing, no determinate universal. Spinozistic substantialism is precluded by the self-negation of the one that is "unable to negate the many but instead depends on them" (Z9 384). So via mutual self-negation the one and the many, whole and parts, are identified (Z13 198, 211–212). Through self-negation the one becomes the many to establish the world of individuals. And this self-negation of the one along the vertical plane means simultaneously the mutual self-negation among individuals on the horizontal level. In negating itself, the world affirms the individuals implaced within; and in turn, the individuals through mutual self-negation contribute to the world's creativity. In the self-negation of the many, the world is one; and in the self-negation of the one, the world is many (Z13 198). The dialectical matrix consists in this mutual (self-)negation of one and many (Z8 371). Self-negation thus mediates the dialectic on all levels and dimensions as a self-opening chiasma. Because the entire dynamism of the world-matrix is founded on this expressive process of the non-substantial medium, the creativity of the world is inconceivable without it.

As I just stated, the vertical dialectic of self-negation translates on the horizontal level into interrelation among individual persons. This includes mutual self-negation between persons operative in interpersonal relationships, as well as between subject and object in cognition. For example, in interpersonal dialectics the self is a person only in recognizing the personhood of the other. Such recognition precludes instrumentalization of the other, although on a certain level objectification is unavoidable because of our bodies. This recognition of the other's otherness qua person, the awareness of otherness mediated by one's self-negation, makes oneself into a person as well (Z6 67). The I is I by recognizing the thou, and this means that the I is I via self-negation and the we is we by reciprocal self-negation (Z6 212–213). Nishida therefore writes that individual persons "relate to one another separated by absolute negation" (Z6 46). We also find mutual self-negation operative in the temporal dimension. Within the continuity of one's self, the unity of personality as the I of today is established by regarding yesterday's I and tomorrow's I as thous (Z6 68). The self is born via self-negation at each moment, being born by dying, making itself anew as its previously made self disappears. Through self-negation, each moment gives way to the next, making the transition possible from the made to the making, from determined to determining, from created to creating (Z6 202). In that respect, self-negation is the medium of the dialectical process not only in space but also in time, allowing for the unfolding of time. The self's individual unity, then, is established both synchronically (with other persons) and diachronically (between moments within oneself) via mutual self-negation between terms. So we see here that the dialectic is mediated through mutual self-negation on the horizontal plane as well, in both spatial and temporal dimensions.

The dialectic of such self-negation can be contrasted with the sublational dialectic of Plato or Hegel that postulates a higher level of being or concept. In Nishida's case, the ultimate field enveloping all dialectical oppositions is in perpetual self-negation to preclude its conception or affirmation as a grammatical subject of statement. Un-objectifiable, it is a place delimited by nothing, the place of absolutely nothing. Determination on any level requires self-negation, and self-negation occurs only on the basis of that self-negating medium of mutual self-negation. And another way in which Nishida articulates that all-pervading self-negation is in terms of the continuity of discontinuity.

The Dialectic of the Continuity of Discontinuity

The interrelation of terms through their mediation in mutual self-negation means that they are continuous in their discontinuity with one another. They are continuous, united, in their discontinuity, that is, their difference, which delimits their respective identities. Hence mutual self-negation, according to Nishida, also means continuity of discontinuity (hirenzoku no renzoku). This is to be contrasted with the continuous self-identity of a substance. The self-determination of the dialectical universal, Nishida asserts, entails neither mere continuity (identity) nor mere discontinuity (difference) between the determined and co-determining individuals but the continuity of their discontinuity (Z6 13, 202).

For individuals to oppose each other and work on each other, they must be independent of each other and hence discontinuous. Yet their mutual working also requires some sort of continuity. A continuity of discontinuity that mediates mutually independent yet inter-dependent individuals would be their place, basho (Z7 17–18). For example, there is a continuity of discontinuity in our interaction with our environment, wherein we make things through the bodily manipulation of tools. Here the body becomes a tool, and in turn the tool becomes an extension of the body, and in its interaction with things, the body becomes a thing of the world (Z8 31, 32). At the same time, the world becomes a tool, a realm of instruments for our use, as well as an extension of our bodily selves (Z8 52–53,

67). The body mediates our relation to other tools, and tools mediate our relation to the environment of things. Through body and tool, self and environment are interconnected, and there obtains a certain continuity among them. Yet the things that we make and use stand apart from us so that there is a rupture in this interconnection, discontinuities amid continuity, uniting man and world. Hence Nishida characterizes "technics" (*gijutsu* 技術) as involving this continuity of discontinuity among body, tool, thing, and world (Z8 64). Another example is the relationship between self and thing via desire, whereby one moves to realize one's inner desire by making its outer object accord to one's subjectivity, but there is simultaneously also an absolute rupture or difference between one's inner subjectivity and its outer object as other. That other is not oneself, one does not possess it, and there is an unpassable abyss separating oneself from one's other. Yet one desires it. Desire thus entails both continuity and discontinuity between self and object, inner and outer, mediating their connection and separation.

The continuity of discontinuity operates not only spatially but in the temporal dimension as well. Nishida applies it, for example, to the issues of temporal moments, personal continuity, and historical epochs. For Nishida, time is neither a mere sequence of now-points nor a static continuity. Time as perpetually perishing is essentially discontinuous in its flow. Motion or change entails that discontinuity of time, and any notion of temporal unity or continuity must take this into account. For Nishida, this means dialectical unity in self-negation. That is, the dialectical process moves from actuality to actuality in a continuity of discontinuity (Z8 90). Each moment as independent of others passes to give way to the next. As we saw in the previous section, the self-negation of each moment constitutes the unity of time, and this also means the continuity of discontinuity in time (Z6 210). Each moment of self-determination is a moment of unique creativity that cuts off the past to move from the made to the making. The affirmation of that moment is thus also its self-negation that engenders the new in a continuity of discontinuity. With this understanding of time, Nishida sought to account for the contradictory nature of motion in time that Aristotelian substantialism failed, in his view, to adequately explain.

In that unity of time as a continuity of discontinuity, there is also the unity of personhood, the constitution of the individual self (Z8 5). The individual person in different times is neither merely continuous nor merely discontinuous with himself or herself. Every moment in personal continuity, the I of yesterday and the I of today, is distinct from the other. What one did twenty years ago, or even yesterday, may seem foreign to oneself today. It is as if the I of yesterday and of today are different persons encountering one another. In that sense the I at each moment rises and falls, appears and disappears. Yet the I is united so that the whole of its moments is simultaneously one and many, continuous and discontinuous. The personal self is always an on-going process of unification in the focal point of its present, a self-determination at each moment vis-à-vis past and future. The individual affirms its identity in that present moment in relation to past and future as a continuity of discontinuity. As persons, Nishida declares, we are continuities of discontinuities (Z6 49). The acting self united in this discontinuous flow of the present is thus "living by dying": "In order to be connected with the following moment, as a continuity of discontinuity, we must die at this moment and enter into nothing. But without dying in this sense, there is no I. . . . We live only by dying in the present" (Z6 231). This means that although it is determined by the past, at each present moment the I, regarding yesterday's I as a thou, is also free to act in discontinuity with that past and thus move from the made to the making. Implaced in the present, the self's creative act marks the transition from made I to making I. It is in this sense that the I is a continuity of discontinuity, living by dying (Z6 32). Nishida repeatedly emphasizes, however, that the self-determination of the self in internal time cannot happen without its co-determination with other selves. The unity of the self-consciousness of the personal self occurs in its implacement within the sociohistorical world (Z6 32). The individual is individual only vis-à-vis other individuals, a continuity of discontinuity extending in the spatial horizon. We can accordingly understand the self's constitution as resulting from a crisscrossing chiasma of continuities of discontinuities both in time and in space. Dialectic at all levels, of time and space, happens as a continuity of discontinuities.

The continuity of discontinuity likewise applies to epochs in collective history. Each epoch is neither the simple result of the previous one nor a mere preparation for the succeeding one. It has its own independent meaning within the whole of history (Z9 390). With the self-negation of each momentary event (or epoch), time, and hence history, unfold in a continuity of discontinuities (see Z8 84–85). And just as personal identity entails a continuity of discontinuity not only in time but also in space, the space-time chiasma here applies also to cultural worlds or societies as both historical and interacting with other cultural or social worlds. Neither continuity nor discontinuity, whether in time or in space, is unambiguous.

Discontinuous beings form a continuum on the basis of such non-substantial mediation—their continuity of discontinuity—implaced on the "placial" medium (*bashoteki baikaisha* 場所的媒介者) of nothing (Z7 19, 109). Again, as I suggested earlier, this is what Nishida has in mind when he speaks of the "substantiality" or "substrativeness" (kitaiteki) of the dialectical world in its self-negation (Z8 99). Precisely as basho, place, delimited by nothing, is the medium a "standing under" (*sub-stantia*) as a place that is no thing. Its self-negation as thing, or in Buddhist terms its emptiness of substance or own-being (svabhāva), is precisely what allows for the inter-continuity among discontinuous individuals. In explicating the radical dialectic of the concrete, whether in terms of self-negation or in terms of the continuity of discontinuity, Nishida thus still has in mind his earlier conception of the place of nothing. The notions of nothing, self-negation, and continuity of discontinuity all refer to one another and together make possible the "inconceivable" conception of a "contradictory self-identity" (mujunteki jikodōitsu 矛盾的自己同一), my next topic of discussion.

The Dialectic of Absolutely Contradictory Self-Identity

A major theme throughout the 1930s and 1940s whereby Nishida explicates the manifold inter-dimensionality of the world-matrix is his conception of contradictory self-identity (mujunteki jikodōitsu). The importance of this concept is shown by the fact that it becomes conceived by many as synonymous with Nishidian philosophy. It was already clear from his earliest works before the 1930s that, in Nishida's mind, self-determination implies contradiction (*mujun* 矛盾). Self-determination and self-contradiction go hand in hand in that the former requires a form of self-negation that alters the current state of things into what it is not. This is a development of what he earlier discussed in terms of a primal pre-dichotomized holistic unity ("pure experience"). It is an extended attempt on Nishida's part to think and articulate that pre-reflective concrete whole. But in the 1930s Nishida is explicitly formulating the inner contradiction of that concrete in its dialectical unfolding via external interaction. For example, in 1933 (*Tetsugaku no konpon mondai*) Nishida conceives of the determination of the interactive world in terms of a "dialectical unity" (*benshōhōteki tōitsu* 弁証法的統一) or "self-identity of opposites" (*sōhansurumono no jikodōitsu* 相反するものの自己同一) (Z6 53, 55). He finds that the world contains contradiction and that it determines itself dialectically in its contradictions (Z6 123). His claim is that dialectical movement (*benshōhōteki undō* 弁証法的運動) is conceivable only in terms of that self-identity of opposites (Z6 48). Reality involves the union of opposites in a contradictory identity, whereby opposites imply and determine each other (Z6 47, 344). By the late 1930s he comes to think of this world in dialectical movement as a world of contradictory self-identity (Z8 20), and he conceives that contradictory self-identity in terms of the interrelations between one and many, universal and individual, world and actors—an interrelationship that moves the world of individuals from the made to the making (e.g., Z8 318–319, 367–368). For example, life involves the dialectic of birth-and-death, generation-and-extinction, and health-and-illness. He states in "Ronri to seimei" that historical life is a dialectical process involving these opposites, whereby it goes on determining itself in self-contradiction (Z8 72–73, 80). In his 1939 essay "Zettai mujunteki jikodōitsu" Nishida explicitly unifies the various expressions he has been using since *Tetsugaku no konpon mondai* for the internal logical structure of the dialectical world—"self-identity of opposites," "self-identity of mutual contradictories," "self-identity of opposing directions," "self-identity of opposing activities," "dialectical self-identity," "self-identity of absolute contradiction," and so on—under the phrase "absolutely contradictory self-identity" (zettai mujunteki jikodōitsu), and it becomes one of the major themes of his philosophy from the late 1930s to the 1940s.

The historical world as a dialectical world, Nishida says, possesses the contradictory self-identity of one and many, of whole and parts, of universal and individuals, and also of outer and inner, or objective and subjective (Z8 239–40). Each pair of these opposites is one dialectically, not monistically or substantially. The point is that neither member of each pair is real on its own. Each is real only in relation to the other as co-relative, co-determining terms. They form each other and are mutually implicative in an organic unity (Z8 331). Again, this means that the concrete as radically dialectical is not substantial, either as a single macrocosmic whole, as in Spinoza's substance, or as many microcosmic atoms, as in Leibniz's monads; either as individual bearers of accidents, as in Aristotle's ousia, or as thinking things, as in Descartes's cogito (Z8 371). All reifications in terms of substance fail to grasp the world's dynamic holism. We might understand what Nishida means if we keep in mind one of the concepts that I touched on earlier, self-negation. We already saw how for Nishida the individual's self-determination involves, in fact, co-determination among individuals, which in turn also means the self-determination of the universal qua world and vice versa. The dialectical universal's dialectical self-determination involves self-identity between the opposites of the environment's (*kankyō* 環境) self-determination, on the one hand, and the individual's (ko 個) self-determination, on the other (Z6 116).[8] The meaning of "universal" (ippan 一般) here, even as "environment," excludes the sense of individuality, and the meaning of "individual" excludes universality, yet these opposites imply each other, and their respective self-determinations coincide with each other. This is possible because self-determination is also self-negation, and what mediates the encounter between opposites is their mutual self-negation on the basis of the non-substantial medium of their mediation, the place of nothing. Opposing or independent terms are united within a whole mediated through mutual self-negations. The whole is one in the self-negation of the many and is many in the self-negation of the one (Z10 145). That whole as their non-substantial medium allows for their continuity of discontinuity, their contradictory self-identity. In the world of interacting persons, opposing actors interact on the basis of mutual self-negation. In mutual self-negation, they are identified in their co-dependency as belonging to a whole. The world that moves in self-contradiction thus possesses such "a self-identity of absolute contradiction" (Z8 367). The dialectical universal as the logical structure of such a world, while determining itself via self-negation, remains self-identical through its self-contradictions as a contradictory identity of individuals and universal, mediated through self-negation.[9] Nishida thus views concrete reality, in its radically dialectical nature, as self-contradictory. And this obtains only because the real for Nishida ultimately is not a substance but a place of nothing.

Within the space-time matrix, there are focal points of creativity mirroring and expressing that contradictory self-identity of the concrete whole (Z8 327). As a self-determination of that whole, the individual self born into its dynamic matrix must also be a contradictory self-identity. Just as the world entails an absolutely contradictory self-identity between the oneness of its whole and the plurality of individuals, we as individuals in that world are also self-contradictory, partaking in its dynamism (Z8 27, 398, 512; Z9 490). Our contradictory existence microcosmically mirrors the macrocosm's contradictory reality. In other words, the contradictory nature of human existence is in dialectical co-respondence with the contradictory nature of the dialectical world. For example, in being an independent and unique creator, determining oneself while also being interrelated and co-determining with others, the individual person possesses self-identity in the contradiction of many and one (Z8 309). The individual determining itself involves the universal's determination, as well as its co-determination with others. Our identities are constructed vis-à-vis the self-contradictory world. While we form it, because we are implaced within it, we are also determined by it. As creative elements of the creative world, we are both forming and being formed vis-à-vis the world, both the subject of this formation and its means, both for ourselves and for the world, both user and used, manipulator and instrument. Human existence—in its embodied implacement in the world, as well as in its acting intuition as the mode of embodied existence—is thus self-contradictory. This is exemplified in Nishida's statement that desire in the individual's dialectical interaction with the world "is born to die and dies to be born" (Z6 16). As both a continuity and a discontinuity of moments, we live by dying.

Nishida also expresses this contradictory identity of the self in terms of transcendence and immanence: the knower both is implaced in the spatiotemporal world and transcends it in the sense that he or she is a foundational conduit for the world's self-expression. That is, the self is a contradictory identity that expresses the world by transcending it while being immanent in the world as the foundation of its self-expression (Z10 118). Such contradictory identity also points to the self's non-substantiality. In Nishida's mind, this is where Descartes went wrong in his method of doubt when he mistook the reality of the self-doubting self in terms of the grammatical subject. Rather, the self that grasps itself in self-doubt as existing, whereby the thinker is the thought, must have the form of a contradictory self-identity, not of a substance. Reminding us that thinking is a historical event, Nishida states that the indubitable self is not the abstract self of consciousness but the historically formative self that is made and is making. By recognizing this, Nishida claims, we can take Cartesian reflection to a deeper and more concrete level beyond that attained by Descartes, for it is within the dynamic matrix that we are self-aware at the deepest level of our contradictory existence. We can thus take Cartesian reflection as a self-awareness via self-negation that uncovers the self's contradictory self-identity between thinker and thought, subject and object, immanence and transcendence, self and thing, inner and outer, and ultimately life and death, being and non-being. What is indubitably immediate to the self is this contradictory self-identity and not its substantiality (Z10 128).

Both world and self thus possess self-identities of contradiction (Z9 443). And in interaction their mutual contradictory identity unfolds the fate of each other. For Nishida, then, contradictory self-identity is the internal logical structure of the world and its concrete reality, including ourselves, not only in space but also in time. Its logic entails strife. Always involving the tension of contradictories constituting its self-identity, it is never static. Rather, it is always moving in self-contradiction, from present moment to present moment. The world of historical reality in its contradictory identity is a world of endless strife, unfolding in a variety of formations from moment to moment, epoch to epoch (Z7 197–198). The many individuals as creative elements within this world of absolutely contradictory self-identity make history through their interactions. Nishida speaks of this structure operative in the world-matrix as the *logos* of *genesis kai phthora* (generation-and-extinction), bearing in mind the Heraclitean sense of logos as the harmony of opposites in strife and in flux. He is associating Heraclitus's logos, the endless flux that unites opposites, with his conception of the dialectical universal as the logos-structure of the world (Z8 9). And he takes the principle of non-contradiction, emphasized by Aristotle, but which pertains only to the logic of objects (the grammatical subject as substance), to be grounded on this more fundamental logos of concrete reality. In other words, the non-contradictory self-identity of substances emerges as an abstraction only in light of their deeper contradictory self-identity within the world-matrix with its dialectical logos. Yet in this contradictory self-identity, Nishida reminds us that the dialectical matrix of the world is not simply in process. In its dialectical self-identity, the world moves and yet remains still qua nothing in the affirmation of its absolute negation. The world continually moves via its self-contradiction and yet is still in its self-identity; it is both moving and at rest in contradictory self-identity (Z8 493). This, for Nishida, is the logic of reality, taking "logic" (ronri) here in the broad sense to mean the dialectical structure of reality.

This logic of contradictory identity also applies to the structure of judgment and the question of its unity. Logically the mutual exclusivity between grammatical subject qua object (substance that cannot become a predicate) and the predicate qua field of concepts (or epistemological subject that can never be stated as a grammatical subject) would make subsumptive judgments impossible. Aristotle's logic of the grammatical subject (*shugoteki ronri* 主語的論理) accounts for the noematic determination of enduring objects. Kant's logic of the transcendental field of categories, which Nishida calls the logic of predicates (*jutsugoteki ronri* 述語的 論理), accounts for the determining features of subjectivity. Nishida thinks, on the one hand, that Aristotle's logic that substantializes the individual object precludes cognition in virtue of the object's transcendence. But, on the other, he thinks that Kant's critical logic that looks internally in the direction of the predicate pole reduces that individuality to intellectual categories. What is the truly concrete situation of their unity? Both theories are too limited on their own. At this stage in his lifework Nishida founds their unity by taking it beyond his earlier 1920s predicate-oriented formulation of the epistemology of place. He reformulates their unity this time more explicitly in light of the contextual matrix of the world of interactivity as a contradictory identity between grammatical subject and predicate, the transcendent object and the transcendental predicate, epistemological object and subject, world and self, universal and individual. Although the basic idea is the same, this slight alteration in the 1930s reflects further caution on Nishida's part to preclude any uni-directional prioritization of noesis over noema, determining act over determined content, predicate plane over grammatical subject, and epistemological subject over object. Instead, he emphasizes the balance of the two opposing terms in terms of their contradictory self-identity. He wants to avoid engendering any tendency that, on the basis of his earlier predicate-oriented logic, would incline in the direction of an idealist monism or transcendentalism. So Nishida reformulates his earlier position with the emphasis that the true hypokeimenon (subject, substratum), or true universal, is conceivable neither merely in the direction of the grammatical subject nor merely in the direction of the predicate but instead is the primal unity of the world of physical force (constituting substance that becomes grammatical subject) and the world of consciousness (as the field of predicates)—"absolutely self-identical as a unity of absolute opposites" (Z6 186–187, 190).[10] His claim is that the logical structure of judgment and cognition becomes conceivable via this self-identity of absolute opposites. This slight shift in emphasis from predicate to contradictory self-identity coincides with his turn from the concrete universal to the dialectical universal and from the interiority of self-awareness to the exteriority of the sociohistorical world. Again, his purpose is to avoid any mistaking of his theory, in other words, to prevent reduction of the concrete not only to the object (noema, grammatical subject) but also to the epistemological subject with its field of predicates or determining acts (noesis), and to preclude the substantialization not only of things but also of the universal. The identity of the concrete cannot be reified, whether as physical or intellectual, object or subject. Nishida means to account for the dialectical complexity of the concrete that obtains its unity only within the world's dynamic matrix, which is self-contradictory. Its unity of contradictories precludes its conception as a grammatical subject (Z8 76).

Acknowledging that in terms of object logic (the substantialism of Aristotelian logic) the contradictory can never be said to be identical, Nishida in "Dekaruto tetsugaku ni tsuite" (「デカルト哲学について」; "On Cartesian Philosophy") of 1944 explains that contradictory self-identity instead has the sense of self-identity in terms of a place, basho, enveloping the contradictories by transcending them (*Z*10 148). And in *Tetsugaku no konpon mondai* of the 1930s Nishida refers to the idea he made use of in his earlier epistemology that contradictories belong to the same species. Taken alone, each term in mutual contradiction is nothing but a reification of, or abstraction from, their concrete whole. The world in its broadest and deepest significance as a place encompassing everything and delimited by nothing must then envelop and make possible the ontologically most basic contradictory relationship, that is, the opposition of being and non-being. But its preservation of self-identity as a whole, encompassing the absolutely contradictory or opposed, does not mean that they are synthesized or sublated at a higher level. The contradiction and opposition remain. Concrete self-identity is precisely in that tension or strife of contradiction or opposition. That is what constitutes the identity of the world's concrete whole as ultimately neither being nor non-being. Nishida here has not abandoned his earlier heuristic turn away from the grammatical subject. Reality is neither a thing that is nor a thing that is not. He argues in *Tetsugaku no konpon mondai* that Spinoza's *substantia* is simply an absolutization of the subject of predication, presupposing the Aristotelian logic of substance. True self-identity cannot be reduced to the grammatical subject as an objectified substance to which the rule of non-contradiction applies. Instead, it is non-substantial, absolutely nothing. That all is one (*issai ichinyo* 一切一如) does not mean their indiscriminate oneness as substance but rather their contradictory self-identity via mutual self-negation (*Z*8 421). The place of the world and its dialectical unfolding, then, is a non-substantial domain or substratum, a grounding (under)ground, of the contradictory relationship between contradictories, including the ontologically ultimate contradiction between being and non-being (*Z*7 181). Its self-forming formlessness allows for both the universal qua one world and the many individual selves to stand in absolutely contradictory self-identity. Therefore, their creative interactivity "possesses the sense of a place determining itself, as the self-determination of absolute nothing" (*Z*6 122). The self-contradictory identity of the world as a place of absolute nothing, then, is neither merely ontological (being) nor merely meontological (non-being), but, we might say, is an-ontological (absolute nothing) to in turn express itself in its self-contradictory self-determinations in the play of being and non-being. This nothing that is absolute and entails contradiction in its self-identity as it unfolds the world is my next topic.

The World-Dialectic as the Self-Determination of Nothing

From the standpoint of absolutely contradictory self-identity, everything that is is a being but also an expression of the absolute nothing (*Z*8 257). Nishida's theme of the 1930s, as well as of the 1940s, the dynamism of the world-matrix, still makes reference to his theme from the late 1920s, the place of absolute nothing. We need to remember this when we are juxtaposing its dialectic with Hegel's. The difference from his earlier formulations is that now Nishida includes in his discussions of the self-realization of the nothing its externalization in the world's dialectic. The important question that Nishida was led to raise from his discussion of "I and thou" was: How are the individuals in their reciprocal recognition mediated without being dissolved into the universal's determination? The mediator cannot be a substance, in which case it would be another individual, but on a grand cosmic scale, as in the case of Spinoza's substance qua nature, as I have already mentioned several times. It would be incapable of permitting the independence of individuals, as well as their inter-dependence. Nishida solves the issue by recourse to his concept of the absolute nothing. The medium is the absolute nothing that can determine itself through its self-negation to make room for the reciprocal determinations of individuals while, at the same time, retaining its self-identity. Hence Nishida states that the true universal that mediates the process of living by dying and the continuity of discontinuity in the reciprocity of individuals is the "universal of nothing" (*mu no ippansha* 無の一般者) (*Z6* 14). By this Nishida does not mean a "universal" that is simply opposed to the particular. Rather, it is a "universal of universals" (*ippansha no ippansha* 一般者の一般者) that envelops universal and individual, enfolding the reciprocity between the concrete universal's determination of the individual and the universal's reverse determination by the individual. Hence it is another name for the dialectical universal, except that here its non-substantiality and self-negation are made explicit in its designation as a nothing. He states that the "universal of nothing" is the "universal of universals . . . that determines itself in absolute negation" (*Z6* 14). As we saw earlier, the medium for the continuity of discontinuity in the mutual determination among individuals is absolute negation (*zettai hitei*) (*Z6* 18). In terms of basho, this means the absolute nothing. The manifold inter-determinations of the dialectical matrix involving mutual self-negation occur as "a determination of the universal of nothing" (*mu no ippansha no gentei* 無の一般者の限定) (*Z6* 13–14). Thus when Nishida claims that this universal is the true substantia (*Z6* 40), we need to remember the non-substantiality of such "substance." At the bottom of the truly dialectical world, there is nothing (*mu*) (*Z6* 306). The nothing as such is no longer simply the "true self" at the bottom of self-awareness but the foundation of the world that enables the reciprocity of individuals through its absolute negation (i.e., self-negation).

In death we enter into this absolute nothing, and in birth we emerge out of it (*Z8* 401). Every moment as a moment of contradiction implies the struggle between life and death, and the world in its continuity of discontinuity of moments thus involves an on-going determination of absolute nothing—a "determination of that which is without a determiner" (*genteisurumononakimono no gentei*) or a

"determination without determiner" (*genteisurumononaki gentei* 限定するものな
き限定) (Z6 15, 20–21, 116, 149, 162, 307–308; Z7 12, 205; Z8 408). This allows for its
limitless creativity, creating from its store delimited by nothing. Creation is thus
the self-determining act of what is absolutely nothing (Z6 127). The notion of a
dialectical universal developed in *Tetsugaku no konpon mondai* and throughout
the 1930s radicalizes the dialectic of the concrete universal's self-determination
only because at the same time it refers to the place wherein individuals and their
inter- and reverse determinations with the universal transpire. That place in its
non-substantial nothingness is the field that makes room for their interactions,
their contradictory self-identity, their continuity of discontinuity. Their medium
is the dialectical universal only qua this place of absolute nothing (Z6 253). Only
as a "universal of nothing" (mu no ippansha) can it allow for their self-identity in
contradictory inter-determinations (Z6 39).

The self-determination of nothing thus forms the kernel of the manifold dialectic of the dialectical universal. In other words, it makes possible the manifold
dialectical determinations: the universal's self-determination, the individual's
self-determination, the universal's determination of the individual, individuals'
co-determination of one another, and individuals' reverse determination of the
universal. Only a field in its non-substantiality can enfold individuals without
mitigating their uniqueness. Only a universal that is nothing qua place can allow
for its individuals to be determinants. Hence the individual person partaking in
the world can be truly free and creative in the world's self-creativity out of its nothingness. And by virtue of the world's abyssal (un)ground, the process is endless
and there is perpetual unrest, which, however, in existential terms can also mean
a world of anxiety, a world of doubt (Z7 206). The focal point of that unrest and
creativity in terms of time is the present.

The Dialectic of Time: Its Enfolding and Unfolding in the Present

As we have already seen, time plays a significant role in Nishida's understanding
of the dialectic of the concrete. During the 1930s he develops the dialectic of time
in conjunction with the dialectic of the world. Temporal determination involves
all the dialectical characterizations I have examined: self-negation, continuity of
discontinuity, and contradictory self-identity. The medium for this dialectic of
time is the present (genzai 現在). In the dimension of time, the present plays the
same mediating role that place plays in the spatial dimension. Time moves irre-
versibly in a straight line from present to present, each momentary present determining itself discontinuously from the previous and the next (Z8 368–369). In
determining itself, it negates itself to give way to the next, whereby in contradictory identity its self-affirmation is its negation, its rising is its falling. Thereby, the
present transcends itself to move from present to present, from actuality to actu-

ality, without ever returning to what has passed, even for an instant (*Z5* 184, 218, 230, 268; *Z8* 225, 236). In its continuity, time is then discontinuous as a continuity of discontinuities. Nishida contrasts this nature of time with the mechanistic viewpoint that sees process as moving from cause to effect (from past to future) and with the teleological view that sees movement as occurring from potentiality to actuality (or from future to past) (*Z6* 18–19, 70; *Z8* 98, 329, 384–385). Each present moment is not merely the preparation for what follows nor simply the consequence of what precedes. Rather, the present is ontologically independent. As such, it is discontinuous with every other moment. Yet in its momentariness it negates itself to make way for other moments of the present. And what goes for each moment goes for time in its greater dimensions as well. History is thus also a continuity of discontinuity from one self-determining epoch to the next (*Z8* 145). The present era is neither simply the result of the previous epoch nor merely a preparation for the following one. It has its independent significance and meaning that rise and fall vis-à-vis other epochs (*Z9* 390). In each epoch, at each moment, the present must yield in transition to what it previously was not, yet it is always present, an "eternal now" (*eien no ima* 永遠の今), as the place for its ongoing self-determination. The now is that focal point of its self-determination. And this, in Nishida's mind, is what establishes time in its irreversibility and unpredictability.

The present therefore is the true substantia of time (*Z6* 65). Nishida views past and future, the innumerable moments, as paradoxically co-existent within that concrete present as their locus (*Z7* 162; *Z8* 368–369). In enveloping them, the present as the eternal now determines them both (*Z6* 45; *Z7* 57). The eternal now envelops the whole of time, creatively determining itself in each momentary now: the self-determination of the present envelops past, present, and future (*Z6* 70). Nishida had adumbrated an earlier version of this in his "Basho" essay of 1926. There it is the eternal nothing (*eien no mu* 永遠の無) that accounts for irrepeatable time and *creatio ex nihilo* (*Z3* 437–438). And in *Mu no jikakuteki gentei* the self-awareness and self-determination of absolute nothing in the temporal dimension become the self-determination of the present, the eternal now, establishing time (*Z5* 109, 112, 145, 147). Just as the nothing envelops being, the eternal present envelops time, both operating as a place. The present as such an absolute locus or basho contains an infinity of possibilities to be actualized via its self-negation. It is a medium filled with innumerable possibilities for determining past and future. Only thus can Nishida speak of the co-presence of past and future in the present (*Z7* 61–62, 63, 176; *Z8* 86–87). By "eternity" (*eien* 永遠), then, Nishida cannot simply mean eternal unchangeability but rather the absolute nothing or non-substantiality, an abyssal indeterminacy, that determines itself everywhere (*Z5* 228). We might say that it is the *nihilo* of *creatio ex nihilo*. The world as a whole arises from that eternal present (*Z5* 104–105). Nishida's view here is, in fact, an extension of Augustine's conception of time,[11] whereby past, present, and future are all contained within, and understood in light of, the present (*Z5* 145, *Z7* 173). But his conception of time also comes exceptionally close to Dōgen's (道元) notion of time, for example, in terms of "abiding in a dharma-position" (*jūhōi* 住法位) or "being-time" (*uji* 有時).[12] Nishida's present in this role of the medium of time is the "absolute present" (zettai genzai). He identifies it with the place of nothing as the place from which time flows from present to present in its envelopment of past and future. Each succeeding momentary present, then, is somehow juxtaposed within the present as it determines itself. Time unfolds as the inner self-determination of this all-enfolding eternal present (*Z6* 160). Therefore, the self-determination of the eternal present (*eien no genzai* 永遠の現在), the self-determination of the medium of the continuity of discontinuity, and the self-determination of the dialectical world or dialectical universal are all different ways of expressing the same thing: the self-determination of the place of absolute nothing (*Z7* 124). They all involve self-determination via self-negation, whether of the universal into individuals or of the eternal present into each moment (*Z8* 95). And in turn, they each involve their reverse determination, whether of the universal by the individual or of the eternal present by each moment.

The moment-to-moment self-determination of the present, in terms of the personal self, means its temporal non-substantiality. We already saw this in the discussions of the continuity of discontinuity and of self-negation as applied to the person. In time, the self continually dies while being born and is born while dying. Every moment in time is a moment of birth-and-death for the self (*Z5* 161). As I already stated, the temporal being of self-existence is thus self-contradictory in that moment of rising and falling, being born and dying (*Z7* 274). It is also the moment of encounter, for the personal self, between its being determined vis-à-vis the past and its freedom vis-à-vis the future. Even as our actions are determined out of the past and toward the future, we act in the present; the time we live is always of the present, and this allows for a margin of unpredictability. At every decisive moment of the present we negate determination from the past to create a new present that will determine the future. And in light of that present we even change the meaning of the past (*Z6* 19). In this meeting of past and future in the present, the now proves to be a point of de-cision[13] that cuts off the past and creates the future. It is what makes possible free creativity (ex nihilo) in the face of the open future and escape from environmental determinations necessitated by the past (*Z5* 289). We die at each moment to the past (its determination) to give birth to the future (in free creativity). The individual's free will, then, is established in this dialectical fact of living by dying (*Z5* 195, 233). One sees this, for example, in a master musician who, having attained the ability to play an instrument by previous practice along with inborn talent, can also freely improvise new sounds and rhythms. Nishida also explains this dialectic of time in terms of

"I and thou." In the determination by the infinite past, one encounters within the present one's past as absolute other, a "past thou." Past thou and present I encounter one another dialectically (Z5 326–327). And in this encounter with one's past as a thou, Nishida finds the dialectical source of the ought in one's responsiveness or responsibility to that infinite past in the immediate present, just as one finds it in the thou of another person one faces (Z5 327–328). One's past is an other to one's present, determining one's present self, yet also in understanding that past in light of the present, one in turn determines the past, re-interpreting it. The I of yesterday and the I of tomorrow are both thous vis-à-vis the I of today (Z5 339). Through the I of each moment regarding all other moments as thou and hence seeing the self's continuity precisely in its otherness, the unity and freedom of personhood are paradoxically established (Z5 343, 351). And this takes place as the self-determination of the present: "Our life . . . , in the sense of the present determining itself, is born as the self-determination of the eternal now . . . , determined as a continuity of discontinuity" (Z5 280).

If the present is the foundation of concrete reality, equivalent to the place of nothing in temporal terms, then it must also possess contradictory self-identity. In its self-determination the present is self-contradictory (Z5 207). In its momentary self-determination, the present begins as it disappears, it "lives by dying," as a continuity of discontinuity (Z5 208). The present contains the non-present of past and future in its determinations. And it is the locus where made and making, determined and determining, determination and freedom, are also in contradictory identity. In addition, the present possesses the contradictory self-identity of the many (innumerable moments) and the one (the whole of time) (Z8 368–369). The non-substantiality of the present, encompassing the dimensions of time in its self-negation, continually giving way to the presencing of the non-present, generates the flux of time, accounting for the changes of the world. Yet amid this flux the present is at rest (Z8 90). Only in this sense of moving while still, manifest in the world's movement-in-stillness and whereby the whole of time is both one and many, is the present the eternal substantia of time. Contradictory identity, as we have seen in previous sections, is possible for Nishida on the basis of the non-substantiality he characterizes as an un-delimited nothing. Therefore, the "substance" of time is non-substantial. Only in its non-substantiality as a field un-delimited by anything can the present envelop past, present, and future as its self-differentiations. Only as absolutely nothing does it envelop the flowing of time (Z5 294–295). It is in that sense that the present is bottomless, determining itself from itself, escaping noematic constraints in its abyssal nature as an *Ortzeit,* "place-time" (*bashoji* 場所時) (Z5 116).

Taken in that sense, Nishida tells us, time is spatial, and space in turn envelops time in its self-negation. This is another instance that Nishida characterizes as a contradictory self-identity in the sense that space and time in their conceptual definitions are mutually exclusive yet mutually implicative in their concrete reality. With his concept of the present as the medium for the mutual self-negations and interrelations of all temporal dimensions, for example, past, present, and future, Nishida has spatialized time. But he has also extended that spatialization to signify time's cross section, or chiasma, with space. That is, he comes to view the fullness of the present, in its implicit containment of the world, as spatiotemporal (*Z5* 193). In the inseparability of history and society, time thus already involves the spatial. To that spatiotemporality of the world matrix I now turn.

The Dialectic of the Space-Time Matrix: The Sphere without Periphery

In his characterization of the concrete world in its logos-structure as dialectical, Nishida comes to conceive its concrete whole as a sphere encompassing time and space. The place of absolute nothing as that non-substantial medium that is one and eternal in its self-negation is at the same time the world of the many interdetermining one another both synchronically and diachronically. That is, the space-time oneness of the dialectical world unfolds in the spatial many (individuals) and the temporal many (moments) and without prioritization of one over the other. We are caught up in its dialectical whirl, where its spatiotemporality obtains both macrocosmically and microcosmically (*Z7* 174).

As noted in the previous section, the unfolding of time already involves the world's spatiality, whereby each is established as "space qua time, time qua space" (*Z7* 120). Nishida states in *Tetsugaku no konpon mondai* that true dialectical determination is not found simply within the temporal unity of the personal self but between dialoging persons within the present, that is, "I and thou," "not between the temporal but rather the spatial, between subjectivity and objectivity" (*Z6* 107). He repeatedly emphasizes that the self-determination of the self in the interiority of time cannot happen without the exteriority of its co-determination with other selves. Just as an individual person determines himself or herself via time, that person is also determined by his or her environment and interactions with others in an environing space, that is, the sociohistorical world (*Z6* 32, 104, 217). Nishida uses the metaphors of "linear" (*chokusenteki* 直線的) and "circular" (*enganteki* 円環的) to characterize the temporal and spatial natures of the concretely real. The dialectical universal's determination in terms of the individual establishes the world of the personal self in a linear process, and the dialectical universal's determination in terms of the universal establishes the sociohistorical world that spatially environs us in a circular fashion (*Z6* 128). The dialectical universal involves both.[14] Nishida states that the linear determination in time as a sequence of moments also entails a circular determination in the synchrony of interrelations within time (and also space) as whole (*Z7* 14). Concrete time is not merely linear but is the self-manifestation of a whole that spatially envelops its linear development; time entails spatiality (Z6 68; Z8 503). This metaphor of a spatial circularity involved in time at its root allows us to envision the fullness of each moment as saturated with implications and possibilities of the world at large.[15] This means that in the world-matrix the direction of diachrony immediately implies the direction of synchrony; time implies space and vice versa. Therefore, we cannot conceive of inter-determination merely in terms of a dialectic of process (Z6 74),[16] for it also entails spatial relationships (*kūkanteki kankei* 空間的関係) (Z6 73). The world-dialectic in its determinations must encompass both the linear and the circular, that is, "longitudinal-latitudinal" determination (*tate no gentei, yoko no gentei* 縦の限定、横の限定), or, more simply put, historical and social dimensions (Z6 258). The dialectic is of a crisscrossing chiasma of linear-circular, temporal and spatial inter-determination, from which each may be abstracted (e.g., Z7 9–10, 55, 64, 198; Z8 233).

This concrete inseparability between spatiality and temporality provides the basis for Nishida's critique of Bergson in *Tetsugaku no konpon mondai*. He argues that Bergson's conceptions of "pure duration" and "creative evolution" lack any genuinely dialectical character that could accurately portray concrete non-duality. He describes Bergson's "pure duration"[17] as resulting from the maximization of individual determination and the minimization of environmental determination; it subsumes universal determination within individual determination (Z6 114–115). Nishida finds Bergson's conceptions of creative evolution, the élan vital, and pure duration all to be conceptions of an activity from within, interior to the self, from the standpoint of individual subjectivity and its internal flow of time that subsumes the physical, the spatial, and the environmental (Z6 121). Yet the élan vital becomes conceivable only in relation to the environment via the body (Z10 186–187). And pure duration must still involve environmental determination, a spatial dialectic of discontinuity and mutual self-negation (Z6 64, 102–103, 115, 117–118, 263; Z8 89, 376).[18] Of course, it is questionable whether Bergson ever denied the connection between internal time and the external environment.[19] Nishida uses Bergson as a target, perhaps as a straw man, in order to advance his argument for the extension of the dialectic into the spatial world.

The place of absolute nothing thus determines itself spatially and temporally in the dialectical matrix. To depict that space-time matrix, Nishida borrows from Pascal's characterization of nature as an infinite sphere[20] to metaphorically call it a circle without a periphery, or with an infinite periphery, and without any central point (*chūshintennaku shūhennaki en* 中心点なく周辺なき円). Instead, its focal center is everywhere or every point within (Z5 148–149, 184, 282, 283; Z6 163). This infinite or endless sphere (*mugendai no kyū* 無限大の球, *mugen no kyū* 無限の球), in determining itself, envelops both the flow of time and the expanse of space (Z6 107–108, 250–251; Z7 121). Its self-determination establishes the unique creativity of both each individual standpoint and each momentary present, among innumerable other focal points of space-time, each concentrating and saturated by the whole. Therein, in its self-determinations, self-differentiations, and self-dichotomizations, the endless process of dialectic obtains (Z5 153). Such complexity in its overdetermining dialectic precludes reduction, reification, hypostatization. And its determination in each here and now wherein we always find ourselves is never thoroughly fixed. The sphere is abyssal in its openness. On this basis Nishida can conclude that true dialectics cannot rest on any determinate standpoint. Instead, it requires a concrete standpoint that is a standpointless standpoint (*tachibanaki tachiba* 立場なき立場) (Z7 167). It is neither a materialism nor an idealism but instead what he calls a "dialectic of Heraclitean realism" (*herakureitosutekina jitsuzaironteki benshōhō* ヘラクレイトス的な実在論的弁証法) (see Z8 328, 336).[21]

7 The Dialectic of Religiosity (the 1940s)

WHAT NISHIDA CALLS "religion" (*shūkyō* 宗教) was a concern from the beginning of his writing career and was already an issue underlying his discussions of pure experience, epistemology, interpersonal relations, and the historical world. But Nishida fully develops the explicitly dialectical aspects of "religiosity," in its connection with the world-matrix, only in the last period of his oeuvre, during the mid-1940s up to his death. One might say that his attempt to answer this question of religion in relation to the dialectical matrix marks the apex of all his philosophical efforts. We find the first obvious attempt on Nishida's part to establish such a dialectic of religion vis-à-vis the world-dialectic in his 1944 essay "Yoteichōwa o tebiki to shite shūkyōtetsugaku e" (「予定調和を手引きとして宗教哲学へ」; "Toward a Philosophy of Religion with Pre-established Harmony as Guide"). And his 1945 essay "Bashoteki ronri to shūkyōteki sekaikan" (「場所的論理と宗教的世界観」; "The Logic of Place and the Religious Worldview"), which was his last completed work before his death, recaps and summarizes the main ideas of his philosophical lifework, especially ideas developed from the 1920s and 1930s concerning judgment and knowledge, the historical world, and the nothing, while relating them to that ultimate question of religion. Nishida's appropriation of religious ideas— both of the East and of the West, that is, Buddhism and Christianity—while developing his dialectic of religiosity is most noticeable in these two essays of the mid-1940s, both included at the end of the final volume of his *Tetsugaku ronbunshū* (『哲学論文集』; *Philosophical Essays*), published in 1945. In these works we see Nishida striving to discern what the essence of religion is while focusing on the theme we saw earlier of death and finitude in the contradiction of human existence. It is important to realize here that by "religion" Nishida thus has in mind something quite specific. It has to do with an existential sense of self-contradiction in the tension of life-and-death or the impermanence one feels in the depths of self-awareness. Religious awareness means the knowledge of one's own death, self-negation as constitutive of one's identity, whereby "I am myself by knowing my own death" (Z10 333). What religions call "God" or "absolute," then, for Nishida is what that finite self immediately faces in those depths of self-awareness, that is, the alterity of the source of being and knowing, the wherein in which we find ourselves always already, always in excess of our attempts at conceptual reduction.

On that basis religion becomes man's relationship to that source or ground of reality. In Nishida's terms this is a place delimited by nothing. Nishida unpacks all of this with a further exposition of his dialectic in relation to religion. In this chapter I will discuss the dialectic we find in both works, and some others, from this period.

The Monadology of Inter-Expression

Nishida in the works of the 1940s expands on the world-dialectic of interactivity that he developed in the 1930s, but now he further emphasizes the aspect of expression (hyōgen 表現) belonging to that dialectic of inter-determination. Implaced in the world, we find ourselves confronting one another and things in mutual determination. Nishida takes such mutual determination in terms of mutual expression and in terms of the world's self-expression (Z10 303, 319). We are constituted accordingly as we partake in the world's expressive act, mirroring the world's expression in our own expressive acts. Nishida spoke of the dialectical world as a world of expression in the previous decade as well, but now the connection with religiosity is made explicit, for to conceive of the universal-individual, world-self relationships in terms of expression is also to conceive of the relationship between two self-expressive persons, that is, God and man. In other words, this idea directly ties in to the dialectic of religiosity that Nishida systematizes in these essays of the 1940s.

As in the 1930s, Nishida during the 1940s divides that world (sekai 世界) into three layers of reality, from the most abstract to the most immediate: the material (*busshitsuteki* 物質的) world of quantifiable mechanical force, the biological (*seimeiteki* 生命的) world of life, and the historical (*rekishiteki* 歴史的) (or sociohistorical) world of human interactivity (Z10 298–299). The most concrete is the last world of human interactivity, the sociohistorical world. Therein we ourselves are things-at-work (*hatarakumono* 働くもの) in the context of our mutual relations. The world understood merely mechanistically in terms of matter or merely teleologically in terms of life is an abstraction of that world of interactivity that we concretely live. Recall that this is the world that in the 1930s Nishida described as possessing the contradictory self-identity (zettai mujunteki jikodōitsu 絶対矛盾的自己同一) between one and many while also being the self-determination of the place of absolute nothing (zettai mu no basho 絶対無の場所). In the 1940s Nishida goes on to identify the meanings of both these concepts—absolutely contradictory self-identity and absolute nothing—with what he regards as "God" (*kami* 神) or the absolute (zettai 絶対) itself.

Nishida explicates the concrete world, in its contradictory self-identity, as neither simply material-mechanistic nor merely biological-teleological, neither just physical nor utterly ideal—each opposition reflecting only a limited aspect of the world as concrete whole. Instead, it is a world of expression (Z10 309). We saw in chapter 6 how the world's contradictory identity is mediated by the mutual self-negations of its constituents, as well as of itself. Nishida now claims that the world founded on self-negation is a world of expression: the nothing expresses itself in the multiplicity of beings. Everything as such is a thou (*nanji* 汝) escaping one's grasp in its self-expressions (Z6 57). This becomes a major theme during the 1940s. Developing his earlier ideas about mirroring, Nishida emphasizes this function of expression as what characterizes the reciprocity between world and individual—as opposed to merely mechanistic causality or mere representation—in the dialectic between the one and the many (Z10 118–119). The self-formative world is a self-expressive world (Z10 348). The world's determination in the individual is its expression in the individual, and conversely the self expresses itself in the world by transforming the world. Individuals mutually determine themselves through expression as well. Thus in their mutual encounter things are expressive of themselves, of one another, and of the world. This also means that the expressive and the expressed are one in contradictory self-identity (Z10 310). The world as a whole enveloping the multiplicity of oppositions and contradictions constitutes a single coherent world. But each of the many things within the world—the ant, the sun, one's desk, one's boredom—contradicting and opposing one another, expresses that world in its own manner. Out of the variety of these things, however, it is the I in its act of self-awareness that creatively expresses the world's contradiction and partakes in its self-formations. The individual human self in this capacity, then, at each moment is the expressive focal point (*shōten* 焦点, *hyōgenten* 表現点) of the world, its momentary self-determination (*shunkanteki jikogentei* 瞬間的自己限定) (Z10 114, 299, 301, 355). The self is a self-expressive element of the world forming itself in self-expression. The individual's expressive act is thus simultaneously creative vis-à-vis the world. And, in acting intuition, the self intuits the world's self-expressive forms (Z10 173). So each self-expressive point (*jiko hyōgenten* 自己表現点) of the whole is also its point of self-awareness (*jikakuten* 自覚点) (Z10 180). The absolutely contradictory self-identity between the one world and the many individuals, then, is founded on the fact that the two terms do not just stand opposed to one another, but that the many individuals are implaced within that world as its focal points of expression.

To describe this, Nishida, especially in his essay "Yoteichōwa o tebiki to shite shūkyōtetsugaku e" of 1944, makes use of Leibniz's concept of monads and their pre-established harmony. He appropriates Leibnizian monadology to describe his conception of the world's contradictory self-identity between one and many. Nishida conceives the human individual as a monadic point that concentrates the world's self-mirroring; it serves as a microcosmic mirror of the macrocosmic whole. This mirroring is what is also understood in terms of expression, so that the self is the world's expressive monad (Z10 94, 299). Each monad is a focal point that thoroughly mirrors, from its own unique vantage point, the holistic one in its self-expression and self-creation (Z10 177). Each of us is thus born in the world to express it in unique fashion. This also means that each monadic self possesses the quality of a single world within itself (Z10 300, 305). Each individual-at-work vis-à-vis one another, expressing the whole, is thus simultaneously a monad and a single world. We are implaced in the world, but the world is within us as well. Hence we are always in touch with the world's absolutely contradictory self-identity within ourselves (Z8 362). The individual self as microcosmic-monadic focal point thoroughly mirrors within itself the macrocosmic world's contradictory self-identity (Z10 301).

Leibniz, according to Nishida, also explicated his monadology in terms of "expression" or something like it.[1] But the difference between Leibniz and Nishida is that while for Leibniz, the monad's expression is its representation of the world, for Nishida, the individual's expression of the world means its creative act as a creative element of the creative world. And while for Leibniz, the monad is a windowless "metaphysical point," a substance,[2] for Nishida, the monadic self is a creative point (*sōzōten* 創造点) of the historical world, an expressive point of the world's self-expression, interrelated dialectically with other such points (Z10 107). The Leibnizian monad is an indivisible substantial unity that expresses or "represents" the variety of compounded and outwardly extended material phenomena by concentrating them into its simple and internal immaterial unity. Nishida, in contrast, characterizes his monadology as a "creative monadology" to distinguish it from Leibniz's "representational monadology."[3] One might say that it is a monadology of dialectical interaction among chiasmatic points within the dialectical matrix. Kosaka Kunitsugu, commenting on Nishida, characterizes this standpoint of creative monadology as both a "worldism" and an "individualism" in that the individual's expressive creativity and the world's expressive creativity move together, or inter-resonate, in non-distinction: in their mutual expression, the world is expressing itself in the individual, and the individual is expressing itself in the world.[4] From this standpoint, whole and individual are dynamically one. It is in that sense that the I, in each of its momentary acts of consciousness, is an expressive monad of the world.

Nishida underscores the dialectical complexity of this monadology by incorporating, along with its spatial aspect, the temporal dimension. That is, the monadic point is not merely an individual subsisting through linear time but rather the singular moment of its expressive and creative act of self-awareness. Each act of awareness, as a living moment of creativity, actively mirrors the whole of space-time from its own unique vantage point. This also means that the monadic spatio-temporal focal points mirror one another in expressive reciprocity throughout the matrix of space-time. The self-expressive whole simultaneously means the reciprocity of inter-expression between those individual monadic points (Z10 98). Not only the self vis-à-vis other individual selves but also each moment of its acting and self-awareness vis-à-vis its past and future is a monadic point within the inter-expressive webwork of space-time. Each act of self-awareness reveals one's life-and-death, the contradiction of existence, and the deeper the self-awareness, the more fully one expresses the concrete reality of the world's abyssal nature. The self-aware act in its spatiotemporal singularity vis-à-vis the infinite whole of space-time, then, is a microcosmic vector of macrocosmic self-expression.

As in the dialectic of the 1930s, such mutual expression also means mutual self-negation. In negating itself, the individual through its self-expression allows for the world to express itself. Monadic individuals in their mutual expressions form the world through their mutual negations. But this conversely means their self-negations serving as the world's self-expression. Everything, including our individual personal selves, is then holistically one in self-negation (Z10 159–160; also Z10 352–354). The whole, in its holistic oneness, expresses itself in self-negation as individuals oppose and interrelate in mutual self-negation (Z10 162–163). In that reciprocity between the holistic one's self-negation into the plurality of individuals and the many individuals' self-negations in the holistic one, the whole mirrors and expresses itself within itself, with each individual serving as its unique point of self-expression (Z10 166, 168). In this way Nishida thus depicts the world's contradictory self-identity between one and many as an inter-expressive whole:

> What are at work on one another in that world, each contains within itself a single focal point of the world. They go on forming the entire world by standing opposed to one another as [each] a single world determining itself self-expressively and in reciprocal self-negation. In other words, each, as an angle of the world, constitutes the single world by relating to and determining one another. The concrete world, i.e., the historical world, existing and moving on its own, contains the focal points of the world within itself, and continually transforms itself by taking these dynamic focal points as its centers. (Z10 305)

In each self-aware act and from its perspectival point, we dynamically express that dialectical matrix of the whole world within ourselves. The self as the expressive monad of the world in this way constitutes the focal point of the world's self-expression.

Nishida thus takes expression to be the structural medium on the basis of which both cognition and acting are to be understood; they are both expressions of the world.[5] But as I mentioned earlier, in distinction from Leibniz, expression for Nishida means the creative act that dialectically moves from the created to the creating, the made to the making via self-negation. On the basis of such interactivity of expressive acts between individuals and objects, actors and acted on, expressers and expressed, history unfolds. Each expressive moment of the process of the reciprocity between self and world is a moment of the historical world's self-formation via moment-to-moment mutual self-negation. Therefore, the monad in Nishida's case is not a substance, as in Leibniz. And neither is the self-expressive monad, or the harmonious whole of interrelated monads (the world), Aristotle's hypokeimenon. Self-expression happens in self-negation; it is non-substantial (Z10 158).

Nishida translates this monadology of inter-expression into religious terms in a variety of ways, most notably the medieval mystical notion of an infinite sphere (*mugen kyū* 無限球). For example, in "Bashoteki ronri to shūkyōteki sekaikan" of 1945 he comes to view each monad as a mirroring self-expression of God in his "pre-established calculus" of divine creation.[6] In "Dekaruto tetsugaku ni tsuite" (「デカルト哲学について」) of 1944 as well, Nishida characterizes this as a contradictory self-identity between the finite and the infinite, between self and God (see Z10 134). In 1945 he describes this as the absolute expressing itself in the relative, the transcendent becoming immanent. Adding to his earlier appropriation of Pascal's infinite sphere, Nishida again makes reference to Pascal and expresses the idea that we are the world's singular focal points (*isshōten* 一焦点) mirroring or expressing the entire world as well as its eternal past and eternal future in the self-determination of the absolute present (Z10 340–341). The world of the absolute present, therefore, is a sphere of infinite radius (*sphaera infinita*) and no circumference (*shūhennaki mugendai no kyū* 周辺なき無限大の球), having its center everywhere (Z10 103, 301).[7] The entire universe, past, present, and future, endlessly creates itself through the infinity of its individual focal points within its infinite sphere. We are those innumerable monadic points in the infinite sphere without periphery or circumference, as momentary determinations of the absolute present (Z10 340–341). Nishida is thus taking Leibnizian monadology in a direction that accords with the mystical notion of Pascal—and earlier of the medieval theologian Nicholas of Cusa—of that infinite sphere. Nishida also makes use of Nicholas's description of God as a "coincidence of opposites" (*coincidentia oppositorum*), namely, the infinite sphere as irreducible to any particular being while simultaneously fullest in being (Z10 110).[8] Accordingly, Nishida likens the place of absolutely contradictory self-identity, the world of the absolute present, and historical space all to this infinite sphere, mirroring itself within itself without substratum (*mukiteiteki* 無基底的) (Z10 322). All these applications and meanings of the metaphor come together in Nishida's conception of the absolute present that qua the macrocosmic whole of space-time corresponds to each of its infinite microcosmic centers. God as such is the infinite formless form forming itself, as in Spinoza's "*natura naturans = natura naturata*,"[9] mirroring and expressing itself in the countless monads (Z10 95). What in religious terms is God's revelation thus is the self-expression of the absolute in the monadology of inter-expression (Z10 320). It is from this inter-expressive relationship between the I (and its acts) and the world in light of that infinite sphere that Nishida seeks to understand the phenomenon of "religion."

The Logic of Soku-hi

Throughout his works of the 1940s Nishida construes "religion" (shūkyō) specifically in the paradoxical form of contradictory self-identity that the sacred or the
absolute takes in its manifestation in the ordinary and everyday. That is, the absolute, God, is not to be reduced to, or objectified as, something transcendent
standing opposed to the self. Instead, it is in an "immanent transcendence"
(*naizaiteki chōetsu* 内在的超越), wherein we find ourselves implaced or, in religious
terms, embraced in its compassion. In other words, Nishida in these works is explicitly associating the religious notion of God with his concept of the place of
absolute nothing. Nishida accordingly conceives of the religious relationship between self and absolute in terms of his key concept of mutual self-negation. Even
earlier, in the late 1930s, for example, in "Rekishiteki sekai ni oite no kobutsu no
tachiba" (「歴史的世界に於いての個物の立場」; "The Standpoint of the Individual in
the Historical World") (1938), Nishida expressed correspondence between absolutely contradictory self-identity and the God of religion (Z8 346). In the 1940s he
develops this way of understanding the religious relationship or "religiosity" in
terms of what he calls the "logic of soku-hi" (sokuhi no ronri 即非の論理).

In order to explain his dialectical logic, Nishida in these works of the 1940s,
for the first time in his career, makes explicit reference to the Buddhist doctrines
of the *Prajñāpāramitā sūtras*. This provides him with an avenue for contrasting
his dialectic to that of Hegel, despite his appropriation of Hegelian terminology
throughout his career. Instead of looking to Hegel as the source of his "absolute
dialectic," Nishida suggests that it can be traced to a form of logic found in the
Prajñāpāramitās (Z10 317). Nishida here is most certainly indebted to his many
conversations with his friend D. T. Suzuki when he refers to the "*Prajñāpāramitā
logic of soku-hi*" in "Bashoteki ronri to shūkyōteki sekaikan" (e.g., Z10 333). The
term *soku-hi* (即非), the Japanese reading of the Chinese *chi-fei*, connotes the conjunction or inseparability in "is and is-not" or "affirmation-yet-negation," the
structural bi-conditionality or non-duality in their mutual reference and inter-
dependence. It expresses the dialectical identity of absolute contradictories, that
is, affirmation or "is" (*soku* 即), on the one hand, and negation or "is-not" (*hi* 非),
on the other. And this is founded on the Mahāyāna notion of the emptiness
(śūnyatā) or non-substantiality of the real.[10] Nishida understands his idea of basho
as designating the locus of that dialectical structure.

The paradoxical logic of soku-hi becomes most pronounced in Nishida's discussions of the absolute or God. He states that an absolute that stands opposed to
the relative would itself be relative (i.e., to the relative) and hence not truly absolute. No being can stand against the absolute to relativize it. Standing unopposed
by any being, the true absolute must be beyond all oppositions. "Absolute" (zettai
絶対) means that it is ab-solved, cut off (*zetsu* 絶) from all opposition (*tai* 対). In
opposing absolutely nothing, it is absolute being (yū 有), yet in being un-opposed,

as un-delimited and hence indefinite, it is nothing (mu 無) determinable. The absolute, then, possesses the contradictory self-identity of being and nothing (Z10 315–316). Its self-identity is self-contradictory. Nishida explains that in its opposition by nothing, the absolute determines itself only through its self-negation that makes room within itself for co-relative beings (Z10 315–316). Because the absolute cannot be objectified in opposition to the relative, it instead bears within itself the relative in its self-negation or self-contradiction (Z10 315–316). In other words, this is a further extension of his earlier notion of place as delimited by absolutely nothing, determining itself in self-negation. The Nishidian absolute thus is a self-negating nothing. He defines it as "the absolutely contradictory self-identity that contains its absolute negation within itself" (Z10 321), God qua absolute nothing, then, entails its internal negation to encompass its opposite. Rather than negating the relative, the absolute "inverts itself into the form of the relative" (Z10 316). In possessing itself through self-negation, the absolute one expresses itself in the world of the innumerable many. And this is the true God's act of creation. The real God cannot be just utterly transcendent and self-sufficient, eternally unchanging beyond the world of transience. God must empty himself in self-expression and thus create. God substantialized, then, is no true God. Its oneness must be non-substantial, allowing for the contradictory self-identity between one and many, absolute and relative.[11]

For Nishida, God must be absolutely non-substantial, no-thing. And in its self-negation, we are reminded of the Mahāyāna notion of the emptiness of emptiness (śūnyatāyāḥ śūnyatā) that denies sva-bhāva ("self-nature," "own-being") even to emptiness itself. Stating in "Yoteichōwa o tebiki to shite shūkyōtetsugaku e" of 1944 that the true God, rather than being the so-called God, must instead be what the mystical theologians of the West had called *Gottheit*, Nishida immediately adds "the emptiness [śūnyatā] of the *Prajñāpāramitās*" to this equation (Z10 104). In the following year ("Bashoteki ronri to shūkyōteki sekaikan") he claims that the absolutely contradictory self-identity of God, as containing absolute negation, is best expressed by the *Prajñāpāramitā* dialectic of soku-hi (*hannya no sokuhiteki benshōhō* 般若の即非的弁証法) (Z10 321). To express this, Nishida, in the manner of the *Prajñāpāramitā sūtras*, states that because

> God . . . is absolutely nothing, He is absolutely being. . . . Hence . . . because there is the Buddha there are sentient beings and because there are sentient beings, there is the Buddha; and because there is God as creator there is the world as creation, and conversely because there is the world as creation, there is God. (Z10 316; see also 324–325)

With the absolute's self-inversion into the relative via self-negation; the transcendent is thus the immanent, and God is simultaneously everywhere and nowhere. This is a development of his earlier notion of the self-determination of the place of absolute nothing, whereby the transcendent is immanent and the immanent is transcendent (Z9 469).[12] To support this paradoxical view, Nishida further quotes the following passage from the *Diamond Sūtra:* "Because all dharmas are not all dharmas, they are called all dharmas; because the Buddha is no Buddha, he is the Buddha; because sentient beings are not sentient beings, they are sentient beings" (Z10 316–317). Nishida reads this passage in accordance with his previous discussions from the 1930s of the inter-determination and reverse determination between universal and individual via self-negation, in other words, the idea that while the universal determines the individual, it in turn is determined by the co-determination of individuals.[13] And he applies that reading to the theistic notion of God that results in an un-orthodox, or rather quite "non-theistic," understanding of "God." In the 1944 essay "Kūkan" (「空間」; "Space") as well, Nishida equates that absolute negation qua affirmation of absolute nothing, in its absolutely contradictory self-identity, with the true emptiness of Buddhism (*bukkyō no shinkū* 仏教の真空) (Z10 157). So he takes the *Prajñāpāramitā sūtras*'s logic of soku-hi as already expressing the paradox of absolute self-contradiction (Z10 317).

In distinguishing this Mahāyānist aspect of his dialectic from Hegel's noematic dialectic, Nishida describes his idea of absolutely contradictory self-identity as belonging to the framework of the eightfold negation (*happu* 八不) developed by the Indian Mādhyamika and Chinese San-lun schools (Z10 317).[14] The four double negations (of is, is-not, both is and is-not, and neither is nor is-not) denying any assertion that can be made about anything provides a middle path between attachment to being as substantial and the utterly nihilistic rejection of being. The systematization of this method of negation can be traced back to the prime representative of Indian Madhyamaka, Nāgārjuna, who calls into question every sort of postulation of being (qua substance or svabhāva) and correlates emptiness (śūnyatā) and dependent origination (pratītya-samutpāda). As such, it is a variant of the soku-hi structure of the *Prajñāpāramitā* mode of thinking. But Nishida's unique contribution here is in taking that Buddhist logic of soku-hi and applying its structure to themes found in Christianity, as well as to one's existential concern vis-à-vis death. Nishida, for example, appropriates the Christian language of *kenosis,* the self-emptying of God, to illustrate the same paradox of the concrete depicted by the *Prajñāpāramitā* logic while conversely applying that logic of soku-hi in his interpretation of Christian kenosis (Z10 317).[15] The result is his dialectical concept of the "inverse correspondence" between God and man, absolute and relative.

The Dialectic of Inverse Correspondence

Throughout the 1930s Nishida alluded to the connection between the self-contradiction in the depths of one's self and what he considered the issue of "religion" or "religiosity." In the mid-1940s he explicates this more fully in the dialectical terms of inverse correspondence (gyakutaiō 逆対応) between the absolute and the finite self. We might even take the notion of generation-and-extinction in relation to the place of absolute nothing in the "Basho" essay of 1926 as a conceptual precursor of this idea of inverse correspondence. Nishida now views the unfolding of the self-determining world, encompassing individual persons, thoughts, and events, explicitly in light of the absolute's self-negation (qua nothing) as its expressions. And he takes this further in terms of place as the absolute enveloping the individuals of the world as it makes room for them. Place as absolute nothing determines, negates, and transforms itself within itself into the activities of the many individuals, which in turn become expressed in each individual's self-awareness. This is a development of Nishida's previous notion from the 1930s of reverse determination (gyaku gentei 逆限定), whereby the universal's self-determination is its determination of individuals, which conversely, however, is the individuals' self-determinations and moreover the individuals' determination of the universal. Nishida has now translated this dialectical matrix of inter-determination into the explicitly religious terms of the interrelationship between God and man in light of the existential concern of man qua finite existence vis-à-vis death. To designate this interrelationship in its religious significance, Nishida coins the new phrase "inverse correspondence" (gyakutaiō).

Man as finite confronts and touches God as infinite only in death, that is, negation. This is the relationship that Nishida designates by the term "inverse correspondence." Earlier, in 1938 ("Rekishiteki sekai ni oite no kobutsu no tachiba"), Nishida explained the encounter between God and man as occurring internally within the self in terms of the individual's internal mirroring of the world's contradictory self-identity as its monadic focal point, its perspective (Z8 362). That is, man and God stand in absolutely contradictory self-identity (Z10 104–105, 111). In the interior depths of his life, man lives in self-contradiction vis-à-vis death. And it is on this basis of self-contradiction—microcosmic self-contradiction mirroring macrocosmic self-contradiction—that man as relative being encounters the absolute. But in his finitude man, from his side, is incapable of treading on the path of this encounter to God; there is no path leading from man to God (Z8 365; Z10 104). A gap of eternity separates man from God. But, as stated in the previous section, that which simply transcends the finite is not truly absolute. Rather, the true absolute must be that which envelops us and that wherein we are implaced (Z8 365; Z10 105). God qua absolute must mediate itself in its encounter with relative existence via self-negation predicated on non-substantiality. The absolute's de-substantializing nothingness thus serves as the place, basho, for that meeting between absolute and relative. By becoming self-aware of the self-contradiction of life in its deepest root vis-à-vis death, man penetrates to his existential source at the place where he meets God in self-negation. Nishida in 1938 took this to be the essence of "religion" (shūkyō) (Z8 365). But in 1945 he develops this idea further in terms of the dialectic of inverse correspondence between absolute and relative. Just as man meets God in death, God meets man in self-negation, or, in Christian terms, via *gratia* (grace) and agapē and symbolically portrayed as Christ—that is, God's incarnation in, and death as, man. God and man via mutual self-negation thus are in inverse correspondence (Z10 325). Just as God possesses himself in self-negation, we as images of God exist as God's self-mirroring self-negations. Although they are separated by eternity, man and God are hence unmediated in their inverse correspondence. Nishida illustrates this simultaneity of transcendence and immanence in both "Bashoteki ronri to shūkyōteki sekaikan" and "Yoteichōwa o tebiki to shite shūkyōtetsugaku e" with a saying of the Zen master Myōchō (Daitō Kokushi): "Buddha and I, parted through a billion *kalpas* of time, yet not separate for a single instant; encountering each other the whole day through, yet not encountering each other for an instant" (Z10 104, 317).

The dialectic of God's self-negation is such that God, as the true absolute, is simultaneously absolutely being and absolutely nothing in contradictory identity: "Because . . . [God] is an absolute nothing, it is an absolute being. . . . It becomes being in being absolutely nothing" (Z10 316). God is nowhere to be found in this world, yet he is everywhere. Nishida states that "the true absolute exists there where it inverts itself as thoroughly relative" (Z10 316). In other words, God is present in his inverse correspondence with ourselves. The absolute is absolute in becoming thoroughly relative. Through self-negation God paradoxically exists in the many individuals, omni-present in the world of co-relativity (Z10 316). As absolute being, rather than transcending the co-relative beings, God encounters and embraces them (Z10 333, 344). Despite its transcendence and invisibility, the absolute is thus within this world and immanent in man: "The truly dialectical God is the God that is thoroughly immanent while thoroughly transcendent, thoroughly transcendent while thoroughly immanent" (Z10 317). In self-withdrawal God envelops the world as its place (basho), for only as place can God be both transcendent and immanent. Nishida takes this to be expressed both in the Christian terms of grace, agapē, and the incarnation and in the Pure Land Buddhist terms of compassion (Z10 321, 345). Agapē is God's love that saves humanity in self-sacrifice, that is, his incarnation and death as man. In Christianity the absolute's self-negation thus translates into kenosis,[16] God's self-emptying absolute love expressed in both the creation and the redemption of the world (Z10 317, 345–346, 349).[17] Absolute love (*zettai ai* 絶対愛) embraces all, both the wise and the foolish, the good and the evil. That is, it embraces its opposite: in his absolute agapē God descends even to the utterly diabolical (Z10 321, 345). Nishida declares that the absolute, in whatever religion, must manifest this sort of love (Z10 345). What in Christianity is God's love in Buddhism translates into the Buddha's infinite compassion. In Pure Land terms this would be Amida's deep wish to save the sinful more than the saint.[18] And in general Mahāyāna thought we may link such contradictory self-identity in the absolute's transcendence and immanence to the non-duality between saṃsāra and nirvāṇa.[19] The absolute's self-negation is possible in each religion only because the real God is really Gottheit and the real Buddha is empty; that is, the absolute is non-substantial, and it can contradict itself in its non-substantiality. Nishida thus equates God qua absolute with the formless source of the world constituting its self-formations in self-negation. And in enveloping everything thus generated, God is really the place of absolute nothing (Z10 329).

Now man's confrontation with God requires the utter denial of all that is human; the only avenue to God is utter self-negation (Z10 315; Z13 235).[20] This means death to one's ego. Living, then, for man, is already dying. But in such death one is born to one's true self; one realizes the "real" self (Z10 335). In other words, in confronting one's impermanence or non-substantiality, "eternal death" (*eien no shi* 永遠の死), one becomes aware of one's existential finitude, and one authenticates oneself in the singularity of one's being in space and time (Z10 314). Nishida takes this penetration into the core of one's interior contradictory self-identity to be the meaning behind what Zen calls "seeing into one's nature" (*kenshō* 見性) (Z10 352–353). It opens up and brings forth the abyssal nothing at the core of one's self and wherein one hovers, the nothing that absolutely negates one's self-being. One realizes that oneself at bottom is groundless: "At the bottom of itself, where there is nothing, the self, thoroughly nothing, responds to the absolute one in inverse correspondence" (Z10 355). Only insofar as one confronts that deep self-contradiction vis-à-vis death, one's nothingness, in the questioning of oneself whereby one's existence becomes an issue, does one enter into the dimension of religiosity, which Nishida also identifies as the true issue of philosophy (Z10 312–313). Only humans can have this explicit awareness of their existential self-contradiction establishing their being. Because that self-contradiction within the self is the raison d'être of the self's existence, its awareness constitutes one's authenticity as a self (Z10 314, 324). Nishida, however, takes this interior self-contradiction of human existence—God's self-negation that establishes man (*kami no jikogentei to shite ningen no seiritsu* 神の自己限定としての人間の成立)—to be also the meaning behind the Christian concept of original sin universally inherited by humanity (Z10 342),[21] for the story was that in eating from the "tree of knowledge," man "becomes like God" (Genesis 3). That is, man within himself must mirror the self-contradiction of the absolute. Hence in proportion to the degree of self-awareness, one experiences angst in virtue of that self-contradiction in the depths of one's existence (Z10 111). In Christian terms this is the awareness of sin. As one grows in self-awareness, one becomes increasingly aware of the internal contradiction, the existential sorrow (*hiai* 悲哀) or tragic condition of human existence, until one reaches the self's abyssal "vanishing point" (*shōshit-suten* 消失点) (Z10 356). This is what for Nishida is the beginning of religious aware-ness, a conversion of life or a religious turning of the mind (*shūkyōteki kaishin* 宗教的回心) (Z10 111; also Z10 312–313). This also means, in religious salvific terms, that the one most fully aware of his inner evil or sin is more likely to be "saved" than the one fully confident in self-righteousness. In other words, there must be corresponding self-negation on both sides of the salvific act: self-doubt on the part of the saved and self-sacrifice on the part of the savior. Only to the extent that the self becomes nothing in the will's self-abnegation does one touch on the absolute in inverse correspondence to the absolute's self-negation. In other words, it is more difficult for the morally confident to attain such religiosity "than for a camel to enter through the eye of a needle" (Matthew 19:24). But this can be translated into Zen terms as well. Pure Land devotionalism appears to be the form of Buddhism most comparable to, or compatible with, Christianity as the religion of grace. But Nishida has already claimed in the mid-1930s that *satori* (悟り enlightenment, awak-ening) in Buddhism is really no different (Z7 210).[22] In addition, he reminds us here, as well as in 1939, of Dōgen's statement that "to study the Buddha's way is to study the self, and to study the self is to forget the self" (Z8 512, 514; Z10 336). Further—as alluded to earlier—he interprets Zen's speaking of "seeing into one's nature" (ken-shō), accordingly, to refer to the absolute's self-negation that establishes oneself, one's self-possession in what transcends the self, self-affirmation in self-negation (Z10 352–353).

Only then, in the attainment of religious awareness that is a selfless self-awareness, does one come to face God. Only in death does the relative face the absolute, does the self face God (Z10 314–315). In facing the abyss that engulfs the instantaneous twinkle that is one's life within the dark nothing, one faces God. In dying to oneself—as ego, own-being, or substance, that is, to one's substantial-ized self—one realizes one's true nature as the self-negation of the absolute. Man faces God only as God's mirror image. What this means, as Nishida signifi-cantly points out, is that one's religious turn occurs not from oneself but from the calling voice (*yobigoe* 呼び声) of God or Buddha (Z10 325). In self-negation one simultaneously discovers that it is happening as God's absolute (self-)negation (Z10 326). God and man, in contradictory self-identity, thus meet in the bottom-less depths of mutual self-negation in inverse correspondence.[23] Since the issue of religion arises only in our confrontation with the tragic, the finitude of exis-tence, true religion, from Nishida's standpoint, cannot be about self-betterment through self-reliance. Quite to the contrary, the significance of works through one's own efforts must be downplayed. In this Nishida sees a parallel between the Christian concept of original sin and the True Pure Land sect's rejection of self-power (*jiriki* 自力). Both the Christian view of the fall of man and the True Pure Land Buddhist view of man's deluded and desirous nature express and exemplify this idea that man in his fallen state cannot encounter the absolute without self-negation. We are intrinsically sinners and deluded. The attitude of pure self-reliance gets us nowhere. The point for these religions is that we can be saved only by reliance on the infinite compassion of Amida Buddha or the infinite grace of God in Christ. Nishida finds in both religions this motif of salvation whereby one meets the absolute only by sinking into the self-aware depths of existential contradiction qua finite being. Religious self-awareness thus arises in all three religions—Christian, Pure Land, and even Zen—through the prāxis of self-negation as opposed to self-affirmation.[24]

The more one realizes one's sinful nature, the more one faces God. One must take this to the furthest extent so that one no longer regards even self-negation as one's own doing. In facing God, it is rather God and not oneself that is doing the facing. Man, in his finitude, his foolishness or sinfulness, on his own can make no contact with the absolute. Self-awareness of one's finitude or limitation must be taken as supported by the working activity of the absolute. Nishida expressed a similar idea much earlier when he claimed that the world's self-awareness and the individual self's self-awareness coincide: "When the world becomes self-aware, our self becomes self-aware, and when our self becomes self-aware, the world becomes self-aware" (Z9 528). But what comes into view here is the a-symmetry from the human perspective in the religious relationship between the absolute and man. God's working is expressed in man's working, man's working is supported by God's working, and they work together via mutual self-negation. In mutual self-negation the finite self and the infinite absolute work together in inverse correspondence as dialectically one. But from man's side, this means that, in his working toward salvation (or enlightenment), the absolute is already at work; it is the doing of the absolute. In Pure Land Buddhism's terms the sinner's search for help from—and dependence on—an other coincides in inverse direction with Amida's will to help the sinner.[25] That is why Nishida states that "the religious spirit occurs not from oneself but is the calling [yobigoe] of God or Buddha . . . , the working activity of God or Buddha" (Z10 325). Nishida finds this "call" paralleled in both the Christian notion of the Word (logos) of God and the Pure Land concept of calling Amida's name (*myōgō* 名号). The calling for help that mediates the reciprocity between savior and saved—for example, calling on the Buddha's name (myōgō) in True Pure Land Buddhism (Z10 350)—is already the absolute's salvific call. The point is that deliverance from delusion or sin requires divine self-negation—whether taken as God's love or Buddha's compassion—in inverse correspondence with the individual self's self-negation. In Lutheran terms this means faith (*fides*) vis-à-vis grace (*gratia*) as opposed to works; in Pure Land Buddhist terms it means enlightenment via reliance on other-power (*tariki* 他力). In 1935, in "Zushiki setsumei" (「図式説明」; "Schematic Explanation") for *Tetsugaku ronbunshū dai ichi* (『哲学論文集第一』; *Philosophical Essays, Vol. 1*), Nishida had already made this point, albeit briefly, that while there is conversion on the part of man and grace on the part of God, one is to realize that one's religious seeking is not by means of one's ability but rather by means of grace. In 1945 Nishida cites Luther in this regard that faith is God working in us so that by killing the old "Adam" (i.e., in admitting one's original sin) within us, we are made to live entirely anew in God (Z10 336).[26]

We must remember, however, that doing on the part of the absolute, operating behind selfless self-negation in man's conversion experience, is also its own self-negation. Just as a relative being cannot face the absolute without dying to itself and passing into nothing, the same is true in the reverse direction for the absolute. It cannot simply transcend, that is, be relative to, the relative. The working activities of wanderer and savior are in correspondence. But two distinct substances, self-affirming positivities, can never meet. The co-respondence must occur via mutual self-negation that is a mutual opening up to each other. In mutual expression one faces the absolute at the extreme limit of one's individual will, and God, conversely, faces oneself in his absolute will. The dynamic of religious conversion points to that reciprocal non-duality between absolute and relative, God and self, in the conjunction of divine grace or enlightened compassion with one's selfless exertion. Nishida thus finds in both the Christian experience of faith and the Buddhist experience of enlightenment an expression of the inverse correspondence between the absolute (God or Buddha) and the relative (the individual self). But he understands both in terms of the "logic" that he traces back to the *Prajñāpāramitās*.

So here, with this theory of inverse correspondence, Nishida in the 1940s has furthered the implications of his notion of absolutely contradictory self-identity. The notion of inverse correspondence was a radicalization of the notion of absolutely contradictory self-identity. Perhaps, as Kosaka claims, Nishida felt that absolutely contradictory self-identity alone was not sufficient to express the paradoxical correlation between absolute and self as especially manifest in the sphere of religion. Hence he formulated the new phrase "inverse correspondence" to express how absolute and individual, even as they are "separated by an eternity," are in contact "inversely" in reciprocal self-negations.[27] In order to preclude any possibility of hypostatizing or reifying its aspect of self-identity, Nishida has drawn our attention to the complementarity of mutual self-negation whereby the corresponding work on both contradictory or opposing ends cannot be mistaken for self-affirmative acts. They are identical only dialectically in their respective self-negations of any substantial identity. That dialectical correspondence of their working activities is a fitting together of enveloping and enveloped, place and implaced. The "correspondence" in "inverse correspondence" refers to their mutual fit in implacement. The relative, which is a consequence of the self-negation of the absolute, negates itself in being enveloped by the absolute as the absolute negates itself. Absolute and relative thus inversely correspond via mutual self-negation. The correspondence of absolute and relative is inverse but is reciprocally so in the sense of a fit between macrocosmic place and implaced microcosm, moving in both directions on both sides.

In that respect we still see Nishida working in these formulations of inverse correspondence to articulate his philosophy of the place of nothing that he had initiated in 1926. If we remember that the absolute in its un-delimited nothingness is ultimately the place of the world, we can also understand the absolute's self-negation in inverse correspondence with relative beings in the sense of a self-inverting space, or a self-withdrawal that makes space, for beings. It is the relationship of implacement between place and implaced that allows the gap of eternity separating absolute and relative to be crossed. Thereby, the absolute qua enveloping place can embrace beings in its immanent transcendence. Nishida retains his old theory that place in its self-contradictory self-negation as absolutely nothing—beyond being and non-being—envelops every oppositional relation, providing the medium for oppositional interactions. Nishida is thus applying to the implicit dualism in religion the basho theory that he had formulated decades earlier for crossing the dichotomy in epistemology.

Although Nishida shows, as we saw earlier, that inverse correspondence is certainly not foreign to Zen, perhaps it is more easily detectable in the other religions that he discusses, the two devotional religions of grace, Protestant Christianity and True Pure Land Buddhism. In that case, what aspect of his dialectic of religiosity approaches the sensibility of Zen? One possibility is his concept of the "depth in the ordinary" (*byōjōtei* 平常底). Yet in the peculiar fashion of his cross-cultural religious syncretism, we find it combined with the Christian term "eschatology." I now turn to this strange concept of the "eschatology of depth in the ordinary."

The Eschatology of Depth in the Ordinary

Nishida during the 1940s continues his discussions of time from the 1930s in terms of the absolute present, but he reformulates the interrelationship between the arising and the perishing monadic-like instants, on the one hand, and the place-like eternal present that embraces them, on the other—in light of their inverse correspondence—in terms of the dialectic of religiosity. As in the 1930s, he takes the absolute present as sustaining the world at each moment, giving birth to it anew, whereby the historical world unfolds from the made to the making at each moment. But now he attends more to identifying that absolute present in religious terms as God.[28] On this basis he can view each individual self, at each moment, as God's unique self-determination (Z10 92, 114). This also means that each of our acts, in self-awareness, expresses the absolute present's self-determinations whereby the eternal past and the eternal future it enfolds are unfolded into the light of the present (Z10 300). In that moment of the present we live time in immediacy with what decades earlier Nishida had characterized in Hegelian terms as the self-determination of the concrete universal. Nishida now depicts this in its religious significance as the inverse correspondence between absolute and finite. The reality of the concrete is in that present moment, which is thus saturated with religious significance and existential meaning, for it is in that present that one dies and is reborn as a reflection of God.

It is in that sense that Nishida in "Bashoteki ronri to shūkyōteki sekaikan" characterizes the absolute present in its self-determination, borrowing Christian terminology, as *eschatologisch* (eschatological, *shūmatsuronteki* 終末論的) (Z10 354; see also 337). He explains, however, that by "eschatological" he means something different from its Christian sense, where it is wont to be conceived teleologically in relation to a transcendent object functioning as telos or end. He thinks of the eschatological rather in terms of the absolute's immanent transcendence (naizaiteki chōetsu) within ourselves, in its inverse correspondence, whereby "we are in accordance [*ouzuru* 応ずる] with the absolute one by transcending ourselves" (Z10 355). The individual person's self-negation is in co-respondence[29] with the self-negation of the absolute present. The self, as a historical individual, in thus facing the absolute as its self-contradiction in the present moment (absolute present), the self in its religious self-awareness as God's self-negation, is eschatological. Our actions, being historical as self-determinations of the absolute present, are eschatological as well. And place itself, in that absolute present and in its explicitly existential or religious significance as the existential matrix wherein we realize the absolute and the absolute realizes itself in us, is thus eschatological. Eschatological urgency here is not in light of some distant future but rather of the present. In other words, the *eschaton*, the "end," is now at every moment, saturated with significance, in the absolute's self-determination. The world in its dynamic concrete immediacy, as an absolute present, is in that sense eschatological.

In thus re-interpreting the meaning of "eschatology," Nishida draws a connection to the Zen-like understanding of the "ordinary and everyday" as manifest in the present moment. Every point in space, at each moment, is the creative point of the absolute's self-determination, established in its self-negation of the eternal past and the eternal future, a self-negation of its eternity (Z10 101). As we saw in chapter 6, it is here in the present that Nishida views the world as moving from the made to the making, the point in time when, as creative elements of the self-creative world, we transcend past conditioning and create the future anew (Z10 346). In Zen terminology that present is the locus of the ordinary. It is therein that the simultaneity of transcendence and immanence, the self-determination of the absolute present, is manifest. Nishida expresses that immeasurable depth of non-substantiality (*mukitei* 無基底), available in the utterly ordinary, in the

Zen-like terminology of "depth in the ordinary" (byōjōtei) (Z10 356).[30] He takes it, as the self's most concrete reality, to be the deepest foundation of personhood that is nevertheless manifest at the shallowest surface of one's being (Z10 358). The most primordial is in the utterly routine; it does not transcend the actual as something higher and beyond. The moment of authentic self-awareness, exhausting the self in self-negation, whereby self-transformative conversion freely takes place, is hence unmediated in that deep root of oneself in the utterly ordinary. It is in that sense that self-awareness mirrors the absolute whole in one's concrete present, one's monadic point in space-time expressing the macrocosmic whole. The present one lives in the here and now possesses an immeasurable depth, yet it is ordinary, not super-ordinary. Kosaka in his commentary on Nishida explains that while "inverse correspondence" expresses the religious relationship between the absolute and the finite self with emphasis on the working activity of the absolute, "depth in the ordinary" here expresses the standpoint of religion in the state of "seeing one's [true original] nature" (kenshō) or "[religious] conversion of mind" (*eshin* 回心), that is, the state of religious self-awareness on the side of man.[31] For Ueda Shizuteru, it signifies our state of implacement in that religious relationship of absolutely contradictory self-identity with the absolute.[32] It is the standpoint of conversion arrived at in self-negation in one's ordinary and everyday existence.

Nishida discovers the eschatological in this ordinariness, for it is therein that we are always in touch with both the inception and the termination of history; we eschatologically stand on the beginning and the end of the world at each moment (Z10 105). There, in the momentary present, we are in contact with the world's beginning and end, the alpha and the omega of the self, its birth-and-death, generation-and-extinction, wherein the eternal past and the eternal future meet in the absolute present (Z10 357). It is the place, basho, of "our realization of the absolute and of the absolute's self-realization."[33] It is in this sense of the ordinary containing at its core its self-negation and self-contradiction vis-à-vis the absolute matrix of space-time that Nishida describes the finite self's inverse correspondence with the absolute in the strangely syncretic Zen-Christian terms of "the eschatology of depth in the ordinary" or "eschatological depth in the ordinary" (*shūmatsuronteki byōjōtei* 終末論的平常底) (Z10 357). As microcosmic creative elements mirroring the macrocosmic creative world, and as expressive monadic focal points of the self-expressive world, we are thus in touch with the absolute at every moment in inverse correspondence and in eschatological depth in ordinariness.

In conclusion, one might say that the ideas of inverse correspondence and eschatological depth in the ordinary take the logic of contradictory self-identity further in the existential and religious dimensions while infusing it with concrete content more immediate in our living selves. But at the same time, in that concern for religiosity, one finds a certain consistency in the final essay of 1945 with his maiden work, *Zen no kenkyū*. In both works it is what Nishida calls the "religious" that provides the key to the concrete basis of the real. There is also a continuity with his epistemology of 1926 in his concern with place, which he opposes to the Aristotelian object qua grammatical subject. Looking back to his earlier theory, Nishida in his final essay refers to the predicate pole as determining itself in contradictory self-identity (Z10 318–319). But in addition, Nishida now characterizes the self of consciousness as mirroring, in its acting, the contradictory self-identity of the world as the world's self-determination. The self of consciousness with its field of predicates finds itself always already implaced within, and determined by, the world as the place wherein it dwells, the self-forming sociohistorical world that is the most immediate to ourselves (Z10 308). Furthermore, however, the dialectical matrix of that world in its self-affirmation qua grammatical subjects in the object-plane (noema) and its self-negation in the predicate pole, the plane of acts of consciousness (noesis), is hence in contradictory self-identity (Z10 308–309). And that dialectic, the contradictory self-identity of the concrete, is what Nishida here reformulates in the 1940s in the religious terms of the infinite sphere of inter-expression, inverse correspondence between absolute and finite self, and eschatological depth in the ordinary. It is in these formulations of the dialectic of religiosity that the Mahāyāna Buddhist influences, as opposed to Hegelian dialectics, along with a certain reading of Christianity, are most evident. Now that we have engaged in a detailed study of dialectics in Nishida, we are ready to move to the next part of this study, in which I assess Nishida's work in its engagement with Buddhism and with Hegel, as well as where it diverges from these influences, and in light of the globalized situation of (post/hyper-)modernity today. We are also prepared now to embark on a more creative reading of Nishida.

PART III

CONCLUSIONS

8 Nishida and Hegel

Now that we have discussed the dialectic in each period of Nishida's oeuvre in detail, we are prepared to look more directly at the issue of Nishida's relationship to Hegel and to Mahāyāna Buddhism. We are also prepared to give a general assessment of his philosophical work, in its so-called dialectical aspect, in light of its unique stance as more than merely Hegelian or merely Buddhist. Finally, I would like to address some questions about Nishida's dialectics in regard to the kind of terminology or language Nishida employs and in regard to what the dialectic of place may have to offer us today in the context of a globalizing world. This and the following chapters will cover these issues. Stylistically they may differ from the previous chapters in that philosophically they will be more ambitious. In this chapter we look at the relationship of Nishida's dialectic to Hegel's dialectic, and in chapter 9 we look at its relationship to Buddhist Mahāyāna ideas of non-duality. But because this necessitates a discussion of his dialectical theory of religion in general, we will also look into his reading and incorporation of Christianity. In chapter 10 I develop Nishida's dialectical philosophy in terms of "chiasmatic chorology" on the basis of the chiasma and the chōra as the matter (*Sache*) of his thinking. This is where our reading of Nishida will move beyond traditional exegesis and bring him into the light of contemporary philosophical issues, especially of Continental philosophy. This will also lead us to raise the issue of Nishida's appropriation of the philosophical terminology of nineteenth-century German philosophy, primarily that of Hegel's dialectics. To what extent does that terminology adequately express what he was thinking? Is there a better way to express the matter of his thought so that it will speak to us in our contemporary philosophical context? In chapter 11 I will tackle that issue of the language of Nishida's dialectic, as well as of its logic and the meaning of "contradiction." I will end my discussion with a look into where Nishida positioned his dialectical thought in relation to the world context, especially in terms of the geo-politics in which he found himself at that time. What might we derive or extract from it in light of our contemporary situation in the global world? This will allow us to make an assessment of what Nishida's work has to offer us today. The reader must therefore be forewarned that while parts 1 and 2 were more expository, the chapters in part 3, especially chapter 10, will be more original and challenging.

In the previous chapters I have discussed in detail the dialectic in Nishida's thinking as it manifests itself in the various stages of his oeuvre. In those manifestations of the dialectic we can discern a slew of influences from, and references to, Western and Eastern sources, especially Hegel and Buddhism. Commentators have noted that one of Nishida's goals was to articulate certain truths experienced in the Eastern traditions, for example, Zen meditation practice, in the terminology of Western philosophy.[1] For example, Nishida employed the language of nineteenth-century German philosophy, most notably that of Hegelian dialectics (together with Neo-Kantian epistemology). Even in regard to content, Nishida, as we have seen, in his attempt to bridge the gap left open by Kantian dualism, appropriates, for example, the general Western terminology of the universal and its relation to the individual (or the particular) and especially the Hegelian conception of the self-differentiating concrete universal. One cannot deny the importance of the concrete universal in the unfolding of Nishida's dialectic. Yet the notions of the nothing that we always find in the background of his dialectics and of the radical interrelationality that unfolds during the 1930s both indicate a nearness to the Mahāyāna worldview, as Nishida seems to suggest in his final essay of 1945. So the question arises: To what extent is Nishida Hegelian, and to what extent is he Buddhist? Is his dialectic simply a version of Hegelian dialectical philosophy? Is it a form of Mahāyāna thought? In this chapter I will examine the dialectic of Hegel and its relationship to Nishida. In chapter 10 I will investigate how Mahāyāna Buddhism relates to Nishida.

In the genesis of his thought, as we have seen, Nishida underwent the influence of many Western philosophers. The catalyst that spurred his philosophical project, as I discussed, was the issue of epistemological dualism. But Hegel is probably the one figure of Western thought whose significance to Nishida is consistent throughout Nishida's writing career. Throughout his oeuvre Nishida expresses both his affinity to and distance from Hegel's philosophy. In his earlier works Nishida's references to Hegel tend to be for the purpose of corroborating his own thoughts with similar ideas. And in what appears to be an afterword added to his one essay that directly thematizes Hegel's philosophy, "Watashi no tachiba kara mita Hēgeru no benshōhō" (「私の立場から見たヘーゲルの弁証法」; "Hegel's Dialectic as Seen from My Standpoint") of 1931,[2] Nishida acknowledges his debt to Hegel. Therein he states that much of his thought was inherited or learned from Hegel and that his thinking is closer to Hegel's than to anyone else's (*Z7* 277–278). Nishida expresses his nearness to Hegel in another work of the same period (1932), *Mu no jikakuteki gentei* (『無の自覚的限定』; *The Self-Aware Determination of Nothing*). Yet their views are far from consonant, as he also implies in his 1931 essay on Hegel.[3] Once he formulated his philosophy of place in the late 1920s, Nishida began to distinguish his dialectic from that of Hegel's. As he develops his dialectical thought through the 1930s and into the 1940s, he increasingly expresses disagreement with Hegel. This is not to deny, however, the strong presence of Hegel that remains even in his critique of that philosopher. In the following sections I will investigate the dialectical ideas and aspects in Hegel's thought and their influence on, or rejection by, Nishida, contrasting and comparing their views in respect to the following points: opposition, contradiction, and negation; the concrete universal; the conceptualism of the absolute idea; the subjectivism of the absolute spirit; the rationalism of the self-completing circle of reason; substantialism and (grammatical) subject logic (or object logic); and metaphysical hierarchy and the hegemony of the universal. Insofar as these points in Hegel support, refer to, and imply one another, there will be some overlap in content among the sections.[4]

Dialectic, Opposition, and Negation

In Western philosophy we can trace dialectics to Plato's Socratic dialogues. In the *Republic, dialektikē* (διαλεκτική) is one of the higher modes of knowledge, whereby, in taking each hypothesis as a stepping-stone and asking "Why?" one moves upward toward an intuitive view (*noēsis* νόησις) that could render a universal account, a logos, for things. That view is of the all-comprehensive *idea* (ἰδέα) of the Good that explains everything and authenticates all other particular forms of knowledge. Hegel inherits from Plato this idea of the art of dialectic, but for him its dia-logic is not founded on a dialogue between two interlocutors and their distinct views but rather on the basis of contradiction, the opposition of premises that lead to further consequences. Rather than taking the formal logical principle of non-contradiction, along with the principles of identity and of the excluded middle, as ontological absolutes that point to a reality of unchanging and independent essences (substances), Hegel's point was to comprehend them within the context of a dialectical dynamic, involving the development of the process of thought and of reality. Nishida inherits from Hegel this appreciation of the dynamic whole, as opposed to the static and formal, but proposes to take its dethronement of absolutes further than even Hegel imagined possible.

Central to Hegel's dialectical analysis is the recognition that the principle of non-contradiction is the principle of identity negatively stated: "$X = X$" implies that X is not not-X. The relation of X's self-identity is established through a negative relation to not-X, that it is itself in not being not-X. Its identity is thus not immediately given. But X's self-identity cannot merely be in its not being not-X. Hence "$X = X$" is no tautology but an affirmation made possible through a double negation, a "negation of negation."[5] Hegel thus rejects any conception of identity as simply atomistic, as unrelated to anything else. Rather, identity always involves a negative relation of exclusion to the other, exclusion of its own non-existence. The self is found in and through its other.[6] Things are not self-subsistent but are established through the mediation of reciprocal negation and are thus united in a state of mutual tension (*WL2* 121/*SL* 497, *WL2* 126/*SL* 502, *WL2* 131/*SL* 506, *WL2*

376/*SL* 726). Hegel thus affirms the logically contradictory character of reality, but he comprehends this dialectically rather than in the abstract terms of formal logic. It does not mean the logical incompatibility between fixed atomic entities but rather the co-relativity of categories. What exists concretely, for Hegel, as such is never fixed or atomic; it exists "with difference and opposition in itself. . . . Contradiction is the very moving principle of the world" (*EL* §119z 174). That tension of contradiction, such as in motion that involves the contradiction between "here" and "not-here," which is also a contradiction between "is" and "is-not," is what serves to drive the world's unfolding. Hegel thus states, "Motion is *existent* contradiction itself" (*WL2* 59/*SL* 440).[7] These are points taken up by Nishida. The main difference, however, is that in Hegel's case that system of the dialectic is to be comprehended under the perspective of a complete concept, which is the substance driving the entirety of the dynamic.

We find dialectics in Nishida's thinking from the beginning of his career, although he did not always characterize his thinking with the term "dialectic" (benshōhō 弁証法) until later. The relationship to Hegel was there from the start as well. Although commentators differentiate Nishida's "logic" as a "logic of paradox" or "paradoxical logic of irresolvable contradiction" from Hegel's "logic" as a "logic of dialectical synthesis,"[8] we ought to keep in mind that Nishida came to use the term *benshōhō* to describe his way of thinking and characterized the reciprocal relationships between opposites found in reality as a "dialectical process." In the early 1920s, for example, in *Geijutsu to dōtoku* (『芸術と道徳』; *Art and Morality*), Nishida refers to Hegel when he is arguing that the self-cognition of the cognitive process involves a necessary contradiction (*Z3* 153). He comes to use the term "dialectic" to emphasize that negativity. As in Hegel, contradiction for Nishida drives the dialectical process of reality and thought. Like Hegel's cases of dialectical contradiction, Nishida's examples of contradiction are often experiential rather than formal-logical. A prime example here is the self-contradiction felt in the religious sphere vis-à-vis one's death. Yet it is that existential contradiction between life and death that can also be understood in, or translated into, the terms of the logical contradiction between being and non-being, affirmation and negation.

When Nishida is contrasting his dialectic with Hegel's, he likes to characterize his system as an "absolute dialectic" (zettai benshōhō 絶対弁証法). By this he means a radicalization of dialectical thinking. He takes Hegel's dialectic to be insufficiently dialectical. "Dialectic" for Hegel means the rational process that gradually resolves oppositions between conflicting positions through what he calls "sublation" (Aufheben, Aufhebung). It involves, on the one hand, the negation or canceling (*Negieren*), ceasing or ending (*aufhören lassen, ein Ende machen*), of the partiality of the positions leading to their opposition and, on the other, the preservation (*Aufbewahren*) of their essential truth that overcomes their opposition, elevating them to a more comprehensive truth (*PG* 90/*PS* 68; *WL*1 94/*SL* 107). This means a reconciliation between the opposing terms. With each sublation, the all-encompassing truth about the whole becomes more and more manifest. But that progression toward the whole truth assumes its end in a telos that drives it. That is, Hegel's system is predicated on a pre-given concept (Begriff) operating from above as it drives the sublations of all oppositions toward the realization of itself in its absolute self-conception (*sichbegreifen*, "self-conceiving") of the entire process. The dialectical process is here founded on this concept that anticipates and grasps the entire dynamic and realizes itself in it. I will cover this conceptualism in greater detail in a later section. From Nishida's perspective, the contradiction here in its conceptual sublation is not a genuine contradiction, nor is it truly lived. The negation involved therein is not absolute.

In opposition to any such totalizing concept, Nishida includes in his dialectical understanding of the historical world an acknowledgment of the autonomy of the individuals engaging in interaction (aihataraki 相働き) to constitute that dialectical unfolding of the world (e.g., *Z*9 13–24). This dialectic, founded on mutual self-negation, allows for genuine reciprocity between the opposing terms, including the relationship between universal and individuals. As we saw in the previous chapters, the individual in occupying the "extreme limit" or "extremity" (kyokugen 極限) of the universal's self-determination counter-determines (gyaku gentei 逆限定) the universal. While living under the influence of the social world wherein the individual is born and acts, the individual as a free person is also self-determining. And in that freedom he or she remodels his or her social environment. Individual persons are just as much agents of history as the world taken as a whole. The individual, then, is not simply a pawn for the "cunning of reason" in history. Of course, in underscoring that radical reciprocity, Nishida does not want to over-emphasize the individual in a manner that would turn it into a metaphysical absolute. Rather, individuals as very much a part of the dialectical matrix are just as self-contradictory as the world. In any case, the pluralism involving true individuals along with their radical reciprocity would seem inconceivable in the Hegelian system traditionally construed. This radical interrelationality in Nishida's dialectic is predicated on the fact that the dialectical universal (benshohōteki ippansha 弁証法的 一般者) embracing its terms here ultimately is no self-conceiving concept but instead entails an un-conceptualizable nothing (mu 無) environing them as their place (basho 場所), enveloping the entire dialectical process. Thus we must distinguish Nishida's discourse of the implacement or envelopment of contradictories from Hegel's discourse of the resolution or sublation of contradictories in an all-encompassing concept. For Hegel, the absolute at the end of the dialectical process is the concept that reconciles all opposites, including the dichotomies between subject and object, mind and matter, self and thing, man and nature, ideal and real. Their ultimate reconciliation in the idea of the whole is the dialectical goal. For Nishida, however, opposites as interrelating bi-conditionals are implaced within an enveloping place of nothing. Both agree that "truth is the whole," of which parts are but moments. Both strive for a holism that is concrete in encompassing those parts or moments as real elements and that is dynamic in realizing itself in those parts or moments. But for Hegel, that whole is encompassed within an absolute concept; for Nishida, that whole is an abyssal place delimited by absolutely nothing that furthermore expresses itself in those moments as autonomous individuals. In Hegel, the dialectical movement culminates in the conceptualization of its whole. In Nishida, the dialectical movement is enveloped by its place encompassed by nothing. The whole is a non-conceptualizable non-concept always lying in the background, behind us, and never made present before us. A look at Nishida's appropriation of one of the Hegelian terms for that whole should help us further understand this subtle difference.

The Concrete Universal

Nishida had been making use, directly or indirectly, of the Hegelian concept of the concrete universal (gutaiteki ippansha 具体的一般者) ever since his maiden work, *Zen no kenkyū* (『善の研究』; *Inquiry into the Good*) of 1911. Recall from the previous discussions that both thinkers looked to the undifferentiated whole as it determines and forms itself from within in self-differentiation. It is the primal judgment (Urteil) that is the primordial division (Ur-Teilung), articulating its whole in elements (*WL2* 264–308/*SL* 623–663). In his opposition to the Kantian premise of an ultimate duality between mind as form and matter as content, Nishida found much use for that Hegelian notion of the concrete universal, providing the ground of judgments. It is from his initial appropriations of Hegel's concrete universal that Nishida then goes on to develop his theory of the place (basho) wherein opposing terms are implaced.

Hegel's concrete universal contains its own principle of individualization (*WL2* 245–264/*SL* 605–622), whereby it differentiates itself while maintaining self-identity. In its primal differentiation (Ur-Teilung) it is the substratum of the judgment (Urteil) whereby it articulates itself into its elements and their relations. On this basis Hegel affirms the identity expressed in the copula between the grammatical subject and the predicate and between the individual and the universal (*EL* § 166 231, § 175z 240). Nishida inherits and appropriates this Hegelian notion of the concrete universal before and after developing his basho theory (e.g., *Z3* 331, 409; *Z8* 93). We find it already conspicuous in *Zen no kenkyū* (1911). Here, as opposed to his later, more mature stance, Nishida appears quite sympathetic to Hegel's conceptualism. A main theme of *Zen no kenkyū* is Nishida's formulation of what he calls "pure experience" (junsui keiken 純粋経験) as the fundamental reality before the subject-object split. Nishida takes this reality as ultimately referring to a universal that grounds individual consciousness while it transcends each consciousness as but a moment or stage in its self-differentiation: "The fact of pure experience means that the so-called universal realizes itself" (Z1 22). The immediate experience one lives is partaking in the self-development of that infinite whole, containing infinite possibilities. He then adds that what he means here is what Hegel calls the "concept" (Begriff). In other words, Nishida here views the Hegelian concept as naming the same unifying power that underlies what he understands in terms of pure experience: "Since our pure experience is a systematic development, the unifying force working at its root must immediately be the universality of the concept itself" (Z1 22), and "The universality of the concept is . . . the unifying force of concrete facts" (Z1 22). Nishida also refers to Hegel in this work as stating that true individuality does not exist apart from universality, and that the determined universal (*bestimmte Allgemeinheit*) is what becomes the individual. This is an obvious reference to the idea of the concrete universal. Nishida, however, immediately adds that individuality cannot be expressed through abstract concepts, although it can be clearly expressed by an artist's brush or a novelist's pen (Z1 149). One might then ask to what extent Hegel's universal is sufficiently concrete to express what Nishida has in mind.

Nishida eventually develops his interpretation of the concrete universal in terms of a place or field, basho, and comes to understand the universal's principle of individuation in light of its being the place of implacement that envelops the implaced. This is an idea for which he also acknowledges a debt to Plato's concept of chōra in the *Timaeus.* This placiality, its basho nature, which must be assumed and cannot be stated as the subject of a judgment, is what for Nishida makes the universal concrete (Z3 431–432, 439, 523, 526–527). For both Hegel and Nishida, while the abstract universal abstracts from specific differences, the concrete universal permits those differences as its internal self-determination.[9] It is in that sense that the grammatical subject of a judgment is the universal. The question, however, is whether that self-determining concrete whole is ultimately to be understood qua idea as an all-comprehending concept—which, furthermore, can be noematized into a grammatical subject—or qua basho in its all-embracing undelimitable placiality. Nishida thus eventually develops his distinct notion of the dialectical universal. He comes to view its self-determining process as involving something more than Hegel's concrete universal and distinguishes his concept of the dialectical world (benshōhōteki sekai 弁証法的世界) from Hegel's universal (Z8 82). For Nishida, the self-differentiating universal entails an undifferentiated place presupposed by conception. As the place of the conceiving act, that place cannot be conceived. It exceeds all attempts to think it. Nishida argues that Hegel's logic failed to explicate this sense of the placiality that every conceptual universal must presuppose, the placiality that a true concrete universal in developing (*entwicklen*) itself into the individual must involve, as enveloping (*enthalten*) the individual. In ignoring that enveloping or environing background of implacement, Hegel's logic is still an "object logic" (taishō ronri 対象論理) guided by its focus on the grammatical subject (Z4 335). We need to acknowledge the dark field surrounding the light of conception, the unsaid or unthought behind every subject of discourse. To the extent that he objectified the universal qua concept vis-à-vis the individual, Hegel, from Nishida's perspective, had not yet extricated himself from the subject-object dichotomy that he was trying to overcome. Hegel was still conceiving his universal noematically, as some thing qua object transcending, and subsisting under, its unfolding process. Nishida, by contrast, is interested in the holistic field that theorizing acts must implicitly refer to as their wherein—that which, noematically speaking, is no-thing.

Nishida was certainly inspired by Hegel's application of the concrete universal to history as what unfolds the dialectical process of its realization, but he found the transcendence of Hegel's universal in its manipulation of individuals (i.e., "the cunning of reason"), precluding genuine reciprocity with individuals, one-sided and hence abstract, not truly concrete. Instead, Nishida found the concrete world to be founded on our bodily interactivities. It is not a world unfolding an absolute concept to realize its telos. Concrete dialectics for Nishida, then, is the world's self-determination that is at the same time its determination via interdetermining individuals (Z8 93). In the formula that equates universal and individual, Nishida thus emphasizes, contra Hegel, their reciprocity: the universal's self-determination, the individual's self-determination, and their interdetermination of each other. That is, Nishida has radicalized the dialectical nature of the concrete universal in the direction of what he comes to call the dialectical universal, the chiasmatic matrix of the dialectical world, whereby its self-determination as individuals involves the self- and co-determinations of those individuals. On this basis Nishida can state that the "substratum" (kitai 基体) of the dialectic is such that "one is many and many is one" (ichi soku ta, ta soku ichi「一即多、多即一」), the dialectical universal that he distinguishes not only from abstract universals but also from Hegel's concrete universal (Z8 82). In differentiating his concept of the dialectical universal from Hegel's concrete universal, Nishida in the late 1930s (e.g., Z8 82) underscores both the radical reciprocity of his absolute dialectic and its placiality making room for that reciprocity—both of which he finds lacking in Hegel. The dialectical universal for Nishida points to the place (basho) for those multiple interacting individuals and their dialectic. Both universality qua place and true individuality, in their concreteness, thus elude the grasp of abstraction or conception.[10] Nishida initially seems to have been inspired by Hegel's concept of the concrete universal in its idea of a self-differentiating undifferentiated reality. Yet that dynamic of the concrete—its chiasmatic nature of over-(inter-)determination—for Nishida proves to exceed any conceptual grasp. This is why, in contrast to Hegel, the dialectical process for Nishida is irreducible to any rational structure or the self-realization of reason. He states that reason is dialectical only on the basis of facts determining themselves; that is, the concrete comes first, not any concept (*Z7* 274).

Conceptualism: The Self-Conceiving Concept or Idea

By "concept" (Begriff), Hegel means the concrete universal in its rational structuring of reality. The world is structured according to conceptual necessity. Its substantial structure, accordingly, is derived solely from that concept. Hegel takes this conceptual structure to be the essence or nature of things, the true substance of reality amid the complexity and contingency of appearances and fleeting manifestations. It is the logos or inner necessity behind whatever is, externally realizing itself in transient forms. But that essence qua concept is only for thought. In his attempt to bridge the Kantian dichotomy, Hegel appears to reduce reality to thought (*WL1* 14–15/*SL* 35–36). Yet as the absolutely self-subsistent matter (Sache), this can be no mere human thought finitized in the face of the world (*WL1* 18–19/*SL* 39). The concept grounds the sublational unity of identity and difference, self and other, in its grasping of totality (*Totalität*) (*EL* § 119z 174, § 121 175; see also § 160 223). It is not that the form of thought imposes itself on an independently existing material, but that the totality of the concept, as free and infinite form, already contains within itself the principle of matter (*EL* § 128z 185). This totalizing concept exists in itself, and in grasping or conceiving itself, knowing itself, it is for itself. Hence it is *an und für sich* (*PG* 301/*PS* 253; *WL1* 30–31/*SL* 49). In this self-sufficiency it is infinite, not finite. This all-encompassing concept that is the substance of reality as a whole is what Hegel also calls the absolute idea (*Idee*) providing a rational vision of the conceptual necessity of that whole (*WL2* 483–506/*SL* 823–844).

The idea, then, represents the systematic totality of reality, its inner reason, underlying and guiding the entire dialectical dynamic. The core of reality is this concept that rationalizes the whole: "What is not rational has no *truth,* or what is not conceived *is* not; thus when reason speaks of an *other* than itself, in fact it speaks only of itself" (*PG* 389/*PS* 333). It is the formula that becomes externalized as real, the non-material force relating everything together, whereby everything in time and in space can be conceptually grasped as a whole. As such, it is the concrete universal. And judgment (Urteil, *Urteilen*) is its primordial division (*Ur-teilen,* Ur-teilung) (*WL2* 267/*SL* 625). The end of the entire dialectical process, culminating in its all-encompassing concept, is this idea's self-realization, the self-conceiving concept (*der sich begreifende Begriff*) grasping itself in the totality of its system, comprehending itself in its realization (*WL2* 504–505/*SL* 842–843; *EL* § 243 296). Moreover, by the concept's self-conception Hegel also means the self-consciousness of the absolute spirit or mind (Geist) (*WL2* 224/*SL* 586). The idea as self-consciousness is Geist—the spirit not merely of individual man but of the cosmos. Its self-comprehension encompasses both its manifestation as real and its conceptual necessity as rational. Thus "The idea is truth which is *an und für sich*" (*EL* § 213 274), "The truth of the finite is . . . its ideality," and "Every genuine philosophy is idealism" (*EL* § 95 140). The absolute for Hegel is the one idea that in the act of judgment differentiates itself into its elements, which in turn return to that idea as their truth (*EL* § 213 275). The point of Hegel's "absolute idealism," then, is that everything in the world manifests this idea of rational necessity—ontologically prior to its manifestations, as in Plato's realm of ideas—for the realization of its rational self-consciousness. And that is precisely the direction in which Nishida does not want to go.

Nishida, like Hegel, wants to overcome the Kantian dichotomy between subject and object, concept and reality, but he rejects Hegel's idealism of an all-comprehending idea that would cement that gap, that is, ideally. In search of the concrete whole, Nishida looks instead to our pre-conceptually or pre-theoretically lived experience. As already mentioned, the early Nishida of *Zen no kenkyū* (1911) seems to regard the universality of the Hegelian "concept" (Begriff)—"the soul of the concrete" (*die Seele des Konkreten*) (*WL2* 242/*SL* 602; *Z1* 22)—as identical with what he has in mind when he is speaking of that spontaneously evolving whole of reality as "pure experience" (*Z1* 22). He states that the universality of the concept is the unifying force grounding the unfolding of pure experience. As in Hegel's concrete universal, it is from that self-unfolding whole of pure experience that judgment emerges through its divisions into the grammatical subject-predicate or the epistemological subject-object. Yet we can still discern an emerging distinction here in what they emphasize: concept or idea, on the one hand, and intuition or experience, on the other. The difference is obvious when we notice that for Hegel, truth qua whole means the conceptual comprehension resulting from, but also driving, the entire dialectical process. It is the telos. In contrast, truth for Nishida is immediate. For both, it is the whole. For Nishida here, pure experience as immediacy is the most concrete and hence truth itself, while for Hegel in his *Phenomenology of Spirit*, sensible certainty (*sinnliche Gewißheit*) is not yet truth but its abstract beginning.[11] What Nishida means here by "universality" that unifies and grounds pure experience cannot in the end mean the same as Hegel's absolute concept.

With the maturation of his ideas, especially with the formulation of his theory of place, Nishida seems better equipped to express where his understanding diverges from Hegel's. We can more easily distinguish Nishida's self-forming formlessness that is a place (basho) from Hegel's self-forming form that is a self-conceiving concept (Begriff). The concept, Hegel states, "is everything" (*alles*). The concrete universal determining itself is the concept's "universal absolute activity" (*allgemeine absolute Tätigkeit*) and "absolutely infinite force" (*schlechthin unend-liche Kraft*), to which nothing can offer resistance or opposition (*WL2* 186/*SL* 826). In its totalizing power, its hegemony is universal. But from the Nishidian stand-point the question is whether such a concrete universal qua idea or concept can truly subsume concrete individuality without extinguishing or covering over the individual's trans-rational or trans-conceptual singularity.[12] This is the issue of Hegel's alleged pan-logism—already raised by his Neo-Kantian critics, such as Lotze—and his implicit Platonism that ontologically prioritizes the con-cept. To this we can oppose what Nishida means by place. Nishida also repeat-edly speaks of Hegel's dialectic as a "dialectic of process" (kateiteki benshōhō 過程的弁証法), by which he seems to mean the sublational process that unfolds in time toward final resolution. Nishida instead looks to the present as the locus or place for the simultaneity of contradictories in their co-existence. True dialectic, Nishida emphasizes, is of existence itself, activity in the present, not merely the rational process of thought working itself out in time. Rather than looking to the conceptual resolution of contradictories, Nishida looks behind them to their en-vironing wherein that must always be assumed as their implicit context. Nishida thus starts from a standpoint distinct from Hegel's by looking not to the concept of the rational necessity of everything but to place, the implicit wherein of everything. As the concept of rational necessity, the concrete universal imposes on, and destroys, the trans-conceptual singularity of individual beings. In con-trast, the place delimited by nothing envelops beings in their unique singulari-ties and contradictions by withdrawing itself, receding into the dark—śūnyatāyāḥ śūnyatā.

Nishida does acknowledge his debt to Hegel for the notion of a concrete logic manifesting itself in the reality of historical unfolding. History, for both think-ers, proves to be the self-realization of something absolute, although for Hegel that self-realization is also the self-grasping of the concept. This is also the point on which Karl Marx contended with Hegel and instead looked to history's material conditions rather than the ideal. Nishida thus also acknowledges his closeness here to Marx and the dialectical materialists in their opposition to the Hegelian idea. Like Marx, Nishida positions that idea—contra Hegel—in the stream of history that self-formatively moves via historical facts (*Z7* 276). Nishida's conviction is that the focus of dialectic should not be speculation but facticity. The individual ele-ments interacting to create history are its agents, not any ideality or concept. And what embraces them to make room for their interactivity is place. The universal's self-determination in those individuals entails its self-negation, presupposing their place that allows for their autonomous activities that in turn counter-determine the universal. In other words, place here envelops both the universal's self-determination as individuals and counter-determination by individuals. In that sense its transcendence is immanently real; it is concrete as the world of interactivity. Hegel as well claims that the idea is immanent in the world as its rational structure unfolding history. The concreteness of Nishida's world history is, however, far more convincing in that Nishida founds it on the embodied activities of man working on the environment, re-structuring it through the manipulation of things as tools. While he agrees with Hegel that we are determinations of the universal or absolute, Nishida also emphasizes the autonomy of ourselves as world-creative historical bodies rather than mere manifestations of the self-consciousness of absolute spirit. His dialectic is a dialectic of individuals with bodies interacting in the world. What is "absolute" for Nishida is only the place for such interactivity. Nishida maintains his opposition to Hegel's dialectic of the idea up to the end of his life when in the essay "Kūkan" (「空間」; "Space") (1944) he claims that his logic of place, which is a logic of the self-formation of the endlessly creative historical world, is the reverse of Hegel's dialectical logic (Z10 172–173). Yet while Nishida approaches Marx in this opposition to Hegelian idealism, he also wants to avoid the position of mere materialism. He does not want to reduce the absolute to mere matter and history to its mechanical movements. At the root of history is neither mere concept nor mere matter. Neither idealism nor materialism leads to the position of absolute dialectics. Neither Hegel's nor Marx's dialectics, for Nishida, then, is true dialectics (Z6 275).

In distinction from both Hegelian and Marxist dialectics, both of which he calls the "dialectics of being" (*yū no benshōhō* 有の弁証法), Nishida characterizes his dialectic as a "dialectic of nothing" (*mu no benshōhō* 無の弁証法) (e.g., Z5 123). As opposed to a rational or conceptual necessity behind the historical and dialectical process, Nishida intimates something a-rational lying at the abyssal bottom of reality, whereon facts transpire in their singularity and individuals act freely. Hegel's logic, in contrast, takes the absolute qua infinite being as its archē, in the affirmation of which finite being reaches extinction. But this being as such, from Nishida's standpoint, is still a being conceived in opposition or contrast to nonbeing. Both are conceived or thought. Being and nothing as opposed to each other are both conceptually determined vis-à-vis each other. True nothing, however, transcends both as the implicit place making their interrelational or oppositional co-implacement possible. As such, it cannot be intellectually determined or conceived. But neither can this abyss be mere materiality conceived as the opposite of ideality. As place, it encompasses both thought and reality and their interaction. For Nishida, it is such interactivity from the enveloping nothing that unfolds history. It is not that history is dialectical because of its underlying reason, but rather that reason is dialectical because of the way facts inter-determine themselves within that nothing (Z7 274).

For Nishida, an essential feature of the place of nothing, as we have already seen, is its incapacity to be stated as a grammatical subject of a judgment (Z3 468–469, 521). We can contrast this view with Hegel's view of the self-conceiving concept. Hegel's idea is the concept that grasps itself as its subject.[13] For Nishida, this means that it is still objectified as noema, still being treated as a grammatical subject (*Z5* 130; *Z6* 40–41). It is not yet the final predicate that "can never become a subject." Nishida's place, in contrast, as the always implicit wherein of every subject of judgment and delimited by nothing, is un-determinable or un-definable. If identity involves the reciprocity of inter-determining self-determining individuals, no concept can ground self-identity. The complexity of the dialectic exceeds conceptuality. The concretely real, for Nishida, ultimately can be no concept or object of thought or subject of judgment. Rather, it is the place wherein individuals relate and interact. Because it is nothing definite, it can enfold individuals in their transrational singularity. Hegel's dialectic, by contrast, is a dialectic of the idea or thought, a dialectic of "being," and a dialectic of (a telos-driven) process incapable of genuine self-contradiction or self-negation (*Z5* 123). It lacks "absolute negation" (zettai hitei 絶対否定) (*Z9* 68–69). This is because genuine self-contradiction or self-negation would presuppose the indefiniteness of Nishida's "nothing," a place that can encompass contradictories. Rather than understanding reality in light of rational necessity that would resolve contradictories, Nishida takes what he calls "the history of life" to encompass any such reason or conceptual understanding. From that perspective, Hegel's logic is an abstraction from concrete life (*Z7* 275). In contrast to Hegel's totalizing dialectic, Nishida's holistic dialectic recognizes the irreducible and un-reifiable complexity of the all-encompassing context. In self-reflection, Nishida's system therefore also acknowledges its own in-completion; that is, its grounding place is not objectifiable but is an abyssal nothing.

Subjectivism: The Self-Knowing Subject or Absolute Spirit

As mentioned earlier, for Hegel, the culmination of the concept's dialectical development in the teleological idea is the self-consciousness of what he calls Geist—spirit or mind—not of any individual human being, but mind in the macrocosmic level, which he also equates with the God of Christianity. At the root of reality, driving everything, is the implicit rationality of the all-conceptualizing idea, which in turn is the "complete self-clarity of *Geist*" in all.[14] Hegel's universal is this self-knowing absolute subject. Everything else is drawn out of its self-development. The whole is the self-movement of the absolute spirit (*absoluter Geist*), identified with the one universal reason, the rational structure of the world. All differences between opposites emerge from this movement, whereby reason or spirit articulates and recognizes itself: "Reason [*die Vernunft*] knows itself and deals only with itself so that its whole work, as well as its activity, lies in itself" (*DFSg* 17/*DFSe* 87). As "thought thinking itself," the concrete universal's self-differentiation is the working out of the thought process of Geist, whereby its dialectical principle externalizes itself for, and the opposing views of realism and idealism are unified in, its total self-vision (*PG* 542–543/*PS* 472–473). The idea as the self-conceiving concept (*der sich begreifende Begriff*) grasping the totality of itself as the all-permeating pattern in its self-reflective self-consciousness is thus subjectivity (*WL2* 504/*SL* 842). Hegel in his *Phenomenology* re-defines and assimilates the Spinozistic substance that he critiqued as mere self-identity and as lacking dialectical determination into this dialectical subject, Geist. Although Nishida agrees with Hegel's critique of Spinoza, he finds this absolutizing reconceptualization of the subject to be an objectification, a return to self-identity as noema, substance qua grammatical subject (*Z9* 79). That is, the subjectivization of substance is in fact the substantialization and objectification of the epistemological subject. It is still not free from being something (*etwas*) and hence is not yet the concrete that in itself remains undifferentiated.[15] Hegel's universal, then, conceived as *absoluter Geist,* again is not concrete enough.

As a counter to the substantialism of Spinoza and Schelling, Hegel meant to re-direct our attention to the reality of subjectivity. But if Hegel's conception of the concrete universal in terms of an absolute spirit does not escape being an objectification, neither does it then escape the standpoint of subjectivism. This is so even when it is supposed to ground the unity of subjectivity and objectivity (*EPM* §§ 575–577 314–315). In seeking rational subjectivity behind reality and thus abstracting from the concrete life of individuality as multiple, bodily, and working in the world, Hegel's dialectic inclines toward subjectivism and mere formalism (*Z7* 274). For Nishida, the real world is not a world mediated or posited by the one mind of the absolute. Instead, it is mediated by absolute negation via the continuity of discontinuities between its elements. The one embracing those many elements does so only as their field or place, the nothing in their background, rather than as a self-positing subjectivity. Nishida would rather conceive the dialectic from the more concrete standpoint of practice on the basis of the historically constitutive interactions of individual persons on that field. The formative and creative universal must not be set above the concrete world; rather, it emerges dialectically as inseparable from the on-going dialectical formation of the world of the many.

Hegel equates "absolute spirit" with the self-knowing God (*PG* 564/*PS* 492–493). Theologian Karl Barth, however, has raised the objection that in making rational necessity an essential feature of God, Hegel has left no room for grace founded on God's freedom.[16] That is, in Hegel's system God cannot genuinely give to man, contrary to an essential component of Christian belief. Nishida, by contrast, in his work from the mid-1940s, takes into consideration this graciousness of the God of religion while interpreting it along the lines of soku-hi logic as freely giving in radical self-negation. Of course, for Nishida, this ultimately points to a non-person beyond God, the place of absolute nothing, rather than a theistic-personal God. He develops this idea in light of his notion of the absolute as place delimited by nothing, self-negating to make room for beings, allowing for their inverse correspondence with God. One might then say that the impersonal nothing as enveloping place allows for the personal God's embracing love. As opposed to the self-illuminating light of a self-conceiving consciousness that is Hegel's God, Nishida's God thus entails a dark abyss. But in its transcendent alterity it is simultaneously immanent as the place wherein we always already find ourselves embraced.

Modeled on intellectual rationality, Hegel's absolute spirit, as reason grasping itself in self-conscious clarity, one might say, is an idealizing self-projection of man as rational thinker. But it fails to account for man's being-in-the-world as a concrete working body. Nishida's absolute, as we have been seeing, by contrast, is no spirit or mind (Geist) modeled on the cogito but rather the un-objectifiable non-reason of nothing (Z5 123). It is no "world spirit" guiding historical events with its "cunning of reason." Its self-awareness (jikaku 自覚) points to its own darkness, its irreducible un-delimitation. The light of cognition always presupposes that darkness as the formlessness giving form and light. If Hegel wanted to maintain, against Spinoza and Schelling, that the absolute or the true is not only substance but also the epistemological subject qua spirit, Nishida strove to show that it is rather the environing place enveloping and determining any substance qua grammatical subject, as well as any epistemological subject knowing it and itself qua spirit. In this way Nishida opposes Hegel's subjectivism of the self-illuminating spirit to acknowledge instead the finitude of light and form on the basis of a radical non-subjectivism.

The Rationalism of the Self-Completing Circle

In opposition to the German Romantics, who looked to intuition or imagination to found the unity of man and nature, Hegel advanced his vision of the rationality of reality that culminates in the absolute spirit's self-cognition. This understanding of reason and how it operates in history leads Hegel to his unique metaphor of the circle (*Kreis*) to explain his whole system. Reason (*Vernunft*) is what bridges the dichotomous gap between consciousness and nature in its all-encompassing vision of the rationality of everything real. Hegel, in his preface to his *Philosophy of Right* (1821), thus states the principle of his philosophy of history as follows: "The rational is actual and the actual is rational" ("Was vernünftig ist, das ist wirklich; und was wirklich ist, das ist vernünftig") (*GPR* 14/*PR* 10).[17] Reason is not only within our consciousness but lies everywhere in the dynamism of its realizations in nature and history. Reason as such, Hegel states, is the substantial (*das Substantielle*) (*WL1* 29/*SL* 48). The rationality underlying all, in its self-grasping, is the world's subjectivity, Geist, the spirit living through our rational thinking as it recognizes itself in nature. In grasping the rational ordering of nature, we are thus taking part in reason's self-cognition. On this basis of universal reason underlying external reality, Hegel can claim—in opposition to Kantian dualism—that being and thought are ultimately one. The real or actual (*wirklich*) at its deepest level, in its underlying necessity, is rational since rationality necessitated it. Hegel's starting point, his archē, is thus rationality. By contrast, Nishida's starting point is the dark unintelligibility or a-rationality situating our implacement. Nishida refuses Hegel's identification of reason and reality. Just as the grammatical subject is implaced in the predicate and the noema is enveloped by noesis, reason is implaced in concrete human life. In Nishida's view, at the bottom of reason there lies the deep contradiction of human existence (*Z7* 276). To explain his distinct view, Nishida makes metaphorical use of the circle (*en* 円) as well, but he takes it in its spatial significance as place rather than in the sense of a temporal self-enclosure. The two circles, as we shall see in the following, are quite distinct.

We might take the contrast between Nishida's a-rationalism and Hegel's rationalism here in terms of a circle that is open or closed. For Hegel, the telos of world history is the self-realization of reason in the world that manifests the rationality of the whole in the clarity of its own light. What is realized is the self-grasping—the concept's self-conceptualization or the spirit's self-consciousness—of the entirety of the process: "The movement is the circle that returns into itself [*der in sich zurückgehende Kreis*], the circle that presupposes its beginning and reaches it only at the end" (*PG* 559/*PS* 488); "The true . . . is its own becoming, the circle [*der Kreis*] that presupposes its end as its aim and has it for its beginning and is actual only through its execution and end" (*PG* 20/*PS* 10); "The result is the same as the beginning only because the *beginning* is the *purpose*" (*PG* 22/*PS* 12). The whole dynamic for Hegel is thus a circle (*Kreis*), a circular motion (*Kreisbewegung*). The dialectic moves toward the closure—the conclusion (*Schluss*)—of its process, making a circle in realizing its inherent goal. Telos is inherent in the beginning, however, only as a potential, an impetus toward its realization. History in that sense is still a progression, but with its self-culmination accomplished in its conceptual or theoretical recapitulation, the self-recognition of reason in history as its complete self-realization, accomplished in man's historical consciousness. While history is progressive, in looking back at itself, the spirit that drives history makes rational sense of itself. The goal of reason as this principle is to recognize itself in this total reality, and history is the process wherein this self-recognition of reason occurs. The progression reaches culmination via closure within a conceptual circle, a circle that conceptualizes its pre-conceptual beginnings.

The suggestion Hegel makes in his *Encyclopedia* is that it is precisely philosophy, and as the science (*die Wissenschaft*) that realizes the totalizing view, that mirrors the world as a whole. It forms a circle that embraces all the particular philosophical principles and sciences in a single intelligible system with a common rational framework, a theoretical system that explains all reality by starting from the single principle of reason. The whole process is a progression toward its all- and self-comprehensive idea, the concept of its truth. Its realization is the self-grasping of the entirety of the process in the absolute concept. The dialectic moves toward the closure of its own process, making a circle, closing in on itself in its self-conceiving (sichbegreifen) end: It "returns into itself and reaches the point with which it began . . . [and] exhibits the appearance of a circle which closes with itself" (*EL* § 17 23; see also § 15 20).[18] For Hegel, both history and philosophy, then, are one big rational circle that is meant to account for everything real, an absolute conceptualization of the whole. Just as it is for Nishida, truth for Hegel, then, is the whole. But Hegel's conception of the whole binds the development of reality and knowledge. For Hegel, the whole means the totality of a system as a completed circle. In contrast, Nishida's whole is an in-completable sphere, a circle without periphery, extending into the unaccountable and the unknown. Hence while Hegel's whole is infinite, its infinity in possessing a definite structure is a whole that can be grasped from within in self-conceptualization. It is determined by its internal rational necessity. In accounting for itself, its self-rationalization, Hegel's infinite here is self-enclosing; it is a self-completing circle. Nishida's infinite, in contrast, is open.

We thus contrast Hegel's circle as closed in assuming the completion of the whole (in the concept, idea, spirit) and Nishida's circle as open, allowing for the whole's in-completion (as the un-objectifiable, ineffable place delimited by nothing). An essential difference from Hegel's self-completing system is that Nishida's system is without system; that is, it is not complete, cannot be completed, and necessarily allows for its in-completion. The telos presupposed in Hegel's dialectic, in already assuming its realization, closes the dialectical circle. Nishida's dialectic, in contrast, as founded on the self-negation of each moment, allows for genuine novelty and change, rupturing the bind of each determination. The focus here is not on a future telos but on the present in its inconceivable or un-conceptualizable singularity of the moment. Therein lies the spontaneity, the freedom, that Nishida emphasizes. It is on this basis that the made becomes the making to counter-determine its determining universal. The whole of the dialectical dynamic thus opens up a space reaching beyond Hegel's closed circle. The "double aperture," as Robert Carter calls it,[19] of the singularity of the individual or the moment, on the one end, and the un-delimited whole, on the other end, escaping conceptual determination on both ends, precludes the closing of the circle. Nishida's circle, in contrast to Hegel's self-closing circle, as boundlessly open is thus an-archic and a-teleological. The open sphere without periphery and without center perpetually undermines and de-stabilizes any totalizing edifice.

This difference between openness and closure may be what Nishida has in mind when he distinguishes, throughout the 1930s, between his dialectic of place (bashoteki benshōhō 場所的弁証法) and Hegel's dialectic of process (*katei* 過程).[20] Following Nishida's lead, many of his Japanese commentators, such as Kosaka Kunitsugu and Nakamura Yūjirō, have also emphasized this distinction.[21] The reason is not always stated clearly, and the distinction can be misleading in that Nishida's dialectic also involves process in the historical world's temporal unfolding, while Hegel's dialectic also involves the idea's external manifestations in space. One might clarify this distinction in the following manner. For Hegel, the dialectical process is a self-completing process, presupposing the whole in its completion, progressing toward its resolution of contradictions in that presupposed completion. And that Hegelian whole, conceptualized in the idea, from Nishida's perspective is an objectification. That whole in its objectification as a grammatical subject requires implacement within an environing openness as its place. And that open field, its always implicit wherein, would have to be mirrored in each present moment of the process, opening it anew at each moment, precluding its closure in some teleological future. Its placiality, open at each moment, is such that it allows for the simultaneity of opposites in their mutual reference as biconditionals, in turn referring to their site of co-implacement. It precludes having to drive them toward future sublations and ultimately to a culminating telos.[22] Nishida's understanding of time is thus focused on the present on the basis of that all-encompassing placiality. In a 1938 lecture Nishida charges Hegel with ignoring that dialectical significance of the present moment (Z13 22). A dialectic of inter-determination among independent individuals and involving contradictory self-identity thus cannot just be a dialectic of "process" of the Hegelian sort. Nishida's point is that it cannot be founded on a conceptual circle that completes itself in due time. The concrete situation that enfolds the reciprocity of opposing elements must have the sense of being their place, their site of co-implacement. Nishida takes this to be the true sense of the self-determination of the dialectical universal as occurring in the present (Z6 75). Hegel's dialectic is still teleological, future oriented in its focus on time while recollecting the past, a modern secular development of pre-modern eschatological thinking. The suggestion is that Hegel's self-enclosing circle (of time) requires Nishida's boundless circle (of place) as its environing wherein.

Substantialism and the Logic of the Grammatical Subject (Object Logic)

In his 1931 essay on Hegel ("Watashi no tachiba kara mita Hēgeru no benshōhō"), Nishida raises as one of his major contentions the issue of the objectification of the un-objectifiable, what he calls "the logic of the (grammatical) subject" (shugoteki ronri 主語的論理) or "object logic" (taishō ronri). Nishida charges Hegel's dialectic with objectifying the absolute, perpetuating the dualism it attempts to eradicate. In objectifying the absolute, it makes it into a noema, a determinate being, that can be made into the grammatical subject of a statement. A real dialectic, Nishida claims, must sever itself from any such standpoint (*Z7* 277–278). Instead of the affirmative determination of a being, true dialectic would have to involve the affirmation of negation in the mutual negation among terms, whereby social interactivity is made possible. The absolute qua place would be the field for such interactivity of mutual self-negation. During the 1930s Nishida goes on to conceive what he calls an "absolute dialectic" that would recognize the grounding of individual self-identity in that reciprocal determination (*Z6* 40–41). This inevitably involves the un-objectifiable field of implacement. By contrast, Hegel's all-encompassing concept,[23] which grasps its developmental totality by sublating its individual moments, according to Nishida, still does not escape being objectified. In its self-conceptualization, whether we call it *Idee* or *Geist,* it is objectified as something specific, even as a universal, set over and above individuals (*Z6* 41). Nishida, however, de-substantializes the universal into a non-objectifiable "predicate" as ultimately implying the place wherein genuine inter-relationality (interactivity, inter-determination) obtains. This model of reality recognizes the complexity of the manifold of interrelationality and thus precludes reifying claims in regard to both the individual and the universal. Rather than reifying the whole as a metaphysical substance or as an ultimate subject of judgments, Nishida looks to the complex facticity of the concrete as an undelimitable context, enfolding and unfolding any apparent reifications or abstractions (*Z7* 274–275).

For Nishida, the focus on the grammatical subject or object, as we recall, is connected to the metaphysical substantialism traceable to Aristotle. It is also related to the general post-Platonist Greek identification of being with form and substance, that is, reality as possessing self-subsistence and definite form. Hegel's metaphysics reflects this affirmation of substantial being while incorporating Cartesian and Spinozist developments of the notion of substance into his notion of the self-conceiving concept whereby "substance is (epistemological) subject." Moreover, Hegel attaches a dynamic structure to that concept in its self-realization. But for Nishida, substance in this significance still means the grammatical subject, what can be stated. Hegel's logic, even if in certain respects it is a logic of concrete reality, still cannot help being "Greek" (*Z6* 62). It is still an object logic, a logic of noema. Nishida finds Marxist philosophy to be no different in this respect as well, failing because of its materialism to think through the meaning of social and historical reality, that is, concrete reality (*Z6* 139).

Nishida states that as long as being is conceived in terms of an object or as a grammatical subject—despite Hegel's equation at the beginning of his *Logic* of pure being and nothing as immediately selfsame (*dasselbe*) (*WL1* 67/*SL* 83)—it cannot be identical with nothing. Taken noematically, being and nothing cannot be one. But neither can being qua noema or object give rise to becoming. Nishida is here thinking of his sense of the indeterminate determining itself. Being and nothing are one only in the sense of nothing determining itself as beings. Being for Nishida is the self-determination of the nothing, the self-forming formlessness. What noematically is nothing (i.e., no thing) is determined in its self-determining as being (*Z7* 268–269). And that is how Nishida re-interprets Hegel's assertion that the truth of being (Sein) and nothing (*Nichts*) is becoming (*Werden*) (*WL1* 91–92/*SL* 104–105; *Z7* 269). The concrete for Nishida always involves this becoming or self-determination of nothing. But in its prior formlessness it escapes reduction to any propositional subject. Hence even Hegel's self-conceiving concept or self-cognizing spirit cannot do it justice. As always already assumed, the concrete perpetually eludes any such self-objectification. Instead, in order to hear that self-determining nothing, Nishida prescribes a de-focusing away from the grammatical subject, that is, in the direction of what he calls "predicate," "the predicate that does not become a grammatical subject." Any objectification remains but a partial view to, or abstraction from, that concrete whole. True dialectical unity of being and nothing, as that holistic context of our interactivity, cannot be thoroughly conceived in the noematic direction, the objectifying direction that transforms it into a subject of utterance, a thing (*Z6* 245). Nishida sees Hegel's dialectical logic as remaining trapped within such an Aristotelian orientation to the grammatical subject. For this reason he claims that his logic takes a stance that is the reverse of Hegel's substantialist dialectics (*Z10* 133–134).

Metaphysical Hierarchy and the Hegemony of the Universal

Nishida's adoption of dialectics to express the formativity of world-realization departs from Hegel's dialectic also in that its radical interrelationality precludes the sort of metaphysical hierarchy that would result from the universal's prioritization qua Geist or Idee. Hegel's universal determines itself in the individual, but it also has the sense of subsuming individuals. Yet because Hegel's universal is ultimately the idea of the whole, its precise relationship to real individual thing-events in the world remains precarious. In what sense does the ideal posit the real? To bridge the gap between thought and reality by means of thought seems one-sided. It would be an imposition of form on matter, universal over individual. As concept or idea, and as spirit in its self-knowing, the universal in Hegel still assumes primacy over individuals. Individuals, in turn, are left unfree as mere abstractions of that absolute principle (*Z13* 169, 501). Because the conception of a rational necessity operating behind the dialectical process extinguishes any genuine freedom of the individual person (*Z5* 119), there can be no sense of the individual's reverse determination (gyaku gentei) of the self-determining universal. Nishida makes the same criticism when the focus is on history as well. For Hegel, reason underlying history is what guides its course, manipulating the passions of individuals to work toward realizing its telos.[24] The true agent of history is not the individual person but universal reason manipulating the individual. Autonomy is only in the individual's identification with the absolute spirit as its self-recognition. For Nishida, this eliminates the autonomy of individuals as free creators of the world. Nishida, by the 1930s, thus opts instead for a genuine reciprocity between universal and individual, place and implaced, a dialectic transpiring within an *ur*-place delimited by nothing. For Nishida, the individual's free act is the world's self-determination, and vice versa, in dialectical interdetermination. Because the absolute is nothing but the field or place of individuals, history is made by the free acting of individuals qua historical bodies, moving as creative elements of that world's self-creativity. Nishida claims that his dialectic, in contrast to Hegel's, thus permits the individual to be thoroughly individual (Z10 105). He states that despite its hegemonic posturing, "Hegel's universal cannot truly subsume the individual. To that extent it cannot avoid being abstract" (Z6 41). No universal, conceived as concept, can exhaust the individual's transrational (i.e., trans-conceptual) singularity, its utter uniqueness with its creativity and self-contradiction. Nishida reiterates this point even in the 1940s ("Dekaruto tetsugaku ni tsuite" 「デカルト哲学について」, 1944), saying that Hegel's universal falls short of grasping the individual practical self who undergoes the dialectic of life-and-death (Z10 132–133). At the bottom of each individual person lies the tragic (*higekiteki* 悲劇的), his or her deep self-contradiction, the inner conflict that no universal concept can subsume and resolve (Z5 119). On this basis Nishida repeats his criticism of Hegel from the early 1930s to the early 1940s that Hegel's dialectic, centered on the conceptualized universal, fails to account for that concrete reality of the individual self; it remains abstract (Z6 41; Z9 144, 379, 381).[25]

While failing to account for individuality, Hegel's dialectic also fails to account for any genuine interrelationality of the concrete (Z5 138; Z10 317, 331; Z13 168, 229). A true dialectic, Nishida argues, must be radically relational to account for the complex inter-determinations between individuals and environment, their mutual self-negations. In this schema there is no dominant universal functioning as metaphysical principle. Instead, there is the place of co-implacement (Z5 270–271). Nishida seeks to explain the interrelationships involving the self-determining concrete universal and the autonomous individual in light of his notion of the manifold determinations of the dialectical universal and of place as enfolding individuals and their interrelations (Z13 110). The universal is desubstantialized in its concreteness, pointing to the space of the world of individuals. The self-determination of the dialectical universal is precisely the dialectical world as consisting of the interactivity of independent individuals, a world of the self- and inter-determination of individuals. That is, the universal in determining itself in the individuals entails its self-negation that makes room for those interrelating self-defining individuals. From the other side Nishida views the individual as breaking through the universal's determination on the basis of the singularity of the moment cut off from both past and future. Only in the present can the individual as a monadic point of space-time counter-determine the universal and make its transition from the made to the making. The nothingness at the concrete base of reality allows for the novelty of the moment. Nishida views his dialectic of the present as accounting for this, in contrast to Hegel's dialectic of future-oriented (and past-gathering) teleology.

Nishida's absolute thus does not exercise hegemonic domination over, or subsumption of, individuals. The concrete whole is absolute (zettai 絶対) only in the sense that it is absolved of all positive predications or determinations, cut off from (zetsu 絶) delimiting oppositions (tai 対). Its only attribute is its self-negation that makes room for beings (Z10 315–316). As the place of absolute nothing, it is thus characterized by its self-contradictory relationship with co-relative beings. It engages in mutual self-negation with individuals. The result is the radical dialectics of inter-determination both horizontally among individual thing-events and vertically between them and itself as their field. The vertical dimension of the dialectic, even while involving universal-individual interrelationality, is non-hierarchical, for its inter-determination happens via mutual self-negation. Nishida thus opts for a model of reality that is radically relational and precludes abstract generalizations. On this basis—that there is no absolute positivity or substantiality, and that the absolute negates itself and as such is non-substantial—metaphysical hierarchy is deconstructed. It is only in this sense that Nishida accepts Hegel's statement that the individual is the universal, that is, as entailing radical reciprocity. And thus individuals can stand without losing their singularity or autonomy under universal law. Like Laozi's *dao* ("way"), the absolute rules without ruling; it rules by letting its subjects rule themselves. But at the same time, we must not forget, individuals are also de-substantialized. The world is predicated on such mutual self-negation.

Final Thoughts Concerning Nishida and Hegel

Although Nishida has borrowed terms, concepts, and even the idea of a "dialectic" from Hegel in his concern to surmount Kantian dualism, it is clear that by the commencement of his mature thinking in the 1930s, he has come to distinguish his dialectics, which he calls "absolute dialectic" (zettai benshōhō), from Hegel's. The distinguishing features of Nishida's absolute dialectic, for example, its foundation in the notions of place, absolute nothing, and absolute negation and its radical reciprocity in the dialectical universal or inverse correspondence, extend beyond the purview of Hegelianism. Nishida uses the term "dialectical" (ben-shōhōteki 弁証法的) to describe the radical interrelationality and non-substantiality of reality in regard to both its whole and its individual elements. In that radical relationality or chiasma, opposites remain in tension as mutually referring bi-conditionals. By contrast, Hegel's dialectic is a dialectic of the process of sublation of opposites, resolving them into its all-encompassing, self-grasping concept. Nishida's absolute, however, is no such concept but instead the place enveloping the interrelations and oppositions. The place encompasses any such would-be sublational process. His absolute dialectic is thus a dialectic of place (bashoteki benshōhō). Nishida views Hegel's dialectic instead as a dialectic of the process of sublation. But the sublational process, as we saw, is also a process of self-objectification in its self-conceptualization that makes itself and the entire process into the subject of self-knowing judgment, that is, subject in both senses as knower (epistemological) and known (grammatical). In this self-objectification, it tacitly perpetuates the dualist standpoint of *theoria* that sees its subject matter out there. Nishida's dialectic of place instead acknowledges that which cannot be seen or objectified but must be assumed as implicit, the irreducible and un-reifiable holistic situation as the wherein of all being and thinking. While necessarily assumed, it cannot be made into an object or grammatical subject, even in the self-conception of an absolute idea, for such an idea must always still assume its unstatable wherein. And this wherein, from Nishida's perspective, is the world's non-substantiality that allows for the autonomous creativity of interacting individuals implaced in it. Nishida's "self-formation of the formless" allows for the freedom of the individual in the radically dialectical manifold of reciprocity. This is quite different from the idea's ordering of the historical world as its material. In short, Nishida takes Hegel's dialectic to be a dialectic of the idea and of process and distinguishes his dialectic instead as a dialectic of place and of nothing, which is also a dialectic of concrete self-contradictory (or: paradoxical) existence, a dialectic of the a-rational as opposed to rational necessity (Z5 122–123).

In conclusion, Nishida's dialectic, in contrast to Hegel's dialectic as traditionally construed, encompasses a radical interrelationality and inter-determination that precludes self-closure in any self-conceiving concept. The chiasmatic complexity of the interrelationality is such that it cannot be reduced to an idea, even an absolute one, and cannot be hypostatized, whether as an absolute subject or substance. The dialectic he develops in the 1930s thus remains true to his original idea of a "self-forming formlessness" in the concrete. His dialectic is not that of a series of sublations that culminate in an all-encompassing concept but instead a dialectic of place, the always implicit wherein that cannot be objectified or reified. To regard Nishida as a Hegelian or his work as a kind of Hegelianism, even if he makes use of Hegelian formulas and terms, is misleading, especially because Nishida himself repeatedly distinguished his position from Hegel's throughout the 1930s. The matter of his thinking here—the dialectic of radical reciprocity with the motifs of the nothing, negation, and interrelationality or inter-determination—instead may possess greater affinity to the non-dualist ideas of Mahāyāna Buddhism, traceable to the *Prajñāpāramitā sūtras*. Toward the end of his life, in "Ronri to sūri" (「論理と数理」; "Logic and Mathematics") of 1944, Nishida thus claims that his dialectic "assumes a standpoint in reverse to that of Hegel's—*it is Buddhistic*" (Z10 59).[26] To this Buddhist aspect of Nishida I now turn.[27]

9 Nishida, Buddhism, and Religion

Nɪsʜɪᴅᴀ ᴛʜʀᴏᴜɢʜᴏᴜᴛ ʜɪs philosophical career, as I have already mentioned, was concerned with what he called the "religious" (shūkyōteki 宗教的) or "religiosity" (shūkyōsei 宗教性). At the beginning of his philosophical career he wrote in his preface to *Zen no kenkyū* (『善の研究』; *An Inquiry into the Good*) that religion is "the end [*shūketsu* 終結] of philosophy" (Z1 6). For Nishida, religion is the dimension referring to the deep contradiction one feels in the depths of one's existence. It has to do with the fact of one's implacement within and on an endless openness and bottomless abyss while encountering one's own annihilation, death. According to one commentator, the statement that "religion is the end of philosophy" means that "philosophy ends in religion, or returns to religion."[1] Nishida did not, however, fully develop this issue thematically until his final works in the 1940s. In general, before the 1940s, we find Nishida somewhat reserved in referring to religious texts, especially those of the Eastern traditions, in contrast to the Western philosophical sources he frequently cited. Nevertheless, both Kyoto School followers and Western disciples of Nishida have repeatedly pointed to a "Buddhist metaphysic," reformulated in the language of Western philosophy, hidden within Nishida's formulations. Although it may be too simplistic to read Nishida's entire project as nothing but a modernized version of Mahāyāna metaphysics, I think that any serious student of Eastern thought would recognize Mahāyānist components in Nishida's dialectical thinking. They are there even before the final essays of the 1940s, in which Nishida acknowledges more openly some sort of connection. We can find references throughout his career to classical Buddhist texts, such as the *Diamond Sūtra* and the *Prajñāpāramitā sūtras* in general, the *Rinzairoku*, and the *Mumonkan*, and to Buddhist thinkers like Shinran, Nansen, Rinzai, Daitō Kokushi, Dōgen, and others.

In discussing Nishida's relationship to Buddhism, one can first point to his practice of Zen meditation, which he began in 1897 and continued from his late twenties through his thirties. He spent some time training in Zen at the Engaku-ji in Kamakura, where his school friend Suzuki Daisetsu (D. T. Suzuki), who later became a world-famous Zen popularizer, was studying. He undertook some *kōan* (公安) training and passed the Zen kōan of mu (無; "nothing") under his Zen teacher in 1903, when he was in his early thirties. Two years later he began his drafting of *Zen no kenkyū*.[2] His Zen practice has been noted by many commentators, even to the point of stereotyping Nishida as a "Zen thinker." Its influence on his thinking, most obviously in his maiden work, *Zen no kenkyū,* is difficult to deny. In the actual text Zen is mentioned very little, but scholars have claimed that they have found implicit references there to kōans from classical Zen texts, such as the *Hekiganroku* (『碧巌録』; *Blue Cliff Record*) and the *Mumonkan* (『無門関』; *Gateless Barrier*).[3] The opening of *Zen no kenkyū,* where Nishida characterizes "pure experience" (junsui keiken 純粋経験) as "to know facts just as they are," without the subject-object split—even if he may have originally adapted the term from William James[4]—is reminiscent of the Zen understanding of enlightenment. Many commentators have thus taken Nishida's philosophy as an expression in philosophical language (the language of Aristotle, Neo-Kantianism, German idealism, Hegel, and Marxism) of his lived experience of Zen.[5] Two years before his death, in a letter to his student Nishitani Keiji (February 19, 1943), Nishida writes that it had been his dearest wish since his thirties to unite Zen and philosophy despite the impossibility this would entail (Z23 73).[6] But in the same letter he also admonishes those who unthinkingly classify his thought as "Zen philosophy."[7] In the same year (July 27, 1943) he also writes to his student Mutai Risaku that his final aim is to connect Buddhist thought and the modern scientific spirit through his logic of place (Z23 123). This interest was not confined merely to the Zen version of Mahāyāna, however; he writes in another letter to Mutai (January 6, 1945), just before beginning work on his final essay ("Bashoteki ronri to shūkyōteki sekaikan" 「場所的論理と宗教的世界観」), that he would like to work on the worldview of Jōdo Shinshū (浄土真宗; True Pure Land school) (Z23 319). In fact, the influence of Pure Land Buddhism cannot be ignored even in his early years. His mother was a serious devotee of Jōdo Shinshū, and the Hokuriku area of Japan, where he was born and raised and taught for a while, is permeated with Shinshū teachings. And early on in his career he associated with colleagues from Ōtani University, a True Pure Land institution, and wrote an essay on Shinran (親鸞) (1173–1263), "Gutoku Shinran" ("Shinran, the Lay Fool") for Shinran's 650th death anniversary, during the same year *Zen no kenkyū* was published (1911).[8] Nor should we ignore the major influence of the True Pure Land thinker Kiyozawa Manshi (清沢満之) (1863–1903) on Nishida during his early years. Nishida had some contact with Kiyozawa when the two cooperated in 1897 to produce an issue of a True Pure Land Buddhist journal.[9] He deeply revered Kiyozawa and intimately mingled with his students at Ōtani University.[10] And alongside Kiyozawa there was also his contemporary Inoue Enryō (井上円了) (1858–1919), another major modern philosophical predecessor of Nishida and also of True Pure Land Buddhist background. Both Kiyozawa and Enryō worked hard to bring Buddhism and Western philosophy into conversation, and Nishida was much indebted to both. What is interesting is that they were both Pure Land Buddhists but constructed dialectical systems using Western philosophical concepts that seem very much in line with Tendai (Ch. Tiantai 天台) or Kegon (Ch. Huayan 華厳) Mahāyāna dialectics.

Many people would not associate Nishida's dialectics with Pure Land thought but, remarkably, it may be possible to trace Nishida's later dialectical evolution in his thinking to both these Pure Land Buddhist thinkers. But it is also the kernel of Pure Land thought that held Nishida's philosophical interest. Just as some have found references to Zen in *Zen no kenkyū*, others have found references to True Pure Land concepts and Shinran's ideas in the same text. Thus not only Zen but also True Pure Land Buddhism supplied an implicit Buddhist background to his maiden work, *Zen no kenkyū*.

After that initial theme of pure experience, throughout the oeuvre of what is called "Nishidian philosophy," from the late 1920s onward, we find plenty of motifs that suggest Buddhist Mahāyāna origins. As the most conspicuous examples, one can mention the unity of opposites or contradictory self-identity, absolute nothing, and mutual self-negation, comparable to the non-dualist notions of inter-dependent origination, emptiness, and mutual non-obstruction found in Madhyamaka, Huayan (Jp. Kegon), and Tiantai (Jp. Tendai) thought. One commentator, Michiko Yusa, has claimed that "the Mahāyāna Buddhist assertion of the radical inter-dependence and inter-penetration of individuals sustains Nishida's fundamental position."[11] The "Basho" essay of 1926 that initiates Nishidian philosophy, in working out a dialectic of negation from the (under)ground of experience, appears to draw from the Buddhist tradition its conception of an absolute nothing (zettai mu 絶対無) that envelops our being qua place. The term "absolute nothing" does not appear in Buddhist literature, but we do find the concept of "nothing" (mu; Ch. *wu* 無) in works of Chan and Zen (禅). After its introduction in 1926 Nishida develops this idea further in his works of the 1930s and 1940s with explicit connections to his religious concerns. His final essay of 1945, "Bashoteki ronri to shūkyōteki sekaikan," especially brings out the religious implications of that idea in a way that makes us feel its nearness to the Mahāhāyana motif of emptiness. But it would be wrong to say that there were no direct references to Buddhism in earlier works. Even during the early years of Nishidian philosophy, for example, in *Ippansha no jikakuteki taikei* (『一般者の自覚的体系』) of 1930, we find Nishida quoting a famous passage from the *Heart Sūtra:* "Form is emptiness, emptiness is form" (Z4 357). Aside from a few such direct references, however, his allusions to Buddhist ideas in the early years are subtle— as in the implicit references noted earlier in *Zen no kenkyū*—and except for the concept of nothing (mu), he makes little direct use of Buddhist terminology, in contrast to his employment of Western philosophical terms. It is only in the works of the late 1930s and 1940s that he makes frequent reference to Mahāyāna Buddhist sources. Most notably, in "Bashoteki ronri to shūkyōteki sekaikan" (1945), he quotes the *Diamond Sūtra* and Daitō Kokushi (大燈國師) (Myōchō Shūhō 宗峰妙超; 1282–1337/1338) (e.g., Z10 316–317) and makes use of ideas coming from Chan texts such as *The Platform Sūtra of the Sixth Patriarch* (『六祖壇經』) and *The*

Record of Linji (Ch. *Linji yü lü*, Jp. *Rinzairoku*『臨済録』), Zen thinkers such as Dōgen (道元) (1200–1253) and Ikkyū (一休) (1394–1481), and the True Pure Land school and Shinran. And certainly the influence of *Prajñāpāramita* notions, at least as conveyed by Nishida's close colleague and friend D. T. Suzuki's readings, is evident as well in his last works. Nishida's debt to Buddhist non-dualism no longer seems so inconspicuous in his last works. Read backward from the standpoint of that 1945 essay, his dialectic even of the mid-1930s appears to express, whether intentionally or not, the non-dualist strand of Mahāyāna philosophy that originated in the *Prajñāpāramitā sūtras*.[12] David Dilworth has pointed out that the non-duality indicated in Mahāyāna thought can never be adequately framed within the dialectical language of Hegel.[13] As we have already seen, Nishida made much use of that Hegelian terminology. Despite that fact, we find evidence that toward the end of his life Nishida saw himself in opposition to Hegelian dialectics as inheriting, but also developing, the standpoint of Mahāyāna Buddhist philosophy (Z10 69).

In this regard, we cannot ignore the close relationship between Nishida and his friend from his student days, the world-famous Zen scholar D. T. Suzuki (Suzuki Daisetsu 鈴木大拙) (1870–1966). As some commentators have noted, Nishida's use of Buddhist sūtras is imprecise, and he does not engage in any kind of textual criticism or exegesis of the Buddhist texts he cites.[14] It is undeniable that Nishida absorbed much of his "academic" knowledge of Buddhism through his association with his lifelong friend Suzuki.[15] Mutai Risaku, who knew them both and witnessed their friendship, writes in his *Shisaku to kansatsu* (『思索と観察』; *Thought and Observation*) that Suzuki and Nishida influenced each other and held in common the view concerning the contradictory nature of reality. Both thinkers found this contradictory nature abundantly manifest within the thought of Mahāyāna Buddhism, including both Zen and Jōdo Shin (True Pure Land). According to Mutai, Nishida highly valued among Suzuki's works *Mushin to iū koto* (『無心と言う事』; *That Which Is Called No Mind*) (1939), *Jōdokei shisōron* (『浄土系思想論』; *A Theory of the Thinking of the Pure Land School*) (1942), and *Nihonteki reisei* (『日本的霊性』; *Japanese Spirituality*) (1944), taking them as exemplary of "religious philosophy." Notice that these books were published during the years when Nishida was making his connections with Mahāyāna thought more explicit. Mutai expresses his belief that Nishida's philosophy of religion in his final essay of 1945, "Bashoteki ronri to shūkyōteki sekaikan," was influenced by his intellectual exchange with Suzuki and his exposure to Suzuki's ideas during the period from the late 1930s to the early 1940s.[16] Especially Suzuki's *Nihonteki reisei* develops what Suzuki calls "the logic of soku-hi" (sokuhi no ronri 即非の論理) (e.g., Z10 316). Nishida began working on his 1945 essay around the same time at which he was given this text by Suzuki. This is significant in that Nishida refers in his essay to what he calls the "logic of soku-hi" of the *Prajñāpāramitā*s. In a letter to Suzuki in the following months (March 11, 1945), Nishida explains how he is writing about religion in an attempt to clarify its conception in terms of his "logic of contradictory self-identity, i.e., the logic of soku-hi" (Z23 348). Nishida also writes in a letter to another student, Hisamatsu Shinichi (April 12, 1945), that in this essay he attempts to show what is unique and excellent about Buddhism vis-à-vis Christianity (Z23 372). It thus appears that through his intellectual exchanges with Suzuki in his later years (late 1930s to early 1940s), Nishida was stimulated to pay more direct attention to the affinity of his thinking with Mahāyāna thought. In a 1938 lecture ("Nihon bunka no mondai" 「日本文化の問題」; "The Problem of Japanese Culture"), for example, while claiming that he did not directly derive his dialectical notion that "one is many and many is one" from Buddhist doctrines per se, Nishida acknowledges that it is an "Eastern way of thinking" found also in the dialectic of Mahāyāna Buddhism. The two ways of thinking—his and that of Mahāyāna—are thus commensurable (Z13 22). It appears that having developed his dialectic along his own philosophical path, with a closer look into these Buddhist doctrines Nishida in his later years came to feel that some deep source common to both had been at work within his thinking. That is, irrespective of whether he had intentionally or unintentionally drawn inspiration from Mahāyāna themes in his earlier works, Nishida through his association with Suzuki had come to feel more strongly than before a deep commensurability between his and Mahāyāna concepts.

We need still to exercise caution, however, so as not to reduce the uniqueness and complexity of Nishida's thinking by categorizing it as nothing but Buddhist or Mahāyāna thought. Notice that Nishida carefully pointed out that his dialectic that "one is many and many is one" does not depend on Mahāyāna Buddhism (Z13 22). To the extent that the stimulus for Nishida's thinking was Western philosophy, even the Zen influence from his meditational practice was never pushed to the forefront for most of his writing career.[17] His philosophizing sought to overcome certain issues, most notably the issue of dualism raised in the works of Western philosophers. His response to them was accordingly articulated in the language of Western philosophy. In this, Nishida saw himself as engaging in a nonsectarian philosophical search for truth. Even his explicit use of Buddhist ideas in his final essay of 1945, as Dilworth notes, moves beyond the sectarian boundaries of traditional Buddhist thought to achieve the status of a world philosophy.[18] And in relation to his usage of Buddhist ideas, especially in his discussion of religiosity in that final essay, we need to also acknowledge his many references to Christianity. In addition to Buddhism, Nishida also studied Christianity, and we find him referring in different works to the Old Testament prophets, the New Testament, Christian concepts of kenosis, agapē, and logos, and Christian thinkers such as St. Paul, St. Augustine, Nicholas of Cusa, Luther, Montaigne, Pascal, Kierkegaard, Dostoevsky, Barth, and Tillich, among others. In his younger years, while he practiced sitting meditation or *zazen* (座禅) and undertook kōan training under Zen masters, he was also an avid reader of the Gospels. This fact that in his encounter with Buddhism Nishida brings Christianity into the picture makes his stance vis-à-vis Buddhism no simple matter. We need to recognize the uniqueness of his dialectical thought, moreover, when it is viewed in light of the history of Buddhist thought. This uniqueness would include, for example, his understanding of the unfolding of history and the role of humanity therein, involving our interaction with the environment and entailing a bodily prāxis that is hence historical in significance. Even his notion of place enfolding everything, including contradictories, while developing the Mahāyāna notions of emptiness and interdependence, goes beyond traditional Buddhist formulations.

In the following sections I will look into the connections between the Nishidian and the Buddhist concepts of nothing and emptiness; contradiction and soku-hi (即非); the dialectical universal and the dharmadhātu of non-obstruction and inter-dependent origination; depth in the ordinary and the present; and myōgō (名号) ("name") and tariki (他力) ("other-power") (along with the comparable Christian notions of kenosis and gratia) and inverse correspondence (gyakutaiō 逆対応).

Emptiness, Nothing, Negation

As I have already mentioned, Nishida's texts in general are short on traditional Buddhist references. The one exception, of course, is the concept of nothing (mu) and its concomitant activity of negation (hitei 否定), appearing throughout his oeuvre ever since the inception of Nishidian philosophy. Mu is a principal concept of Japanese Mahāyāna Buddhism, but Nishida develops it in his own manner in dialogue with Western philosophy and initially independently of any direct references to Buddhist scripture. It is this concept of mu that Nishida often points to when he is distinguishing his dialectic of place from the dialectic of Hegel, which he characterizes as a "dialectic of being [yū 有]." One might then ask to what degree this concept of nothing that distinguishes Nishida from Hegel makes Nishida's thought Buddhistic. It is, however, only in his final years that Nishida comes to examine in detail this concept in its explicitly Buddhist context. The Buddhist source of this idea, nevertheless, is difficult to deny. Dilworth has noticed, for example, a Buddhist antecedent to, and possible influence on, the metaphor of self-mirroring nothing in the Buddhist classic *The Awakening of Faith in the Mahāyāna* (Jp. *Daijō kishinron*『大乗起信論』), wherein the essence of enlightenment is stated to be like an empty space and a contentless mirror.[19] Kosaka has claimed that for Nishida "religious consciousness" (*shūkyōteki ishiki* 宗教的意識) is precisely "the self-awareness of absolute nothing" in the double sense of the genitive, where absolute nothing is both the subject and object of awareness.[20] In Japanese Bud dhism the term *mu* is another way of speaking of the Mahāyāna concept of kū (空), emptiness (śūnyatā), the open sky. Whether Nishida was explicitly conscious of any such influence when he first started using the idea of mu in his early works is another matter. The awareness of a connection, however, shows in his later works. In discussing the self-determination of absolute nothing (zettai mu) in terms of its absolute negation (zettai hitei 絶対否定), Nishida, in one of his later essays from the 1940s, "Kūkan" (「空間」; "Space"), makes a direct reference to "the true emptiness of Buddhism" (bukkyō no shinkū 仏教の真空) (Z10 157). A little earlier, in a letter of November 6, 1939, Nishida appears to have in mind *prajñā*-intuition when he writes that he has always had a deep interest in the vision of emptiness (*kūkan* 空観), a vision on which he would like to build his philosophy (Z19, 1980 ed., 90).[21] One can also notice an affinity between Nishida's characterization of the absolute (zettai 絶対) (that is nothing) as self-negating and Nāgārjuna's notion of śūnyatāyāh śūnyatā, the emptiness of emptiness. As I noted in chapter 8, this is one of the points that distinguishes Nishida's conception of the absolute from Hegel's, for the absolute's self-negation is what precludes in Nishida the subordination of individuals under the universal's hegemony. If the universal were empty, any threat of a unilateral totalization would be perpetually destabilized. In Mahāyāna both the individual (i.e., forms) and the so-called universal (i.e., emptiness) are empty, and this enables their simultaneity or non-duality while disabling any reduction of the one to the other. On this basis one might claim that Nishida's original concept of zettai mu (absolute nothing) certainly does give expression to "the formless" that he states has nurtured the traditions of the East (Z3 255). This in turn makes the connection of mu that has become a "standard hybrid trope"[22] of the Kyoto School with Buddhist metaphysics even more suggestive.

We can distinguish not only Nishida's absolute from Hegel's through its association with Buddhist nothing but also Nishida's Buddhistic concept of the nothing from Hegel's understanding of nothingness. For Hegel, nothingness is relative to being and but a moment within the dialectic of being and non-being in the process of becoming. For Nishida, the nothing is absolute (zettai); as self-forming formlessness it enfolds and unfolds everything else in its creative self-negation. Consciousness cannot function without assuming that pre-given nothing that provides, via its self-determination, the space of its implacement (Z5 82). To explain this, Nishida in his 1945 essay "Bashoteki ronri to shūkyōteki sekaikan" makes use of an ancient Buddhist expression: "With no place wherein it abides, this mind arises" (Z10 329). The mind in authentic self-realization arises in a place delimited by absolutely nothing. Absolute nothing here serves to negate all apparent substances, including the knowing subject itself. The subject or spirit here, then, cannot be absolute; it is always implaced in the pre-given un-objectifiable place of concrete immediacy. Nishida had already in 1931 found self-awareness in terms of nothing, the self-determination of nothing, mu, to be operative behind Hegel's dialectic (e.g., *Z5* 123–124; *Z7* 271). The deepening of self-analysis in light of that dark abyssal place, the place of absolute nothing, eradicates or extinguishes any rationalist attempt to reduce concrete awareness to a self-conceiving concept in Hegelian fashion. What Nishida expresses in the thought of the nothing is rather a self-learning that is a "self-forgetting" in the fashion of the Zen thinker Dōgen, as we shall see later.

This non-substantiality of the nothing is a far cry, however, from any ontological nihilism, for the self-negation of nothing serves to simultaneously affirm the beings it embraces as their place; it makes room for their co-being (*Z10* 315–316). Nishida's motion here is comparable to that of the Mahāyāna middle path—the emptiness of emptiness (śūnyatāyāh śūnyatā) I just mentioned that avoids ontological reification, on the one hand, and annihilation, on the other. For Nishida, it is this self-negation of the absolute that affirmatively establishes the personal self and the world of such individuals. His final 1945 essay states that absolute negation qua affirmation is "God's creation." But since absolute negation here must be mutual, in the reciprocity of inverse correspondence, Nishida expresses this in Buddhistic fashion: "Because there is Buddha, there are sentient beings, and because there are sentient beings, there is Buddha" (*Z10* 324–325). Stating that the true God cannot be simply an utterly transcendent God but rather what the mystical theologians of the West have called Gottheit (Godhead, Godhood), Nishida immediately adds that this "is the emptiness of the *Prajñāpāramitā* [*sūtras*]" (*hannya no kū* 般若の空) (*Z10* 104–105). One might thus say that the entire dialectic of mutual self-negation between absolute and relative, world and beings, universal and individuals, in the non-substantial and de-substantializing matrix of the nothing as place is Nishida's rendering of the non-dualist concept of emptiness (śūnyatā) in explicitly dialectical terms.

I have already noted in discussing the concept of inverse correspondence that the self-negation of the absolute is to be matched by man's own self-negation. Nishida in several of his works makes use of Dōgen's statement that "to learn the Buddha way is to learn the self; to learn the self means to forget the self; and to forget the self means to be authenticated by the ten thousand dharmas" (*Z10* 336; see also *Z8* 512, 514; *Z10* 326). Nishida takes Dōgen's statement as a repudiation of the dogmatic substantialization of the self predicated on self-attachment and further as exemplifying what he means by absolute negation (or self-negation) (*Z8* 512). At the ground of its foundation, where life meets death, the self touches on absolute negation, and one dies to oneself (*Z8* 514). The true self lies where the abstract self, the substantialized ego serving as the subject of consciousness, is negated. Nishida finds this true self in the oneness of body-and-mind in its dynamic interaction with the world, a practical standpoint that cannot be approached through an Aristotelian orientation to the grammatical subject. Breaking away from that Aristotelian orientation, we arrive at a concrete standpoint that is the reverse of that of Hegel's rational or idealist dialectics (Z10 133–134). It is the existential awareness of one's self-contradiction in the depths of one's being, an experience of one's being qua life-and-death, which Nishida also calls the standpoint of "religious self-awareness." He finds this religious self-awareness evident in several different religions. For example, he finds the motif of dying to one's ego not only in Dōgen's Zen but also in the True Pure Land Buddhist idea of relying on other-power (tariki) (Z8 514). In both Dōgen's "forgetting oneself" and True Pure Land's "relying on other-power," one discovers true self-identity in self-negation, one's inner existential strife that is not sublated but rather lived. In discussing self-negation, Nishida also refers to Dōgen's comment (from "Seishi" 「生死」 ["Life and Death"] in *Shōbōgenzō* 『正法眼蔵』) that "this life and death is the life of the Buddha" and Dōgen's notion of "dropping off body-and-mind" (*shinjin datsuraku* 身心脱落) (from "Genjōkōan" 「現成公案」 in *Shōbōgenzō*), as well as to Shinran's concept of "spontaneity through the working of the dharma" (*jinen hōni* 自然法爾) (Z9 75). We can thus say that the paired concepts of nothing and negation bring Nishida's thinking into proximity with that of Mahāyāna, and moreover that Nishida was—or at least became—aware of this closeness. But we should not forget that Nishda also makes reference, in relation to self-negation or emptying, to Paul's statement in his Letter to the Galatians (2:20) that "it is no longer I who live, but Christ who lives in me" (Z9 74). So we cannot deny the presence of a Christian element in his discussion of absolute negation as well.

Contradiction, Soku-hi, and the Middle Path

We noticed earlier the proximity of, and possible connection between, Nishida's conception of the absolute's self-negation—the nothingness of the absolute that he designated absolute nothing—on the one hand, and the Mahāyāna notion of the emptiness of emptiness, on the other. The other major concept of his work that sounds particularly Buddhist is that of absolutely contradictory self-identity (zettai mujunteki jikodōitsu 絶対矛盾的自己同一). Therein one can observe a motif quite conspicuous within Mahāyāna Buddhism: its various formulations of the nonduality between opposites on the basis of their non-substantiality, such as between nirvāṇa and saṃsāra or between śūnyatā (emptiness) and rūpa (form). This is an idea traceable to the *Prajñāpāramitā sūtras*, for example, the well-known statement in the *Heart Sūtra* that "form is emptiness, emptiness as such is form" (rūpam śūnyatā śūnyataiva rūpam). The collapsing of opposites in both Nishida and Mahāyāna treads a middle path that avoids the reification of being as substance, on the one hand, and the annihilation of being into utter nothing, on the other. A major feature of that paradoxical mode of thinking, recognizable in both Mahāyāna and Nishida, is what we might call "double transcendence" or "double negation," a "trans-descendence," which precludes any sort of unilateral reduction, as we have already seen in the Mahāyāna notion of the emptiness of emptiness, and which may be contrasted with a tendency within Hegel toward totalization under a hegemonic universal. Nishida's friend D. T. Suzuki has traced that dialectic of the middle in Mahāyāna to the *Prajñāpāramitā sūtras*, which he finds to be characterized by a mode of thinking that he calls "logic of soku-hi" (sokuhi no ronri). Suzuki's influence on Nishida in this regard is conspicuous in Nishida's final essay, in which he frequently refers to the logic of soku-hi of the *Prajñāpāramitās*. In this section I will discuss the possible connections between Nishida's idea of contradictory identity and Suzuki's logic of soku-hi in light of the Mahāyāna notion of the middle path.

The double negation or trans-descendence—the emptiness of emptiness—just mentioned is what constitutes Mahāyāna Buddhism's so-called middle path. In chapter 2 I noted some of the differences between that middle path of Mahāyāna and the sublational dialectic of Hegel. As opposed to Hegel's dialectic, the nondual middle of Mahāyāna (1) escapes conceptual reduction and (2) involves the simultaneity of opposites as bi-conditionals, which thus (3) allows for genuine contradiction via emptiness as opposed to conceptual resolution. The point of Mahāyāna practice, one might say, is to experience or realize that emptiness. If we contrast Mahāyāna's middle path with Hegel's sublational dialectic, Nishida certainly appears closer to Mahāyāna in content despite his terminology. Nishida, throughout the 1930s and 1940s, declares that his dialectical and holistic understanding of the concrete is neither monism nor pluralism, neither idealism nor materialism, neither teleology nor mechanism, neither universalism nor individualism. He rejects both the Aristotelian reduction of reality to the individual substance and the Platonist subordination of individuals under a universal idea. Each position on its own is an abstraction from the chiasmatic complexity of the concrete. Rather, Nishida's middle position embraces individuality and universality, parts and whole, many and one, and so on in their interrelationality. His dialectical matrix, precluding reduction to any of these terms, as well as to mere being or mere non-being, thus appears to epitomize the Mahāyāna middle. The Mahāyāna middle path avoids the reductive extremes of utter nothing in nihilism (uccheda) and of substantial being in eternalism (śāśvata). Nishida's self-contradictory identity almost appears to be a direct descendant of that Mahāyāna middle that empties both absolute substantiality and utter annihilation, preventing any unilateral transcendence that would annihilate relativity or individuality. Nishida, with his dialectic, treads that middle path.[23]

Having developed the dialectical and middle-treading concept of contradictory identity during the 1930s, Nishida subsequently turns his attention more directly to his religious concerns in the 1940s. He articulates a dialectic of religiosity with explicit textual references to religious sources, especially Buddhist but also Christian. And on the basis of these direct references to religious sources, his dialectic of contradictory identity, together with the newer formulation of inverse correspondence, can be seen in a clearer Buddhist light. For example, Nishida identifies what he had been calling the contradictory self-identity between many and one as the logic that has been operative behind "the religion of Eastern nothing," in which "mind is Buddha." He claims that through that absolutely contradictory self-identity of the world as one and many, each individual self faces the absolute in the present. He explains this in terms of the individual's self-contradiction. The religious understanding that "mind is Buddha" entails that we penetrate this principle of "all is one" by dying to the ego in the depths of self-contradiction (*Z8* 421). On several occasions Nishida refers to Tendai (Ch. Tiantai) Buddhism, with its notion of "three thousand worlds in one thought" (*ichinensanzen* 一念三千), as the model of the principle that "one is many" (*ichi soku ta* 一即多) (e.g., *Z9* 71). With this stance Nishida again sees himself moving in a direction opposite to that of the object logic that he still finds in Hegel. He asserts that a truly absolute dialectic, that is, a dialectic of contradictory identity, is instead to be found in the Buddhist doctrine of the *Prajñāpāramitā sūtras* that gives expression to the intuitive wisdom (prajñā) of the emptiness of all (*Z10* 317, 399). As I mentioned earlier, Suzuki's influence is evident here, and Nishida approvingly quotes Suzuki's explanation of prajñā as a true self-awareness that is the discrimination of non-discrimination (*Z10* 109).[24] Nishida thus detects a connection between his dialectic of contradictory self-identity and the prajñā stance of the *Prajñāpāramitā sūtras* that his friend Suzuki calls the "logic of soku-hi" (sokuhi no ronri). In his final essay Nishida looks to that literature of the *Prajñāpāramitās* and its so-called logic of soku-hi, to which we now turn.

The intellectual exchange between Nishida and Suzuki was one of mutual influence on each other's scholarship. Although Suzuki with his expertise on Buddhism shaped Nishida's understanding of that topic, it has also been suggested that Nishida's philosophy in turn influenced Suzuki's reading of Mahāyāna doctrines. Suzuki had initially stressed the a-rational and experiential dimensions of Zen Buddhism, but by the late 1930s, realizing the importance of its philosophical and doctrinal dimensions, he came to emphasize—perhaps under the influence of Nishida's logic of contradictory self-identity—what he viewed as the characteristic logical structure found in the *Prajñāpāramitā sūtras*, especially the *Diamond Sūtra* (Jp. *Kongōkyō* 金剛経).[25] The logical structure assumes the paradoxical form of equation via negation, which he formulates as "*A* is not-*A*, therefore *A* is *A*."[26] This is the logical structure that Suzuki designates as "the logic of soku-hi [is and is-not]." But just as Nishida's logic may have been a catalyst that formed Suzuki's reading of Mahāyāna doctrines, Nishida on his part repeatedly received instruction from Suzuki about the ideas, literature, and terminology of Buddhism and incorporated them into his works.[27] As I noted earlier in this section, Nishida, in his final essay of 1945, repeatedly made use of Suzuki's reading of the *Prajñāpāramitās* in terms of a logic of soku-hi. But if Suzuki's logic of soku-hi influenced Nishida's view of contradictory self-identity, Nishida's thought concerning contradictory self-identity may earlier have influenced Suzuki's reading of those Buddhist scriptures in light of soku-hi logic. It appears that the exchange of ideas between Suzuki and Nishida was truly reciprocal. Nishida's dialectic, as found earlier in the 1930s, despite its affinity with Mahāyāna non-dualism, was not simply composed out of pre-existing notions he already possessed on the basis of his understanding of Buddhist doctrines. If Mutai's observation of the two thinkers is correct, not only did Suzuki instruct Nishida concerning Buddhist doctrines, but also Nishida's philosophy in turn influenced Suzuki's interpretations of Mahāyāna doctrines. But for such reciprocity to be possible, there must have been something commensurable between Nishida's dialectic and Mahāyāna doctrines to begin with. In a letter to Suzuki (May 11, 1945), Nishida writes that he takes his logic of absolutely contradictory self-identity to be in one aspect the *Prajñāpāramitā* logic of soku-hi (*hannya sokuhi no ronri* 般若即非の論理). He immediately adds, however, that he thinks that something unique and distinct emerges in its determination as the contradictory self-identity of one and many (*Z23* 386). In any case, Nishida during the 1940s—perhaps on the basis of a felt commensurability between the two ideas—begins employing the term *soku-hi* in explicating his notion of contradictory self-identity.

By the 1940s, as a result of his intellectual exchange with Suzuki, we find Nishida fully incorporating the discourse of soku-hi logic into his dialectical philosophy of religion. In elucidating his concepts of the place of nothing, contradictory identity, and inverse correspondence, Nishida appropriates Suzuki's logic of soku-hi while employing passages from Buddhist texts, especially the *Prajñāpāramitā sūtras.*[28] For example, after discussing the absolutely contradictory self-identity between the absolute and the relative, between the absolute's holistic oneness and the manifold of individuals, between the absolute's transcendence of and immanence in the world, Nishida, in that final essay of 1945, "Bashoteki ronri to shūkyōteki sekaikan," refers to Suzuki's reading (*Kongōkyō no zen* 『金剛経の禅』; *The Zen of the Diamond Sūtra*) of the *Diamond Sūtra* as expressing the same paradox in soku-hi logical terms. He quotes the famous passage from the *Diamond Sūtra:* "Because all dharmas [thing-events] are not all dharmas, they are called all dharmas; because the Buddha is no Buddha, he is the Buddha; because sentient beings are not sentient beings, they are sentient beings" (*Z10* 316–317). The point of the *Diamond Sūtra* is that nothing exists in virtue of itself; nothing is ontologically independent; everything is what it is because of its relationship to what it is not. For something to be what it is, it cannot just be what it is by itself. Even the Buddha can never stand on his own as the Buddha. (Or, at least, he does not regard himself as such; he is free of ego-centricity.) And hence the Buddha is Buddha because he is not Buddha.

Nishida applies the soku-hi logic of the *Diamond Sūtra* to God to explain what he means by "absolute." An utterly transcendent God that is without any reference or relation to anything else, as utterly independent in self-identity, is no true God. God cannot be conceived in terms of object logic as such a substance. Just as the dharmas in the *Diamond Sūtra* are dharmas in their emptiness, God must empty himself in order to be God. The absolute must contain self-negation within itself whereby it inverts itself into the relative. The holistic one thus maintains itself in the plurality of individuals. The creativity of the absolute is in the affirmation of God's absolute negation within himself. The divine love that creates the world in self-negation thus cannot be conceived in terms of the object logic of self-affirmative substance. That would reduce God to a non-self-contradictory Aristotelian substance. Rather, God's self-identity as a true absolute is mediated by absolute negation in terms of *Prajñāpāramitā* soku-hi logic (Z10 333). Hence God's relationship with the world or with man is more fundamental than God's self-being.[29] Nishida's God here is thus a dialectical God who is both transcendent and immanent, an absolute that maintains itself in absolutely contradictory self-identity, whereby the absolute "is absolutely being because it is absolutely nothing; in absolute rest because it is in absolute movement" (Z10 335). Already in 1919 Nishida had borrowed a phrase from the fifteenth-century Christian mystic Nicholas of Cusa, *coincidentia oppositorum* (coincidence of opposites), whereby God can be said neither to exist nor to not exist, to express a similar notion (Z14, 1966 ed., 295–300). And in the 1940s he also refers to Kierkegaard's notion of the absolute paradox in the God-man relationship in discussing his own notion of absolutely contradictory self-identity (Z9 189). By 1944, however, Nishida finds this dialectic to be best expressed by the *Prajñāpāramitā* logic of soku-hi and even asserts in a letter that "what envelops the opposite opposition of world and individual in contradictory self-identity is the Buddha . . . , and not the Christian God that is merely in opposition to the individual."[30] He claims that only its thought "thoroughly penetrates such absolute dialectic" to give full expression to absolutely contradictory self-identity (Z10 317, 321; see also 335). He thus regards its soku-hi logic as fully epitomizing the absolute dialectic that he had been contrasting with Hegel's sublational dialectic. And Nishida applies this same soku-hi formulation from the *Diamond Sūtra* to the human self or mind that is in inverse correspondence with God as well. In 1944 ("Yoteichōwa o tebiki to shite shūkyōtetsugaku e" 「予定調和を手引きとして宗教哲学へ」; "Toward a Philosophy of Religion with Pre-established Harmony as Guide"), in order to explain his vision of self-awareness in terms of self-contradiction or self-negation in distinction from the self-affirmative stance of the Cartesian cogito, Nishida quotes another passage from that sūtra: "Because all minds are not minds, they are called mind" (Z10 109).

The two, man and God, finite and absolute, meet in the inverse correspondence of their mutual self-negation so that they are in absolutely contradictory self-identity. To show this, Nishida makes use of a Buddhist saying taken from the Zen master Myōchō (Daitō Kokushi): "Buddha and I, parted through a billion *kalpas* of time, yet not separate for a single instant; encountering each other the whole day through, yet not encountering each other for an instant" (Z10 104). Throughout the 1940s Nishida makes use of this passage in several different works. He seems to understand this passage to mean that when one feels one's separation from God or Buddha, at that moment of utter despair, one in fact is in contact with God or Buddha; and in reverse that when one feels confident that one is in contact with the absolute, one is infinitely separated from it. It illustrates the inverse correspondence of mutual self-negation: one meets God only in dying to one's ego. Nishida returns to this passage several times in order to exhibit the dialectic of religiosity. What makes such a dialectic possible, according to Nishida, is not Aristotle's substance logic but rather the *Prajñāpāramitā* logic of soku-hi.

Within Indian Buddhist philosophy, the first important interpreter of that paradoxical thought of the *Prajñāpāramitā sūtras* was Nāgārjuna of the Mādhyamika school. Scholars usually take this to be the commencement of systematic philosophy within Mahāyāna. This Mādhyamika school further developed what Suzuki and Nishida found in the *Prajñāpāramitā sūtras*. We see, for example, a collapsing of opposites, comparable to Nishida's, in Nāgārjuna's *tetralemma* (four-fold negation of is, is-not, both is and is-not, and neither is nor is-not) and the concomitant theory of the two truths of the relative or conventional (saṃvṛti-satya) and the ultimate or absolute (paramārtha-satya).[31] The tetralemma is meant to disclose the provisional nature (saṃvṛti) of all truth-claims while simultaneously referring to an ultimate truth (paramārtha) in regard to their emptiness, that is, the absence of any permanent eternal essence or substance. A statement, even if it is provisionally true, is ultimately empty in virtue of its provisional nature. Yet because emptiness signifies this lack of ontological independence or ultimacy, it does not point to anything separate and beyond the provisional: "Whatever is dependently arisen, that is emptiness."[32] In that sense, neither is emptiness really ultimate. Both truths, provisional and ultimate, thus refer to the same reality that things are conventionally real but substantially unreal. While they are not utterly unreal, neither are they ultimately real as substances. Hence Nāgārjuna's theory of two truths takes saṃsāra and nirvāṇa to be not two distinct realms but rather alternative perspectives of the same reality of empty phenomena, with neither side possessing its "own-being" or "self-nature" (sva-bhāva).[33] This is the Mādhyamika standpoint of the middle way that collapses the distinction between opposites, such as being and nothing or many and one, via their emptiness without reifying one at the expense of the other or annihilating either for the sake of the other. On the basis of emptiness, reality is "one yet many, many yet one." We find similar sorts of non-dualist collapsing of opposites in later Far Eastern Mahāyāna as well, and this is precisely the standpoint that Nishida inherits in his view of reality as a contradictory self-identity between being and nothing, one and many. His idea of contradictory identity is founded on the same sort of de-substantialization of opposites. That is why some commentators have suggested that Nishida's concept of the place of nothing that negates mere affirmation and mere negation, being and non-being, corresponds to, or may have taken a hint from, Mādhyamika thought.[34] Nishida, in "Bashoteki ronri to shūkyōteki sekaikan," alludes to the Mādhyamika logic of "the middle path." He claims that Nāgārjuna's "negative theology" and his "eightfold negation" (happu 八不)—the systematic denial of all reifying assertions, repudiating the notion of any underlying substance: "neither ceasing nor arising, neither annihilation nor permanence, neither identity nor difference, neither coming-in nor going-out,"[35] which was then further developed by the Chinese San-lun (三論) school that inherited Mādhyamika concepts—along with its cardinal teaching of the non-duality between nirvāṇa and saṃsāra, exhibits a version of the structure of soku-hi logic (Z10 317).[36]

In any case, by the 1940s Nishida has come to view what he calls the place of absolute nothing as a place wherein the logic of soku-hi operates to unfold its characteristic dialectic that shapes the world-matrix of co-originating or mutually dependent opposites. In general, then, in the essays of the 1940s, dealing with religiosity and its dialectic, Nishida suggests a deep inter-resonance between his thought of absolutely contradictory self-identity and Suzuki's understanding of the *Prajñāpāramitā* logic of soku-hi. Seeing the two logics—the dialectic of contradictory self-identity and soku-hi logic—side by side is helpful in reminding us that the "identity" in "absolutely contradictory self-identity" is always mediated by "absolute contradiction," that is, the relationship of mutual self-negation, which in Buddhist terms means emptiness. This is no self-identity that affirms self-substantiality. The whole qua absolute is no totalizing principle that erases or dominates its other or its parts. As I mentioned at the beginning of this chapter, a decade or so earlier, in *Ippansha no jikakuteki taikei* of 1930 Nishida had already expressed this non-substantiality in reference to Buddhist scripture—rare for that time period—by citing the famous *Prajñāpāramitā* equation from the *Heart Sūtra,* "Form is emptiness, emptiness is form" (Z4 357). In that respect he already had some awareness, although he was reticent about it, of the closeness of his thinking to Mahāyāna even before the influence of Suzuki's soku-hi logic in the late 1930s. During the mid-1930s Nishida develops that non-substantial non-duality in a dialectical direction reminiscent of the Huayan (Jp. Kegon) doctrine of the dharma realm of the mutual non-obstruction between thing-events and their patterning (Ch. lishi wuai; Jp. riji muge 理事無礙) and among thing-events themselves (Ch. shishi wuai; Jp. jiji muge 事事無礙). It is this dialectic of non-substantiality that becomes explicated in the 1940s in terms of soku-hi logic with explicit reference to the *Prajñāpāramitā sūtras.* In the next section I will look into possible connections between that Huayan doctrine and Nishida's dialectics.

Inter-dependent Origination and Mutual Non-obstruction

In addition to the general proximity of Nishida's dialectical thought to the so-called soku-hi logic of the *Prajñāpāramitās*, we also find motifs in Nishida's thinking reminding us of the Mahāyāna concept of inter-dependent origination (Skrt. pratītya-samutpāda; Jp. engi 縁起) and some of its East Asian variations, such as the Huayan concept of "mutual non-obstruction" (Ch. wuai; Jp. muge 無礙) that I alluded to at the end of the last section. In Nishida's works from the 1930s (as well as in the 1940s) we notice a conspicuous affinity with these Buddhist doctrines, such as in his concept of the dialectical universal with its fourfold inter-determinations in *Tetsugaku no konpon mondai* (『哲学の根本問題』; *Fundamental Problems of Philosophy*). Nishida in 1933 refers to that similarity between his "dialectical logic" and the dialectics of what he mentions as the "deepest of Buddhist philosophy," Huayan (Jp. Kegon) and Tiantai (Jp. Tendai) (Z13 190). And in his final years he connects the term "expression" (hyōgen 表現) that he uses to address the structure of the historical world (rekishiteki sekai 歴史的世界) to Tiantai and Huayan (Tendai and Kegon) thought (Z10 438) in that simultaneously the particular expresses all other particulars as well as the world, and the world forms itself through such expressions (Z10 370). Indeed, it has been remarked that Nishida kept till his later years a copy of the *Avataṃsaka Sūtra*—an important Indian sūtra for the Chinese Huayan school—he purchased during his college years.[37]

When Nishida is considering the manifold of individuals, he stresses their irreducible individuality. He also reminds us, however, that these individuals are not substances since they are self-negating vis-à-vis one another. This non-substantiality of individuals in their interrelationality appears quite Buddhistic when it is juxtaposed to certain Buddhist notions. The stress on their radical interrelationality that constitutes the identity of each reminds one of the Mahāyāna doctrine of inter-dependent origination that individuals are what they are through their dependence on, and interrelations with, one another. Each lacks its own being (sva-bhāva) or substantiality and as such is empty (śūnya). In turn, the world as a whole is likewise what it is in inter-dependence with its co-constituting individual elements. Both the world and its individuals, whole and parts, have their being in inter-dependence. The being of each is inseparable from its inter-dependence, its lack of ontological independence, that is, emptiness. This doctrine of inter-dependent origination that juxtaposes dependent being to emptiness or the lack of substantiality, one might then say, contains a sort of simultaneity of opposites similar to that we find in Nishida's idea of the contradictory identity between being and non-being, affirmation and negation, that he employs throughout his later (post-1930) works.

Consider the Huayan doctrine of the fourfold dharmadhātu (Jp. hokkai 法界). The manifold determinations of the dialectical matrix in Nishida—the universal's self-determination, the universal's determination of the individual and the individual's reverse determination of the universal, the individual's self-determination, and the individuals' inter-determination—may be translated into Huayan terms with almost the same meanings (li, shi, lishi, shishi; or in Japanese: ri, ji, riji, jiji; 理、事、理事、事事). For example, what Nishida formulated in the 1930s in terms of the universal's determination of the individual and its reverse determination (or counter-determination) by the individual, and then in the 1940s in terms of the inverse correspondence between the absolute and the finite, in Huayan terms would be lishi wuai (riji muge), that is, the mutual non-obstruction between thing-events (shi, ji) and their pattern (li, ri). Thus in explaining his notion of contradictory self-identity, even while discussing Leibnizian ideas, Nishida in 1943 ("Chishiki no kyakkansei ni tsuite" 「知識の客観性について」; "On the Objectivity of Knowledge") refers to that Huayan understanding of lishi wuai and shishi wuai (Z9 416). In Huayan doctrine, it is not that li as a transcendent principle orders the material of shi (thing-events) from above. Li is identical with the patterning of mutual non-obstruction between shi (shishi wuai, jiji muge). Taking li in its properly Chinese significance as that patterning of how things interrelate to one another and are thus mutually distinguished from one another,[38] it is immanent in the realm of the myriad shi. Lishi wuai thus does not entail the uni-directional dominion of a transcendent li over the many individual shi but rather its immanence as the patterning of their interrelationality and mutual difference. Similarly, in Nishida's system of the dialectical universal, the universal is not some transcendent ideal principle ordering its material from above. And just as in Nishida the universal must refer to its non-substantiality, an absolute nothing, in Huayan, the non-obstruction obtaining among individual thing-events (shi, ji) simultaneously manifests the emptiness (Ch. kong; Jp. kū) pervading all, that is, their patterning of interrelationality and mutual difference (li, ri) and hence their full "wondrous being."[39] By contrast, in Huayan terms, Hegel's dialectic is one-sided in allowing only for a transcendent li's domination over shi while ignoring the true immanence of li within shishi. On the other hand, as a self-forming formlessness, Nishida's absolute is shaped by the interactivities of its individual elements. In its non-substantiality, the place of nothing does not exercise domination over the manifold of individuals.

Nishida's dialectic, as we see, thus accounts for the genuine reciprocity of lishi wuai on the vertical plane that is simultaneously shishi wuai on the horizontal plane. Nishida in *Nihon bunka no mondai* (『日本文化の問題』; *The Problem of Japanese Culture*) of 1940[40] mentions Fazang's (法藏) Huayan formula of "the non-obstruction among thing-events" (shishi wuai; jiji muge), as facts determining facts themselves, when he is speaking of the self-determination of the world as an absolutely contradictory self-identity (Z9 73). Nishida contrasts Fazang's shishi wuai (jiji muge) with Hegel's dialectic and underscores their distinction (Z9 8).

Nishida here favors Huayan over Hegel. Just as in Huayan lishi wuai and shishi wuai imply each other, in Nishida's system of the dialectical universal the universal's self-determination means the individual's self-determination, which in turn means inter-determination among individuals and their reverse determination of the universal (e.g., Z6 236–237). Through such radical interrelationality of the world, each individual thing-event is simultaneously what it is (shi, ji), inter-dependent with others (shishi wuai, jiji muge), and expressive of the whole (lishi wuai, riji muge), while the whole simultaneously is expressive of those individual determinations. Nishida's dialectical matrix with its manifold cross-directional chiasma thus appears to fit hand in glove with Huayan's fourfold dharmadhātu. Furthermore, taking off from this comparison, Nishida's notion of the place of absolutely nothing that negates itself to make room for individuals also comes very close to the Huayan understanding of li (ri) as the patterning of emptiness inter-penetrating its terms (shi, ji), whereby their interrelations are described as a non-obstruction (wuai, muge). The entire realm of interrelations, the dharmadhātu or basho (place) in both systems, via non-obstruction or self-negation is empty of substance or svabhāva. In his philosophy of religiosity in the 1940s Nishida trans-lates this reality into what thinkers like Pascal and Nicholas of Cusa called the infinite sphere without periphery or circumference. In Mahāyāna terms, we might in turn re-interpret this sphere in terms of emptiness (kū) as the open sky (kū), perhaps traceable to the idea of the sky as an "open space" (ākāśa) in the *Pra-jñāpāramitā sūtras* that supposedly inspired Nāgārjuna's use of *śūnyatā*.[41]

In light of this discussion, it is interesting to note Suzuki's remark in his introduction to Viglielmo's English translation of *Zen no kenkyū:* "Toward the end of his life . . . Nishida seemed to have felt a new interest in Kegon [Huayan] philosophy. We often talked about it. . . . [Zen's relationship with Huayan/Kegon] is likely to have induced Nishida to take up the study of Kegon and to expound it in his characteristic way of thinking."[42] Whether or not Nishida's formulation of the manifold dialectical universal was directly influenced by the Huayan four-fold, it is clear that he came to notice the proximity of his thinking to Huayan through his conversations with Suzuki in the later part of his life.[43]

Depth in the Ordinary and the Absolute Present

Commentators have repeatedly spoken of Nishida's connection with Zen: Nishida practiced zazen (seated meditation) from his late twenties through his thirties. Nevertheless, as is obvious by now, the actual stimulus for his philosophical work came from his encounter with Western philosophy and the issues it raised. Yet into his philosophical project that had been stimulated by Western philosophy Nishida incorporated what he had learned from Zen, both experientially and doctrinally. We can see his Zen experience filtering into his early conceptions of pure experience. This serves in turn as a foundation for Nishida's later incorporation of Zen thought—found most notably in Dōgen—into his understanding of the absolute present (zettai genzai 絶対現在). Finally, in the last years of his life, references to Zen doctrines become most pronounced in his conception of depth in the ordinary (byōjōtei 平常底). All three—pure experience, the absolute present, and depth in the ordinary—are connected and suggest Zen themes, but here I will focus on the last two, which emerge during the 1930s and 1940s, when Nishida was developing his explicitly dialectical mode of thinking.

I have already noted how Nishida's dialectic not only involves a spatial dimension that encompasses simultaneous terms but also possesses significant implications for a perspective on time in terms of the present. Hegel's view of time is teleological in its orientation to the end, an inheritance of the general Western eschatological perspective deriving from the Abrahamic religions (and before that from the Persian religion of Zoroastrianism). Nishida's view of time, which focuses on the absoluteness of the present, by contrast, is akin to Buddhist notions of time. The teleological premise of the end in Hegel makes his time a closed circle, while it is the focus on the present—a microcosmic condensation of an infinity of possibilities from which past and future flow—that makes time in Nishida open. The genuine novelty it allows for is what permits the individual's reverse determination of the universal, allowing for the transformation of the made into the making. This happens on the basis of the self-negation of each moment vis-à-vis all other moments. And this emptiness of each moment is an idea that one might perhaps trace back—or, at least, relate—to the Buddhist view of impermanence (Skrt. *anitya*), as well as to the *Prajñāpāramitā Heart Sūtra*'s notion of the emptiness of the dharmas. The latter was the Mahayanists' contention against the Abhidharmists' substantialization of successive dharmas that constitute the flow of time. In addition, one also detects the Zen refinement of that idea within Nishida's notion of the absolute present in its enfolding of past and future. This enfolding mirrors the whole of time in its impermanence, whereby there is rest amid movement. The most obvious Zen source here, whom Nishida repeatedly cites, is Dōgen. Dōgen understood time to involve what he called "now" (nikon 而今), "passage" (kyōryaku 經歷), and "abiding-in-a-dharma-position" (jūhōi 住法位). Nishida's understanding of the present in terms of a place comes very close to Dōgen's conception of the configuration of dharma (jūhōi) in the immediate now (nikon), which concentrates the whole of cosmic space-time into a single point by mutual implication in the net of inter-dependence, only to negate itself for the next moment, allowing for the continual passage (kyōryaku) of self-negating moments. In this context, what Nishida means by basho becomes the place of what Buddhism means by impermanence.

But what is most noticeable in the last stages of Nishida's thought (during the 1940s) in terms of concepts borrowed from, or influenced by, Zen is the motif of "depth in the ordinary" (byōjōtei). This idea takes off from the Zen notion of "ordinary mind" (byōjōshin 平常心) that develops the non-duality of saṃsāra-nirvāṇa. What Nishida refers to as depth in the ordinary expresses the dialectic of inverse correspondence between the absolute and the finite in more immediate terms. In explaining this concept, Nishida makes use of a quotation from the Chinese Chan master Linji Yixuan (Jp.: Rinzai Gigen 臨済義玄) (d. 867 CE): "There is no use for the Buddha dharma. Everything is as usual, nothing is different. One shits and pisses, wears clothes, and eats. And when tired, one lies down" (Z10 353). Nishida also refers to the statement of Nanquan Puyuan (Jp.: Nansen Fugan 南泉普願) (748–834) that "the ordinary mind [byōjōshin], just as it is, is the way [Ch. dao; Jp. *dō* 道]" (Z10 359). And even before those two the term "ordinary mind" was used by the Chinese Chan master Mazu Daoyi (Jp.: Baso Dōitsu 馬祖道一) (709–788 CE). Nishida understands that phrase in terms of the absolute present's self-determination and explains that it is therein that the inverse correspondence between self and absolute, or the non-duality between saṃsāra and nirvāṇa (*seishi soku nehan* 生死即涅槃), is realized (Z10 334, 356). But Nishida, perhaps to emphasize the infinite depth that extends beyond any "mind"—as in his earlier notion of the place of absolute nothing that extends beyond the field of consciousness, a depth that is simultaneously manifest in the most commonplace or ordinary—renders his concept as "depth in the ordinary." The point is that the deeply primordial is the concretely real; it does not transcend the world of everyday existence but is right before us. The deep ground is right here in everyday appearances (Z10 359). The ordinary is thus the place of concrete reality, which in spite of its ordinariness holds infinite "religious" significance for Nishida. This is another way of speaking of the immanence of the transcendent.

We also see Nishida further extending that Zen "ordinariness" by adding Christian terminology, coining the phrase "eschatological depth in the ordinary" or "depth in the ordinary in terms of eschatology" (shūmatsuronteki byōjōtei 終末論的平常底). With this phrase Nishida communicates the idea that the absolute's self-negation, in all its worldly or cosmic proportions, happens in the here and now, in the immanent and ordinary reality of our immediacy, whereby our present self-awareness as finite already bears the religious meaning of the "end-times." In other words, the end, the eschaton, is in the here and now. This is also another way of talking about inverse correspondence. As the standpoint wherein one truly finds oneself in self-authentication, Nishida characterizes it as the standpoint of the free will or the freedom of self-conversion and opposes it to Kant's version of the free will whereby reason follows a self-imposed moral imperative. To make his case, Nishida cites the Zen notion of "absolute freedom" (*zettai jiyū* 絶対自由) found in Linji (Jp. Rinzai), whereby one is the self-expression of the absolute (Z10 355). "Absolute freedom" in Rinzai is the standpoint "of always acting freely, in whatever circumstance, by establishing one's identity without being captivated by anything" and "of everything embodying the truth wherever one may be."[44] As Kosaka explains,[45] absolute freedom here is determined neither by instinct nor by reason. Rather, true freedom as such entails one's exhaustive self-negation in the awareness of one's finitude, one's impermanence, as a self-determination of the present. Hence one is free of attachment, even to the self. And this freedom happens not in view of the future but in the present that is ordinary yet eschatological. The connection of Nishida's thinking to Zen, which was there in his earlier works because of his Zen training but remained implicit, thus becomes more pronounced in his later works, especially in the 1945 essay, "Bashoteki ronri to shūkyōteki sekaikan," where he makes explicit reference to Zen thinkers and their thoughts.

Inverse Correspondence and Kenosis, Gratia, Myōgō, and Tariki

Nishida's religious thought was not inspired only by the Mahāyāna ideas that come to expression in Zen. In examining his late works of the 1940s, one notices references to what has often been stereotypically regarded as a form of Buddhism antithetical to Zen, the True Pure Land (Jōdo Shin) school of Mahāyāna Buddhism.[46] This True Pure Land influence is ignored by commentators who would like to present Nishida as the Zen philosopher vis-à-vis, for example, Tanabe Hajime as the True Pure Land philosopher. Moreover, Nishida often conjoins references to these Pure Land ideas and references to Christian doctrines. Both are devotionalist and grace-oriented religions that on the surface appear to be very distinct from the Buddhism of Zen. In discussing these religions, we find Nishida here trying to clarify his dialectical ideas about religiosity in general. The set of Christian ideas that Nishida found inspiration from, and often refers to, is the rubric connecting or encompassing a certain reading of the notions of kenosis, gratia, and agapē, along with logos, that is, ideas belonging to a line of Christian thought that one might trace through St. Paul, St. Augustine, Martin Luther, and Kierkegaard and perhaps up to modern German Protestant theology. In the mid-1930s, in *Tetsugaku no konpon mondai,* as if to pre-view his later concept of inverse correspondence, Nishida speaks of the establishment of the world as an affirmation of absolute negation, a self-determination of an absolute alterity that we as finite beings can also reach through our corresponding absolute negation. The latter happens when in deep anxiety we become aware of our self-contradiction within our depths. Nishida declares this to be the message of Mahāyāna Buddhism. But he also goes on to identify this with what Christianity calls "the Word of God" (Z6 334). Later, in the 1940s, Nishida compares this Christian notion of logos (Word) with the True Pure Land Buddhist notion of myōgō. Both imply a profound sense of absolute alterity in the face of which we are but powerless finite beings. Proper comportment vis-à-vis that excess other on our part would hence be self-negation. Nishida thus relates these ideas found in both religions to his understanding of inverse correspondence.

In his final essay of 1945 ("Bashoteki ronri to shūkyōteki sekaikan") Nishida finds support for his notion of inverse correspondence in the Christian tradition. He takes the statements "The Word became flesh to dwell among us" from the Gospel of John (1:14) and "As in Adam all die, so in Christ all shall be made alive" from St. Paul's First Letter to the Corinthians (15:22) as exemplifying the paradoxical mutual self-negation between God and man (Z10 342, 351). In self-negation God qua logos becomes man in Christ[47] and then dies qua man; and in self-negation man dies to his sinful ego (Adam) so that Christ may dwell in him. In both cases any objectification of God or self qua substance is deconstructed. Nishida also likens Paul's statement in his Letter to the Galatians (2:20) that "it is no longer I who live, but Christ who lives in me" to Shinran's notion of jinen hōni ("spontaneity through the working of the dharma") (Z9 73–74). The religious conversion of sinful and deluded man entails the working dynamic of God's self-emptying (kenosis) that signifies God's divine love (agapē) or, in Buddhist terms, the Buddha's compassion.[48] And simultaneously it also means the existential self-negation of that deluded or sinful self on the part of man. In this way, via mutual self-negation God and man encounter each other. Nishida views this as the meaning of "faith" in Christianity and cites Luther's point that faith as such is not really one's own working but the working of God within oneself. Only through this attitudinal belief that one is not working to help oneself but rather is being helped by God working within oneself can one's sinful ego truly be killed so that one is made anew to live in God. Nishida understands "enlightenment" in Buddhism in a similar fashion. Another Christian thinker, whom Nishida often cites and in whom we may find a comparable understanding of this conversion experience, is Pascal, who stated:

> True conversion consists in self-annihilation before the universal being whom we have so often vexed and who is perfectly entitled to destroy us at any moment, in recognizing that we can do nothing without him and that we have deserved nothing but his disfavor. It consists in knowing that there is an irreconcilable opposition between God and us, and that without a mediator there can be no exchange.[49]

And just as "the finite is annihilated in the presence of the infinite and becomes pure nothingness ... so it is with our mind before God."[50] Such alterity is what undermines the rationalism of a self-thinking thought. In more recent modern Christian thought Kierkegaard especially provides a standpoint antithetical to Hegel's rationalism. Hence in his attempts to understand the self-contradictory or paradoxical nature of human existence, Nishida finds inspiration in Kierkegaard's nineteenth-century polemic against rationalism. To support his dialectic, Nishida takes Kierkegaard's "unity of paradox"[51]—between negativity and positivity, the absolute unlikeness and the absolute likeness between man and God[52]—as what sustains yet simultaneously undermines, from the bottom, Hegel's dialectical logic (*Z7* 275).[53] But in regard to Nishida's interest in the structure of mutual self-negation or inverse correspondence that he finds in the religions, we need to remember that for Nishida it is the relationship of inverse correspondence and its placiality that are more fundamental than God per se, as in mainstream Christianity. For Nishida, it is the absolute qua place that is originary, not the absolute qua God the Father (i.e., as objectified).

The emphasis on the absolute's alterity and one's own finitude in inverse correspondence with each other, although much inspired by Christian ideas, is ultimately mediated through the Mahāyānistic understanding of *śūnyatāyāh śūnyatā* transposed into Nishida's dialectic of self-negation. Accordingly, the notion of God's self-negation, for example, would express the inseparability between saṃsāra and nirvāṇa. But a significant mediator that brings together Christianity and Mahāyāna, in particular, is Shinran's True Pure Land school (Jōdo Shinshū) of lay devotionalist Buddhism, the religious sect of which Nishida's mother was a devout follower. Nishida juxtaposes the two religions, Pure Land and Christianity, when he is speaking of the interrelationship between the absolute and man as occurring solely by means of expression, involving "the Word (logos) of God" (*kami no kotoba* 神の言葉) or "the name of the Buddha" (*Z10* 347, 349–350). Here he compares the Pure Land concept of "calling the name of the Buddha Amida" (myōgō) with the biblical "Word of God" (logos) as both being instances, in separate religious traditions, of a dialectical encounter of contradictory self-identity between God and man or between absolute and finite, that is, their inverse correspondence (*Z10* 351).

Masao Abe thus argues that Nishida's development of the idea of inverse correspondence was stimulated, at least partially, by his interest in True Pure Land Buddhism with its notion of myōgō. Myōgō refers to the act of "calling the name of the Buddha Amida," as well as to the vow made by Amida to save suffering beings who would be calling on his name. In other words, it means at the same time both Amida's salvific voice calling on the sinner and the recitation of Amida's name by the sinner who hears his calling voice. The two calls happen in synchrony. And as in the Lutheran understanding of faith we saw earlier, the sentient being's calling to Amida is conceived to happen under the direction of Amida (*Z10* 351). This idea also exemplifies the True Pure Land school's emphasis on reliance on "other-power" (tariki).[54] When Nishida read Suzuki's *Nihonteki reisei*, he found inspiration not only in its explication of the *Prajñāpāramitā* logic of soku-hi but also in its concept of myōgō. In a letter to Mutai Risaku (January 6, 1945), Nishida expresses his approval of Suzuki's "logic of myōgō" and adds that he would like to conceive it from his own standpoint of contradictory self-identity to consider myōgō as what is heard in the depths of oneself as the self-determination of the absolute present (Z23 319–320). There is also evidence (Z10 356) that Nishida was stimulated by his exchanges not only with Suzuki but also with his student Mutai, who explicates Shinran's notion of absolute other-power and incorporates True Pure Land notions into his exposition of Nishida's theory of place in his *Basho no ronrigaku* (『場所の論理学』; *The Logic of Place*).[55] Another commentator, Kosaka, suggests that Nishida had discovered something in the logic of myōgō that was lacking, or at least not as evident, in his theory of contradictory self-identity, and that this in turn led him to reformulate his idea in terms of inverse correspondence.[56] Nishida does come to take the Pure Land concept of myōgō to coincide with his idea of inverse correspondence. In "Bashoteki ronri to shūkyōteki sekaikan" Nishida states, "The relationship between absolute and man that is thoroughly in inverse correspondence happens by nothing other than the myōgō expression" (Z10 350). And on this basis he can argue, à la Luther, that the religious mind occurs not from oneself but from, or as, the calling voice of the absolute, as "the work of God or Buddha" (Z10 325). In Amida's salvation of the evil man, there is the inverse correspondence between, on the one hand, the sinner's self-awareness of his desiring nature and his heavy load of sin while also believing in salvation by Amida and, on the other, Amida Buddha's original vow and work to save such sinful and wandering beings.[57] This relationship of inverse correspondence—an absolute conversion by means of self-negation—becomes for Nishida the essence of religiosity. In this one can discern the influence of the True Pure Land philosopher Kiyozawa Manshi as well.[58] Through the mediation of that True Pure Land idea of myōgō, it appears that Nishida was attempting a synthesis of Mahāyāna śūnyatā and Christian kenosis and gratia. But the entire synthesis is founded on his system of place (basho). And one might argue that the Christian notions were seen in light of Suzuki's reading of Pure Land Buddhism tinted in turn by his reading of the *Prajñāpāramitās*—which in turn, however, may have been influenced by Nishida's earlier understanding of contradictory self-identity, as suggested earlier.

Final Thoughts Concerning Nishida and Buddhism

As we can see, the relationship between Nishida and Buddhism is no simple matter. On the one hand, Nishida's thought was certainly inspired by his Zen practice of his early years (when he was in his twenties). But it was really in his later years (late 1930s to early 1940s) that through intellectual exchanges with his friend D. T. Suzuki and through Suzuki's books, as well as exchanges with others like his former student Mutai, who was interested in Pure Land Buddhism, that Nishida came to realize and give frequent expression to the closeness of his dialectical ideas to some of the non-dualist doctrines of Mahāyāna. We certainly find conspicuous similarities of his dialectical formulations during the early to mid-1930s to Mahāyāna notions, most notably Huayan's fourfold dharmadhātu of mutual non-obstruction. And we notice explicit references in the 1930s and more frequently in the 1940s to Chan or Zen thinkers like Linji and Dōgen, among others. Nishida was certainly not ignorant of the more important doctrines of Mahāyāna Buddhism, although his knowledge was not necessarily that of a scholar of Buddhism. Buddhism informs his ideas as part of his "general cultural heritage."[59] Nevertheless, this cultural premise becomes more intentional or conscious in his later years, so that in 1944 Nishida characterizes his thinking as "Buddhistic" (Z10 59). In content, his dialectic, centered on self-negation and self-contradiction, is closer in spirit to Mahāyāna than to Hegel. But we ought not to deny Nishida the status of an independent thinker whose creativity cannot be pigeonholed within the confines of "Buddhist thought" or "Mahāyāna thought" or "Zen thought." In *Nihon bunka no mondai* he warns the reader that he is not prescribing a return to the Buddhist logic of the past (Z9 72). What stimulated Nishida's work, for the most part, were issues raised within Western philosophy, most notably the issue of dualism. In his attempts to answer such issues he made good use of concepts and terms borrowed from Western philosophy, mostly nineteenth-century German philosophy. As we have seen, he was very much inspired by the religious thought of the Western world as well and was not necessarily confined to the academic philosophy of that region. Although he does admit to commensurability with Mahāyāna thought, his dialectic thus cannot be restricted to the doctrinal category of "Buddhist thought" for the following two reasons: (1) its eclectic nature, which brings in elements drawn from various sources, both Western and Eastern, thereby constituting his work as a "world philosophy"; and (2) Nishida's creative contributions, especially in his formulation of place, which provides the foundation for his dialectic. It would not do justice to his syncretic and creative intellectual endeavor to reduce it within sectarian boundaries. The nature of his project precludes categorization as simply Buddhist philosophy. Rather, Nishida's work is a true case of cross-cultural or world philosophy, even if it is inspired by Mahāyāna.

The closeness of Nishida's thinking to Mahāyāna thought in his response to the issue of dualism is, of course, undeniable. But much of Nishidian philosophy also extends beyond previous Buddhist formulations. For example, the cross-dimensional complexity of its dialectic that encompasses our bodily interactivity and even the unfolding of history in time—this latter being a dimension that Nishida seems to acknowledge as lacking in Buddhism (Z9 70–71)—and the founding of this dialectic on the notion of place (basho), I think, are uniquely Nishidian developments that cannot be reductively categorized as just Buddhist even if they are relatable in certain aspects to Buddhist notions. In the next chapter I will look into that complexity of inter-determination that is chiasmatic together with its placial aspect as a chōra, borrowing Plato's concept. Although it is commensurable with Mahāyāna notions, Nishida's development of his notion of contradictory self-identity and its placial (bashoteki 場所的) or chōratic nature in conjunction with a bodily prāxis—that is, embodiment as dynamic implacement—encompasses the complexity of a multi-dimensional chiasma that extends beyond the previous formulations of Nishida's forebears, Buddhist or Hegelian. The next chapter will thus move beyond Nishida's formulations to unfold the implications of his thought in a way that may be relevant to our contemporary context. The presentation of its content will thus be more original, philosophically ambitious, and hence challenging in comparison with previous chapters.

In general, if we are to compare and contrast the Hegelianism and the Buddhism within Nishida's thoughts, we might say that much of Nishida's terminology and formulations, as well as certain concepts, has been borrowed from Hegel. Yet we have found many connections of his ideas, implicit or explicit, with Buddhist sources as well. The formulation of a concrete universal and the dialectical language involving the relations between universal and individual are Hegelian, but the non-substantiality brought forth in Nishida's appropriation of that dialectic as an absolute nothing or as a contradictory identity and the radical relationality that undermines any substantiality are closer in content to Mahāyāna doctrines than to Hegel. Nishida's emphasis on individuality, materiality, and the body undercut the residue of Platonist universalism in Hegel. But the extension of that dialectic to the social world of interacting persons and its concomitant ethics, and his interest in the historicity of that world-dialectic, exhibit a concern that is more typical of modern philosophy than of traditional Buddhist discourse. Even if Nishida in his later years occasionally characterized his thinking as "Buddhistic," his thought cannot simply be categorized as a version of Buddhist or Mahāyāna thought. As a marvelous example of a world philosophy, an intellectual product of the encounter between East and West, between Buddhist thought and Western philosophy, Nishida's philosophy, while bringing the two together, stands on its own.

10 The Chiasma and the Chōra

On the basis of the previous two chapters one might surmise the inadequacy of Nishida's appropriation of Hegelian (and, in general, nineteenth-century German philosophical) terminology to capture the content of what he strove to express. The matter that he attempted to expound through the language of dialectical philosophy slips away from its structure, ex-ploding beyond any bounds erected to systematize it. But neither would simply repeating the paradoxical and parabolic modes of traditional Zen discourse be satisfying philosophically. The two aspects of Nishida's thinking that I think confound traditional metaphysical discourse despite the fact that they are essential to his mature philosophy are what I call the "chiasmatic" aspect of, or implied in, his so-called dialectic (ben-shōhō 弁証法) on the one hand, and the chōra that embraces or enfolds it while expressing itself in it, on the other. Combining these two terms, I will take the liberty in the following of presenting Nishida's mature philosophy, what he calls his "absolute dialectic" (zettai benshōhō 絶対弁証法), as a "chiasmatic chorology" in an attempt to better characterize the real matter of his thinking and to suggest that therein lies Nishida's philosophical contribution that makes his work more than a mere appropriation or development of Hegelian dialectics or Mahāyāna non-dualism. I argue that it is because of its chiasmatic and chōratic nature that the Sache he strove to capture and express through the language of dialectical philosophy perpetually slips away from any systemic bounds.[1]

Dialectic and Chiasma

One of the central themes in Nishida's benshōhō is the theme of contradictory self-identity (mujunteki jikodōitsu 矛盾的自己同一), an identity that by its very nature is not static but dynamic, involving the whole of oppositional processes. If dialectical logic involves the interrelationship reflecting a system wherein the terms in relation are what they are only in their interrelations and in the context set by their system, the dialectical whole,[2] Nishida's system may be included in the general category of what constitutes a "dialectic." Certainly, Nishida described his depiction of reality as a "dialectic" (benshōhō). The mature Nishida, in an attempt to preclude misunderstandings of his "predicate logic," emphasizes that true self-identity, in its dialectical nature, can neither be objectified in the direction of what can be stated as a grammatical subject nor simply be conceived in the opposite direction of the thinking subjectivity qua absolute spirit or of absolutizing the predicate qua absolute concept. Rather, he views his dialectic as involving genuine inter-determination that can never be reduced to either side of its terms. And this inter-determination is what Nishida characterizes as mujun (矛盾), "contradiction" or "paradox."

What does Nishida mean by "contradiction" (mujun)? Some commentators have expressed the view that perhaps "contrary" is a better translation of *mujun*.[3] The term *mujun* comes from a Chinese story appearing in the text of *Han Feizi* (『韓非子』) in which a vendor is selling lances (or halberds) and shields. On the one hand, the vendor advertises his lances as so sharp that there are no shields that the lances would fail to penetrate, but on the other, he advertises his shields as so strong and solid that nothing, no lances, can penetrate them. His character-izations are inconsistent; they are contradictory.[4] Nishida's dialectic involves the play between being and non-being, affirmation and negation, in other words, logical contradictories, which from a trans-logical perspective can be seen as bi-conditionals in that each implies the other and conditions the other as the con-tradictory that it is. We have seen how this involves a radical dialectic of mutual self-negation (jiko hitei 自己否定) precluding any conceptual synthetic resolution of the opposites.[5] The mediator is not a sublating concept but mutual self-negation or, from another perspective, their field or place that is nothing. Any sort of self-affirmative act is seen to be predicated on this prior self-negation: the self's affir-mation requires its prior delimitation by environing conditions, a negation that can give shape to the affirmation. Its affirmation is obtained only in self-negation, that is, de-substantialization, to preclude any substantial inter-obstruction of others. The self must come to terms with its fact of finitude or contingency in a self-negation vis-à-vis the world acting on it. And such self-negation, on the part of each individual, mirrors the absolute nothing (zettai mu 絶対無) that is the place, the field, of the world's dialectical self-formations (via self-negations). It mirrors the self-negation of the abyssal place that qua world clears room for the emergence of correlative beings (Z10 315–316). The relationship between the individual and the world involves this radical inter-dependence via mutual self-negation. The entire world is a unity-in-flux of such contradictories, irreducible to any simple identity.

Yet Nishida is also careful to avoid any sort of nihilism that might result from self-negation and that would deny the reality of the world of things. The self-negation is a double negation that is not simply a negation vis-à-vis the positive. Absolute nothing encompasses both negativity and positivity, non-being and being, destruction and creation, as a middle irreducible to either term. The place of the world escapes both reification as substance and annihilation into utter nothing. Insofar as its self-negation is what makes room for beings, creating and affirming them, it is positive. It is a fecund nothing, an un-definable potential that unfolds in its actualizations. As we can see, Nishida's dialectic does involve logical contradiction, but seen from a broader perspectival stance that witnesses the relationship of contradiction. That is, it encompasses logical contradiction but for that reason refuses reduction to the mere terms of being or non-being, *on* (ὄν) or *mē on* (μὴ ὄν), affirmation or negation, positivity or negativity.

Broader and deeper than what can be reduced to the dialectical structure of bi-conditional opposites, Nishida's absolute dialectic, with its multi-dimensional complexity of a self-determining matrix, involves a chiasma of (over-)inter-determinations. By "chiasma" I mean the radical multi-dimensional relationality that Nishida recognizes in reality. Does this chiasma undermine the language of that dialectic? "Chiasma" is a term used in anatomy and genetics and in general refers to a "crossing." The word comes from the Greek *chiazein,* meaning "to mark with an X," the Greek letter *chi* (C, c), and the related noun *chiasma* (χίασμα), meaning "cross-piece," "cross-over," or "X-shape." I use "chiasma" and "chiasmatic" here to refer to the cross-configuration or intersection between the horizontal interrelationality among individuals (relative beings) and the vertical inter-relationality between individuals and what envelops and embraces them—understood in the various terms of place, world, absolute, nothing, and so on—in Nishida. This means also, for example, the various cross-dimensional intersections between the spatial and the temporal, vertical and horizontal, linear and circular, individual and universal, the body and its social and natural environments, and so on that we find in Nishida's thinking. And this certainly includes the dialectic of logical contradiction between being and non-being and between affirmation and negation as well. But the more one attempts to demarcate the boundary between *X* and *~X*, the more incomplete the determination and the more ambiguous and complex the matter is revealed to be. By taking Nishida's "contradiction" (mujun) as a chiasma, we can focus on its character as an inter-dimensional cross section where opposites, including contradictories, meet and condition each other, and as their source out of which they are abstracted. The expression of contradictory self-identity seems to depict, however, only the tip of the iceberg of a vast complexity that is chiasmatic. Although Nishida at times emphasizes logical contradiction in its ontological significance, that is, yes and no as being and non-being—so that even time and space become viewed in their mutual exclusivity (i.e., time is not space and space is not time)—we might also take this as a surface manifestation or expression of a logically irreducible plethora of a manifold in chiasmatic interaction.[6]

"Chiasma" is not exactly the same in significance as "chiasmus." Dictionaries distinguish these two related words. The latter is a figure of speech based on an inverted parallelism, whereby the order of terms in parallel clauses is reversed in one of the clauses (e.g., "one should eat to live, not live to eat"). This sense seems to approach what Maurice Merleau-Ponty tries to capture with his notion of "chiasm," which might be defined as the paradoxical form of a whole composed of parts interrelating in inverse structural orders.[7] Yet in the radical reciprocity of its dialectic, I take Nishida's chiasma to be inclusive of the meanings of chiasmus and the Merleau-Pontyan chiasm, for its multi-layered crisscrossing also involves multiple inversions, albeit with certain irreversible disjunctions between the terms. One notices this, for example, in Nishida's notions of the dialectical inter-determination between individual and environment, of the universal's determination of the individual and its reverse determination (gyaku gentei 逆限定) by the individual, and of the inverse correspondence (gyakutaiō 逆対応) between absolute and finite, as we shall see later.

Even in his earlier works, such as *Geijutsu to dōtoku* (『芸術と道徳』; *Art and Morality*) of 1923, Nishida had already recognized the chiasmatic nature of the concrete in terms of our embodiment that connects our subjectivity with objects while also serving as the locus for the intersection (*kōsa* 交差) between the object-world of cognition and the object-world of volition. The body with its sensibility and motility serves to connect the various object-worlds of facts, truth, reality, beauty, and good, whereby we can enter and exit each world (Z3 246). A little later, in "Hyōgen sayō" (「表現作用」; "The Act of Expression") of 1925, Nishida speaks of the "cross section" (*kōsaten* 交差点) between the ideal and the real in the body where content, expression, and act all intersect. And the world is also such a cross section between volition and cognition (Z3 382). The significance of the body in the 1930s deepens that chiasmatic aspect as an intersection that gathers various forces into a microcosmic creative funnel whereby the world creates itself in our acting intuitions. The body is seer of the world but in turn is also seen as part of the world. It is active and passive in the world's formation—the world here both as subject and as object of formation. The human body thus serves, in its interactivity, as a place of intersection, a chiasma.[8] While he is musing on this chiasmatic nature of the body, Nishida also unfolds the chiasma on a macrocosmic level, taking the creative world to be a world of interaction (aihataraki 相働き) between individuals that are simultaneously active and passive, affirmative and negative, toward each other. Their bodies are thus influenced by others as something made (*tsukurareta mono* 作られたもの) but simultaneously influence others as something creative (*tsukuru mono* 作るもの) (Z8 299; Z10 94, 97–98). Embodiment is at the crisscrossing intersection of the world where the horizontal (interaction with other bodies) and the vertical (interaction with the world as a whole) meet as a chiasmatic axis uniting inner and outer, self and environment, individual and universal, affirmation and negation, subjective and objective, time and space, and so on.

In the manifold dialectic of the dialectical universal (benshōhōteki ippansha 弁証法的一般者), what on the vertical plane is the universal's self-determination and its reverse determination by the individual is, on the horizontal plane, the inter-determinations of individuals belonging to that universal. The chiasmatic inter-reactions between them on these different planes constitute the unfolding of the world-matrix in society and history. The vertical and the horizontal here are inseparable in that they are different ways of speaking of the same dialectical matrix: the universal's self-determination is the individuals' co-determinations, and neither side can be prioritized over the other or reduced to the other. The different directions and planes of dialectical determination are mutually implicative so that the dialectical universal's self-determination means the individual's self-determination, and the individual's self-determination also implies inter-determination among individuals, which in turn also means the self-determination of the universal to constitute the world of those individuals (Z6 236–237). Hence, as Nishida states, the world is thoroughly universal and thoroughly of individuals (Z6 159). The matrix simultaneously is both universal determination and individual determination (Z6 234). We can comprehend that reciprocity involving the self-determination of the universal of nothing and the mutual determinations of individual beings conjoined via contradictory identity and inverse correspondence as an inter-dimensional and inter-directional chiasma. Universal and individual meet in the chiasma of inter-determinations. Moreover, the chiasma in its radical reciprocity—in its reverse determinations, mutual self-negations, and inverse correspondences—involves a chiasmus that must extend in complexity beyond the mere triadic formulas of bi-nomial interplay. What we have here is a chiasmatic intercrossing of dimensions. With its maturation in the 1930s, Nishida's dialectic between subjectivity and objectivity, inner and outer, thus comes to involve the interrelationship between the world as whole and the individual person as the world's elemental part, and between the individual's internal self-determination that Nishida metaphorically characterizes as "linear" in time and the world's external determination metaphorically characterized as "circular" in space. The co-determinations of these various dimensions, whereby "inner is outer and outer is inner," meet in the chiasma of the world-matrix that is neither simply ideal nor merely material.

As we have seen in previous chapters, Nishida characterizes that world-matrix in terms of Pascal's (and Nicholas of Cusa's) infinite sphere without periphery, with everywhere its center.[9] We have to conceive this spherical un-limitedness as being filled chiasmatically with such crisscrossing intersections even while being a "nothing" in substance. The world of matter and the world of consciousness ultimately are what become abstracted out of that chiasmatic sphere as their concrete but empty foundation. And in turn, the embodied individual mirrors that macrocosmic chiasma as a chiasmatic microcosm, the meeting point of the diverse dimensions, caught between the "two abysses of the infinite whole and of nothing."[10]

This chiasmatic sphere certainly has spatial significance, but that "spatiality" also encompasses time, for Nishida understands the "eternal present" (eien no genzai 永遠の現在) as a place that enfolds and unfolds time. I might add here that Nishida's concept of depth in the ordinary (byōjōtei 平常底) from the 1940s also exemplifies this cross-sectional chiasma of temporal and spatial interrelations, horizontal and vertical interrelations, whereby depth is manifest at the surface. Concrete reality is realized in that surface point of the present, concentrating an unfathomable chiasmatic complexity where temporal and spatial axes intercept. I have already discussed how the abyssal nature of that present serves as the source of novelty, as well as of freedom and creativity. The determinist hold of mechanistic causality is thereby loosened. Human creativity as partaking in world formation seems to be predicated on the seizure in self-awareness of the singularity of the here and now vis-à-vis that abyss, realizing the intersection, the chiasma, of spatial and temporal conditions. This singularity that is not the same as individuality[11] but rather the event of be-ing, exposed as finite here and now vis-à-vis its end, its other, faces its own being as constituted—and thus made possible—by an innumerable plurality of interrelations, processes, elements, and events. How precarious and thus precious is one's being, set on a thread or node in the chiasmatic web on the abyss that sets one free.

In his reading of Nishida, Nakamura Yūjirō relegates the horizontal dimension of this dialectic to the moment-to-moment temporalizing sequence of its process unfolding in time.[12] However, since inter-determination also occurs among what are spatially co-relative, we ought to recognize the spatiality of the horizontal as well, allowing for the synchrony of co-determination among events or individuals. The horizontal cannot be restricted to time because interrelations among co-relative beings happen not only diachronically but also synchronically. As Nishida states in *Tetsugaku no konpon mondai* (『哲学の根本問題』; *Fundamental Problems of Philosophy*), the mutual determination of individuals cannot be understood in light of mere process (Z6 74).[13] Furthermore, along with temporality and spatiality, what Nishida means by "place" must encompass the spatiality of both the vertical and the horizontal dimensions. The chiasmatic nature of the world-matrix as place is thus both horizontal, as the spatial field of co-relative beings and the temporal course of successive beings, and vertical in its self-negating inversion that makes room not only for those horizontal relations but also for its relationship qua place with the implaced—or qua absolute with the relative, or qua nothing with beings. While the vertical in the self-emptying process—what Nishida comes to call inverse correspondence—collapses into the horizontal in the interrelations among beings, it simultaneously encompasses the horizontal in giving it space. It is the incalculable complexity in the compounding of these many dimensions—horizontal and vertical, synchrony and diachrony—grounded on an un/grounding abyss, that accounts for unpredictability and indeterminacy in the history of the world (see figure 10.1). So the "spatiality" of the infinite sphere here is really trans-spatial. It encompasses the horizonality of both space and time as media for the interrelations and inter-determinations between individual actors and between individual moments. It also encompasses the sphere's vertical interrelations and inter-determinations with those individual elements

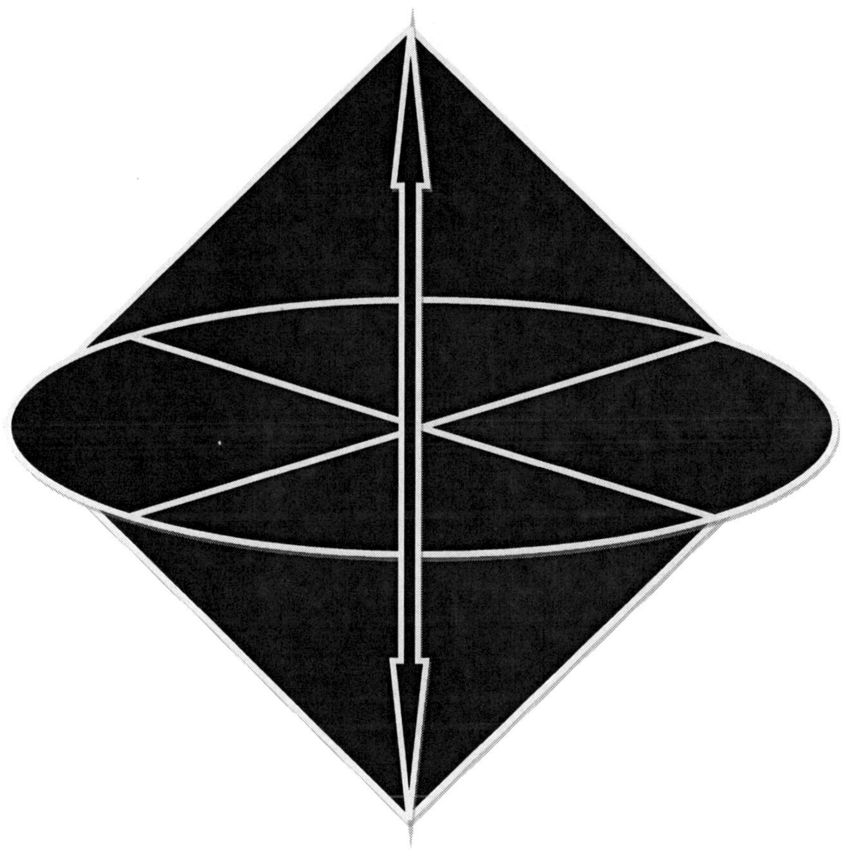

Figure 10.1 The dialectic of place as a dialectic of vertical and horizontal inter-determination:

Zettai mu 絶対無 (absolute nothing) as an undetermined *basho* 場所 (place) that self-negates to make room for beings. Vertical line: *gyakutaiō* 逆対応 (inverse correspondence) and *zettai mujunteki jikodōitsu* 絶対矛盾的自己同一 (absolutely contradictory self-identity); mutual self-negation between nothing and beings, absolute and co-relatives, one and many, place and implaced. Horizontal plane: co-relativity of beings. This plane is both temporal and spatial since the inter-dependence among thing-events entails both diachronic and synchronic relationships.

The place of absolute nothing (*zettai mu no basho* 絶対無の場所) is non-distinct from the place of beings (*yū no basho* 有の場所) and does not transcend it. Beings are inter-dependent both diachronically and synchronically and thus temporally and spatially. In relation to the absolute nothing (as delimited by it or as its self-determination), this place is a circle, or rather a sphere, without periphery or center.

Acting intuition (*kōiteki chokkan* 行為的直観) of the historical body (*rekishiteki shintai* 歴史的身体) dialectically moves from the made/created to the making/creating, expressing the horizontal interrelationship between the individual self and the environment of other individual things and persons, but also expressing the vertical interrelationship between the self-forming world and individuals as its formative elements.

(in space-time). The matrix of the world, the concrete place of reality, is an infinite self-inverting space-time chiasma, an indefinite openness that in itself is both trans-temporal and trans-spatial. Basho or place, then, is this cross-dimensional self-inverting chiasmatic spatiality of the world. But paradoxically, in making room even for its self-negation that in turn makes room for beings—making space for its making space for beings—this space is a space that escapes geometrical representation. As I just stated, it is a trans-temporal and trans-spatial space.

In the late 1930s Nishida also names that structuring of the concrete *logos*. It is the structuring of reality wherein there is inter-resonance via mutual self-negation and contradictory self-identity between universal and individual, whole and part, world and element. Nishida's logos, then, involves the chiasmatic structuring of multi-levels, dimensions, and directions; it really names what exceeds the logical. The world qua dialectical universal is a multi-directional chiasma of inter-dimensional self-negation. First and foremost, before any theoretical abstractions or reductions, we find ourselves implaced within this concrete chiasma, wherein we are born, dwell, and die, and wherein we are generated and perish at every moment on an abyss (Z8 38). We take part in that chiasmatic *legein* (λέγειν) or "gathering," of logos. Only thus can we also speak of the chiasma in one's deep personal and existential dimension—the chiasma in the depths of one's being, where one crosses the threshold between life and death, being and nothing, wherein one directly confronts one's contradictory identity and one's inverse correspondence with the absolute place of one's implacement, the dimension of what Nishida calls "the religious" (shūkyōteki 宗教的) where we come face-to-face with alterity defining our finitude.

The chiasma of inter-dimensional inter-determinations—vertically and horizontally, in linear time and in circular space, microcosmically and macrocosmically—is the world's matrix, the logos of its unfolding. But this matrix, whose elements are mediated by self-negation, is non-substantial, for its radically chiasmatic nature precludes the possibility of substantialization. To construe Nishida's philosophy as comparable to Spinozism and as promoting "one body that is non-dual" (*ittai funi* 一体不二), even if both Nishida and Spinoza look to God as a universal principle, is thus highly dubious.[14] Kosaka Kunitsugu's emphasis on the non-discrimination and equality between self and world, individual and universal, and the utter elimination of any distinction between subjectivity and objectivity, inner and outer, one and many, absolute and relative, and so on, accomplished via an exhaustive self-negation, is somewhat misleading.[15] This still sounds like a kind of monism whereby everything sinks into nothingness. It downplays the tensions between these opposites that are never resolved, whether under an absolute concept or an absolute substance or even under utter nothingness. Nishida distinguishes his thinking from Spinoza's. The difference is obvious when we notice that Nishida's universal is not a substance and escapes being made into a grammatical subject of a sentence. The chiasmatic nature of his dynamic non-dualism precludes any universalizing monism, as well as any self-affirmation, from the other end, regarding the ultimacy of the individual qua substance. As Ueda Shizuteru states, neither the one nor the many, neither monism nor dualism nor pluralism is taken as the foundation.[16] Concrete reality is non-substantial because it is predicated on difference, alterity, and interrelationality. Substance emerges only in abstraction from that concreteness. The path that Nishida treads thus avoids the pitfalls of an absolutizing conceptualism or substantialism, on the one hand, and nihilism, on the other. Nishida's stance is rather what Ueda calls a "dynamic non-foundationalist multi-dimensionalism."[17] Its dynamic tension—the chiasma—is the "Dionysian dance from which gods are born" (Z8 396–397).[18]

Hence we might say that Nishida's philosophy, in its logic of contradictory self-identity—the dialectic of the dialectical universal that is really a dialectic of negation—implies a chiasmology as opposed to Aristotelian ousiology, a logic of substance, that is, a logic of non-contradictory identity. Perhaps the language of the logic of contradiction can then be re-stated in terms of a field of an interacting or inter-folding manifold, a chiasmology, the legein of chiasma. As I mentioned briefly earlier, if "dialectic" is but the interrelationship between two opposites, even as bi-conditionals, it would seem to be a simplification of, or abstraction from, what concretely speaking is a chiasma of multiple disparates, or of an inter-folding manifold of the abyssal place constituting identities through mutual differences in those folds. To take my discussion beyond Nishidian formulations, the dialectic of bi-conditional opposites or contradictories thus ultimately gives way to a chiasma of manifold forces and dimensions in (over-)inter-determination, each term of which precludes reduction to any other in virtue of its own chiasmatic complexity.[19] The crisscrossing of multiple factors on multi-dimensional levels exceeds in complexity bi-nomial oppositions or even the triadic formula of traditional dialectic. The complexity is one of over-determination that threatens to undermine the language of traditional dialectics. Even the primal opposition between being and non-being would have to dissolve into this chiasma of manifold chiasmas, each of which is too complex to be declared merely "being" or "non-being," "is" or "is-not." It is not that there are two distinct absolute principles that we name "being" and "non-being," which subsequently oppose and interrelate to constitute things. Rather, the enfolding-unfolding play of being and non-being, constituting the finitude of things, consists of a chiasmatic manifold of forces or folds, each in turn irreducibly composed of further such chiasmas. The chiasmatic manifold of chiasmas, extending without end outwardly and inwardly, to explode and implode delimiting boundaries, is thus what constitutes the infinite sphere without periphery. The chiasma therefore deconstructs any notion of a substance. One might say that Nishida's logic of place as a logic of the predicate opposed to Aristotle's logic of the grammatical subject is a logic of the chiasma opposing the logic of ousia (substance). The Greek term for Aristotle's substance, *ousia* (οὐσία), is also the abstract noun form for the verb *einai* (εἶναι), "to be." In contrast to the Aristotelian ousiology of being, the chiasmology points to a cross-sectional place of manifold intricate interactivities. This is what surfaces in Nishida's terms of the contradictory identity between *on* (being) and *mē on* (non-being). If Aristotle's ousiology is an ontology, Nishida's chiasmology is an an-ontology implying the enfolding intertwining of *on* and *mē on* within a chiasmatic manifold.[20] That place of chiasma, enveloping the manifold, is what Nishida calls basho. The chiasma (over-)determines that otherwise indeterminate place of nothing. To that place in its self-withdrawing, self-negating character, making possible the chiasmatic (over-)inter-determinations, I now turn.

Place and Chōra

There are ideas among the ancient Greeks comparable to Nishida's notion that to be is to be in a place, to be implaced (Z3 415), as well as to his general notion of a place of nothing. Simplicius quotes Pseudo-Archytas as saying: "All existing things [*ta onta panta*] are either in place [*en topō*] or not without place [*ouk aneu topō*]. . . . It is necessary for other things to be in place, but for place to be in nothing."[21] Nishida's idea is that everything is in a place, every place is in its place, and ultimately everything and every place are encompassed by the nothing: the place of absolute nothing (zettai mu no basho 絶対無の場所). In the beginning of his 1926 essay "Basho," Nishida states that he drew inspiration for this idea from Plato's concept of *chōra* (χώρα) in the *Timaeus* in order to adapt it to the subject-object relationship. In the *Timaeus* (52b), for example, it is said: "Everything that exists must of necessity be somewhere, in some place [*topos*; τόπος] and occupying some *chōra,* and that which doesn't exist somewhere, whether on earth or in the heavens, doesn't exist at all."[22] It may help us understand Nishida's dialectic of place if we examine the implications of this Greek Platonist notion of chōra.

In the initial stages of his basho theory, where his concern is primarily to overcome epistemological dualism, Nishida adapts Plato's chōra to that epistemological subject-object sphere. Thereby he transposes the Platonic ideas into epistemological categories that form sense-matter, and chōra becomes the place qua field of consciousness (ishiki no ba 意識の場) for that interrelationship of form and matter (Z3 415, 498; Z10 59). The source of that general adaptation of Platonic cosmology to Kantian epistemology may be found in Hermann Cohen, who took the sensibly given in terms of Platonic non-being and the forms of thought in terms of being.[23] In working out his idea of place as the field of consciousness, Nishida also appears to be referring to the modern German—Neo-Kantian and even phenomenological—conceptions of *Gebiet* (domain, field), *Region* (region), and *Bewußtseinsfeld* (field of consciousness) (Z3 416–417). But the final place that is delimited by nothing, as we have seen amply by now, would have to envelop both subjectivity and objectivity, or noesis and noema. Husserl's *Region* either implies only noesis or, in Nishida's view, is an objectified, noematized noesis (Z4 191).[24] Thus, although Nishida takes over the Neo-Kantian appropriation of Platonist thought, he regards the field of consciousness as a place of relative or oppositional nothing (sōtai mu 相対無, tairitsuteki mu no basho 対立的無の場所) in relation to its objects, which are thus beings (yū 有).

Ueda Shizuteru understands Nishida's basho to involve a multi-layered structuring of meanings, a horizon of meaning for experience, that constitutes the place wherein one always already finds oneself existing. Each horizon of experience is in itself always limited, implying a "beyond" that constitutes the condition for the horizon's possibility.[25] That "beyond" is always dark and unknowable, un-objectifiable, what Nishida called mu (無; nothing). Yet to acknowledge it is "self-awareness" or "self-realizing" (jikaku 自覚). A significant point here is that in his attempt to construct a complete system of self-awareness that will surmount the gap of Kantian dualism, Nishida has ingeniously allowed for the impossibility of its completion as an aspect integral to his "complete" account.[26] Yoko Arisaka has thus pointed out that Nishida's theory of place is an attempt to construct a theoretical system that is inherently irreducible to thought, that is, theory itself, in virtue of its unreifiable concrete source, a self-grounding principle of un-groundedness, the nothing that horizons as an open system, a "circle without periphery."[27] What Nishida comes to call "the world" (sekai 世界) in the 1930s can then be viewed in light of that final place or horizon of sense (meaning) encompassing myriad other delimited places.[28] If we take the "world" as a delimited and restricted horizon, however, it would imply a further openness enveloping it, itself unrestricted, un-delimited, the open that Nishida calls the place of absolute nothing, which in the world-dialectic of the 1930s takes on the significance of that trans-temporal and trans-spatial space enfolding and unfolding its chiasmology, as I discussed earlier. Our being-in-the-world essentially involves our implacement within the world, which is, in turn, implaced within that open sphere without periphery.[29] On this basis Nishida develops an "absolute dialectic," or what I have called his implicit chiasmology, whence the dialectical implications of his thoughts on place can be drawn. The self-determining open sphere that is the world's matrix is the field, place, of the inter-dimensional, inter-directional, inter-determining chiasma that I touched on earlier. It is this *open*, however, that we may further understand in terms of chōra in its more than merely epistemological significance, for it is here in the later stages of Nishida's thought that the chōratic nature of place, taken in its original Greek sense, becomes manifest. Nishida initiated his philosophy of place with an inward look into the interior depths of the self that opens to an abyssal nothing. As he proceeded through the 1930s, that nothing revealed itself as an un-delimitable opening whereon and wherein the world unfolds in one's interactivities with other beings. As one so acts, one expresses the world's self-formation in one's action. Place understood in this significance does not permit confinement to mere topos and instead entails chōra, but not simply as Plato understood it. Rather, we might also look to its original Greek significance as a contextualizing region or field that encompasses the *polis* (πόλις, city) and sinks its roots into the earth.

Why chōra? The Greek term has been variously translated as "place," "space," "country," "region," "land," or "area." In ordinary non-philosophical and pre-Platonic Greek it connotes the "country" as opposed to or surrounding the city or town. In Plato's *Timaeus* the term is used to mean the "receptacle" (*hypodochē*) onto which the ideas are in-formed or in-scribed to make their particular copies that occupy and give shape to the *kosmos* or "world." Plato variously characterizes chōra as the "nurse" (*tithēnē*) of all becoming (49a),[30] the ultimate "in which" (*en hō*) for all transient and changing things, their "seat" (*hedra*) or matrix (*ekmageion*) (50c).[31] The character Timaeus, after whom the work is named, explains:

> Not only does it always receive all things, it has never in any way whatever taken on any form [*morphē*] like any of those things that enter it. For its nature is to be a matrix [*ekmageion*] for all things; and it is modified, shaped, and reshaped by those things that enter it. These are the things that make it appear different at different times. (50b–c)

That idea of chōra expresses an indefinition that is neither subjective nor objective, neither idea nor thing, neither paradigm nor copy. It is the third "something" or genus—*triton genos* (52a)—necessitated by the relationship between copy (thing) and paradigm (idea), that is, between the formed individual qua "becoming" (*genesis*) and the forming universal idea qua "being" (on), for "the image must be *in* something and made *out of* something other than that of which it is an image."[32] Because it receives the types (ideas) and gives them place, Timaeus names that something "place" (chōra). As all-receiving, it becomes stamped or in-formed by all sorts of intelligible paradigms, the ideas (*eidē*), so that it serves as the receptacle of all formations of things, the wherein of their generation and the whence of their passing. But in itself chōra is neither intelligible (in the order of "being," the ideas) nor sensible (in order of "becoming," the copies) (52a–c). Belonging to neither of the two genres—intelligible-formal or sensible-material— and lacking its own identity, chōra remains un-determined, characterless, formless, amorphous (*amorphon*) (50e). Eugene Fink thus characterizes chōra as "the dark nocturnal space-matter of the universe" (*die dunkle, nächtige Raum-Materie des Weltalls*). While stressing its all-embracing and nurturing nature as "the great mother . . . 'earth'" (*die Große Mutter, die "Erde"*), Fink also characterizes it as "chaos" (*das Chaos*).[33] But it is good to remember that *chaos* for the most ancient Greeks meant "chasm" and implied an opening. Hans-Georg Gadamer suggests that chōra is something like an undifferentiated "that" on which we hit in our immediate experience before identifying what the thing is in distinction from others.[34] Within that formlessness—an empty opening of a formless space—chōra makes room for things, clearing space to be occupied by whatever becomes. I might point out here the verb form of *chōra, chōreō* (χωρέω), which, along with the sense of being in flux, has the sense of making room for another by giving way or withdrawing.[35] In this way it provides an abode (*hedra;* ἕδρα) to all insofar as they are generated; it is their seat of generation and destruction. As the wherein and whence of every this and that, chōra withdraws from any designation as this or that.

Nishida's dialectic of negation is predicated on that amorphous nothingness— the chōratic nature—of place. The chōratic open, which in Mahāyāna translates into the emptiness (kū 空) of the open sky (*sora* 空), in Nishida translates into the place (basho) delimited by nothing (mu). Nishida thus refers to Plato's chōra when he first formulates the concept of place (*Z3* 415). Like chōra, Nishida's basho at its most concrete level eludes positive description, yet in its no-thingness it opens a space for things determined and differentiated from one another and envelops them. It recedes into the dark to make room for the objects of our attention. Because Nishida was inspired by Plato's idea, we ought to acknowledge this chōratic nature of his notion of place. Although some English translators of Nishida have rendered the term *basho* by the Greek-English *topos* and occasionally by the Latin *locus,* and while certainly Nishida also refers to Aristotle's conception of the soul as a "topos of forms" (*Z3* 419),[36] the sense of basho is truly closer to that of chōra than to the defined or delimited place that is topos.[37] In general, for the ancient Greeks, topos is the physical location that a material thing happens to occupy at the moment and that is independent of its being. Chōra, on the other hand, is the field that gives room for such localities and provides the contextual significance for things. It is dynamically involved in the thing's being and as such is ontologically essential to what the thing is. Augustin Berque has characterized this distinction in terms of cartological place (topos) and existential or ontological place (chōra). Plato makes this distinction when he speaks of chōra's thrashing motion, whereby things therein are settled into their distinct *topoi* (52e–53a).[38] But in distinguishing the ontological sense of chōra, Berque clarifies its pre-Platonic significance as a context-providing or meaning-giving ecumene tying the human habitat to its surrounding land or milieu. Chōra in its ontological sense as essential to the formation of beings is thus closer in significance to Nishida's notion of place than is topos.[39]

Yet we also need to acknowledge the difference between Plato's chōra and Nishida's development of it as basho. Chōra in Plato, despite its status as a triton genos, is not neutral. It is a receptacle for the ideas. Hence Plato likens chōra to the mother vis-à-vis the true being (*ontōs on*) of the ideas, or vis-a-vis the *dēmiourgos* (δημιουργός) who handles them, as the father impregnating her, with genesis as their child (50d)—the archetypal image of Heaven the Father and Mother Earth. But this is precisely what led to the Aristotelian duality of form and matter and eventually its Kantian reformulation in epistemological terms that Nishida wants to overcome. On this account Nishida expresses dissatisfaction with the ancient Greeks' failure to attribute any "logical independence" to their notion of "place" (*Z7* 223).[40] For Nishida, place as basho, instead of being on the mere receiving end of formation, is self-forming. Its formlessness is a living creativity that forms itself. Nishida calls it a self-forming formlessness. It is in this sense that it is a nothing (mu) that gives rise to being (yū). Place forms itself via the inter-determinations of things for which it makes room. In distinction from Plato's place as receptacle, Nishida's version of chōra is self-formative but self-formative via its individual elements, whereby the transcendent, the universal, is in fact immanent as their place, a self-negating nothing that allows for their self- and co-determinations by making room for them. In contrast to Plato's hierarchical dualism that subordinates chōra as receptacle, chōra's status as a triton genos is amplified in Nishida as truly neutral and indefinable. The contrast of Nishida's position with Platonic idealism, then, does not necessarily imply a materialism, as in Marxism. We should also remember here that the understanding of chōra as pure matter or *hylē* was an Aristotelian imposition.[41] Plato never characterized chōra as *hylē*.[42] The chōratic nature of a self-withdrawing clearing (*Lichtung*) precludes any such characterization. And in Nishida's position, its clearing makes room for the opposition between the ideal and the material, form and matter. In its nature of giving place to the various interrelations between opposites without itself being subject to the laws it situates,[43] Nishida's basho, as an empty or formless place, is indeed chōratic.

If we look back at that chōra in light of Nishida's dialectic of contradictory self-identity, Jacques Derrida, who most certainly was unaware of Nishida's appropriation, nevertheless comes close to Nishida's conception when he remarks that Plato's chōra seems to defy that either-or "logic of non-contradiction," "the logic of binarity."[44] As a triton genos (52a), the essential space standing behind and enveloping both being (ideas) and becoming (images, things), chōra is neither of the immutable intelligibles nor of the becoming and corruptible sensibles; neither being qua universal transcendent paradigm nor becoming-and-unbecoming beings qua particulars in-formed by or copying the universal paradigm; neither intelligible being nor sensible being. As a dark "beyond" that gives place to their oppositions, it is in excess, irreducible to either opposite.[45] As neither sensible nor intelligible, it then is beyond sense and meaning. Only from and within it can their cleavage, including also that between body and mind, "have and take place."[46] In its withdrawing that makes room, it perpetually slips beyond any reduction to the presence of an *eidos*. As an excess, it is ontologically "nothing," preceding all beings and allowing for all such binary or dialectical determinations. Nishida's basho, as absolutely nothing (zettai mu) that enfolds every opposition, is chōratic in precisely that way, slipping away from any law of contradiction that would reduce it exclusively to being or non-being.

In its movement of clearing space for the happening thing-events, chōra is dynamic, not static. Everything happens in relation to everything else, near and far, in its contextual implacement. Things are predicated on the space wherein they belong, their concrete place. But those environing or contextualizing conditions continually recede the further we inquire after them, without ever revealing any absolute answer or final principle that explains the reason for the way things ultimately are. The clearing continually retreats into the darkness of indefinition. Hence the "absolute" for Nishida is ultimately nothing or a place delimited by absolutely nothing. This idea echoes chōra's rejection of either-or logic, concurring with its ambiguity as the wherein of all beings and their opposites. As the place wherein everything is marked but that itself remains unmarked, chōra is a place without a place, an un-implaced—even if irreplaceable—place.[47]

Place qua chōra, furthermore, implies our embodiment. In terms of Nishida's concept of self-awareness, the self's deepening into that abyssal place is what led Nishida in the late 1920s to realize the self's pre-epistemic interactivity with its environment via embodiment. The human body in this respect, mirroring the place of the world, is itself a chōra. As a microcosm, it takes part in the self-forming of the cosmic chōra. Both world and body, as macrocosmic and microcosmic places, are chōratic. Plato in the *Phaedo* depicts that chōratic nature of the body as taking on the opposites of life and death.[48] For Nishida, similarly, the individual body is the place of the existential contradiction between life and death. But for Plato, the life force that in-forms the receptacle body qua chōra, the *psychē* (ψυχή), is foreign to it. Because of his dualism, the chōra in Plato here is in-formed by something transcending it. But for Nishida, the mirroring of the cosmos's self-formation in the human body is simultaneously man's own active self-doing. The self-forming formlessness happens on the level of the free and creative individual as well, so that within the infinite expanse of chōra, we have chōras within the chōra. Within that chōra as its place, the medial body extends our limits through our chiasmatic interactions with environing nature. The human body is implaced and contextualized within, and mirrors, the world of meanings and its further implacement within an ever-receding and endless amorphous chōra sinking into the earth. Instead of simply being projectors of meaning on the world, we are born into that world of pre-given meanings receding into non-meaning. Meanings are contextualized, and these contexts are contextualized by the succession of further hidden contexts withdrawing from our grasp. In negotiation with that ever-receding environment, we are also actively shaping contexts and meanings as well. But as meaning-giving and receiving subjects, we find ourselves thrown into that contextualizing environment, enveloping the flux of contextualized realities. Eventually the contexts and meanings sink into the a-meaning of nature, earth, contingency, and finitude with which we must come to terms. Within that chiasmatic chōra, what is immediately present to our embodied being is but a drop in the ocean, yet it mirrors and expresses the ocean, itself uncontextualizable, beyond meaning or purpose, with neither archē nor telos, neither beginning nor end.

If chiasma expresses the over-determinate aspect of Nishida's matter of thinking, chōra expresses its under-determinate aspect. Its indetermination is what refuses reduction to *archai* (ἀρχαί) and *telē* (τέλη), principles and ends, or to any terms of opposition. Rather, in its self-withdrawal, its self-negation, it provides a clearing, a space for the chiasmatic unraveling of the many. The unfolding it enfolds is, as Nishida states, "a determination without determiner" (genteisuru-mononaki gentei 限定するものなき限定) (Z6 15, 20–21, 116, 149, 162; Z7 12, 205). Even while it is nurturing the generation of things, then, chōra undermines any claim to a first substance or the hegemony of a universal First. Only when we understand the universal precisely in light of that an-ontological chōratic opening or self-negation qua place, in its formless nothingness, can the idea of a universality—as in Nishida's dialectical universal—permit the irreducible singularity of individuals. Hegel had inherited the primacy of the idea from Plato as what in-forms, orders, the material of world history. Nishida, by taking off from and developing the chōra rather than the ideas in Plato, hoped to overcome that dichotomy between form and matter and its consequent hierarchy with his notion of a self-forming formlessness, a place enfolding its own forms. In opposition to the idealism of Plato and Hegel, or more precisely, their idea-logy (logos of the idea[s]), Nishida thus puts forth what we might call a "chorology."[49] It serves as a dark undertow that pulls apart and tears asunder metaphysical tendencies, whether in Nishida's thinking or in his misguided interpreters, toward reifying absolutes. John Sallis has remarked that the chōra both originates metaphysics and exposes it to its abyss; it engulfs metaphysics as its beginning and end.[50] It both founds and displaces metaphysical posits. Within the space it clears, metaphysical "firsts"—substances, principles, absolutes—are erected but also toppled. Such a chorology of a place of nothing allowing for the crisscrossing inter-dimensionality, the chiasma of being-and-non-being, not only positions Nishida's so-called dialectic beyond previous Buddhist formulations in unfolding their implications but also situates it beyond Hegel's dialectical idea-lism founded on the concept conceiving itself via its dialectical structure. Hence we question the adequacy of a language of dialectical logic that borrows Hegelian terminology to express Nishida's matter of thought, the chiasmatic chōra.

Chiasmatic Chōra

Chōra both supports, or rather engulfs in its gaping abyss, and is constituted by its chiasma. Nishida's mature thought—"the dialectic of place" (*basho no benshōhō* 場所の弁証法)—entails both together as a chiasmatic chōra. Chōra establishes (as well as topples) in its abyss an an-archic economy of generation-and-dissolution whereon quasi-substances and apparent principles (archai) are generated and cease as singular constellations within a chiasmatic concurrence of manifold forces and dimensions.[51] This concrete chiasma of what Nishida calls "absolute dialectic" cannot be expressed adequately in terms of Hegelian dialectics. And place in its nature as a self-withdrawing chōra that founds this dialectic—enfolding and unfolding its chiasma that in turn determines its shape—also escapes the grasp of a conceptual systematic such as that of Hegel's self-conceiving concept or self-knowing spirit. Nishida's basho is the place of dialectics, and his benshōhō is the dialectic of place, together constituting a chiasmatic chorology. It is the place of dialectic because it enfolds the unfolding chiasma, and it is the dialectic of place because chōra determines itself through the dialectic. Furthermore, the complexity of the chiasma—in excess of standard dialectics—involves a chiasm (chiasmus) between place and dialectic, chōra and chiasma as mutually constitutive. Place constitutes its dialectic and dialectic constitutes its place through their mutual self-negations. The self-determination of the (under-)determined chōra is a chiasma of (over-)inter-determinations, a perpetually reconfiguring chiasmatic chōra—as a self- and inter-morphing amorphousness—the sheer complexity of which undermines any final Aufhebung. What we have here, then, is a chiasmology in opposition to Aristotelian ousiology and a chorology in distinction from Platonist and Hegelian idea-logy (i.e., their idealism)—the reticulated space of a chiasmatic chōra. And if it is the principles—rules for thought—that decide what is and is-not, chiasmatic chōra, irreducible in its over- and under-determinations to being or non-being, proves to be the an-ontological origin of both *on* and *mē on* (being and non-being). Both chōra and chiasma here work together to undermine, in Nishida's system of in-completion, any semblance of a metaphysics of self-closure under the postulation of an absolute—whether as idea or concept or Geist or substance. It is the matter of Nishida's thinking that has undermined his repeated attempts to grasp it under the structure of a completed system once and for all. Never reaching its end, his philosophy is thus incomplete and open. To read Nishida in such terms allows us to bring him into an intimate dialogue with the more recent post-Hegelian thinkers of the twentieth and twenty-first centuries, who, in countering the ousiology of traditional Western metaphysics, have also been attending to place, chōra, chiasma, and related or similar issues. Nishida's dialectic of place, then, has something to offer to contemporary Western philosophy. In regard to the relationship of Nishida's chiasmatic chorology to Mahāyāna non-dualism and Hegelian dialectics, we can offer the following conclusions. The grounding and un-grounding of Nishida's absolute dialectic within this gaping chōra qua place, releasing the dialectic's chiasmatic complexity, distinguishes Nishida's dialectic as "absolute dialectic" from Hegel's dialectic. But this absolute dialectic as founded on place also extends beyond previous formulations within Buddhism.

11 Concluding Thoughts, Criticism, and Evaluation

Now that we have discussed in detail Nishida's dialectic, in this final chapter I would like to conclude this work with some evaluation and assessment of Nishida's dialectical philosophy. I ask two challenging questions: (1) To what extent is the language (or terminology) Nishida employed adequate for expressing the matter of his thinking? (2) What does Nishida's thinking have to offer us today? I will discuss the first question in relation to the issues of logic and dialectics in Nishida and the second question in relation to modernity and the contemporary situation of globalization.

Language, Logic, Dialectics

Nishida's theory of place seeks to provide a philosophical glimpse of the concrete standpoint we all live and experience as always already, the ever-implicit wherein of our implacement. Yet this is also the wherein from which we inevitably "fall from grace"—or at least distance ourselves—in the act of reflecting on it. Perhaps this attempt to philosophically formulate the inexpressably concrete is one of the attractions of Nishida's thought. The attempt makes us aware of our finitude and contingency. This brings up the issue of Nishida's mode of presenting that concrete. To what extent is it viable? One might say that one point of Mahāyāna Buddhist practice, such as Zen, is to experience concrete reality in its non-dual or contradictory nature, unmediated by conceptual thought. Paradoxically, Nishida strives to articulate the un-articulable, to speak about what cannot be spoken, to discursively bring the concrete to expression. While telling us to look for it in the direction of the predicate since it cannot be made into a subject of judgment, Nishida cannot help but speak of it himself, treating it as the subject of discussion. Does his mode of locution succeed in portraying that ineffable sphere? This question may be raised more succinctly in regard to the metaphysical and epistemological terminologies he appropriates, especially from nineteenth-century German philosophy—most notably, that of the Neo-Kantians and of Hegel. This includes the conceptual schemata of the universal-individual relationship or of the concrete universal, the logic of contradiction, and the language of a dialectic. Do these terms and phrases do justice to the matter of Nishida's thinking? My concern here is not whether Nishida adequately understood those German philosophers. The point is whether his appropriation of their terms and concepts—Hegelian dialectics, the epistemological hylo-morphism of the Neo-Kantians, or even the noesis-noema scheme of Husserl from the early twentieth century—fits what he wanted to express.

This issue of Nishida's language has to do with the issue of logic and of dialectics in general. Nishida liked to characterize his philosophy both as dialectical (benshōhōteki 弁証法的) and as a kind of logic (ronri 論理). To what extent, then, can the ineffability of his subject matter be rendered in logical form, including dialectical logic? His system was to be a "logic" (ronri) explicated as unfolding in the structure of a "dialectic." In "Watashi no ronri ni tsuite" (「私の論理について」; "Concerning My Logic"), published in 1946 and serving as the afterword to his final essay, "Bashoteki ronri to shūkyōteki sekaikan" (「場所的論理と宗教的世界観」; "The Logic of Place and the Religious Worldview"), Nishida reflects on his dialectical logic as a form of thinking that "clarifies the logic of the historically formative act . . . from the standpoint of our historically active self" (Z10 431). He responds here to those who attack his logic of contradictory self-identity as "not a logic at all." His reply is that his critics are misunderstanding rather than clarifying his dialectic (Z10 431). And in "Ronri to sūri" (「論理と数理」; "Logic and Mathematics"), also from the same period, he views his notion of contradictory self-identity as rendering form to the "logic of nothing" (*mu no ronri* 無の論理) that can be found in Buddhist philosophy (Z10 69). Why did Nishida insist on a "logic"? Nishida's frame of reference was nineteenth-century German philosophy, in the context of which "logic" serves as a synonym for epistemology but can also mean the structure of metaphysics (e.g., in the systems of Kant, Hegel, and the Neo-Kantians). For example, the Neo-Kantian use of the term "logic" (*Logik*) can be traced to Hermann Lotze, who, while doing what we would call "epistemology" (or "theory of knowledge"), refused to use the term "epistemology" because what was called "epistemology" during the 1850s and 1860s in Germany was "psychologistic," or, more precisely, even psycho-physiological, attempts to reduce Kant's transcendental philosophy to nerve-energies.[1] Following Lotze, the Neo-Kantians formulated their epistemology as a kind of "logic" in order to overcome psychologism, the point being that cognition is unrelated to psychological or physiological contingencies. Nishida's philosophy of place takes off from this Neo-Kantian attempt to "logicize" (or: logically found) (*ronrika* 論理化) the dynamic of cognition without reference to the psychology of the subject-knower. Like the Neo-Kantians, Nishida, when he was first formulating his theory of place, felt the need to avoid the charge of psychologism by providing a "logical foundation" (*ronriteki kiso* 論理的基礎) for his ideas that would not call to mind the contingencies of the psyche (Z3 254–255).

Nishida, however, also considered his "logic of place" a kind of "intuitionism" (chokkanshugi 直観主義). In contrast to the Neo-Kantian emphasis on conception, his cognitive theory was to be grounded on a fundamental intuition (chokkan 直観). As he indicated in his preface to the 1927 *Hatarakumono kara mirumono e* (『働くものから見るものへ』; *From the Working to the Seeing*), Nishida believed that with the formulation of his theory of place, he was making a "turn" from his earlier "voluntarism" involving Bergsonian and Fichtean formulations to an "intuitionism" of a "seerless seeing," that is, an intuition of the nothing—the nothing here as both subject and object—that sees through self-differentiation. Such intuitionism as underlying Nishida's "logical founding" is indicative of what lies in the depths of human existence, which Nishida often spoke of as "the religious" (shūkyōteki 宗教的), the extreme limit point of one's existence, one's "vanishing point," where the self-contradiction of one's being in its generation-and-extinction, its radical contingency, is made explicit. Intuition here is the self-seeing of the place (basho 場所) where life meets death. What Nishida calls "the religious" in this significance—what in today's philosophical parlance we may translate as "the existential"—entails the self-awareness of one's finitude vis-à-vis the excess reality of the concrete, the awareness of the nothing wherein one is ultimately implaced and to which one belongs. It seems obvious that this is irreducible to any logical formulation. Place in its concrete whole, in its transcendence, is irreducible to logical formulations and rules of thought.

The issue of the appropriateness of the language of "logic" thus arises especially in connection to Nishida's allusions to that a-rational aspect of place. In the late 1930s (e.g., in "Ronri to seimei" 「論理と生命」; "Logic and Life") Nishida further develops the alleged logic of concrete reality to understand it in terms of the proto-logical structure or logos of the historical world. Furthermore, he understands that latter structure dialectically and comes to elaborate it in terms of contradictory self-identity (Z8 68, 97, 100). Nishida here views what we normally call "logic"—formal logic—to be mediated by logos, which he in turn understands as this dialectic of historical reality. The essence of logic (ronri) as such is generated from the historical world's formative act, logos that is dialectical ("the logic of absolute negation," "the logic of absolute nothing") (Z8 97; Z9 442, 452–453). This leads to the issue of dialectic that structures that logos underlying world history. Nishida—in what Ōmine Akira calls the standpoint of "thoroughgoing logicism" (*tetteiteki ronrishugi* 徹底的論理主義)—attempts to think logic through to its dialectical genesis in life, whereby logic itself is exhausted.[2] Hence the dialectic of logic is established by means of that dialectic of life. In "Ronri to seimei" Nishida states that dialectic means not that logic mediates life but that life mediates logic (Z8 98). A few years earlier, in *Tetsugaku no konpon mondai* (『哲学の根本問題』; *Fundamental Problems of Philosophy*), Nishida states that true logic is not the science of abstract thought but "the science of concrete thought" (*gutaiteki shii no gaku* 具体的思惟の学), and that true dialectic is "the path by which reality explains itself" (*jitsuzai ga jikojishin o setsumeisuru michi* 実在が自己自身を説明する途)

(Z6 172). But at that point during the mid-1930s, Nishida still identifies Hegel with his standpoint. By the late 1930s, however, he comes to view Hegelian dialectics as not thorough, not radical, enough. In Nishida's eyes, the grounding of logic on the concrete reality of life exhausts Hegelian dialectics and exceeds its framework.[3] To what extent, then, does that dialectical structure of life that exceeds Hegelian formulations adequately portray the complexity of the concrete?

David Dilworth has pointed out that the Mahāyāna doctrine of the nonduality between nirvāṇa and saṃsāra cannot be adequately framed in the dialectical language of Plato or Hegel. Noticing the closeness between Nishida and Mahāyāna, Dilworth thus refuses to even speak of a "dialectic" in Nishida.[4] Yet Nishida, in describing his thinking, employs the term *benshōhō* (弁証法), the term commonly used for translating "dialectic" into Japanese. While Dilworth speaks of Nishida's paradoxical logic contra Hegel's dialectical logic, Nishida characterizes his way of philosophizing as dialectic (benshōhō), even if it is ultimately of a different sort from Hegel's. "Paradox" rather translates *mujun* (矛盾), also meaning "contradiction." What Dilworth renders as Nishida's "paradoxical logic" in opposition to Hegel's "dialectical logic" really means a "dialectic of contradiction" in contrast to Hegel's "dialectic of sublation." Nishida views his version of dialectic, which he comes to call "absolute dialectics" (zettai benshōhō 絶対弁証法), as involving genuine self-contradiction or self-negation, in contrast to Hegel's dialectic of sublational synthesis. A related issue, then, is what Nishida means by "contradiction" (mujun). Nishida's "absolute dialectic" is a dialectic of contradiction, as I just mentioned. David Putney has criticized Nishida's concept of a contradictory identity, stating that propositions or concepts cannot really be contradictory unless both sides of the dichotomy are asserted to be true. Nishida, however, does not reject the dichotomy of opposites outright by sublating or resolving the opposition. Nishida's point is that contradictories co-exist in tension, in mutual reference, and within a self-nullifying place. Putney thus concedes that perhaps Nishida's idea should be viewed from a broader perspective.[5] But that broader trans-logical perspective is what we get in Nishida's concept of an un-delimited place (basho) that negates itself to make room for the relationship of contradiction. The Japanese word Nishida employs for "contradiction" is *mujun*. This can be translated as "paradox"—the word that Dilworth prefers, as I have noted—which certainly would give a broader meaning than the merely formal-logical one. This may have been the sense Nishida had in mind when he referred to the mujun of the Heraclitean strife and its logos that underlies world history. The Heraclitean sense here—also pointed to by Nietzsche—is that contradiction (thus taken broadly) is the motor of life, and that the strife of opposites is the source of everything. I certainly agree with commentators who point out that what Nishida means by "contradiction" (mujun) in the phrase "contradictory self-identity" (mujunteki jikodōitsu 矛盾的自己同一) specifically has to do with inter-dependence via mutual negation of opposites, which in turn is more akin to the Mahāyāna "logic of soku-hi" than to anything Hegel meant by "contradiction." At the same time, however, I question whether such a "logic" can be stated to be uniquely Eastern.[6] But the point here is that it is only from that non- or trans-logical paradoxicality that formal-logical distinctions could be derived and hence logical contradiction subsequently obtained. In this respect Nishida does not always clarify the distinction between logical and non-logical opposition—that is, between contradiction in formal logic, on the one hand, and contradiction construed concretely as strife, paradox, or inter-dependence, constituting the logos of the concrete world, on the other.

Yet as I mentioned in chapter 10, the compound *mujun* also comes from a Chinese story in *Han Feizi* (『韓非子』) about a vender selling lances or halberds (*mu* 矛 of *mujun*, pronounced *hoko* in Japanese) and shields (*jun* 盾 of *mujun*, pronounced *tate* in Japanese). On the one hand, he advertises that there are no shields that his lances cannot penetrate; on the other, he advertises that there are no lances that can penetrate his shields.[7] Accordingly, the concept does have the sense of mutually exclusive alternatives.[8] Nishida's point is that such alternatives in their mutual exclusion refer to each other and in that respect are bi-conditionals, and that furthermore, such co-relating terms assume the place of their relationship, even if it is a relation of mutual exclusion. Ontologically the primordial opposition of mutual exclusion would be between being and non-being, and we can transpose this ontological opposition logically into the contradiction between yes and no, affirmation and negation. Nishida often has in mind precisely this ontological opposition, which is also a logical contradiction, although it is more than just that. Furthermore, the logical and ontological senses merge into the existential sense of one's self-contradiction as a finite being in the fact that life entails death, or, in religious terms, that salvation or enlightenment entails the self-awareness of one's inescapable sinfulness or ignorance. What Nishida means by "contradiction" entails all these senses. The problem lies more in Nishida's mode of articulation, which makes use of the language and categories of German metaphysics and epistemology to put forth his thinking as a "logic." This usage tends toward abstraction and reification[9] and away from the concrete, despite Nishida's warnings against abstraction. On this basis one might view Nishida's logic of contradictory self-identity as instead "a complex system of abstractions which tend to defeat themselves."[10] But to fault Nishida for that shortcoming is perhaps unfair if one takes into consideration that he was a pioneer within his milieu (the first generation of Japanese intellectuals trained in Western philosophy) in attempting a project of such immense proportions. What he means by contradictory self-identity is in fact the concrete from which opposing abstractions are made. In any case, one may still ask: Does Nishida's employment of a dialectical terminology serve to fetter and congeal the fluidity or complexity of the concrete into the mere formula of a dialectic?

From the other side, in the face of that abstraction, one might wonder whether the concreteness of the matter of that "concrete logic" or "concrete dialectic" undermines—in escaping—that logicality, its dialectical formulation. One cannot help but ask whether Nishida's dialectical systematic is still a rationalization of the a-rational that ultimately eludes and slips away from the reductive categories of its "dialectical logic." In other words, does Nishida's explication of the paradoxical nature of concrete reality in the terms of a dialectical logic, a logic even of contradiction, really do justice to the chiasmatic nature of its matter that I discussed in chapter 10? Would the underlying chiasma of Nishida's absolute dialectic exhaust the formulation of a dialectic? Can one make the same objection here that Gilles Deleuze leveled against Hegel's *Logic* for conceiving difference in terms of contradiction? Deleuze's point was that difference in itself—diversity, alterity—is not reducible to contradiction.[11] As I stated earlier, what Nishida meant by contradiction is not the same as what Hegel meant and cannot be reduced to formal logical contradiction, although it includes it. Nonetheless, we may still question the adequacy of the language of contradiction, even of dialectics, for the *Sache selbst,* not only of the chiasma but also of the chōra. Can dialectical language of any sort adequately capture and portray the un-delimitedness of that place that is absolutely nothing, its chōratic aspect? Nishida spent over thirty years reconstructing versions of his system, one after another. But in virtue of the nature of its subject matter, the system he attempted to build could never be completed. The language he employed as building blocks for this system repeatedly met its limit in the matter it attempted to structure and express. Its founding touches an undertow that perpetually undermines and threatens to deconstruct its construction. He was erecting his system on that which escapes systematization—a dark ineffable non-substantiality, whose openness can never meet closure. Yet this was Nishida's lifelong philosophical project—the paradox of a philosophical system that allows for its in-completion. Its in-completion is its openness in the face of an irreducible other and in the midst of which it finds itself—the philosophical system along with its thinker—implaced. But in that case, does the dialectic, as an anti-logic, serve to facilitate that opening—at least as a pointer to the ineffable? How might Nishida answer Martin Heidegger's contention that "all dialectic in philosophy is only the expression of an embarrassment"?[12] Certainly dialectic is embarrassing if we limit it to what Maurice Merleau-Ponty termed "bad dialectic"—an assemblage of statements: thesis, antithesis, synthesis—as opposed to what he called "hyperdialectic," a "good dialectic" that recognizes that every thesis is but an idealization that cannot exhaust being. Such a dialectic without synthesis, according to Merleau-Ponty, "envisages without restriction the plurality of the relationships and what has been called ambiguity."[13] That plurality and that ambiguity, coupled with Deleuzean difference, are perhaps what in my reading of Nishida I have been calling the chiasma. And if, as Heidegger contends, dialectic is derivative of tautology as more original,[14] Nishida's self-seeing self-awareness of the undelimitable nothing—the intuition of a seerless seeing—may intimate an answer.[15] Dialectics may be embarrassing if it assumes synthesis under conceptual super-impositions. The absolute dialectical tension that Nishida has in mind, however, entails a complexity that is lived rather than artificial and is more intense and complicated than mere binary opposition—the chiasmatic complexity I discussed in chapter 10 whereby that self-awareness of one amid many can never be fixed into a grammatical subject or concept or substance.

Indeed, if we fully abandon object logic, the dynamism that is the matter of Nishida's thought, exceeding rules of formal or binary logic, may not have to be seen as contradictory. It is self-contradictory only from the logical perspective. It is only under the reification of alternative sides, through their abstraction from the concrete dynamism of their implacement—their chiasma—that they are seen as mutually contradictory. Nishida is not utterly unaware of this, and that is why he points to the place of nothing as their chōratic basis allowing for dialectic, dichotomization, and abstraction. In overstepping the Aristotelian principle of non-contradiction, Nishida's place indicates the concrete context wherein that logical principle can make sense. Its broader view that is neither/nor allows for the narrower focus on each term as contradicting, excluding, the other. It is from that deeper and broader perspective that Nishida speaks of "the religious" as the place wherein one faces the intersection between life and death, being and nothing, where one faces what, logically speaking, is a contradiction in one's existence. So in one sense we can say that place logically is self-contradictory, but in another sense it lies beyond such logical formulations, having surpassed, while making possible, binary opposition.

If the opposing terms of a dialectical relationship are but abstractions from or derivations of their co-implacement in that pre-dichotomized place, the logic of a dialectic (of binary opposition) unfolding from what enfolds them seems to be derivative, a posteriori, in relation to that enfolding place. This brings us back to the basho nature, the chōratic aspect, of Nishida's dialectic. I note again the verb form of *chōra, chōreō,* meaning "to make room." To make room for all that can be grasped via the senses or the intellect, chōra eludes our grasp. Nishida's basho implies an openness that extends into the dark, defying any attempt to conceive it or capture it within some system. We have seen that the matter of Nishida's thinking perpetually slips away from his repeated attempts to systematize it, to complete its structure, in the language of dialectical philosophy. That darkness would precede any logic of a dialectic. Yet we must not forget that Nishida also emphasized the interrelationality of terms that give shape to that openness. But the question here is whether the structure of a dialectic, and not necessarily interrelationality per se, designates a system of thinking imposed on what is pre-dialectical and exceeds such a system.[16] Does the language of "dialectic" shape the matter exceeding its form in the attempt to express it? If dialectics necessarily involves the interrelationship between two opposing terms, even as bi-conditionals, could the relationship be a simplification of, an abstraction from, what concretely is a chiasma involving a multiplicity? The sense one gets from Nishida's key thought motifs, such as the manifold dialectical matrix, the irreducibility of place to being or non-being, and inverse correspondence as mutual self-negation, is that the dialectic of opposing terms is but the tip of an iceberg of what is concretely there. If each of the terms in their mutual contradiction is itself self-contradictory, that is, in their mutual self-negations, this indicates—as I suggested in chapter 10—a chiasmatic complexity that extends beyond the mere dichotomy of opposing terms. The complexity of the concrete, in the chiasma of (over-)inter-determinations, thus exceeds the dialectic. But even if we then take "dialectic" broadly in terms of that trans-dialectical complexity that is chiasma, we might argue that, seen chiasmatically, place and dialectic are co-constitutive. That co-constitution—between the place of dialectic and the dialectic of place—is the chiasmatic chōra.

Thus we return to the fundamental question raised in chapter 10: Can the chiasmatic chōra that is the matter of Nishida's thought be captured by the language of dialectics? Does the multi-dimensional complexity of the self-determining matrix that is the world, as a chiasma of (over-)inter-determinations, along with its nature as an un-delimited place, a self-receding chōra that clears room for those interrelations, undermine the language of a "dialectic"? Does the matter of Nishida's "absolute dialectics" undermine its dialectical structuring? To what degree was Nishida's choice of terms and modes of articulation, borrowed from traditional Western metaphysics, adequate to express his insights concerning concrete reality? The chiasmatic complexity of (over-)inter-determination and the chorological openness of that matter, allowing for perpetual in-completion, work together to undermine any attempt at systematic closure. The matter of Nishida's thinking is in excess of any conceptual or logical system and hence is irreducible even to the structure of a dialectic. The place of dialectic, the dialectic of place, is open, revealing its chiasmatic chōra. It is the unthought and the unsaid lying behind every grammatical subject. Yet despite that dark in-completion, this is what Nishida found to be the most immediate, concrete basis of our existence. It is what must be assumed, pre-conceptually intuited, the contextualizing place that im-places our being in an unhorizoned horizon, the empty sky of openness that Nishida calls the sphere without periphery.

If traditional metaphysical language, the language of logic and of dialectics, fails to capture that chiasmatic complexity and the chōratic openness of place, what would suffice instead? Can we find superior ways to convey what envelops us to ground us even while it escapes our conceptual grasp? Would more "poetical" modes of expression do greater justice to what Nishida wanted to say?[17]

Globalization and the Ethics of Humility

As I stated at the beginning of this work, the world today in its globalization is unfolding its chiasmatic nature as a place of manifold contradictions and oppositions. As Nishida states in "Sekai no shinchitsujo no genri" (「世界の新秩序の原理」; "Fundamental Principles of a New World Order") of 1943, formerly disconnected nations "have been brought into a common world space because of developments in science, technology, and economy" (Z11 445). And in *Nihon bunka no mondai* (『日本文化の問題』; *The Problem of Japanese Culture*) of 1940 he states that nations can no longer stand separately from the world made one by free trade (Z9 10). The technological shrinking of the globe in the past few centuries has torn and erased what previously were cultural and geographic boundaries. Forced to face others like yet unlike ourselves, the spatial contingencies in the constitution of our being, our implacement, previously invisible, become apparent, explicit. The cultural relativity of certain truths previously held to be unquestionable now becomes obvious. As the crossing of borders between formerly isolated worlds becomes increasingly easy and frequent, anxiety grows in the face of broader and more complicated horizons that unfold from the merging and twisting of older ones. No horizon—cultural, religious, political, or ideological—is ultimately self-contained. The present situation, which brings distant horizons into the midst of one another on a global scale, increasingly reveals their emptiness.[18] A certain duplicity is involved in this phenomenon of globalization whereby the globalized market of consumer goods—the pseudo-culture of consumption—drives toward homogenization, on the one hand, and the worldwide network of communication, on the other, flows with proliferating information in the direction that realizes difference on a global scale. What is the relevance of Nishida's dialectic of place to this current state of affairs?

The global spread of technology, as noted by some twentieth-century and contemporary thinkers, such as Martin Heidegger and more recently Edward Casey, reduces the place of human dwelling to calculability, erasing or concealing its unique or singular "homeliness" in the homogeneity of measured space. The world, thus made calculable, is no longer the wherein of our dwelling but becomes reduced to "measurable object-ness."[19] We see this, for example, in the world of capitalism made into a vast market of numerical exchange values. As societies, enamored of an ideology of equality and sameness—colored by the latest fashions and trends—move toward greater homogeneity under this "globalization of capitalism, technology, scientific rationality, and political uniformity,"[20] human beings become uprooted from their traditions, and humanity loses any sense of a grounding in identity.[21] Casey has identified this "homelessness" of the contemporary world as the lack of a primal place, as being without the means of orientation in a complex and confusing world.[22] The increasing sense of placelessness threatens us with disorientation and dispossession.

Yet modern technology's leveling of place, from another perspective, has also led to the unveiling of its contradictions. With the increased speed and efficiency of both physical travel and information exchange—for example, airplanes and the internet—distances are abolished, bringing the far near and displacing human existence into alien lands. On one level, as I just noted, this has led to the globalization of consumer "culture" on a mass scale, threatening with homogenization the unique ways of life of the many indigenous cultures of the world. Mass consumerism that levels everyone to the lowest common denominator makes many long for that home place from which we have been uprooted, the place that would provide a secure ground for our being. But the technological shrinking of the globe at the same time also makes the heterogeneity among cultural places, previously isolated or distant from one other, all too obvious. We thus find ourselves faced with the extreme contrast between the homogeneity of consumer pseudo-culture and the rich multiplicity of differences among world cultures. Globalization involves this double tendency or duplicity between homogenization and the realization of diversity.[23] The increasing pronouncement of difference is countering global homogenization.[24] Forced to face others, each horizon claims autonomy for itself, now threatened with erasure. Modern consumerism's "ideology of equality," in its global expansion, thus seems to be heading toward its exhaustion and destitution. With its globalization, it spreads itself thin as it finds itself displaced from what seemed to be its natural embeddedness or implacement in the world. The hegemony of a principle (the ideology of modernity), in its universalization, in Nishidian terms, finds its extreme limit in its counter-determination by disparates. And in its exhaustion at that extreme point, globalization would reveal the surrounding abyss underlying the ground from which modernity was erected. In Nishida's words, this is the place of nothing.

What can Nishida's thinking offer us today in this context of globalization? What does his dialectic of an open circle or sphere without end provide? When borders crumble and boundaries are being torn down, life can flourish only when people learn to respect others with a sense of humility in the face of mutual differences. Amid these alterations, mutations, and conflicts of traditions and horizons, it may do us well to bear in mind the infinite and irreducible expanse wherein we all are in co-implacement amid differences. Nishida experienced the global heterogeneity or split within his soul as someone growing up in an Eastern culture opening itself up to the world after two centuries of isolation.[25] His philosophical project of overcoming dualism was also a search for a common ground that could contextualize the disparity between East and West on the basis of a deeper unifying source. Ueda Shizuteru claims that the East-West split was exemplified in Nishida's dual activities of Zen meditation and philosophy: "The split was itself his gateway to the 'deeper foundations' of unity."[26] But that foundation can be no universalizing essence that would impose on, and hence erase, mutual differences among elements. It must rather be nothing—that which gives space for co-existence.

From the 1930s up to the end of his life, Nishida sought to extend his theory of place to this arena of globalization and world politics. It is remarkable that when Japan was becoming engulfed in military conflicts in Asia and the Pacific, Nishida attempted to give expression to his vision of a multi-cultural world.[27] In 1935 political discourse became severely restricted by the government. Any statement that could be taken to threaten national policy as religiously sanctioned or to question the primacy of the emperor was suspect. Christopher Goto-Jones thus argues that Nishida's way of dissent within this environment was the philosophical manipulation of conventions and terms, as we shall see in greater detail later.[28] In *Tetsugaku no konpon mondai* of the early to mid-1930s, rather than looking to the domination of a single culture to solve the inevitable and unavoidable encounters between regions and horizons, Nishida looks to their mutual mediation whereby each develops vis-à-vis one another in interrelationship: "True world culture will be formed by various cultures developing themselves through the mediation of the world while preserving their own respective standpoints" (Z6 353). And in *Nihon bunka no mondai* of 1940, the question of inter-cultural encounter is no longer one of "us or them" or even East versus West: "It is not the question of negating Eastern culture by means of Western culture or negating Western culture by means of Eastern culture, nor of enveloping one into the other. Instead, the point is to bathe both in a new light by discovering an even deeper and broader ground" (Z9 91). The depth is to be plumbed via mutual difference and co-relativity. This idea of a "world culture" resulting from inter-cultural encounter culminates in 1943 in his "Sekai no shinchitsujo no genri," in which Nishida promotes the idea of a "global world" as a "multi-worlded" inter-civilizational world-culture.[29] In this global vision of a "multi-world" or "world-of-worlds" (*sekaiteki sekai* 世界的世界), each nation, moving beyond itself but also remaining true to itself, unites with others. There is no single dominating national force, and each culture is able to retain its own way of being, its horizonal world, while simultaneously developing itself and world culture in relation to others in the medium of the world-of-worlds (Z6 353).

In "Sekai no shinchitsujo no genri" Nishida writes:

> For the various national peoples to constitute a global world by transcending themselves while realizing themselves, each must first constitute a particular world by transcending itself and by following its own regional tradition. The world can accordingly form a single global world by the union of these particular worlds, each constituted on its historical foundation. (Z11 445)

Nishida's vision here is no nationalist imperialism, but neither is it an "internationalist globalism" that aims to eradicate or subsume differences under the assumed universality of an allegedly authentic way of being human, be it communism or consumerism: "Each nation or race, possessing its respective world-historical destiny, combines into a single global world while each lives its own unique historical life" (Z11 445). He calls for each nation's simultaneous self-realization and self-transcendence, whereby each reaches beyond itself to participate in erecting a global world. Each nation opens itself up to the world-of-worlds, first by opening to its own concrete regional sphere or "co-prosperity sphere" (*kyōeiken* 共栄圏) (Z11 446) founded on geographic conditions and cultural bonds. The world-of-worlds is to be realized only from the cooperative interrelationship between these particular worlds (*tokushuteki sekai* 特殊的世界), or co-prosperity spheres, precluding the domination of powerful national or multi-national entities.[30] This also means that the "historical life" belonging to the regional traditions and cultures of specific peoples is to be respected.[31] On this basis Nishida foresaw the potential of the twentieth century to be an age when nations of the world would overcome colonialism and undergo a world-awakening.

With no privileged or dominating center, the globe is thus spatialized as a place for the co-implacement of regions. Rather than possessing a universal essence that imposes itself on the various cultures, the globe is their basho, place, wherein they interact and must co-exist. This globalized vision of place is of an *Urkultur* (*genbunka* 原文化)—a term inspired by Goethe—that possesses disparate cultural possibilities in non-distinction, a "nothing" (mu 無), from which they are realized in their mutual differences. In this *Urkultur* Nishida sought a deeper foundation or original source from which spring the branches of East and West (Z9 80; Z13 19–20).[32] Within this space of a primal nothing, cultures of the world interact to dialectically create their own identities vis-à-vis one another, accounting for both deep-rooted commonality and irreducible diversity. Nishida thus writes in 1944 ("Dekaruto tetsugaku ni tsuite" 「デカルト哲学について」) that the path toward the fusion of East and West lies in returning to that primal source of "self-contradiction" and beginning from that standpoint of true "contradictory self-identity" (Z10 138).

Nishida, however, warns in *Nihon bunka no mondai* that one must carefully avoid making one's own country, for example, Japan, into a subject-body (shutai 主体) that would dominate other cultures and countries. To thus attempt to negate them or reduce them according to one's own national standpoint would be imperialism (*teikokushugi* 帝国主義). Rather, one must work vis-à-vis other nations from the standpoint of the world enveloping multiple subject-bodies. Each *kokutai* (国体), or "national polity," must renounce its subjectivization in self-negation. The dialectic of nations in his global vision, then, is one of mutual self-negation. This term *kokutai* has been used in a variety of political significances throughout Japanese history. Goto-Jones argues that Nishida's use of this term, which coincided with its appearance in the document *Kokutai no hongi* (『国体の本義』; *Fundamentals of the National Polity*), published by the Ministry of Education in 1937—in whose authorship Nishida declined to participate—should be read as a moral critique of that document rather than its philosophical elaboration.[33] Rather than being a legal institution, Nishida (in "Sekai no shinchitsujo no genri") viewed kokutai as an organic ethical entity that emerges spontaneously through a people's self-determination, a society that is a historical body (rekishiteki shintai 歴史的身体). Genuine nations as such organic societies—kokutai—would be the natural unit for global affairs.[34] Each such nation comes together with others in mutual determination via mutual self-negation. The country must forgo any aggressive designs and must take care not to impose its own policies on the variety of regional traditions, both within and without (Z9 52, 59, 76–77). Without imposing itself on others, each nation is to learn from others in their interrelations. This is the sense of "self-negation" (jiko hitei 自己否定) extended to the global context. With nations thus transcending their individual self-interested standpoints, global co-existence becomes possible, mediated via mutual self-negation. Nishida was convinced that such global self-negation—a "worldism" (*sekaishugi* 世界主義)—as opposed to self-affirmation for world dominance, would be the reverse of totalitarianism (*zentaishugi* 全体主義) (Z23 386). This was also precisely the point of Nishida's alleged rebuke of the Research Center on National Strategy—according to Tanabe Juri's recollection of Nishida's meeting with army officials at the institute—that a genuine co-prosperity sphere "is definitely not imperialism [teikokushugi]. . . . A co-prosperity sphere coerced while fettering the free will of everyone else would not be a co-prosperity sphere."[35] Nishida distinguishes the co-prosperity sphere from ethnocentrism, which would conceive the world from its own basis to become ethnic egoism (*minzoku jikoshugi* 民族自己主義) and inevitably lead to aggression and imperialism (Z11 449). Although Nishida's text does not—and could not without repercussions—explicitly criticize the official rhetoric, it is clear that in his view the formation of the co-prosperity sphere cannot be forced. Nishida's use of terms such as *kokutai* or *kyōeiken* (co-prosperity sphere)—which at the time were propagated as imperialist ideology—thus was not in the spirit of Japanese imperialism or militarism that would impose its vision of hierarchy on others to assert its hegemony. This was the only way in which Nishida could possibly struggle with the imperialist position of the militarists—through a semantic reappropriation of the meaning of terms.[36] His appropriation is more Mahāyānistic than State Shintō or Confucian in spirit. Rather than imposing the universal on particulars, its vision is of an integration whereby the universal—the world-of-worlds—is formed via the co-participation of the particulars. Hence the resulting world-of-worlds cannot be formed through erasure of national or cultural differences (Z11 447) nor through the universalization of any particular culture, nation, or race or ethnic group over others: "By each nation becoming self-aware of its own world mission, we will be able to construct a single world-historical world [*sekaishiteki sekai* 世界史的世界], that is, a world-of-worlds [sekaiteki sekai]" (Z11 444–445). Each cultural entity, in order to play a part in the world-of-worlds, would have to be true to itself, its own singularity. Only on this basis can the world be truly worldly, a union of distinct particular worlds, a unity-in-diversity permitting the interaction of a plurality of cultures.[37] What Nishida offers here is a pluralistic rather than an imperialistic paradigm, a paradigm founded on cooperation and not domination, and a plurality in interaction rather than one that disperses into isolation. What makes this possible is not some being that is posited as a universal principle, but rather the place of absolute nothing.[38]

In Nishida's thoughts on the co-prosperity sphere and kokutai, despite what the army ideologues might have hoped for, we thus find reference to a de-totalizing undertow of the un-containable and un-systematizable, the globe as a place environed by nothing (mu) to perpetually displace any totalizing, totalitarian inclinations or universalizing claims. We find the chiasmatic chōra that is the matter of Nishida's thinking thus undermining the tendency not only toward absolutization or essentialism in metaphysics but also toward totalitarianism in politics. The sort of ethics one finds here is one of mutual self-negation, an ethics calling for humility vis-à-vis one's others.[39] This vision that would apply an ethics of mutual self-negation, with the concomitant attitude of humility, to the field of world politics is compelling today in this age of global plurality. It calls for an openness in the face of others and caution against attaching oneself dogmatically to one's own stance. Rather than totalizing or absolutizing one's position in self-affirmation over and above others, it calls for a de-totalization in openness to alterity. When this occurs reciprocally, one is no longer necessitated to stake blood and life to defend one's turf or assert one's honor. Nishida's vision here of the world-of-worlds without a doubt presupposes his philosophy of place. Nishida states in "Basho-teki ronri to shūkyōteki sekaikan" that a nation's nationhood lies in its "religious [shūkyōteki] character" as a self-expression or self-formation of historical life (Z10 360, 366). As in his discussions of the "religious" in human existence, by the "religious essence of nationality" here, Nishida has in mind the un-delimited place in its activity of self-negation. In the context of the political arena of nations, it serves as the groundless ground of global co-existence via mutual self-negation.

One is tempted to simply leave the controversy concerning Nishida's relationship to the imperialists at this juncture. Yet thorough and honest scholarship demands attention to certain issues within Nishida's thinking that ought not to be ignored and that are relevant in our attempts to appropriate his thought to our situation. There is a certain tendency in his later works toward cultural essentialism and in particular a Japanocentrism (or Japanism) (*nihonshugi* 日本主義), including his attempts to conjoin his dialectical philosophy with the emperor cult of the state ideology of the time. In *Nihon bunka no mondai* he sets forth Japan as the exemplar of the spirit of self-negation that would envelop its others in order to construct one world through its contradictory self-identity (Z9 57). He adds that this is Japan's destiny as the builder of East Asia and its co-prosperity sphere. He distinguishes the "Japanese spirit" (*nihon seishin* 日本精神) from that of mere "imperialism" (teikokushugi) in that in his vision it is via self-negation rather than through self-imposition of its subjecthood that Japan envelops others (Z9 59). In other words, Japan is to serve as the unique and universalized place (basho) of the world-of-worlds. In "Sekai no shinchitsujo no genri" Japan has the unique responsibility to set up the East Asia Co-Prosperity Sphere and ultimately to spread worldwide the principle of world-of-worlds formation (*sekaiteki sekaikeisei no genri* 世界的世界形成の原理) by cultivating the principle of "eight directions constituting one universe" or "under one roof" (*hakkō iu* 八紘為宇)[40] centered on the imperial household (*kōshitsu* 皇室). This is Japan's world-historical task that lies within its national polity (kokutai) (Z11 450).[41] Japan is singled out as especially capable of playing this role of constructing a "great synthetic culture" (*ōkina sōgōteki bunka* 大きな綜合的文化) because of its nature of being a formless "musical culture" (*ongakuteki na bunka* 音楽的な文化) that has formed itself through centuries of repeated assimilations and transformations of foreign cultures (Z14, 1966 ed., 416–417). Nishida looks to the imperial household (kōshitsu) as symbolizing this capacity to function as the world's dialectical universal and its absolutely contradictory self-identity, serving as the place of absolute nothing to permit the unification of many in one. As evidence, Nishida re-cycles the spurious argument traceable to the Native Learning (*kokugaku* 国学) scholars of Tokugawa Japan that the imperial household has remained constant—as the absolute present (zettai genzai 絶対現在)—amid change throughout the history of Japan in order to draw an analogy between the temporal and the spatial dimensions:[42] It is "the beginning and end of the world. It envelops past and future, and everything, as the self-determination of the absolute present, develops with it at the center" (Z12, 1966 ed., 409). Therefore, "Contained within our nation's Imperial Way [*kōdō* 皇道] is the world-formation principle [*sekaikeisei no genri* 世界形成の原理] of *hakkō iu*" (Z11 446–447). The suggestion is that Japan with its imperial system has a special role to play in the constitution of the world-of-worlds, and that this is its world-historical mission, its essence. One might raise several questions at this point: Is this really an alternative to imperialism? Is there any room within Nishida's dialectics for such an "unchanging essence"? Is Nishida here slipping from "a multicultural cosmopolitanism towards a 'particular universalism,' which in turn all too easily plays into the hands of . . . ethnocentric imperialism against which he so strongly protested"?[43]

I think that we cannot deny that all of this is in tension with the deconstructive element at the core of Nishida's thought. The problem is that this privileging of Japan's status and this essentializing of her characteristics vis-à-vis other nations are countered by Nishida's dialectical philosophy concerning the world and its underlying chiasma. As Gereon Kopf argues, the dialectic of contradictory self-identity can equally apply to any other nation or people.[44] Nishida believed that

Japan was a "culture of the nothing" (*mu no bunka* 無の文化) distinct from the Western "culture of being [*yū* 有]." This was precisely why he believed that Japan could dialectically serve as the "absolutely contradictory self-identity of East and West" (Z6 335). As John Maraldo points out, Nishida's Japanocentrism was a reaction to the Eurocentrism of world powers at the time. But today we can no longer rely on such over-simplifications that divide the world into Eastern and Western hemispheres.[45] This Orientalist dichotomizing, however, is subverted by Nishida's dialectical non-dualism.[46] The irony here, as Kopf contends, is that Nishida's nationalism (i.e., an essentialism) was justified by a philosophy that is subversive and anti-essentialist.[47] But his dialectical non-dualism—what I have called its underlying chiasmology—would pull asunder any such attempt to set one nation above others as the exemplar of those principles of self-negation, contradictory identity, or chiasma on a universal scale.

Another important and related issue is Nishida's emphasis on the centrality of the nation-state in general, an emphasis that tends toward an essentializing as well. The concept of the nation is a product of modernity, and even within Japan as it emerged out of two centuries of isolation to converse with the world and embrace modernization, the sense of nationhood was contingent on various factors, such as the assimilation of ethnic or cultural minorities and regional identities and the erasure of their sense of difference. While Nishida's concept of a "world-of-worlds" addresses the issue of a world of many cultures—which in turn seem closely identified with nations—he ignored the issue of multi-ethnic states and the possibility of multi-cultural nations, as well as multi-national corporations, none of which are out of the ordinary today.[48] Our sense of national boundaries and identities today is much less fixed or rigid and much more fluid than before.

If we want to be true to Nishida's core insights concerning place and dialectic and apply them to our contemporary world, we cannot take every word of his for granted. We need to discard his Japanocentrism and reverence for the imperial household even as a symbol. In addition, we ought to resist his tendency toward cultural essentialism and reification of the nation-state. Only then can we develop his conception of the world-of-worlds in a way relevant to our contemporary situation. But these essentialist tendencies within Nishida's thinking are undermined by the chiasmatic chōra working as their undertow to pull them asunder. The chiasma implicit within Nishida's concept of world qua place facilitates the development of such a world, especially when it is augmented through cross-cultural and cross-epochal conversations that would bring Nishida into dialogical—or multilogical—partnership with a variety of other thinkers from different periods, regions, and schools of thought. The point is to realize an open place that privileges no center, the world as an open sphere—open in the sense that it precludes closure and absolutism. It is possible to have profoundly differing values informing our lifestyles and yet co-exist peacefully.[49] My attempt here has been to bring out the radicalness of his dialectic, its chiasma, to loosen the hold of essentialism and dissolve any residual absolutism.

As I come to the close of this study, let us recall the main issue that spurred Nishida's thinking. Initially, there was the epistemological issue of how one crosses from one's mind to the source of the material of what one knows, the thing-in-itself, in its independence from what we impose on it. This was the dualism of Western epistemology that pressed Nishida to formulate and develop his theory of place. But from the 1930s on, this issue of bridging the gap of separation increasingly took on an ethical significance that in the global confrontations of the 1940s also became a political issue. Hence in the early 1940s, immediately before beginning work on his dialectic of religiosity, Nishida was also attempting a dialectical theory of the global world. The global and political here still boil down to the ethical issue of how we are to communicate, interrelate, and mutually respond to one another without imposing our ego-centricity on our others, that is, how one makes contact with one's other without forcing oneself on the other. Nishida's thought—with its idea of self-negation on the part of both the individuals implaced and the implacing place—implies an ontology that can found such an ethical posture vis-à-vis one's other. As suggested earlier, rather than a substantializing position that would affirm and assert one's own absolutized truth-claim over and above others in self-affirmation, it sets forth a posture of reciprocal humility on the basis of its an-ontology that acknowledges one's finitude in being-in-the-world. This posture of reciprocal humility allows for co-implacement amid others in an empty space permitting multiplicity and difference. Faced with the lack of ground amid the manifold claims to the title of the absolute, we are called to an ethos of humility to cultivate the groundless opening for conversation. It is in this sense that we look to Nishida's place of nothing, in its self-negation, to preclude privileging and universalizing one way of being over others and instead to encourage such an ethical stance for co-dwelling. And this doubtless applies to the human world's relationship to its natural environment as well.

Just as there is violence toward indigenous cultures in modern times of global homogenization, there is violation directed against nature in man's plundering of the environment without concern or respect for the place of nature or of our place within nature. The posture that attempts to colonize nature and rape its sources of energy for the sole purpose of consumption becomes questionable in the face of environmental hazards. In spite of the will-to-power whereby man "exalts himself to the posture of lord of the earth,"[50] nature always exceeds his grasp. Nishida's concept of the world-matrix qua place, understood in light of an ecological dynamism, becomes suggestive here, that is, to no longer regard ourselves as ontologically independent of and separate from our natural environment but rather as partaking in its dynamic ecology. The issue again is one of humility: to no longer regard nature as mere stock material for our technical and instrumental reasoning, but instead to comport with nature in mindfulness of our finitude, with our debt in mind, our origination in the source of our being. The result would engender a more wholesome and healthier ecological co-existence with beings of the earth, both alive and inanimate.[51] Yet we must admit that to open the world as a world-of-worlds in intimacy with nature is no easy task. It is an ongoing responsibility that involves working for dialogue, conversation, and cooperative interactivity with our others, both human and non-human.[52]

Closing Thoughts

We find ourselves today surrounded by the ever-increasing multiplicity of truth-configurations sounding in the global web of communication-and-information, competing for universal and eternal validity. Amid the confusion in the global encounter of worldviews, religions, philosophies, ideologies, truth-claims, and ways of life, the question thus arises: What is one's place in the midst of others, the position one occupies within the environing world? How or where does one fit? Over a century ago Japan as a nation was asking similar questions concerning its implacement in the world. Nishida as a thinker tried to make sense of that period of inter-epochal and inter-horizonal chaos. As Japan underwent radical changes in its appropriation of foreign influences, straining to synthesize different cultural horizons of the globe, for example, East and West, Nishida's thinking reflected that environing circumstance. What, then, does he offer us today?

Looking at Nishida's philosophy of place as a whole, in its chiasmatic and chōratic aspects, I think that an understanding of reality in terms of a field or place—whether taken internally or externally, mentally or physically, taking into consideration all the complexities of reality—an abyssal (under)ground that is ultimately un-delimited or undifferentiated to encompass differences and delimitations, has something to offer us today, especially when we find ourselves faced with the (post-)modern world of multiplicity, un-groundedness, and uprootedness. And the understanding of place in terms of an absolute nothing, or in the face of absolutely nothing, I think, allows for, or takes into cognizance, the finitude of human reason vis-à-vis our existence in the world, the alterity of the source of being and knowing that is always in excess of human conception. We ought to be listening to what sounds from the chōratic depths of the abyss unfolding its chiasmatic (inter-)manifold.

Nishida Kitarō was at the forefront in the intellectual confrontation between, and synthesis of, East and West at the turn of the twentieth century. His dialectic was born out of his philosophical readiness to cross cultural and intellectual boundaries. Now we have entered into another century as globalization, for better or worse, continues its advance. Nishida's thinking is not totally irrelevant to our contemporary situation. As a marvelous synthesis of its cross-cultural inheritances,[53] his philosophy serves as a model for today's philosophizing to germinate even further possibilities of thoughtfulness in the face of the world. But it is much more than a mere "synthetic product of Zen and Hegel." The source of the distinct ways of being and thinking, East and West, that Nishida sought is what they must assume, despite differences, as the wherein of their being-in-the-world. While its nature remains non-substantial and un-objectifiable, its formlessness provides the space allowing for the co-being of truly different ways of being and thinking. This is what Nishida attempted to express with his notion of basho or place, which is thus quite distinct from Hegel's absolute concept and for which Hegelian formulations are inadequate. And despite its Buddhistic nature, as acknowledged by Nishida, Nishida's work is more than just that. In its character as a creative philosophy of global proportions, Nishida's work surpasses categorization as merely Hegelian or merely Buddhist.

In short, I may summarize the conclusion of this present work as follows. Nishida, in his attempt to surmount Kantian dualism, was led to Hegel's dialectical terminology and formulations, for example, in the notion of a concrete universal or in the universal-individual relationship, whether in the structure of judgment or in the historical unfoldings of the world. Yet the core ideas of Nishida's dialectic, for example, in its founding on the notions of place, absolute nothing, and absolute negation and in its radical reciprocity, expressed in notions such as the dialectical universal or inverse correspondence, extend beyond the purview of Hegelianism. Nishida's dialectic, centered on self-negation and contradictory identity, in content is closer in spirit to Mahāyāna Buddhism. Although Nishida does admit to commensurability with Mahāyāna, as I stated above in chapter 9 we nevertheless ought not to confine his philosophy to the doctrinal category of "Buddhist thought," for the following two reasons: (1) its eclectic nature, which brings in elements drawn from various sources, Western and Eastern, thereby constituting his work as a "world philosophy," and (2) Nishida's creative contributions, especially in his formulation of place, which provides the foundation for his dialectic. But I might also mention here the chiasmatic chōra implicit in the second point that seems to suggest a reciprocal co-founding of place and dialectic—understood in their broader and deeper significance, respetively, as chōra and chiasma—rather than a simple grounding of one on the other. Basho or place in its nature as a self-withdrawing chōra escapes the grasp of a conceptual system, such as that of Hegel's self-conceiving concept or self-knowing spirit/mind. The (un)grounding of Nishida's dialectic in this notion of place, enfolding and unfolding the chiasmatic complexity of the dialectic to in turn shape and form the chōra, is what distinguishes Nishida's "absolute dialectic"—his chiasmatic chorology—from Hegel's dialectic while also extending beyond traditional Buddhist formulations.

Lexicon of Key Non-English Terms

Chinese

Chan 禪: Zen (Jp.): East Asian school of Mahāyāna Buddhism emphasizing meditation. The name comes from the abbreviation of the Chinese transliteration (*channa* 禪那) of the Sanskrit *dhyāna* for "meditation."

chifei 即非: is/not, is and is-not, affirmation-yet-negation, *sokuhi* (Jp.)

dao 道: way, *dō* (Jp.)

fajie 法界: realm of truth/reality, *dharmadhātu* (Skrt.), *hokkai* (Jp.)

Huayan 華嚴: Kegon (Jp.): East Asian school of Mahāyāna Buddhism emphasizing the interpenetration of all and based on the *Avataṃsaka Sūtra*. The name comes from the Chinese translation of the Sanskrit *avataṃsaka* for "flower garland."

kong 空: emptiness, *kū* (Jp.), *śūnyatā* (Skrt.)

li 理: patterning, patternment, *ri* (Jp.)

lishi wuai 理事無礙: non-obstruction between thing-events and their patternings, *riji muge* (Jp.)

San-lun 三論: *Sannron* (Jp.): a Chinese school of Buddhism based on Madhyamaka

shi 事: thing-event/s, fact/s, phenomenon/a, *ji* (Jp.)

shishi wuai 事事無礙: non-obstruction among thing-events, *jiji muge* (Jp.)

shishi wuai fajie 事事無礙法界: dharma-realm of non-obstruction among thing-events, *jiji muge hokkai* (Jp.)

Tiantai 天台: Tendai (Jp.): East Asian school of Mahāyāna Buddhism based on the *Lotus Sūtra*.

wu 無: nothing, *mu* (Jp.)

wuai 無礙: non-obstruction, *muge* (Jp.)

German

abbilden: reproduce, copy, to form an image of

absolute, ursprüngliche Identität: absolute, primordial unity

absoluter Geist: absolute spirit

abstrakte Allgemeinheit: abstract universal, *chūshōteki ippansha* (Jp.)

Allgemeinheit: universality, *ippansei* (Jp.)

Anstoß: (sensory) impingement

an und für sich: in- and for-itself

Aufheben: sublation, sublating

Aufhebung: sublation

begreifen: grasp, conceive

Begriff: concept

bestimmte Allgemeinheit: determined/determinate universal

bilden: form
Erlebnis: lived experience
eschatologisch: eschatological, *shūmatsuronteki* (Jp.)
etwas: something
Gebietskategorie: domain category
Gebietsprädikat: domain predicate
Gegend: region
Geist: spirit, mind, *seishin* (Jp.)
Geltung: validity
Gemeinschaft: society, *shakai* (Jp.)
Gottheit: godhood, godhead
hinauswerfen: project
Idee: idea
konkrete Allgemeinheit: concrete universal, *gutaiteki ippansha* (Jp.)
Kreis: circle
Lichtung: clearing
Logik: logic
Nichts: nothing
Nichtseiende: non-being
objektive Geist: objective spirit, *kyakkanteki seishin* (Jp.)
Ortzeit: place-time, *bashoji* (Jp.)
Prädikat: predicate
Sache: (subject) matter
Seiende: beings, entities
Sein: being, to be
Selbstentäusserung: self-externalization
sichbegreifen: conceive oneself, grasp oneself, thus self-conception, self-conceiving,
    self-grasping
Sinn: sense, meaning
Sollen: ought, *tōi* (Jp.)
substratlose Tätigkeit: non-substantial/substratumless act
Tathandlung: fact-act
Totalität: totality
unmittelbare anschauliche Erleben: immediate intuitable lived experience
Urkultur: primal/originary culture, *genbunka* (Jp.)
ursprüngliche synthetische Einheit: original synthetic unity
ursprüngliche Teilung: primordial differentiation/division
Urteil: judgment
Ur-teil: primal/primordial division
Ur-teilen: primal/primordial division
Ur-Teilung: primordial differentiation/division
Vernunft: reason
Werden: becoming
Wert: value
wirklich: real, actual
Wirklichkeit: reality
Wissenschaft: science, knowledge

Greek

agapē ἀγάπη: love
archē ἀρχή; pl.: *archai* ἀρχαὶ: principle
chaos χάος: chaos, chasm
chiasma χίασμα: cross section, intersection
chōra χώρα: place, region
chōreō χωρέω: make room
dēmiourgos δημιουργός: demiurge
dialektikē διαλεκτική: dialectic/s
eidos εἶδος: idea, form
einai εἶναι: to be
eschaton ἔσχατον: end
genesis γένεσις: becoming, generation
genesis kai phthora γένεσις καὶ φθορά: generation-and-extinction
hylē ὕλη: matter
hypokeimenon ὑποκείμενον: substratum
idea ἰδέα: idea, form
kenosis κένωσις: emptying
legein λέγειν: to speak, to gather
logos λόγος: order, structure, word, account
mē on μὴ ὄν: non-being
morphē μορφή: form (as distinguished from *hylē*)
noema (*noēma*) νόημα: object of thought/cognition
noesis (*noēsis*) νόησις: understanding, intuition (in ancient Greek philosophy),
        knowledge or cognitive act (in Husserl)
on ὄν: being
ontōs on ὄντως ὄν: true being
ousia οὐσία: substance, beingness
poiēsis ποίησις: production, making
polis πόλις: city
prāxis πρᾶξις: practice, human activity
psychē ψυχή: life-force, soul, psyche, mind
telos τέλος; pl.: *telē* τέλη: end, goal
theoria θεωρία: observation, contemplation, looking at
theōsis θέωσις: deification, human transformation to attain likeness to, or union with, God
topos τόπος: place
triton genos τρίτον γένος: third genus

Japanese

ai 愛: love
aihataraki 相働き: interaction, mutual working
aru ある、有る: is, exists, to be
ba 場: field
baikai 媒介: mediation, medium

basho 場所: place

bashoji 場所時: place-time, *Ortzeit* (Germ.)

basho no benshōhō 場所の弁証法: dialectic of place

basho no ronri 場所の論理: logic of place

bashoteki 場所的: placial, pertaining to place

bashoteki baikaisha 場所的媒介者: placial medium, mediation via place

bashoteki benshōhō 場所的弁証法: dialectic of place, placial dialectic

bashoteki ronri 場所的論理: logic of place, placial logic

benshōhō 弁証法: dialectic/s

benshōhōteki 弁証法的: dialectical

benshōhōteki busshitsu 弁証法的物質: dialectical matter

benshōhōteki chokkan 弁証法的直観: dialectical intuition

benshōhōteki ippansha 弁証法的一般者: dialectical universal

benshōhōteki ippansha no sekai 弁証法的一般者の世界: world of the dialectical universal

benshōhōteki ronri 弁証法的論理: dialectical logic

benshōhōteki sekai 弁証法的世界: dialectical world

benshōhōteki tōitsu 弁証法的統一: dialectical unity

benshōhōteki undō 弁証法的運動: dialectical movement

bukkyō no shinkū 仏教の真空: true emptiness of Buddhism

busshitsuteki sekai 物質的世界: material world

byōjōshin 平常心: ordinary mind

byōjōtei 平常底: depth in the ordinary

chōetsuteki ishi 超越的意志: transcendental will

chōetsuteki jutsugo 超越的述語: transcendental predicate

chōetsuteki jutsugomen 超越的述語面: transcendental predicate plane/pole

chokkan 直観: intuition

chokkanmen 直観面: plane/pole of intuition

chokkanshugi 直観主義: intuitionism

chokusenteki 直線的: linear

chokusetsu 直接: immediate, immediacy

chūshintennaku shūhennaki en 中心点なく周辺なき円: circle without a central point or periphery

chūshōteki ippansha 抽象的一般者: abstract universal, *abstrakte Allgemeinheit* (Germ.)

danzetsu 断絶: rupture

dō 道: way, *dao* (Ch.)

eien 永遠: eternity, eternal

eien no genzai 永遠の現在: eternal present

eien no ima 永遠の今: eternal now

eien no ima no jikogentei 永遠の今の自己限定: self-determination of the eternal now

eien no mu 永遠の無: eternal nothing

eien no shi 永遠の死: eternal death

en 円: circle

enganteki 円環的: circular

engi 縁起: (inter-)dependent origination, *pratītya-samutpāda* (Skrt.)

eshin 回心: (religious) conversion/turn of mind

genbunka 原文化: primal/originary culture, *Ur-Kultur* (Germ.)

genteisurumononaki gentei 限定するものなき限定: determination without determiner

genteisurumononakimono no gentei 限定するものなきものの限定: determination of that which is without a determiner

genteisurumono nakushite jikojishin o genteisuru 限定する物無くして自己自身を限定する: self-determination without a determiner

genzai 現在: the present

gijutsu 技術: technics, technology

gutaiteki ippansha 具体的一般者: concrete universal, *konkrete Allgemeinheit* (Germ.)

gutaiteki shii no gaku 具体的思惟の学: science of concrete thought

gyaku gentei 逆限定: reverse determination, counter-determination

gyakutaiō 逆対応: inverse correspondence

hakkō ichiu 八紘一宇: see *hakkō iu*

hakkō iu 八紘為宇: eight directions constituting one universe, eight directions under one roof

handan 判断: judgment

hannya no kū 般若の空: emptiness of the *Prajñāpāramitā* (*sūtras*)

hannya no sokuhiteki benshōhō 般若の即非的弁証法: *Prajñāpāramitā* dialectic of is/not

hannya sokuhi no ronri 般若即非の論理: *Prajñāpāramitā* logic of is/not

hansei 反省: reflection

happu 八不: eightfold negation

hatarakumono 働くもの: things at-work, that which works, the working/acting

herakureitosutekina jitsuzaironteki benshōhō ヘラクレイトス的な実在論的弁証法: dialectic of Heraclitean realism

hi 非: not-, is-not, negation

hiai 悲哀: (existential) sorrow

higekiteki 悲劇的: tragic

higekiteki narumono 悲劇的なるもの: that which is tragic

hirenzoku no renzoku 非連続の連続: continuity of discontinuity

hitei 否定: negation

hitei no hitei 否定の否定: negation of negation

hito to hito to no musubitsuki no sekai 人と人との結びつきの世界: world of interacting persons

hokkai 法界: realm of truth/reality, *dharmadhātu* (Skrt.), *fajie* (Ch.)

hontai 本体: substance

hyōgen 表現: expression

hyōgenten 表現点: expressive point

ichinensanzen 一念三千: three thousand (worlds) in one thought

ichi soku ta 一即多: one is many, one qua many

ichi soku ta, ta soku ichi 一即多、多即一: one qua many, many qua one; one is many, many is one

ippan 一般: universal, universality

ippan gainen 一般概念: universal concept

ippansei 一般性: universality, *Allgemeinheit* (Germ.)

ippansha 一般者: universal

ippansha no ippansha 一般者の一般者: universal of universals

ishi 意志: will, volition

ishiki 意識: consciousness

ishiki no ba 意識の場: field of consciousness

issai ichinyo 一切一如: all is one

isshōten 一焦点: singular focal point/s

ittai funi 一体不二: one body (that is) non-dual

ji 事: thing-event/s, fact/s, phenomenon/a, *shi* (Ch.)

jiji muge 事事無礙: non-obstruction among thing-events, *shishi wuai* (Ch.)

jiji muge hokkai 事事無礙法界: dharma-realm of non-obstruction among thing-events, *shishi wuai fajie* (Ch.)

jikaku 自覚: self-awareness, self-realization, self-awakening

jikakuten 自覚点: point of self-awareness

jiko hitei 自己否定: self-negation

jiko hyōgenten 自己表現点: self-expressive point

jiko mujun 自己矛盾: self-contradiction

jinen hōni 自然法爾: spontaneity through the working of the dharma

jinkaku 人格: person, personality, character

jiriki 自力: self-power

Jōdo Shinshū 浄土真宗: True Pure Land school/sect

jūhōi 住法位: dwelling/abiding in a dharma-position, configuration of dharma

junsui 純粋: pure, purity

junsui keiken 純粋経験: pure experience

jutsugo 述語: predicate

jutsugomen 述語面: predicate pole/plane

jutsugoteki ronri 述語的論理: logic of predicates

kami 神: God

kami no kotoba 神の言葉: the Word (*logos*) of God

kankyō 環境: environment

katei 過程: process

kateiteki benshōhō 過程的弁証法: dialectic of process

Kegon 華厳: Huayan (Ch.)

kenshō 見性: seeing into one's (original) nature

kitai 基体: substratum, substance

kitaiteki 基体的: substantial, substrative

ko 個: individual

kōan 公案: riddle/puzzle used in Zen to meditate on

kobutsu 個物: individual thing

kōdō 皇道: Imperial Way

kōi 行為: activity, action, acting

kōiteki chokkan 行為的直観: acting intuition

kōiteki jiko 行為的自己: acting self

kojin 個人: individual person

kokugaku 国学: Native Learning (school)

kokutai 国体: national polity, national body

kōsa 交差: intersection

kōsaten 交差点: cross section, point of intersection

kōshitsu 皇室: (Japanese) imperial household

kū 空: emptiness, *kong* (Ch.), *śūnyatā* (Skrt.)

kūkan 空観: vision of emptiness

kūkanteki kankei 空間的関係: spatial relationships

kyakkanteki seishin 客観的精神: objective spirit, *objektive Geist* (Germ.)

kyakkanteki tōitsu 客観的統一: objective unity

kyōeiken 共栄圏: co-prosperity sphere

kyokugen 極限: extremity, extreme limit

kyōryaku 經歷: passage

kyū 球: sphere

minzoku jikoshugi 民族自己主義: ethnic egoism

mu 無: nothing, *wu* (Ch.)

muge 無礙: non-obstruction, *wuai* (Ch.)

mugendai no en 無限大の円: circle without periphery

mugendai no kyū 無限大の球: infinite sphere, endless sphere, *sphaera infinita* (Lt.)

mugenkyū 無限球: infinite sphere

mugen no kyū 無限の球: infinite sphere, endless sphere

mujun 矛盾: contradiction, paradox

mujunteki jikodōitsu 矛盾的自己同一: contradictory self-identity

mujunteki tōitsu 矛盾的統一: contradictory unity

mukitei 無基底: non-substantiality

mukiteiteki 無基底的: without substratum, substratumless

mu no benshōhō 無の弁証法: dialectic/s of nothing

mu no bunka 無の文化: culture of (the) nothing

mu no ippansha 無の一般者: universal of nothing

mu no ippansha no gentei 無の一般者の限定: determination of the universal of nothing

mu no ronri 無の論理: logic of nothing

myōgō 名号: (Amida's) name (to call upon)

naizaiteki chōetsu 内在的超越: immanent transcendence

nanji 汝: thou

nihon seishin 日本精神: Japanese spirit

nihonshugi 日本主義: Japanism, Japanocentrism

nikon 而今: now, here-and-now

Nishida *tetsugaku* 西田哲学: Nishidian philosophy

oitearu basho 於いてある場所: place of implacement

oitearu mono 於いてあるもの: the implaced, that which is placed

onchō 恩寵: grace

ōyake no basho 公の場所: public place

rekishiteki genjitsu no sekai 歷史的現実の世界: world of historical actuality

rekishiteki kūkan 歷史的空間: historical space

rekishiteki seimei 歷史的生命: historical life

rekishiteki sekai 歷史的世界: historical world

rekishiteki shintai 歷史的身体: historical body

ri 理: patterning, patternment, reason, principle, *li* (Ch.)

riji muge 理事無礙: non-obstruction between thing-events and their patternings, *lishi wuai* (Ch.)

ronri 論理: logic

ronrika 論理化: logicize, logically found, logicization
ronriteki kiso 論理的基礎: logical foundation
sagyōteki yōso 作業的要素: operative elements
satori 悟り: enlightenment
seimei 生命: life
seimeiteki sekai 生命的世界: world of life, biological world
seishin 精神: spirit, *Geist* (Germ.)
seishi soku nehan 生死即涅槃: saṃsāra is nirvāṇa
sekai 世界: world
sekaikeisei no genri 世界形成の原理: world-formation principle, principle of world formation
sekaishiteki sekai 世界史的世界: world-historical world
sekaishugi 世界主義: worldism
sekaiteki sekai 世界的世界: multi-world, world-of-worlds
sekaiteki sekaikeisei no genri 世界的世界形成の原理: principle of world-of-worlds formation
shakai 社会: society, *Gemeinschaft* (Germ.)
shakaiteki rekishiteki 社会的歴史的: sociohistorical
shakaiteki rekishiteki jijitsu 社会的歴史的事実: sociohistorical fact
shakaiteki rekishiteki sekai 社会的歴史的世界: sociohistorical world
shiki soku zekkū 色即是空: form is precisely emptiness
shinjin datsuraku 身心脱落: dropping off body-and-mind
shin no chokkan 真の直観: true intuition
shin no mu 真の無: true nothing
shin no mu no basho 真の無の場所: the place of true nothing
shintai 身体: body
shōmetsu 生滅: generation-and-extinction, life-and-death
shōshitsuten 消失点: vanishing point
shōten 焦点: focal point
shōuchū 小宇宙: microcosm
shugo 主語: (grammatical) subject
shugo no ronri 主語の論理: logic of the (grammatical) subject, subject logic
shugoteki ronri 主語的論理: logic of the (grammatical) subject
shugoteki ronrigaku: 主語的論理学: logic of the (grammatical) subject
shūhennaki mugendai no kyū 周辺なき無限大の球: infinite sphere without circumference
shūketsu 終結: end
shukyaku gōichi no ten 主客合一の点: the point of subject-object union
shukyaku mibun 主客未分: subject-object non-differentiation
shūkyō 宗教: religion
shūkyōsei 宗教性: religiosity
shūkyōteki 宗教的: (the) religious
shūkyōteki ishiki 宗教的意識: religious consciousness
shūkyōteki kaishin 宗教的回心: religious turning of the mind
shūmatsuronteki 終末論的: eschatological, *eschatologisch* (Germ.)
shūmatsuronteki byōjōtei 終末論的平常底: eschatological depth in the ordinary
shunkanteki jikogentei 瞬間的自己限定: momentary self-determination

shutai 主体: subject (as active and embodied), subject-body

sōhansurumono no jikodōitsu 相反するものの自己同一: self-identity of opposites

soku 即: is (as copula), qua, affirmation

sokuhi 即非: is/(is) not, is and is-not, *chi-fei* (Ch.)

sokuhi no ronri 即非の論理: logic of is/not

sora 空: sky

sōtai mu 相対無: relative nothing

sōtai mu no basho 相対無の場所: place of relative nothing

Sōtō Zen 曹洞禅: A sect of Zen Buddhism founded in Japan by Dōgen but continuing the lineage of Chinese Caodong Chan (曹洞禅).

sōzōteki sekai no sōzōteki yōso 創造的世界の創造的要素: creative element/s of the creative world

sōzōten 創造点: creative point

tachibanaki tachiba 立場なき立場: standpointless standpoint

tai 対: opposition, opposed, oppose

tairitsuteki mu 対立的無: oppositional nothing

tairitsuteki mu no basho 対立的無の場所: place of oppositional nothing

taishō ronri 対象論理: object logic

taishōteki ronrigaku 対象的論理学: object logic

tariki 他力: other-power

tate no gentei 縦の限定: longitudinal determination

ta to ichi no zettai mujunteki jikodōitsu 多と一の絶対矛盾的自己同一: absolutely contradictory self-identity of many and one

teikokushugi 帝国主義: imperialism

Tendai 天台: Tiantai (Ch.): A Japanese school of Mahāyāna Buddhism founded by Saichō, based on Tiantai Buddhism in China.

tōi 当為: ought, *Sollen* (Germ.)

tōitsu sayō 統一作用: unifying activity

tokushuteki sekai 特殊的世界: particular world

tsukuraretamono kara tsukurumono e 作られたものから作るものへ: from the made to the making

u 有: being/s

uji 有時: being-time

watashi to nanji 私と汝: I and thou

yobigoe 呼声: calling voice (of God/Buddha)

yoko no gentei 横の限定: latitudinal determination

yū 有: being/s

yū no basho 有の場所: place of being/s

yū no benshōhō 有の弁証法: dialectic/s of being

yū soku mu 有即無: being qua nothing

zazen 座禅: sitting meditation

Zen 禅: Chan (Ch.): Japanese school of Mahāyāna Buddhism, the Japanese version of Chinese Chan. Sometimes this Japanese name, however, is used to refer to Chinese, Japanese, and other East Asian versions.

zentaishugi 全体主義: totalitarianism

zetsu 絶: cut off, ab-solved

zettai 絶対: absolute
zettai ai 絶対愛: absolute love
zettai benshōhō 絶対弁証法: absolute dialectic
zettai genzai 絶対現在: absolute present
zettai hitei 絶対否定: absolute negation
zettai ishi 絶対意志: absolute will
zettai jiyū 絶対自由: absolute freedom
zettai mu 絶対無: absolute nothing
zettai mujunteki jikodōitsu 絶対矛盾的自己同一: absolutely contradictory self-identity
zettai mu no basho 絶対無の場所: place of absolute nothing
zettai no dokuritsu 絶対の独立: absolute independence
zettai no jiyū 絶対の自由: absolute freedom
zettai ta 絶対他: absolute other

Latin

cogito: I think
coincidentia oppositorum: coincidence of opposites
creata et creans: created and creating
creatio ex nihilo: creation out of nothing
emanatio: emanation
fides: faith
gratia: grace
locus: place
natura naturans: naturing (creative) nature
natura naturata: natured (created) nature
sphaera infinita: infinite sphere, *mugendai no kyū* (Jp.)
substantia: substance, standing-under

Sanskrit

ākāśa: open space
anitya: impermanence
āśraya: locus, basis
catuskoti: tetralemma
dharma: thing-event, momentary constituent of reality, *shi* (Ch.), *ji* (Jp.)
dharma: truth (of reality), *fa* (Ch.), *hō* (Jp.)
dharmadhātu: realm of truth/reality, *fajie* (Ch.), *hokkai* (Jp.)
kalpa: eon, epoch, time-period
nirvāṇa: release, freedom
paramārtha: ultimate
paramārtha-satya: ultimate/absolute truth
paratantra: dependent
parikalpita: imaginary

parinispanna: consummated
prajñā: (intuitive) wisdom
pratītya-samutpāda: (inter-)dependent origination, *engi* (Jp.)
rūpa: form, phenomenon
rūpam śūnyatā śūnyatāiva rūpam: form is emptiness, emptiness is form
saṃsāra: realm of reincarnation
saṃvṛti: provisional, relative, conventional
saṃvṛti-satya: relative/conventional truth
śāśvata: eternalism
śūnya: empty
śūnyatā: emptiness
śūnyatāyāh śūnyatā: emptiness of emptiness
svabhāva: own-being, self-nature, substantiality
tathatā: suchness
uccheda: nihilism

Notes

Introduction

1. I am not denying the unity that holds together the so-called Nishidian philosophy of his mature years. The division is purely for the sake of convenience, allowing us to focus on the different formulations he developed in each period in order to conceptualize and discuss what he was ultimately concerned with throughout his philosophical life.

2. For example, Nishitani Keiji (西谷啓治) and Nishitani's student Ueda Shizuteru (上田閑照). I return to this question at the end of this work. However, the nature and scope of this work prevents me from engaging in a detailed examination at the philosophies of Nishitani and Ueda in relation to Nishida. I will render the names of Japanese authors according to the traditional Japanese ordering of family name first and personal name second. However, I will render the names of Japanese authors or scholars who reside in the West and have done most of their work in a Western language according to the Western format of personal name first and family name second.

3. Of Buddhist schools, along with the Chinese Huayan school, Kūkai's Shingon Buddhism seems close to Nishida's chiasmatic complexity in encompassing embodiment and prāxis within its micromacrocosmic version of the Mahāyāna "logic of emptiness." Yet Nishida does not seem to have been influenced by Kūkai. For a comparison of Nishida and Kūkai, see Krummel, "Embodied Implacement in Kūkai and Nishida."

4. For the following details on and differences among these different methods of division, see Sueki, *Nishida Kitarō*, vol. 1, pp. 6–13.

5. All my references to Nishida's works in Japanese will be to the volumes from the most recent editions of the collected works of Nishida: *Nishida Kitarō zenshū* (Tokyo: Iwanami, 2002–) unless otherwise noted. They will be indicated in the text in parentheses by *Z* followed by the volume number. Other texts will be cited in notes.

6. This scheme actually may be close to Tanabe Hajime's fourfold division of Nishida's work: (1) "pure experience"; (2) "self-awareness"; (3) "place"; and (4) "dialectical world." See Kosaka, *Nishida Kitarō o meguru tetsugakusha gunzō*, p. 102.

7. The English publication is Nishida, *Intuition and Reflection in Self-Consciousness*. The Japanese original can be found in *Z2*. I prefer to render the Japanese term *jikaku* (自覚) as "self-awareness" rather than "self-consciousness." *Ishiki* (意識) is the word that would be translated as "consciousness."

8. The English publication is Nishida, *Art and Morality*. The Japanese original can be found in *Z3*.

9. The English publication is Nishida, *Fundamental Problems of Philosophy*. The Japanese original can be found in *Z6*.

10. The English translation of this final essay constitutes the main portion of Nishida, *Last Writings*. The Japanese original can be found in *Z10*.

11. Aside from this way of dividing his oeuvre into periods, one also ought to recognize that there is a significant break between the works before "Nishidian philosophy" and the works that came to make up "Nishidian philosophy," in other words, between the second and the third periods. I will not go into the details of this turn in his thought here since it will distract

from my immediate purpose. I refer the reader to Krummel, "*Basho,* World, and Dialectics," in Nishida, *Place and Dialectic,* pp. 3–48. This book includes the English translation of two essays, "Basho" (1926) from the third period and "Ronri to seimei" ("Logic and Life") (1936) from the fourth period.

1. From Aristotle's Substance to Hegel's Concrete Universal

1. Aristotle, *Metaphysics* 7.1–3.1028b–1029a39, in Aristotle, *Basic Works of Aristotle,* pp. 783–785.

2. See Renford Bambrough's introduction in Aristotle, *Philosophy of Aristotle,* p. 33; and Reck, "Aristotle's Concept of Substance in the Logical Writings," p. 7.

3. Aristotle, *Categories* 5.2a14–19, in Aristotle, *Basic Works of Aristotle,* p. 9.

4. Aristotle, *Categories* 5.2b5f, in Aristotle, *Basic Works of Aristotle,* p. 9.

5. Aristotle, *Metaphysics* 4.2.1003b5–7 and 1003a33–35, respectively, in Aristotle, *Basic Works of Aristotle,* p. 732.

6. It is interesting to note here that the term "category" (*kategoria* κατηγορία) means "predicate," that which is said of something, in ancient Greek. The first category, substance, in that sense is not really a category since it can never be a predicate. As the subject of which something is said, that which has something predicated of it, it is *to kategoramenon.* See Aristotle, *Categories,* ch. 5. Also see Reck, "Aristotles Concept of Substance," p. 9.

7. Aristotle, *Metaphysics* 4.7.1012a25, in Aristotle, *Basic Works of Aristotle,* p. 750.

8. Parmenides, *Parmenides of Elea,* frag. 2, pp. 54–55, and frag. 8, pp. 64–76. See also Kirk, Raven, and Schofield, *Presocratic Philosophers,* pp. 244–246, 248–253.

9. Aristotle, *Physics* 1.6.189a29–33, in Aristotle, *Basic Works of Aristotle,* p. 229.

10. Aristotle, *Physics* 2.9.200b32–3.1.201a3, in Aristotle, *Basic Works of Aristotle,* p. 252–253. As a metaphysical truth holding primarily of substances, the principle of non-contradiction thus plays a role exceeding the merely formal-logical. On this, see Cresswell, "Non-contradiction and Substantial Predication," pp. 169–170; Lukasiewicz, "Aristotle on the Law of Contradiction," p. 58; and Anton, *Aristotle's Theory of Contrariety,* pp. 51–52, 62, 63, 92. Lukasiewicz states that for Aristotle, "the changing world of sense perception may contain as many contradictions as it pleases; but beyond it there lies another, eternal and immutable, world of *substantial essences,* intact and safe from the ravages of contradiction" (p. 58).

11. Aristotle, *Metaphysics* 4.4.1007a20, in Aristotle, *Basic Works of Aristotle,* p. 739.

12. Aristotle, *Categories* 2.1b3–8, 5.2a10–13, and 5.2b15–17, in Aristotle, *Basic Works of Aristotle,* pp. 8, 9, and 10.

13. See Aristotle, *Categories,* 5.2b5–6, in Aristotle, *Basic Works of Aristotle,* p. 9; and *Metaphysics* 12.1.1069a25, ibid., p. 872. On this, see also Anton, *Aristotle's Theory of Contrariety,* pp. 60–61.

14. See Aristotle, *Metaphysics* 7.3.1028b36, in Aristotle, *Basic Works of Aristotle,* p. 785; and *Posterior Analytics* 2.19.100a16–100b3, ibid., p. 185.

15. These included life philosophy, phenomenology, the Vienna Circle, and the Frankfurt school, among others. See Makkreel and Luft, *Neo-Kantianism in Contemporary Philosophy,* pp. 4–5.

16. I am assuming here the Kantian distinction between transcendental and transcendent. By the former I mean the a priori principles, forms, categories, and so on inherent to the mind that are prior to, and conditions, empirical experience. By the latter I mean that which is beyond human experience and cannot be known.

17. Two figures foremost in this work are Theodore Kisiel and Steven Galt Crowell. Both have spelled out this connection in numerous works.

18. See Crowell, "Transcendental Logic and Minimal Empiricism," pp. 155–156 and 172n26 for the following as well. Lask's list of dualities includes, among others, sensible-supersensible, sensible-intelligible, appearance–true actuality, appearance-idea, matter-form, matter-mind, finite-infinite, conditioned-unconditioned, empirical–super-empirical, relative-absolute, nature-freedom, nature-reason, and temporal-eternal. See Emil Lask, *Die Logik der Philosophie und die Kategorienlehre* [*The Logic of Philosophy and the Doctrine of Categories*] (1911), in Lask, *Sämtliche Werke*, vol. 2, p. 5, on the following as well.

19. See also Lotze, *Logic in Three Books*, vol. 2, § 316, pp. 208–209; § 320, pp. 217–218; and § 341, p. 269.

20. Lask, *Logik der Philosophie*, p. 6.

21. Ibid., pp. 60, 83.

22. E.g., see ibid., pp. 178–179.

23. Nishida will consequently refer to Lask's "alogical lived experience" as a kind of basho that envelops within itself the opposition between form and matter (*Z3* 418).

24. Lask, however, was prevented from doing so when he was killed at the young age of forty, fighting for Germany on the eastern front during World War I. For more on Nishida's debt to Lask, as evident especially in his 1926 "Basho" essay, see my introduction to Nishida, *Place and Dialectic*, esp. pp. 13–14, 20–21.

25. For example, the species extracted from its individual members and the genus opposing the species in biological classification are both abstract universals, while reason as operative within the activities of human beings is a concrete universal. See Hegel, *Encyclopedia Logic*, in *Hegel's Logic*, § 163 Zusatz, pp. 227–228. The example is borrowed from Kosaka, *Nishida Kitarō no shisō*, p. 160 and p. 363n132. I will say more about Hegel's "concrete universal" in chapter 2.

26. Hegel, *Encyclopedia Logic*, § 166, p. 231.

27. The meaning of these paradoxical terms should become clear in part 2 of this work.

28. By *noema-noesis* I have in mind the pairing found in Husserl, loosely speaking, between the object of thought or cognition and the cognitive act (or, more precisely, the mind's act of intending).

29. In this respect it appears that Nishida was not familiar with Husserl's later theories on inter-subjectivity or the life-world.

30. This is evident, for example, in Bergson, *Matter and Memory*, where Bergson argues against both materialism and idealism and against the division between extended, divisible, and multiple matter, on the one hand, and the unextended pure unity of the mind, on the other, taking note of the inseparability among mind, organism (i.e., the body), and environment. We are in the midst of the surrounding environment, as one part in a greater whole, taking part in the rhythmic flow of surrounding matter via perception (centripetal motion) and action (centrifugal motion) vis-à-vis environing matter. Bergson distinguishes this movement with its "concrete extensity" as prior to "homogeneous space." The origin of one's independence and freedom vis-à-vis that continuous flow of surrounding matter has to do with human perception's capacity to prolong in memory the duration of that movement affecting it and the human capacity to act on its basis. For Bergson, the mind-body relation or the subject-object distinction thus boils down to the difference in degrees of duration in the vibrations of "continuous extensity," a difference in the "rhythm of time." Like Nishida, Bergson was also responding to Neo-Kantian dualism. See Bergson, *Matter and Memory*, pp. 11–12, 43–44, 71, 77, 178, 186, 235–236, 278–279, 289, 295.

31. For example, in *Time and Free Will*, Bergson explains "pure duration" as the form of lived succession of our states of consciousness inter-permeating one another as a whole. See

Bergson, *Time and Free Will*, p. 100. In this work Bergson establishes the priority of pure duration as such over what he calls "homogeneous space." See also pp. 104 and 229.

32. See Bergson, *Matter and Memory*, pp. 11–12, 71, 278–279, 289.

33. See ibid., p. 295.

34. I will provide a more detailed discussion of the concept of "continuity of discontinuity" in chapter 6.

35. See Haldane, *Philosophical Basis of Biology*, especially lecture 1, "The Axiom of Biology."

36. Kim, "Logic of the Illogical," p. 28.

2. Hegelian Dialectics and Mahāyāna Non-dualism

1. Kim, "Logic of the Illogical," pp. 27–28.

2. See ibid., pp. 25 and 27.

3. Hegel did use triadic formulas and owed much to Fichte's formulations, which involved the terms of thesis-antithesis-synthesis. However, Hegel did not use those exact terms of thesis-antithesis-synthesis except when discussing Kant's triads, i.e., the four groups of categories, each consisting of three concepts, with the third concept arising from the combination of the other two.

4. *Aufheben* or *Aufhebung* has also been translated as "supersession," "superceding," and "transcendence."

5. In this chapter I will identify Hegel's works as follows: *DFSe = The Difference between Fichte's and Schelling's System of Philosophy; DFSg = Differenz des Fichteschen und Schellingschen Systems der Philosophie; EL = Encyclopedia Logic*, in *Hegel's Logic; GW = Glauben und Wissen oder Reflexionsphilosophie der Subjektivität in der Vollständigkeit ihrer Formen als Kantische, Jacobische und Richtesche Philosophie*, in *Werke in zwanzig Bänden*, vol. 2; *MF = Mancherlei Formen, die bei dem jetzigen Philosophieren vorkommen*, in *Werke in zwanzig Bänden*, vol. 2; *NL = Natural Law; NR = Über die wissenschaftlichen Behandlungsarten des Naturrechts, seine Stelle in der praktischen Philosophie und sein Verhältnis zu den positiven Rechtswissenschaften*, in *Werke in zwanzig Bänden*, vol. 2; *PG = Phänomenologie des Geistes; PH = Philosophy of History; PS = Phenomenology of Spirit; SL = Science of Logic*, trans. A. V. Miller; *WL1 = Wissenschaft der Logik*, pt. 1; *WL2 = Wissenschaft der Logik*, pt. 2. The lowercase *z* denotes *Zusatz*, notes taken by students based on Hegel's lectures and added to the original text.

6. This self-enclosure of the circle of dialectic may be noticeable to a certain extent in Plato as well. See the *Republic*, wherein Socrates describes the dialectic as an upward advancement that culminates in the origin, the first principle (*archē*) (533c–d). Through the process of dialectic, Plato states, reason grasps the *archē*, the origin or first principle of everything (511b). See Plato, *Complete Works*, pp. 1132 and 1149. Plato's dialectic thus also proceeds toward the beginning of everything, including itself. Hegel's contribution here was in formulating this culmination in terms of an explicit self-grasping of the origin.

7. However, this was before the Neo-Kantian movement that Nishida was primarily responding to. In fact, the Neo-Kantian movement developed partially in response to Hegel.

8. Hegel, *System der Sittlichkeit*. For the English, see Hegel, *System of Ethical Life and First Philosophy of Spirit*.

9. The full title in English of this work is *Natural Law: The Scientific Ways of Treating Natural Law, Its Place in Moral Philosophy, and Its Relation to the Positive Sciences of Law*.

10. On this, see Pinkard, *Hegel,* pp. 118–220.

11. Hegel provided two versions of his system of logic, of which the *Science of Logic* was the first one, first published during 1812–1816. The second version constitutes the first part of his system of science, the *Encyclopedia,* first published in 1817.

12. It is interesting to contrast this with Nishida's non-substantialist notion of basho that allows for a "contradictory self-identity." I will discuss this in the ensuing chapters.

13. This is obviously a departure from Aristotle's conception of self-identity as founded on that substantiality of the individual. The individual is the primary substance without which both its accidental characteristics or qualities and the secondary substance, i.e., the universal to which it belongs, cannot exist. The universal must inhere in the individual, and in that sense Aristotle prioritizes the individual as the primary substance.

14. Hegel thus distinguishes this concrete universal from the abstract universal that remains a mere conceptual form imposed on its subject matter in thought. In remaining opposed to the particular, it proves to be yet another particular (*EL* § 80z 113–115).

15. In the *Science of Logic* Hegel thus also speaks of the concept as "soul and substance" ("Seele und Substanz") (*WL2* 486/*SL* 826).

16. I do not, however, want to deny other possible ways of reading Hegel. For example, one might emphasize the unknown future rather than the retroactive circularity of the recognized. The past is known, but not the future. Realization then may also be viewed as inexhaustible and in that sense irreducible to any concept or consciousness. Since the alleged telos is detected only retrospectively, teleology itself is constituted in recollection, with a view to the past— justifying past sufferings in light of the present only in their de-legitimation, their sublation. The future, however, is still unknown. On this, see Heller, *Theory of Modernity,* p. 21. Hegel, however, in viewing history retroactively, regarded its culmination as the self-grasping concept, the absolute idea. This is the point in Hegel's dialectic that I want to emphasize vis-à-vis Mahāyāna non-dualism and, in chapter 8, vis-à-vis Nishida's dialectic.

17. See Dilworth, "Introduction," p. 2.

18. "Form" (*rūpa*) here designates the material or phenomenal "thing-event." "Emptiness" (*śūnyatā*) is generally taken to mean the lack of "own-being" or "self-nature" (*svabhāva*), or ontological independence, namely, substance.

19. "Chinese translation" ought to be put in quotation marks here. Some scholars suggest that the original was first composed in Chinese and then translated into Sanskrit. In any case the identification of or equation between form and emptiness may have to do with the lack of a copula in the Chinese language. This suggestion was made to me by Shigenori Nagatomo.

20. The Indian Buddhist texts will be identified as follows: *MMK* = Nāgārjuna's *Mūlamadhyamakakārikā; MS* = Asanga's *Mahāyānasaṃgraha; TK* = Vasubandhu's *Triṃśikā; TN* = Vasubandhu's *Trisvabhāvanirdeśa.*

21. See Nāgārjuna's *Mūlamadhyamakakārikā* (*Root Verses/Stanzas on the Middle*) in Nāgārjuna, *Fundamental Wisdom of the Middle Way;* and in Nāgārjuna, *Nāgārjuna, the Philosophy of the Middle Way.*

22. In his *Mūlamadhyamakakārikā* Nāgārjuna applies his tetralemma to various subject matters, such as time, self, Buddha, and causality.

23. A major target of Nāgārjuna here was the substantialism and dualism of the Abhidharmist schools, such as the Sarvāstivāda, that dichotomized reality into the conventional (what appears to be real) and the ultimate (the atomic or elemental thing-events, *dhamma*s [Pali; Skrt. *dharma*s], that constitute the apparent). Nāgārjuna's aim was to return Buddhism to its original "middle way" of refusing dichotomies and refusing attachment to either of the alternative positions.

24. In other words, one must realize that emptiness is not something ultimate to cling and become attached to.

25. In Asaṅga's *Mahāyānasaṃgraha* (*Compendium/Summary of the Mahāyāna*) and Vasubandhu's *Trimśikā* (*Thirty Songs*) and *Trisvabhāvanirdeśa* (*The Teachings/Treatise on the Three Own-Beings*). For the English, see Asanga, *Summary of the Great Vehicle by Bodhisattva Asanga;* and Vasubandhu, *Seven Works of Vasubandhu.*

26. In his *Mohe Zhiguan* (Jp. *Makashikan* 『摩訶止観』) (*Great Insight into Dwelling in Tranquility*). In the following I am relying on Paul L. Swanson's commentary. His relevant citations are to the *Taishō shinshū daizōkyō,* volume 46, 24a3–6, 24a13–15, 24c8–11, and 24c21–26. See Swanson, *Foundations of T'ien-t'ai Philosophy,* pp. 117–120.

27. *Dharmadhātu* also means "the realm of thing-events [*dharmas*]" seen from the point of view of the *dharma* or the true nature of reality.

28. *Li* has traditionally been translated into English as "principle," "reason," or "universal" and mistakenly compared to Plato's concept of idea (*eidos*) or Aristotle's form (*morphē* μορφή). But we ought to be aware of the distinction of the Chinese concept of li from these Western notions. The etymological origin of the term points to the line pattern of grain one observes in a piece of wood or stone such as jade. One might thus understand li in the sense of the crisscrossing lines of interconnection constituting the coherence or order that differentiates an individual thing while simultaneously relating it to others. In Buddhist terms this means interdependent origination and hence emptiness. Its relationship to *shi,* the individual phenomenon or thing or occurrence, then, is not the same as the relationship between the universal qua idea and the particular qua individual thing, e.g., in Plato. The li-shi relationship is really the relationship between things and their inter-dependence or emptiness. This vertical interrelationship becomes further expressed in Nishida in terms of the relationship between nothing and beings, whole and parts, absolute and relative, place (basho) and implaced, universal and individual, world and individuals, and so on.

29. In his *Fa-jie-guan-men* (『法界観門』) (*Gate of Insight into the Dharmadhātu* or *On the Meditation of the Dharmadhātu*). In the following I am basing my interpretation primarily on the commentaries and short translations in Chang, *Buddhist Teaching of Totality,* and Oh, "*Dharmadhātu.*" Relevant passages (for example, see T45.652c28, 653c16f, and 653c25f) are cited in these works and are found in the third patriarch Fazang's (法藏) (643–712) commentary on Dushun's *Fajieguanmen* in his *Huayan Fapudixinzhang* in *Taishō shinshū daizōkyō,* volume 45 (T45.652a–654a). See also Cook, *Hua-yen Buddhism.*

30. In his *Huayan fajie xuanjing* (『華嚴法界玄鏡』) (*Mirror of the Mystery of the Avatamsaka* or *Great Exegesis of the Huayan Sūtra*).

31. See Masao Abe's commentary on this in *Zen and Western Thought,* p. 4. He is quoting Aishin Imaeda, ed., *Gotō egen* [Ch. *Wudeng Huiyuan*] (Tokyo: Rinrōkaku shoten, 1971), p. 335. Abe inserts the word "really" in the final concluding lines to say "mountains are really mountains, waters are really waters." The word does not appear in the original, and in fact, this insertion could lead to a misunderstanding. The point is not that they are ultimately, i.e., really, what they are. They are not ontologically independent (substances, essences). Rather, the point is that they are what they are in their emptiness, i.e., their inter-dependent origination. But rather than signifying their "nothingness," this means their "suchness."

32. In Dōgen's *Shōbōgenzō* (『正法眼蔵』) (*Treasury of the Eye of True Teaching* or *Treasury of the True Dharma Eye*).

33. The following is primarily based on Shigenori Nagatomo's analysis, presented in a seminar. See also Mizuno Yaoko's annotation in Dōgen, *Shōbōgenzō,* p. 53. For the English, see Dōgen, *Heart of Dōgen's "Shōbōgenzō,"* p. 40; and Dōgen, *Shōbōgenzō: Zen Essays by Dōgen,* p. 32.

34. On this and the following, see Kosaka, *Nishida Kitarō no shisō*, pp. 279–285.
35. See Suzuki, *Kongōkyō no zen*, p. 15.
36. See Suzuki, "Reason and Intuition in Buddhist Philosophy," p. 18.
37. I will examine this interaction between the two more closely in chapters 7 and 9.
38. See Kim, "Logic of the Illogical," p. 23.
39. See Verdú, *Dialectical Aspects in Buddhist Thought* and *Philosophy of Buddhism*.
40. Verdú, *Dialectical Aspects in Buddhist Thought*, p. 3.
41. See ibid., pp. 57 and 235–236. Even the notion of the *ālayavijñāna* becomes seen as "an eastern replica and forerunner of the Hegelian absolute 'idea,'" encompassing all aspects of reality in the identity between absolute and relative. See Verdú, *Dialectical Aspects in Buddhist Thought*, p. 5. He also finds the "true infinite," containing within itself the finite as the indeterminate's "power of self-determination," in the notion of the *tathagata-garbha* in the *Dacheng qixin lun* (Jp. *Daijō kishinron* 大乗起信論) (*Awakening of Faith in Mahāyāna*). See Verdú, *Philosophy of Buddhism*, p. 33.
42. See Verdú, *Philosophy of Buddhism*, pp. 36–37.
43. This is according to Gino K. Piovesana, "Contemporary Japanese Philosophy," p. 230, but Piovesana does not provide bibliographical information for this quotation.

3. Pure Experience, Self-Awareness, and Will

1. See Ueda, "Pure Experience, Self-Awareness, 'Basho,'" p. 68. This article is a translation of a chapter from Ueda's *Nishida Kitarō o yomu* (Tokyo: Iwanami, 1991).
2. For English translations of this work, see Nishida, *Inquiry into the Good*, trans. Masao Abe and Christopher Ives; and *Study of Good*, trans. V. H. Viglielmo. The more recent translation by Abe and Ives is far superior.
3. In "Does 'Consciousness' Exist?," James defines "pure experience" as "the instant field of the present . . . only virtually or potentially either object or subject as yet. . . . It is plain, unqualified actuality, or existence, a simple *that*; and the doubling of it in retrospection into a state of mind and a reality intended thereby, is just one of the acts." See James, *Writings of William James*, pp. 177–178. The essay originally appeared in *Journal of Philosophy, Psychology, and Scientific Methods*, vol. 1, no. 18 (September 1, 1904). The two thinkers, starting from the premise that there is only one primal stuff that is "pure experience," approach one another in their claims that objects of cognition are but abstractions from that originary experience that is concrete. For example, James explains knowledge as but a relationship between the parts of pure experience: one term becomes the subject or knower, and another term becomes the object known. See "Does 'Consciousness' Exist?," pp. 170, 172.
4. See Schopenhauer, *World as Will and Representation*.
5. The word *ri*, which in modern Japanese has come to mean "reason," has its origin in ancient Chinese thought and was developed by Neo-Confucianism and Kegon (Chn: Hua-yen 華厳). Buddhism, in which it had the sense of the patterning of the interrelationships between thing-events. See Krummel, "Transcendent or Immanent?"
6. On this, see Fujita, "Nishida Kitarō to Hēgeru," p. 162.
7. On this, see Ogawa, "Kyoto School of Philosophy and Phenomenology," pp. 214–215.
8. On this, see Ueda, "Pure Experience, Self-Awareness, Basho," pp. 69–71.
9. Keeping in mind William James's discussions of the place of things experienced and of the unity of the world and his referencing of C. A. Strong's idea of a common space as the medium of interaction between things, we can surmise that James's writings on "pure experience" may have contributed to the later germination and sprouting in Nishida of that notion of "place"

(basho). See James, "World of Pure Experience," pp. 195, 213, and n. 70. The article was origi-nally published in *Journal of Philosophy, Psychology, and Scientific Methods,* vol. 1, no. 20 (September 29, 1904) and no. 21 (October 13, 1904).

10. For the English translation, see Nishida, *Intuition and Reflection in Self-Consciousness.* This translation, however, is not always accurate.

11. For the English translation, see Nishida, *Art and Morality.* Unfortunately, this transla-tion is not always accurate.

12. Royce, *World and the Individual.* Royce's idea that facts are "what they are by virtue of their place in a self-determined system of facts, whose totality is . . . [the] Absolute" also re-minds one of the theory of place that Nishida would initiate in the late 1920s and continue to develop throughout the 1930s and 1940s. See Royce, *World and the Individual, Second Series,* p. 17.

13. See Fichte, *Science of Knowledge,* pp. 38, 41. This notion of an originary self-positing act coupled with intellectual intuition also provides the seed for Nishida's later notion of acting intuition.

14. As just stated, a Neo-Kantian influence is evident in this understanding of the ought, for the Neo-Kantians took the ought not merely ethically but in logical terms to mean validity. And even before the Neo-Kantian movement per se, this idea can be traced to Hermann Lotze. See Lotze, *Logic in Three Books,* vol. 2, pp. 209–210 and 267–268. But in the same way in which Nishida here collapses the logical (ought) and the ontological (is) in his interpretation of Fichte, so does Emil Lask, who was also very much influenced by Fichte and was a major influence on Nishida.

15. See Arisaka and Feenberg, "Experiential Ontology," p. 184; and Kopf, "Between Iden-tity and Difference," p. 98.

4. Dialectics in the Epistemology of Place

1. Fichte, *Science of Knowledge,* pp. 108–109.

2. Here Nishida even refers to Hegel's *Encyclopedia,* § 166, which speaks of judgment as the differentiation of the concept (Begriff). But the question is, can we equate Nishida's con-crete universal with Hegel's if what Hegel means is "concept"?

3. Again we need to be aware of the subtle relationship between basho at its most concrete level and what Nishida means by "universal" (ippansha), which he does not always carefully delineate or make clear. In discussing judgment in the 1925 essay "Hatarakumono" (「働くもの」; "That Which Works") in the same volume, Nishida explains how the system of self-determining universal concepts requires at its root a self-identity that contains its own principle of individ-ualization, allowing for self-differentiation. He states that a universal concept (*ippan gainen* 一般概念) enveloping the mutually distinct is required for their differentiation. And the contra-diction of two concepts requires an "objective unity" (*kyakkanteki tōitsu* 客観的統一) envelop-ing them (*Z3* 400). Nishida then speaks of what unifies contradictory concepts as the basho or place of the generation-and-extinction, rise-and-fall, of concepts, which is also what establishes beings by becoming nothing (*Z3* 402). So it appears that Nishida here speaks of basho in terms of universal concepts or certainly at least in relation to them. The distinction between the most concrete basho and universals qua concepts is not as clear in the first passage. In the second passage, however, Nishida seems to make a subtle distinction between that basho enveloping universal concepts and those implaced concepts. It is important to remember that basho at its most concrete level is not a concept.

4. For Hegel, however, the abstract universal is reached through the exclusion of the particular features distinguishing individuals while retaining what is common to them. See Hegel, *Hegel's Logic*, § 163, p. 227.

5. Ibid., § 166, p. 231.

6. In an analogous sense the Neo-Kantian Paul Natorp attempted to recapture the dynamic concrete life of the subject of experience that gets lost through the process of objectification. See Natorp, *Allgemeine Psychologie nach kritischer Methode*, p. 191. He had to do this without thematizing the subject, which would kill its lived immediacy or flow, in a method that involves the "turning inside out" (*Umstülpung*) of objectification. On this, see Luft, "Reconstruction and Reduction," pp. 65–66. Yet one might say that Nishida went further in that for him, the turning away from the object (grammatical subject) ultimately entailed attending to the place that encompasses both the object and the subject of experience, both the subject and the predicate of judgment.

7. On basho as "horizon," see Ueda, "Pure Experience, Self-Awareness, 'Basho,'" p. 80.

8. This relationship between the predicate plane and the concrete universal is also subtle and not as clear as it should be. In the 1927 essay "Shirumono" (「知るもの」; "That Which Knows") in the same volume, Nishida makes an equation among (1) the no-longer-determinable universal grounding the concrete universal, (2) the predicate pole that becomes the predicate but not the subject, and (3) the place of nothing. He states that when we view the predicate pole as containing the transcending object—what becomes the grammatical subject but not the predicate, i.e., Aristotle's substance—the universal is concrete (*Z3* 523). So the transcendental predicate pole that envelops the individual, the grammatical subject, is a concrete universal. He then speaks of the concrete universal's triadic movement in affirmation, negation, and the negation of negation, which is its contradictory unity (*Z3* 528). But in speaking of the universal that grounds the concrete universal—the universal in its self-determination or in its triadic movement—in terms of the predicate pole that encompasses the transcendent object qua grammatical subject, Nishida obviously means basho. So one might try to add precision to Nishida's explanation here by clarifying that the place of nothing is what envelops that dynamism of the concrete universal. But we also have to be careful not to separate that basho from everything else, including the concrete universal's self-determinations, and not to make it into something utterly transcendent without any immanence.

9. This is what Martin Heidegger would call "the ontic." Heidegger, like Nishida, was very much influenced by Emil Lask.

10. See Emil Lask, *Die Logik der Philosophie und die Kategorienlehre*, in Lask, *Sämtliche Werke*, vol. 2, pp. 5–6; and Crowell, "Transcendental Logic and Minimal Empiricism," p. 172n26.

11. See Lotze, *Logic in Three Books*, vol. 2, §§ 316–317, pp. 208–209, 211; § 320, pp. 217–218; and § 341, p. 269.

12. See Lask, *Logik der Philosophie und die Kategorienlehre*, pp. 60, 83.

13. See Schürmann, *Heidegger on Being and Acting*; and Schürmann, *Broken Hegemonies*. This is my appropriation of Schürmann's ideas in reading Nishida. Schürmann, as far as I am aware, had no knowledge of Nishida's philosophy.

14. Here I use the Greek prefix *an-* to denote absolute irreducibility not only to the ontological (i.e., beings) but also to its negation denoted by the Greek prefix *me-* (i.e., the meontological as non-being). Hence the an-ontological encompasses both being and its opposite, non-being, both the ontological and the meontological.

15. That is, one's lived experience before theorizing about that experience in the epistemological terms of subject and object or the grammatical terms of subject and predicate.

16. Tanabe's critique appears in *Nishida sensei no oshie o aogu* (「西田先生の教えを仰ぐ」), published in *Tanabe Hajime zenshū yon maki* (『田辺元全集四巻』; *Tanabe Hajime Collected Works*, vol. 4). My discussion here relies on Fujita, "Nishida Kitarō to Hēgeru," pp. 164–166, 168.

17. On the nature of this "logical contradiction," see Kopf, "Between Foundationalism and Relativism," p. 26 and n. 5.

18. Ibid., p. 27.

19. Ibid., p. 31.

20. Nishida also applies the same sort of analysis that he directed at the structure of judgment when he is looking at the syllogistic relationship between propositions. He accordingly regards the universal enveloping judgments as enveloped by the universal of syllogisms, which is also thus shown to be self-contradictory (*Z3* 529–531, 548).

21. See Wargo, *Logic of Nothingness*, pp. 123, 136, 155, 160.

22. I disagree with Wargo's use of the term "resolution" or "resolve" to characterize this seeing of contradiction from the deeper level. See ibid., p. 160.

23. On this, see Arisaka, "System and Existence," p. 44.

24. This is in fact a reference to Pascal's notion of an "infinite sphere." See Pascal, *Pensées*, § 199 (§ 72), p. 60. In later works Nishida will characterize this as a "sphere" (*kyū* 球) as well.

25. See his afterword to the 1931 essay "Watashi no tachiba kara mita Hēgeru no benshōhō" (*Z7* 278).

5. The Dialectic of the World-Matrix Involving Acting Persons

1. On this and the following, see also Fujita, "Nishida Kitarō to Hēgeru," pp. 170–171.

2. In fact, Josiah Royce anticipates this idea when he says, "The true world . . . is the world of socially interrelated Selves." See Royce, *World and the Individual, Second Series*, p. 107. Nishida occasionally refers to Royce throughout his oeuvre.

3. See also Fujita, "Nishida Kitarō to Hēgeru," p. 176. Hegel's term for ethical norms as embodied in society was *Sittlichkeit*. By "objective spirit (or mind)" (*der objective Geist*) Hegel meant the common spirit of a social group as embodied in its institutions and permeating the consciousness of individual members. See Hegel, *Hegel's Philosophy of Mind*, §§ 483–552, pp. 241–291.

4. When Nishida speaks of "phenomenology," he predominantly has in mind Husserl and occasionally the early Heidegger. But he remained ignorant of the later Husserl and his notion of the life-world (*Lebenswelt*), as well as of Heidegger's post–*Sein und Zeit* developments. And he was just as unaware of any of the other major post-Husserlian phenomenological developments because his life ended in 1945.

5. This is from a 1935 lecture included in the 1966 edition of the *Zenshū* volumes. I was unable to locate it in the newest edition that began publication in 2002.

6. See Haldane, *Philosophical Basis of Biology*, e.g., pp. 13–14.

7. I will discuss this concept in greater detail in chapter 6.

8. As I discussed in preceding chapters, William James was a major influence on Nishida's conception of pure experience. Here, however, we also find James anticipating Nishida's idea of the active body as mediating our being-in-the-world when he writes as follows: "The world experienced (otherwise called the 'field of consciousness') comes at all times with our body as its centre, centre of vision, centre of action, centre of interest. Where the body is is 'here'; when the body acts is 'now'; what the body 'touches' is 'this'; . . . The body is the storm centre, the origin of co-ordinates, the constant place of stress in all that experience-train.

Everything circles round it, and is felt from its point of view." See William James, "Experience of Activity," in James, *Writings of William James*, p. 284n180. (The essay was James's 1904 presidential address to the American Psychological Association and was first published in *Psychological Review*, vol. 12, no. 1 [January 1905].) In fact, this is also an interesting point of mutual convergence with Maurice Merleau-Ponty's theory of body and perception. On this, see Kazashi, "Bodily Logos."

9. On the body as mediator, see Kosaka, *Nishida Kitarō no shisō*, pp. 221–222.

10. Similar notions of the microcosmic mirroring of the macrocosm are found in many writers, among whom I might note the Romantic thinkers of Germany immediately preceding Hegel, such as Herder and Goethe, and before them in the Renaissance. The spirit expresses itself in external nature and comes to full expression in human consciousness that reflects the whole. See Taylor, *Hegel*, p. 43. Nishida, however, takes this in a different direction predicated on his notion of absolute nothing. A closer precursor of Nishida in this respect might be the ninth-century founder of Shingon Buddhism, Kūkai (空海).

11. On this, see, Kosaka, *Nishida Kitarō no shisō*, p. 199.

12. On this, see ibid., p. 202.

6. The Dialectic of the World-Matrix Involving the Dialectical Universal and Contradictory Identity

1. On this, see Fujita, "Nishida Kitarō to Hēgeru," p. 169.

2. Some commentators have identified only four. For example, see Kopf, "Between Foundationalism and Relativism," pp. 31–32. To Kopf's fourfold forms I am, however, adding the mutual determination of individuals as an important feature of this dialectic that we should not neglect. Each of the fivefold forms can be translated into one of the fourfold mutual non-obstructions of Huayan (Kegon) Buddhism. I will discuss this in a later section, as well as in later chapters.

3. In virtue of this reverse determination, and also of what Nishida in the 1940s call "inverse correspondence" (gyakutaiō 逆対応), the chiasmatic nature of Nishida's dialectic also proves to be chiasmatic; that is, the chiasma also encompasses the nature of a "chiasmus," or, in Merleau-Ponty's terms, a "chiasm," a radical reciprocity. See chapter 10 on these concepts.

4. See Hegel, *Encyclopedia Logic*, in Hegel, *Hegel's Logic*, § 166, p. 231.

5. I will return to this topic in detail in chapters 7 and 9.

6. E.g., René Descartes, *Principle of Philosophy*, pt. 1, principle 51, for example, in Descartes, *Philosophical Works of Descartes*, vol. 1, p. 239.

7. Does Nishida mean by this that we literally transform into those things metaphysically? To consider this just a metaphor, however, may fall short of what he really means. I take him to mean here the pre-reflective realization in acting intuition of the lack of any essence within oneself that would substantially separate or isolate oneself from those other things. It is the realization of the relationality (i.e., in Mahāyāna terms, "emptiness") of one's being vis-à-vis other beings.

8. See Fujita, "Nishida Kitarō to Hēgeru," pp. 174–176.

9. In 1939 Nishida again uses the German dialectical terminology—as used by Fichte and Hegel—of *an und für sich* ("in-and-for-itself") to characterize such contradictory identity (e.g., Z8 390).

10. "Zettai ni sōhansurumono no tōitsu toshite zettai no jikodōitsu" (絶対に相反するものの統一として絶対の自己同一) (Z6 187).

11. Augustine, *Confessions* 11, 20, p. 235.

12. In addition to "abiding in a dharma-position" (jūhōi) and "being-time" (uji), Dōgen's understanding of time involves the concepts of "here-and-now" (*nikon* 而今) and "passage" (*kyōryaku* 經歷). The gist of his view, the complexity of which I cannot really do justice to here, is that each moment is mutually distinct yet implicative of all the others as a microcosm that focuses or condenses the whole of space-time-being into one momentary point.

13. "De-cision" here should not be taken anthropomorphically in its ordinary sense as something "we" do. Rather, it should be taken literally as the dividing point or "break," *caesura,* where past and future meet and separate.

14. See Fujita, "Nishida Kitarō to Hēgeru," pp. 174–176.

15. Again, this is an idea reminiscent of Dōgen's notions of time, especially "being-time" (uji) and "abiding in a dharma-position" (jūhōi).

16. Dilworth translates the term *kateiteki benshōhō* (過程的弁証法) here as "dialectical process." See Nishida, *Fundamental Problems of Philosophy,* p. 47. But the meaning is really "dialectic of process," having the significance of a certain type of dialectic, namely, a dialectic unfolding diachronically, as opposed to a dialectic that would involve synchronic terms. The former involves the temporal dimension, and the latter involves the spatial dimension. Ultimately Nishida's dialectic of the world-matrix involves both.

17. In *Time and Free Will* Henri Bergson defines what he means by "pure duration": "The form which the succession of our conscious states assumes when our ego lets itself *live,* when it refrains from separating its present state from its former states . . . , [forming] both the past and the present states into an organic whole" (p. 100); "A succession of qualitative changes, which melt into and permeate one another, without precise outlines, without any tendency to externalize themselves in relation to one another, without any affiliation with number; it would be pure heterogeneity" (p. 104); and "Duration . . . , restored to its original purity, will appear as wholly qualitative multiplicity, an absolute heterogeneity of elements which pass over into one another" (p. 229).

18. For example, Nishida in "Ronri to seimei" contrasts his acting intuition as "circular" (enganteki) with Bergson's pure duration and creative evolution as "linear" (*chokusenteki*) (Z8 89).

19. As I mentioned in chapter 1, Nishida's critique of Bergson may seem unjustified when it is seen in light of Bergson's discussion of mind, body, and environment in *Matter and Memory* of 1896. Nishida's intended target is most certainly Bergson's *Time and Free Will* (1889), in which Bergson distinguishes duration as qualitative and intensive from space as quantifiable extension. Edward Casey has pointed out the irony in Bergson's assertion of the primacy of durational time in human experience in that in the previous year in his Latin dissertation Bergson had taken up the topic of Aristotelian *topos.* But in *Time and Free Will* the temporocentrism of modern Western philosophy is reinforced. See Casey, "Smooth Spaces and Rough-Edged Places," p. 288. In *Time and Free Will* Bergson differentiates, on the one hand, quantitative multiplicity as applicable only to magnitudes and involving the intuition of space and, on the other, qualitative multiplicity as belonging to states of consciousness that are unquantifiable. That qualitative multiplicity unfolds in continuous succession, without distinction, in an "organic evolution" that constitutes "duration," whereby the heterogeneous moments interpermeate one another (*Time and Free Will,* pp. 105, 110, 120, 226). In that respect it is an occurrence of pure interiority. The difference is between "simultaneity . . . , mutual externality without succession," and "succession without mutual externality" (pp. 226–227); between simultaneity, extensity, and quantity, on the one hand, and succession, duration, and quality, on the other (p. 240). In other words, Bergson reduces spatiality to the quantitatively measurable

and homogeneous "pure extension" and takes the qualitatively heterogeneous intensity as belonging to temporal duration. Later, in *Creative Evolution* (1907), Bergson characterizes spatiality as a "degrading of the extra-spatial [i.e., pure duration]" and reduces it to the self's extension into the fixed and mutually external "in place of the tension it possessed as an indivisible active will" (p. 171). He views spatiality qua extension as emerging in the shift from "tension to extension . . . , freedom to mechanical necessity" (p. 195). Therefore, "*Extension . . .* appears only as a *tension* which is interrupted" (p. 201). But such reduction of spatiality ignores its pre-theoretical modes that we have direct access to in our concrete existence—whether conceived in terms of alterity or exteriority, embodiment, world, or the place or space of clearing wherein things appear and wherein we find ourselves implaced. When Bergson speaks of pure duration as pure heterogeneity (e.g., *Time and Free Will*, p. 104), one might ask whether such heterogeneity would not also have to involve the lived spatiality of alterity in one's encountering of the other-than-I. In its lived aspect, that spatiality is not quantifiable and escapes reduction to geometrical extension. We notice a groping toward such an understanding of spatiality in such later twentieth-century thinkers as Heidegger, Emmanuel Levinas, Merleau-Ponty, and most certainly Nishida. Bergson, moreover, seems to ignore, at least in *Time and Free Will*, the dialectical intersection of duration with that space of our concrete dwelling that Nishida describes in terms of basho and the dialectical world.

20. See Pascal, *Pensées*, § 199 (§72), p. 60.

21. He opposes this to Leibniz's idealism of monadology.

7. The Dialectic of Religiosity

1. Leibniz in his *Discourse on Metaphysics* (1686), § 12, refuses to reduce the substance of bodies to extension, e.g., size, figure, or motion, and claims that instead we must recognize in them something akin to the soul that serves as the principle of identity for bodies. See Leibniz, *Discourse on Metaphysics, and Other Essays*, pp. 11–12; and Leibniz, *Discourse on Metaphysics, Correspondence with Arnauld, and Monadology*, pp. 18–19.

2. See Leibniz, "New System of the Nature of the Communication of Substances, as Well as the Union That Exists between the Soul and the Body (27 June 1695)," in Leibniz, *Shorter Leibniz Texts*, pp. 68–77, pp. 69–70. Also see p. 73, where he says: "There are only *atoms of substance,* that is to say, real unities absolutely devoid of parts, which are the sources of actions, and the absolute first principles of the composition of things, and as it were the ultimate elements of analysis of substantial things. They can be called *metaphysical points:* they have *something vital* in them, and a kind of *perception,* and *mathematical points* are their *points of view* for expressing the universe."

3. On this, see Kosaka, *Nishida Kitarō no shisō*, pp. 233–234 and p. 365n161.

4. See ibid., p. 234.

5. All of this is a development of Leibniz's notion of expression in his monadology. See Leibniz, *Monadology, and Other Philosophical Writings*, pp. 156–157, §§ 56–57; p. 158, § 62.

6. See Dilworth, "Introduction," p. 32.

7. Before Pascal this idea was expressed by Nicholas of Cusa (1401–1464). See Nicholas of Cusa, *De docta ignorantia* (On Learned Ignorance), in *Nicholas of Cusa: Selected Spiritual Writings*, bk. 1, ch. 21, pp. 116–120. Nicholas's claim here that the universe's circumference is nowhere and its center is everywhere in fact derives from a twelfth-century pseudo-Hermetic text, "The Book of the XXIV Philosophers." Later, Giordano Bruno in the sixteenth century and Pascal in the seventeenth century borrow this idea. But none of these writers cite the original

source from which they took this idea. Edward Casey discusses this in *Fate of Place*, pp. 116–117, 385nn43–44.

8. Nicholas states: "Because the absolutely maximum is absolutely and actually all that can be, and it is without opposition to such an extent that the minimum coincides with the maximum, it is above all affirmation and all negation. It both is and is not all that is conceived to be, and it both is and is not all that is conceived not to be. . . . The absolute maximumness, to which nothing is opposed and with which the minimum coincides, is infinite" (Nicholas of Cusa, *On Learned Ignorance*, bk. 1, ch. 4, p. 92).

9. I.e., nature as creator or cause and nature as creation or effect. For Spinoza, God is the creator manifest in his creations, His essence is expressed therein, and therefore he is "nature" in both senses. See, e.g., Benedict de Spinoza, *The Ethics*, pt. 2, definition 1, in Spinoza, *On the Improvement of the Understanding; The Ethics; Correspondence*, p. 82.

10. On this, see Dilworth, "Introduction," p. 27; and Kopf, "Between Identity and Difference," p. 83.

11. One might compare Nishida's notion of God or the absolute here with Luce Irigaray's radical re-interpretation of Spinoza's notion of God as an "ultimate envelope . . . that envelops him/herself (and everything else)" with itself (Casey, *Fate of Place*, p. 329): "*that which is its own place for itself, that which turns itself inside out and thus constitutes a dwelling (for) itself . . . that which provides its own envelope*" (Irigaray, *Ethics of Sexual Difference*, p. 85). One might also bring Nishida's idea into a conversation with Jean-Luc Nancy's notion of the displacement or replacement of God by its place that is now empty, an emptiness co-extensive with infinite space. See Nancy, *Inoperative Community*, p. 149.

12. "Naizaiteki naru mono ga chōetsuteki ni, chōetsuteki naru mono ga naizaiteki ni" (Z9 469).

13. See chapter 6 for discussion of this dialectic of the "dialectical universal" that entails its reverse determination by individuals even while it determines them.

14. "Neither ceasing nor arising, neither annihilation nor permanence, neither identity nor difference, neither coming-in nor going-out." This appears at the beginning of Nāgārjuna's *Mūlamadhyamakakārikā* in the dedicatory verses. See Nāgārjuna, *Nāgārjuna, the Philosophy of the Middle Way*, p. 101; and Nāgārjuna, *Fundamental Wisdom of the Middle Way*, p. 2. See also Dilworth, "Nishida's Final Essay," pp. 360–361. This is not exactly the same as the four double negations (is, is-not, both is and is-not, and neither is nor is-not) that the Buddha also made use of.

15. The term *kenosis*, meaning to empty oneself, appears in Paul, Letter to the Philippians 2:6–8. See note 17 in regard to the controversy concerning this.

16. *Kenosis* derives from the Greek word *kenon*, "void."

17. Nishida, of course, was unaware of the more recent debates in the twentieth century in regard to the issue of God's incarnation as evidenced in the New Testament. Hans Küng shows that the distinction between the Son of God and God the Father is maintained everywhere in the New Testament, and that there is no mention of the incarnation of God himself. It is always God's Son or Word who became man, never God himself. In Paul's Letter to the Philippians 2:6–8, where the idea of *kenosis* appears, it is not, strictly speaking, the *kenosis* of God but rather of Christ: "Christ Jesus . . . emptied himself [or: made himself nothing], taking the form of a servant, being born in the likeness of men." And it is only fifty years after Paul that an ambiguity then appears in the Gospel according to John, where its prologue mentions the eternally pre-existing *logos* (Word)—that is, "as God in God's being"—becoming "flesh," as man. See Küng, *Does God Exist?*, pp. 684–685. Nevertheless, Abe Masao suggests that Christ's *kenosis* has its origin in God's *kenosis* as a loving God and cites Karl Rahner's notion of God who creates by emptying himself. See Cobb and Ives, *Emptying God*, pp. 9, 14.

18. This is called *akuninshōkisetsu,* "the doctrine that [even] the evil person has the chance for salvation," meaning that the evil person is Amida's true object of salvation. Although the expression *akuninshōki* does not appear in any of Shinran's writings, its idea is expressed variously in his works. For example, in *Tannishō* (*A Record in Lament of Divergences*), paragraph 3, Shinran says, "Amida made the vow, the essential intent of which is the evil person's attainment of Buddhahood. Hence, evil persons who entrust themselves to other-power [*tariki*] are precisely the ones who possess the true cause of birth. . . . Accordingly he [Amida] said, 'Even the good person is born in the Pure Land, so without question is the person who is evil'" (Shinran, *Collected Works,* vol. 1, *The Writings,* p. 663). See also paragraph 16. See also Suzuki, *Collected Writings on Shin Buddhism,* p. 135; and Dobbins, *Jōdo Shinshū,* 37, 53–54, 70–71, 75, 193. However, some claim that this doctrine can also be traced to Hōnen. See Fujimoto, "Study of Honen's Doctrine of Evil Persons as the Object of Salvation." See the discussion of this doctrine in the context of Nishida in Asami and Sakurai, *Nishida Kitarō,* p. 143. The main point of this idea is the overcoming of self-righteousness that relies on "self-power" (*jiriki*), an overcoming that Nishida transposes into what he calls "self-negation."

19. Dilworth has described this as Nishida's "hermeneutical repossession" of the Mahāyāna saṃsāra-nirvāṇa non-duality. See Dilworth, "Introduction," p. 36.

20. Nishida had already made this point in a lecture in 1933 (Z13 235).

21. In this passage (Z10 342) from "Bashoteki ronri to shūkyōteki sekaikan," Nishida first understands Adam's "original sin" of eating the fruit from the "tree of knowledge" as God's self-negation that establishes humanity. He then associates this with his idea of the "self-contradiction" (*jiko mujun* 自己矛盾) that is at the source of man's establishment.

22. Nishida here may be dispelling the stereotypical portrayal of Zen as a religion of "self-power" or "self-reliance" (*jiriki*) in opposition to Pure Land as a religion of "other-power" (*tariki*) or Amida's "grace" (*onchō* 恩寵). That becomes clear in his statement in the 1945 essay that religion primordially is not founded on "self-reliance" or "self-power" (Z10 326).

23. Nishida's concept here of inverse correspondence and, along with it, his understanding in terms of self-negation of the Christian idea of divine incarnation may show some influence of Kierkegaard's notion of the "absolute paradox" that he opposes to Hegel's sublational dialectics in both *Fear and Trembling* and *Concluding Unscientific Postscript.* See, e.g., Kierkegaard, *Concluding Unscientific Postscript,* on the paradox of "eternal essential truth" in its "relationship to an existing individual" (p. 183); "The eternal truth has come into being in time: this is the paradox" (p. 187); and "That God has existed in human form, has been born, grown up, and so forth, is surely the paradox *sensu strictissimo,* the absolute paradox" (pp. 194–195).

24. A similar sort of dialectical ethics of self-negation is suggested by another religious tradition that Nishida did not examine. The sixteenth-century Jewish mystic Isaac Luria spoke of God's voluntary self-withdrawal that made room for creation. In more recent Jewish authors, such as Hans Jonas and Harold Kuchner, this becomes God's voluntary self-relinquishing of omnipotence to permit the actualization of human freedom, with all its perils and dangers. See, for example, Luria, *Kabbalah: A Study of the Ten Luminous Emanations;* Jonas, "The Concept of God after Auschwitz"; and Kuchner, *When Bad Things Happen to Good People.* In Eastern Christianity the Christ figure is taken more explicitly to mirror that self-abnegation of God in the human realm as an examplar or model for human *theōsis* (θέωσις) ("deification"), that is, the transformation of humanity to attain likeness to, or union with, God. One might then take Nishida's dialectic here as advocating an ethics of humility in our mutual interactions.

25. See Kosaka, *Nishida Kitarō no shisō,* p. 78.

26. This point, emphasized by the Protestant Reformists Martin Luther and John Calvin, is also an idea traceable to St. Augustine and St. Paul. Paul described his conversion experience as having died to his old self ("Saul") so that Christ might live in him. See Paul's *Letter to the Galatians* 2:19–20.

27. See Kosaka, *Nishida Kitarō no shisō*, pp. 287–288.

28. Of course, Nishida already did this in his earlier works as well, but this identification now has a clear place of belonging in the philosophy of religion he systematizes in these last essays.

29. Here we must not take the verb "respond" to be something undertaken by the volitional self. Rather, the correspondence or co-respondence is prior to what might be reduced to the individual's activity. In other words, the dialectical interrelationality, the concrete whole, in its dynamism is prior.

30. This idea is traceable to the Chinese Chan master Mazu Daoyi (馬祖道一; Jp.: Baso Dōitsu) (709–788) and his notion of "ordinary mind" (*byōjōshin*平常心). Nishida refers to related ideas in Linji Yixuan (臨濟義玄; Jp.: Rinzai Gigen) (d. 866/867 CE) and Nanquan (南泉; Jp.: Nansen) (748–834). I will discuss these again in chapter 9.

31. See Kosaka, *Nishida Kitarō no shisō*, pp. 295, 298.

32. See Ueda Shizuteru, "Gyakutaiō to byōjōtei," in Ueda, *Nishida tetsugaku*, pp. 376–377.

33. Dilworth, "Introduction," p. 15.

8. Nishida and Hegel

1. See Arisaka, "Beyond 'East and West,'" p. 240.

2. Although the afterword was probably added immediately before the publication of *Zoku shisaku to taiken* in 1937.

3. Fujita Masakatsu states that Nishida's characterization of his standpoint as an "absolute dialectic" (zettai benshōhō) or "dialectic of place" (bashoteki benshōhō) is on the basis of his recognition of this overlapping of "nearness" and "farness" between his dialectical thinking and that of Hegel. See Fujita, "Nishida Kitarō to Hēgeru," pp. 163–164.

4. In this chapter, similar to what I did in chapter 2, I will identify Hegel's works as follows: *DFSe* = *The Difference between Fichte's and Schelling's System of Philosophy*; *DFSg* = *Differenz des Fichteschen und Schellingschen Systems der Philosophie*; *EL* = *Encyclopedia Logic*, in *Hegel's Logic*; *EPM* = *Hegel's Philosophy of Mind*; *GPR* = *Grundlinien der Philosophie des Rechts*; *PG* = *Phänomenologie des Geistes*; *PH* = *Philosophy of History*; *PR* = *Hegel's Philosophy of Right*; *PS* = *Phenomenology of Spirit*; *SL* = *Science of Logic*, trans. A. V. Miller; *WL1* = *Wissenschaft der Logik*, pt. 1; *WL2* = *Wissenschaft der Logik*, pt. 2. The lowercase *z* denotes *Zusatz*, notes taken by students based on Hegel's lectures and added to the original text.

5. On this, see James Lawler, "Hegel on Logical and Dialectical Contradictions," pp. 19, 22.

6. See ibid., pp. 22, 24, 39. This idea that the determination of each entity or idea is via negation is a development of a conception inherited from Spinoza, that all determination is negation.

7. "Die Bewegung der daseiende Widerspruch selbst ist" (*WL2* 59).

8. For example, see Dilworth, "Introduction"; and also Kozyra, "Paradokkusu ronri no nihirizumu," pp. 93–94, 100.

9. For Hegel, the concrete universal (konkrete Allgemeinheit) allows for specific differences, while the abstract universal (abstrakte Allgemeinheit) abstracts from them (*EL* § 163z 227).

10. Strictly speaking, however, one ought to distinguish basho from what we ordinarily think of as a "universal." What Nishida means by basho is un-delimited by any universal. Nevertheless, he seems to have basho in mind when he speaks of the "universal of universals" or the "universal of nothing" (Z6 14).

11. On this, see Funayama, *Hēgeru tetsugaku to Nishida tetsugaku*, p. 21.

12. On this question, see, e.g., Masao Abe, "Nishida's Philosophy of 'Place,'" pp. 365–366; and Masao Abe, "Logic of Absolute Nothingness," pp. 170–171.

13. And "subject" here can simultaneously have two significances: grammatical and epistemological.

14. Taylor, *Hegel*, p. 569.

15. See Masao Abe, "Nishida's Philosophy of 'Place,'" p. 366; and Masao Abe, "Logic of Absolute Nothingness," pp. 171–172.

16. Barth, *From Rousseau to Ritschl*, p. 304.

17. For this, Hegel has been accused by the Neo-Kantians, among others, of a kind of pan-logism.

18. To an extent, this self-enclosure of the dialectical circle can be found in Western philosophy even before Hegel. See chapter 2, note 6.

19. See Carter, *Nothingness beyond God*, p. 32.

20. See, for example, "Watashi no tachiba kara mita Hēgeru no benshōhō" of 1931 (Z7 278) and also his 1938 lecture "Nihon bunka no mondai" (The Problem of Japanese Culture) (Z13 22).

21. See Kosaka, *Nishida Kitarō no shisō*; Nakamura Yūjirō, *Nishida Kitarō*; and Nakamura Yūjirō, *Nishida Kitarō no datsukōchiku*.

22. Nakamura Yūjirō regards this as a trans-temporal simultaneity with respect to the horizontal process of Hegel's dialectic. In Nakamura's reading, Nishida's dialectic accordingly is, in fact, a meta-dialectic that relativizes Hegel's dialectic of process by enfolding it within its own dialectic of place (bashoteki benshōhō). See Nakamura Yūjirō, "Nishida Kitarō no shūkyōron to rekishiron" ("Nishida Kitarō's Theory of Religion and Theory of History"), in Nakamura Yūjirō, *Nishida Kitarō no datsukōchiku*, pp. 238–239, and in *Nishida Kitarō II*, pp. 222–223. This leads Nakamura to conclude that Nishida's dialectic is really not dialectical. The question, then, is how one is to define "dialectic." If we take the meaning of "dialectic" in a broader sense as involving the interrelations between opposites in general, then this co-relationship between the field of nothing and the co-relative terms implaced within it is certainly dialectical, as Nishida claims. Yet one might still question whether that dialectical language adequately expresses the content matter of Nishida's thought.

23. Hegel distinguishes such a concept from ordinary ones in his *Encyclopaedia Logic* (EL §9 13, §160z 223–224) and in his *Science of Logic*, "On the Concept in General" (WL2 213–234/SL 577–595).

24. E.g., "The special interest of passion is . . . inseparable from the active development of a general principle" (PH 32).

25. For example, in Hegel's conception of the state, the state is absolute, while the individual is its abstraction. Fujita Masakatsu, however, states that the individual's free will is Hegel's starting point in his *Philosophy of Right* (*Grundlinien der Philosophie des Rechts*). What Hegel states here (§ 4) is that the will as the place and origin of right is free. And the basis of that right is mind (*das Geistige*) (GPR 28/PR 20). Hegel's point was that the system of law embodied in the state or civil society was necessary to actualize that freedom. According to Fujita, Nishida's critique of Hegel might then provoke the retort that it is rather Nishida's understanding of the individual that is abstract in lacking any consideration of the concrete content of that freedom,

including various rights and relations that would actualize it and contradictions that might alienate it. See Fujita, "Nishida Kitarō to Hēgeru," pp. 179–180.

26. The emphasis is mine.

27. A couple of recent discussions of the Hegel-Nishida relationship that take different approaches than mine, both published as I was finishing this book, are Schultz, "Nishida Kitarō, G. W. F. Hegel, and the Pursuit of the Concrete"; and Suares, *Kyoto School's Takeover of Hegel.* Both works are worth looking at.

9. Nishida, Buddhism, and Religion

1. Nīgata, *Mu no hikaku shisō,* p. 274.

2. On these biographical details, see Takemura, *Nishida Kitarō to Bukkyō,* pp. 14–16, 20.

3. See Fujita, "Significance of Japanese Philosophy," p. 14.

4. See James, "World of Pure Experience."

5. E.g., see Arisaka, "Beyond 'East and West,'" p. 240.

6. On this and the difficulties of uniting the discursive activity that is philosophy with the practical path that is Zen, see Yusa, "From *Topos* to Environment," p. 115.

7. On this, see Takemura, *Nishida Kitarō to Bukkyō,* p. 21.

8. See ibid., pp. 4, 48–49, 58–59.

9. Goto-Jones, *Political Philosophy in Japan,* p. 142n15.

10. See Takemura, *Nishida Kitarō to Bukkyō,* p. 76. See also Goto-Jones, *Political Philosophy in Japan,* p. 44, on the following.

11. Yusa, *Zen and Philosophy,* p. 249.

12. The *Prajñāpāramitā sūtras,* "Great sūtras of the wisdom that reaches the other shore," were a series of about forty Mahāyāna scriptures gathered together, from the centuries before and after the start of the Common Era, all dealing with the realization of *prajñā,* the intuitive wisdom in regard to certain truths, such as emptiness and dependent origination. The best known are the *Diamond Sūtra* and the *Heart Sūtra,* and their most important interpreter was Nāgārjuna.

13. Dilworth, "Introduction," p. 28.

14. See Cestari, "Between Emptiness and Absolute Nothingness," p. 329; and Kopf, "Critical Comments on Nishida's Use of Chinese Buddhism," p. 326.

15. See Kopf, "Critical Comments on Nishida's Use of Chinese Buddhism," p. 314.

16. See Mutai, *Shisaku to kansatsu,* pp. 150, 151, 154–155. See also Kosaka Kunitsugu's discussion of this in *Nishida Kitarō no shisō,* pp. 277–278.

17. See Funayama, *Hēgeru tetsugaku to Nishida tetsugaku,* p. 18.

18. On this, see Dilworth, "Introduction," pp. 34–35.

19. See Dilworth, "Nishida Kitarō," p. 474. See also Aśvaghosha, *Awakening of Faith Attributed to Aśvaghosha,* pp. 42–43.

20. See Kosaka, *Nishida Kitarō no shisō,* p. 75.

21. This letter appears in the 1980 edition of Nishida's *Collected Writings* (*Zenshū*), but had not yet appeared, at the time of this writing, in the most recent series that began publication in 2002.

22. Arisaka, "Beyond 'East and West,'" p. 240.

23. Along with the influence of Nishida's friend D. T. Suzuki, the influence of one of Nishida's precursors in modern Japanese philosophy, Inoue Enryō, and his application of Buddhist concepts to philosophy, e.g., in his theory of the logic of mutual inclusion (or "theory of mutual containment and inclusion") and his notion that contradiction is truth, undoubtedly played a part in the development of Nishida's thinking here. See, e.g., Inoue, "View of the Cosmos,"

pp. 623–627, esp. pp. 625–626. The particular situation of Nishida's relationship to Buddhism and Western philosophy becomes complex when we notice that Nishida seems to have inherited the filtering of Buddhist concepts through Western philosophical terminology that we find in this pioneer of modern academic philosophy in Japan. For example, Inoue explained the relationship and distinction between the *dharmas* or "forms of things" and *tathatā* as their "essential nature" in terms of the relative and finite, characterized by distinctions, for the former, and the absolute and infinite, characterized by non-distinction, for the latter. See ibid., pp. 619–623.

24. Nishida also adds that in the West, Nicholas of Cusa's learned ignorance (*docta ignorantia*) comes closest to this idea. See Nicholas's *On Learned Ignorance (De docta ignorantia)*, in Nicholas of Cusa, *Nicholas of Cusa: Selected Spiritual Writings*, pp. 85–206.

25. *Vajrachchedika-sūtra* from around the second or first century BCE. This scripture propounds the idea of the emptiness or lack of selfness or substantiality in all reality and opposes the conceptual understanding of reality in terms of such self-being or substance. The work was said to be sharp like a diamond in that it cuts away all unnecessary conceptualization to bring one to enlightenment, hence its title.

26. See Suzuki, *Kongō-kyō no Zen*, pp. 380–383. The full formulation of this "logic of *prajna*-intuition" is given in English as follows: "A is not-A, therefore A is A." See Suzuki, *Studies in Zen*, pp. 119–120.

27. On this interaction between the two, see Mutai, *Shisaku to kansatsu*, pp. 150–156. See also Kosaka's depiction of this exchange as witnessed by Mutai (in his *Shisaku to kansatsu*) in Kosaka, *Nishida Kitarō no shisō*, pp. 276–277. Mutai's discussion of their interaction shows the reciprocity and mutual influence between the two thinkers.

28. Nishida had already been making much use of the Japanese expression *soku* throughout his earlier works as a copula that joins opposites in their simultaneous mutual independence and contradiction, for example, in the self-determination of the world and the self-determination of the individual (in the 1930s), to illustrate their contradictory self-identity. On this, see Nishitani, *Nishida Kitarō*, p. 195. Thus Nishida's adoption of Suzuki's soku-hi logic at this stage meshes well with that use of the copulative *soku* in explicating contradictory self-identity.

29. Ueda Shizuteru calls this an "*Ur*-relation" (*genkankei* 原関係) in "Gyakutaiō to byōjōtei," in Ueda, *Nishida tetsugaku*, pp. 381–382.

30. The letter is addressed to Mutai Risaku and dated December 22, 1944. See Takemura, *Nishida Kitarō to Bukkyō*, p. 106.

31. Nāgārjuna, *Mūlamadhyamakakārikā*, chapter 24, verses 8–9. See Nāgārjuna, *Fundamental Wisdom of the Middle Way*, p. 68; and *Nāgārjuna, the Philosophy of the Middle Way*, pp. 330–331.

32. Nāgārjuna, *Mūlamadhyamakakārikā*, ch. 24, verse 18 in Nāgārjuna, *Fundamental Wisdom of the Middle Way*, p. 69; and *Nāgārjuna, the Philosophy of the Middle Way*, p. 339.

33. Nāgārjuna, *Mūlamadhyamakakārikā*, ch. 25, verses 19–20, in Nāgārjuna, *Fundamental Wisdom of the Middle Way*, p. 75; and *Nāgārjuna, the Philosophy of the Middle Way*, pp. 366–367.

34. See Matsumoto, "Absolute, Relatives and Nothingness," p. 77.

35. This appears at the beginning of Nāgārjuna's *Mūlamadhyamakakārikā* in the dedicatory verses. See *Nāgārjuna, the Philosophy of the Middle Way*, p. 101; and Nāgārjuna, *Fundamental Wisdom of the Middle Way*, p. 2.

36. On this, see Dilworth, "Nishida's Final Essay," pp. 360–361 and n. 17.

37. See Takemura, *Nishida Kitarō to Bukkyō*, p. 86.

38. See Krummel, "Transcendent or Immanent?"

39. I am primarily basing my interpretation on the commentaries and short translations in Chang, *Buddhist Teaching of Totality*; and Oh, "*Dharmadhātu*," with relevant passages from

the *Taishō shinshū daizōkyō*, vol. 45 (T45.652a–654a). In the following I am also relying on Cook, *Hua-yen Buddhism*.

40. This 1940 version is longer than the 1938 lecture with the same title.

41. In the *Astasāhasrikā Prajñāpāramitā sūtra*, *śūnyatā* (emptiness) is used synonymously with space. See McCagney, *Nāgārjuna and the Philosophy of Openness*, pp. xix–xxi, 25–26, 35, 58. We might also remember here that the Chinese translation of *śūnyatā* as *kong* (Jp.: *ku*) has also the connotations of "sky" and "space."

42. Suzuki, "How to Read Nishida," p. v.

43. We need to acknowledge, however, that, as Gereon Kopf remarks, Nishida interprets Huayan terminology in his own terms without providing any deep analysis of Huayan philosophy. See Kopf, "Critical Comments on Nishida's Use of Chinese Buddhism," p. 317.

44. Kosaka, *Nishida Kitarō no shisō*, pp. 371–372n203.

45. Ibid., pp. 296–297.

46. The True Pure Land sect (Jōdo Shinshū) of Buddhism was a sect founded by Shinran (1173–1262) as an offshoot from the Pure Land school (Jōdo-shū) of Hōnen (法然) (1133–1212). The original Pure Land practice was based on the recitation of a formula for venerating Amida Buddha (Buddha Amitabha) that was to lead one to rebirth in Amida's Pure Land through Amida's grace. While the Jōdo-shū regards recitation as strengthening the devotee's faith in Amida, the Shin sect sees it as an act of gratitude for Amida's exertion to save the individual, a radicalization of reliance on "other-power" (tariki). Nishida appropriates Suzuki's interpretation that the devotee's act of recitation is Amida working through the devotee, an idea that Nishida in turn compares to Christian grace in Paul, Augustine, and Luther.

47. On the controversy concerning this reading of the Bible see note 17 of chapter 7.

48. In a 1932 letter Nishida even states that "the self-awareness of nothing" has the significance of *agape*. See Takemura, *Nishida Kitarō to Bukkyō*, p. 65.

49. Pascal, *Pensées,* § 378 (§ 470), p. 110.

50. Ibid., § 418 (233), p. 121.

51. Søren Kierkegaard, "The Absolute Paradox: A Metaphysical Crotchet," in Kirkegaard, *Philosophical Fragments*, esp. p. 59.

52. In other words, the unity of humanity between Adam, the fallen sinful man, and Christ, the risen God-man (savior-saved).

53. In his critique of Hegel's dialectic, Nishida here also turns to the younger theological Hegel, who, as is noticeable in his *Theological Essays*, had experienced deep distress in regard to the issue of fate. Nishida suggests that it is this experience that Hegel later grasped systematically in terms of his logic (Z7 275). See Hegel, "Der Geist des Christentums und sein Schicksal" ("The Spirit of Christianity and its Fate") (1798–1800), in Hegel, *Werke in zwanzig Bänden*, vol. 1.

54. On this, see Kosaka, *Nishida Kitarō no shisō*, p. 285.

55. See Mutai, *Basho no ronrigaku*. In addition, Masao Abe suggests that Mutai's ideas stimulated Nishida to develop his notion of "inverse correspondence." See Abe, "'Inverse Correspondence' in the Philosophy of Nishida," p. 331.

56. See Kosaka, *Nishida Kitarō no shisō*, pp. 286–288.

57. See ibid., p. 291.

58. Takemura suggests that Kiyozawa's explication of the Buddha's other-power that grounds one's generation and extinction in the world may have provided an impetus for Nishida's concept of inverse correspondence, and he argues that inverse correspondence was a logicization of True Pure Land devotional concepts. See Takemura, *Nishida Kitarō to Bukkyō*, pp. 54, 76.

59. Cestari, "Between Emptiness and Absolute Nothingness," p. 330.

10. The Chiasma and the Chōra

1. In preparing to write this chapter, I was much inspired by the questions and suggestions I received from participants at two conferences where I presented earlier versions of it: the International Conference on Japanese Philosophy as an Academic Discipline, held at the Chinese University of Hong Kong in December 2011, and the Seventh Annual Meeting of the Comparative and Continental Philosophy Circle, held in San Diegeo, Calif., in March 2012. In particular, I would like to thank Inaga Shigemi, Kazashi Nobuo, and Bret Davis. I also would like to mention here that a modified version of this chapter is scheduled to appear as "'The Place of Nothing' in Nishida as *Chiasma* and *Chōra*" in the journal *Diaphany*. And figure 10.1 that appears in this chapter is a slightly altered version of a figure that appears in another forthcoming article of mine, "Embodied Implacement in Kūkai and Nishid" in *Philosophy East and West*.

2. See Israel, *Language of Dialectic and the Dialectics of Language*. See also G. S. Axtell's discussion of Israel's definition in "Comparative Dialectics," p. 176.

3. E.g., Heisig, *Philosophers of Nothingness*, p. 66.

4. The text in which the story appears was written during the end of the Warring States period (ca. 222 BCE) or the beginning of the Qin (Jp.: Shin) Dynasty (221–206 BCE), the first unified state of China. See Han Fei Tzu, *Complete Works*, vol. 2, p. 143.

5. We should also keep in mind here that "radical" comes from the Latin word *radix*, which refers to "the root of things."

6. This means that even the basic contradiction between life or birth and death might be viewed as a bifurcation and inseparable intertwining of bi-conditionals within a complex chiasma of multiple processes on a variety of levels (e.g., social-ethical, physical, biological, etc.). Here I do not intend to dismiss the existential significance in Nishida of one's encounter with death in its alterity and negation of the self. The plurality into which one disperses in death and out of which the unity of the self is born in itself can be viewed as the otherness of the not-self.

7. An example suggested by Andrew Feenberg in his discussion of this would be history as what is "drawn" by the subject and what "draws" the subject. See Merleau-Ponty, *Visible and the Invisible*, pp. 130–155, esp. p. 138; Arisaka and Feenberg, "Experiential Ontology," p. 202; and Feenberg, "Experience and Culture," p. 38. Some work has been done on the Merleau-Pontyan notions of *chiasm* and flesh (*la chair*) from his posthumous work *The Visible and the Invisible* and on their possible convergence with ideas found in Nishida Kitarō, as well as Mahāyāna Buddhism more broadly. For more discussions bringing them into dialogue, see the essays in Park and Kopf, *Merleau-Ponty and Buddhism*.

8. Compare this Nishidian sense of the body with Merleau-Ponty's notion of the duplicitous body as sensed object, a thing among things, on the one hand, and as sentient, the subject who senses them, on the other. But it can touch and see them only because it is tangible and visible. The lived body (*corps vécu*) is involved in reciprocity with its environment. It belongs to the world—the touching hand "takes place among the things it touches" (Mereleau-Ponty, *Visible and the Invisible*, hereafter *VI*, p. 133; see also pp. 137–138). It is involved in the "circle of the touched and the touching" (*VI* 143), "the coiling over of the visible upon the seeing body, of the tangible upon the touching body" (*VI* 146). Body and world overlap as they share the same flesh (*chair*) (*VI* 248). This exchange or reversal between perceiving body and perceived body is the Merleau-Pontyan chiasm between me and world (*VI* 215), sensing and sensed interwoven, intertwining, as one flesh. Thus the active body extends into its surroundings and at the same time is an extension of the world (*VI* 255). What unites them—body and world—is flesh, an "identity within difference" (*l'identité en différence*) (*VI* 225), "*chiasm and Ineinander*"

(*VI* 268). That unity, flesh, is an ambiguity of alternation differentiating itself into subject and object in the articulation of the visible, moving from silence to expression. These are obvious points of possible convergence with what I have been calling Nishida's chiasma, although my development of this notion of chiasma in Nishida pre-dates my discovery of Merleau-Ponty's idea of chiasm. For relevant discussions, see, for example, Kazashi, "Bodily Logos," pp. 112–113.

My reading of acting intuition as bodily chiasma also brings Nishida into proximity with Merleau-Ponty, for example, in the latter's notion of the world's flesh (la chair) in the lived body's reciprocity with the environment. For Nishida, we see things as our body acts. For Merleau-Ponty, the body sees but also moves as a thing among things within the visible world. See Merleau-Ponty, *Primacy of Perception*, pp. 162–163; and also relevant discussions in Kazashi, "Bodily Logos," pp. 113–114, 118; and Stevens, "Self in Space," pp. 133, 137–139.

9. See Pascal, *Pensées*, § 199 (§ 72), p. 60. Before Pascal this idea was expressed by Nicholas of Cusa. See Nicholas of Cusa, *De docta ignorantia* (On Learned Ignorance) in *Nicholas of Cusa: Selected Spiritual Writings*, bk. 1, ch. 21, pp. 116–120. On this see note 7 of chapter 7.

10. Pascal, *Pensées*, § 199 (§ 72), p. 61.

11. Nishida failed to make this distinction.

12. See Nakamura Yūjiō, *Nishida Kitarō*; and Nakamura Yūjirō, *Nishida Kitarō no datsukōchiku*. The former was republished as *Nishida Kitarō I*, and the latter was republished as *Nishida Kitarō II*.

13. The original reads: "Tann naru kateiteki benshōhō kara kobutsu to kobutsu to no sōgōkankei to iūmono wa kangaerarenai" (Z6 74). On the problem of David Dilworth's translation of this, see note 16 in chapter 6.

14. See Kosaka, *Nishida Kitarō o meguru tetsugakusha gunzō*, chs. 3–5; and Kopf's critique of it in "On the Brink of Postmodernity," p. 138.

15. Kosaka, *Nishida Kitarō no shisō*, pp. 301–302.

16. Ueda, "Pure Experience, Self-Awareness, Basho," p. 67.

17. Ibid.

18. Nishida here is referring to an idea found in Harrison, *Themis*, pp. 13–14.

19. I do not mean to simply deny the significance of contradiction, which is such a major theme in Nishida. Nishida was fond of speaking in terms of opposites and contradictions, even setting up questionable dichotomies such as that between the stereotypical East and West. But the complexity of reality that contradiction points to exceeds mere binarism. It is in virtue of that complexity that each term of opposition loses its self-identity that would distinguish it from its other. The more detailed or precise our attempts to determine and demarcate the boundary line between X and $\sim X$, the more incomplete our attempt to determine it becomes, and the more complex and ambiguous the matter reveals itself to be. Nothing has substance, everything is empty, and a multiplicity of factors constitute the way things are. What reality entails, and what Nishida's dialectical formulations imply, is a chiasma that ruptures dichotomies and deconstructs dialectical formulas. For example, the contradictory self-identity between the many and the one that is fundamental to Nishida's later thought, when analyzed, reveals an infinite sphere (mugenkyū 無限球) of innumerable centers, each a "one and many." Yet I do not mean to diminish the existential significance—underscored by Nishida—of one's encounter with the alterity of death that negates oneself and releases one's individuality. That opposition, however, is simultaneously vis-à-vis multiplicity. The otherness of the not-self therein is the plurality into which one disperses and out of which self-unity is constituted. The contradictory self-identity of one and many, as well as the self-other opposition, thus breaks into a multiplicity of multiplicities, multiples of multiples of multiples, without end, without ever reaching a solid one, without substance. And the field of this endless multiplicity, the situation that is of emptiness, is the place of nothing.

20. I neologize the term "an-ontology" to characterize this structure of basho as what Nishida calls absolute negation. We cannot call it "meontology" because μὴ (*mē*) is still a conditional adverb (e.g., "I think not"). I use "an-ontology," in contrast, to mean the structure encompassing both *on* and *mē on*, or being and non-being, ultimately referring to the place of absolute nothing.

21. See Sambursky, *Concept of Place in Late Neoplatonism,* pp. 36–37. More recently, American phenomenologist Edward Casey wrote in *The Fate of Place:* "Place: we are immersed in it and could not do without it. To be at all—to exist in any way—is to be somewhere, and to be somewhere is to be in some kind of place" (p. ix), and "Implacement is a sine qua non for things to be" (p. 4). One might also compare Nishida's conceptions of place in its various manifestations with Henri Lefebvre's studies of space that aim to discover the "spatial" unity between the various "fields" of the physical, the mental, and the social. See Lefebvre, *Production of Space,* p. 11.

22. Plato, *Timaeus,* in Plato, *Complete Works,* p. 1255. The translation is by Donald J. Zeyl.

23. See Takeda, "Brief Note on Nishida's Doctrine of Universals," p. 499 and n. 7.

24. On the Neo-Kantian notion of *Gebiet,* see Emil Lask, *Die Logik der Philosophie und die Kategorienlehre* (1911), in Lask, *Sämtliche Werke,* vol. 2, pp. 60–61, 82–94; and on Husserl's *Region,* see Husserl, *Ideen,* bk. 1, pt. 1, ch. 1, §§ 9–10, in Husserl, *Ideas Pertaining to a Pure Phenomenology and to a Phenomenological Philosophy, First Book,* pp. 18–23.

25. Ueda, "Pure Experience, Self-Awareness, Basho," p. 80.

26. On this and the following, see Arisaka, "System and Existence," p. 44.

27. Cf. William James's statement "A system, to be a system at all, must come as a *closed* system." William James, "The Will to Believe," in James, *Writings of William James,* p. 724.

28. Certainly in the early period of Nishida *tetsugaku,* basho or place in a certain sense is the true self found in the depths of oneself. But in the later periods that place constitutive of the self is extended in an outward direction to mean the world in the sense of milieu or ecumene. This is what I find compatible, as I will show in the following, with the original Greek sense of chōra. But the sense of basho as the existential root of one's finite self is here retained.

29. On the world's implacement in an "unrestricted openness," see Ueda, "Pure Experience, Self-Awareness, Basho," pp. 78–79.

30. Plato, *Complete Works,* p. 1251.

31. This and the following are from Plato, *Complete Works,* p. 1253. The translation here is slightly modified on the basis of Casey, "Smooth Spaces and Rough-Edged Places," p. 271; and Sallis, *Chorology,* p. 108.

32. Gadamer, *Dialogue and Dialectic,* pp. 174–175.

33. Fink, *Zur ontologischen Frühgeschichte von Raum-Zeit-Bewegung,* pp. 187–188. Here I might mention the etymological link between the Greek terms *chōra* and *chaos* (χάος). The latter derives from the verb *chainō* (χαίνω) for "open," and in Hesiod's *Theogony,* chaos still means "chasm" rather than simply "disorder." See Jammer, *Concepts of Space,* p. 9; and Cornford, *Principium Sapientiae,* p. 194 and n. 1. See also Casey, *Fate of Place,* p. 345n13.

34. See Gadamer, *Dialogue and Dialectic,* p. 174.

35. On this, see Sallis, *Chorology,* p. 118.

36. See Aristotle, *On the Soul (De anima),* 429a15, in Aristotle, *Basic Works of Aristotle,* p. 589. See also *Metaphysics* 1032a35–b1 (ibid., p. 792), where he speaks of the artist's soul as wherein the form of artificial products (the essence of each thing) lies; and *De anima* 406a16–20 (ibid., p. 543), where he speaks of the soul as itself having a place (topos).

37. I am not advocating here, however, the translation of *basho* as *chōra* as opposed to *topos.* On the question of translation, I am in favor of rendering *basho,* which is used in ordinary Japanese, with the ordinary English word "place." My point in this chapter, however, is that

the ultimate place in Nishida, what he calls *zettai mu no basho* (the place of absolute nothing), can be characterized as chōratic.

38. To be more precise: through chōra's violent thrashing motion, bodies (*sōmata*) are separated out, the dense and heavy sinking down and the light and rare floating upward, each to its own place (topos) to settle (52e–53a). Nor should Plato's chōra be conflated with Aristotle's topos from the *Physics*, as Sallis (*Chorology*, p. 115) warns. There have been numerous studies on this chōra-topos distinction that Nishida scholars who wish to translate *basho* as *topos* ought to be aware of: Casey, *Fate of Place* and "Smooth Spaces and Rough-Edged Places"; Sallis, *Chorology*; and, most notably, Berque, "Overcoming Modernity, Yesterday and Today"; Berque, "Offspring of Watsuji's Theory of Milieu (*Fūdo*)"; Berque, "Ontological Structure of Mediance"; and Berque, *Écoumène*. To make his case, Berque in turn refers to various experts in the field: Pradeau, "Être quelque part, occuper une place"; Brisson, *Le même el l'autre dans la structure ontologique du "Timée"*; and Boutot, *Heidegger et Platon*. At the same time, however, Berque faults Plato's idealism for making chōra into an amorphous receptacle of forms to conceal its originary dimension of spatiality that harbored the sense of "region" (*Gegend*) and that can be found in the pre-Socratic philosophers, as well as in the later Heidegger. See Berque, *Fūdogaku josetsu*, p. 43n24; and Berque, "Overcoming Modernity, Yesterday and Today," pp. 94–95.

39. I take this position in spite of Berque's critique of Nishida. Berque ignores the complex world-dialectic in Nishida, as well as Nishida's discussions of our concrete interactivity with the environment.

40. This also relates to their different ways of conceiving being in relation to place. For Plato, what requires place is not being per se but rather "becoming" (genesis), which is only relatively being. The *Timaeus* establishes the radical distinction of true (or absolute) being (ontōs on) from becoming. While that which becomes and perishes needs chōra as its place, true being—the ideas—transcends this condition. For Nishida, in contrast, being (yū) is always relative, and what is absolute is the nothing that envelops and unfolds beings. This leads us to the question of the absolute (zettai 絶対) in Nishida. As Berque shows, chōra for the ancient Greeks before Plato was concrete. Hence Berque criticizes Nishida for absolutizing chōra and making it abstract in the concept of basho or mu. See Berque, "Overcoming Modernity, Yesterday and Today," p. 92. In fact, when Berque translates Nishida's *mu* as "non-being-thereness" or as "absence," he misses what is essential for Nishida in the concept of mu: its double or self-negation. Throughout his critique of Nishida, Berque ignores the complex dialectic that plays out in Nishida's later works. Nishida appears to have inherited the terminology of the absolute (zettai) and the relative (sōtai), with its metaphysical connotations that we can trace to Western philosophy, from Inoue Enryō (井上円了). Inoue was making use of Western concepts in his attempt to translate Buddhist concepts into philosophical terms. But we need to keep in mind here the literal meaning of the two sinographs, *zetsu* (絶) and *tai* (対), combined as *zettai* (絶対): "cutting off opposition." "Absolute" understood in this sense would not be separate, or abstracted, from the relative but rather in its midst. It is in the midst of beings emerging in its space of self-negation. It is the concrete space of the world. Opposition occurs within it. It permits opposition. Hence it is not absolute in the way ontōs on is absolute for Plato.

41. See Aristotle, *Physics* 4.2.209b11–17, in Aristotle, *Basic Works of Aristotle*, p. 272.

42. John Sallis (*Chorology*, p. 151) explains that after Aristotle this conflation between matter (hylē) and chōra was furthered when Plutarch in *On the Generation of the Soul in the Timaeus* claimed that it is "corporeal being" (sōmatos ousia) that Plato called the chōra and hedra (abode) of all generated things (5.1014c–d), to link the material (hylikon) to chōra (6.1014e). See Plutarch, *Plutarch über die Seelenschöpfung im Timaeus*, pp. 28–29. Much later, Plotinus comes to take this identification for granted. See Plotinus, *Enneads*, 2.4.1, p. 92.

43. That is how Jacques Derrida characterizes *chōra*. See Derrida, "*Khōra*," p. 90.

44. Ibid., p. 89. It has been suggested that Derrida may have been influenced by another Japanese thinker in his reading of Plato's chōra, the architect and theorist Isozaki Arata (磯崎 新), who has been relating chōra to Nishidian concepts for several decades now. The main theme of his theoretical work is the pre-modern Japanese concept of *ma* (間), which he relates to Plato's chōra while also making references to Nishida's basho and contradictory identity. See, for example, the 16mm film *Ma: Space-Time in the Garden of Ryoan-ji,* directed by Iimura Takahiko, for which Isozaki wrote the text narrative. See also Isozaki, "Ma: Japanese Time-Space." Isozaki engaged in dialogue with Derrida at several conferences. In 1992 both attended the "Anywhere" conference in Yufuin, Japan, where Arata spoke on chōra in relation to ma, making use of the Nishidian motif of contradictory identity. See Isozaki, "Demiourgos in Anywhere"; and also Derrida's piece from that same conference, "Faxitexture." In the following year, 1993, Derrida published *Khora,* wherein he makes use of Nishidian-sounding motifs, e.g., the unity of opposites.

45. The expression *epekeina tēs ousias* (επέκεινα της ουσίας, "beyond being") was used by Socrates in the *Republic* to refer to *to agathon* (τὸ ἀγαθὸν, "the good"). Derrida, however, points out the possibility of extending the expression to chōra. He bases this on a passage where Socrates speaks of how the liberated prisoner, having exited the cave, could turn his gaze upward and "be able to look upon the sun—not in its appearances . . . or in some other base [hedra], but the sun itself by itself in its own chōra . . . and behold how it is" (*Republic* 516b). On this, see Sallis, *Chorology,* pp. 113–114n23; and Derrida, "Tense," pp. 73–74.

46. Derrida, "*Khōra*," p. 103; see also pp. 92–93.

47. Derrida speaks of *chōra* as an "irreplaceable and unplaceable place." See ibid., p. 111.

48. In fact, this may explain the later conflation of *chōra* with materiality or corporeality.

49. I am borrowing this term from John Sallis's discussion of the *chōra* in *Chorology.*

50. See ibid., p. 123.

51. I also want to mention here John Maraldo's use of the terminological pairing "chiasm" and "chasm," similar and perhaps comparable in some ways to my pairing here of "chiasma" and "chōra," which I came across after having developed my idea independently of his. His pairing comes up in the context of a discussion of Nishida's theory of time and in particular the concept of the absolute present in Maraldo, "Absolute Present," pp. 1–17 (from the back flap). He brings up the possibility of characterizing the absolute present (zettai genzai 絶対現在), on the one hand, as a chiasm that allows the multiple dimensions of time and history to emerge; and, on the other, characterizing it as a chasm that engulfs historical time and submerges its significance (p. 2). The chasm beneath history permits the present to contain infinite time and to negate it (p. 4). Yet the "Now is the crossover, the chiasm, of an irrevocable past that defines the present, and a future ever different from it that renders it un-definitive. This Now is the Absolute Present. . . . It determines itself as historical reality. . . . This Now opens a chasm beneath history" (p. 9). We might re-state this in our terms: the chiasma both unfolds from the present moment and over-determines it. But it is the chōra, in its abyssal indeterminacy, wherein the chiasma occurs that allows for the unpredictability of time and history and for novelty to arise.

11. Concluding Thoughts, Criticism, and Evaluation

1. See Lotze, "Philosophy in the Last Forty Years" (1880), p. 467.

2. On this, see Ōmine, "Gyakutaiō to myōgō," p. 425. Ōmine here states that this was the stance behind what Nishida called his "dialectical logic" (*benshōhōteki ronri* 弁証法的論理) or "logic of place" (bashoteki ronri 場所的論理).

3. See ibid., pp. 425–427.

4. See Dilworth, "Introduction," p. 28. Nevertheless, some scholars have expended much effort in trying to assimilate Buddhist non-dualist thought to Hegelian sublational thought. Alfonso Verdú's works exemplify such attempts. See Verdú, *Dialectical Aspects in Buddhist Thought;* and Verdú, *Philosophy of Buddhism.*

5. See Putney, "Identity and the Unity of Experience," p. 149.

6. On this, see also points made by Nitta, "Nishida tetsugaku ni okeru 'tetsugaku no ronri,'" pp. 37 and 49n2.

7. Han Fei Tzu, *Complete Works,* vol. 2, p. 143.

8. To understand it merely as "contrary" would not do it justice.

9. On this, see Putney, "Identity and the Unity of Experience," p. 150.

10. Ibid., p. 154.

11. "Everywhere, couples and polarities presuppose bundles and networks, organized oppositions presuppose radiations in all directions. . . . Everywhere the depth of difference is primary. . . . Space and time display oppositions (and limitations) only on the surface, but they presuppose in their real depth far more voluminous, affirmed and distributed differences which cannot be reduced to the banality of the negative. . . . Underneath conflict, the space of the play of differences." Deleuze, *Difference and Repetition,* p. 51. See also Leonard Lawlor's preface to Hyppolite, *Logic and Existence,* pp. xi–xii.

12. "Alle Dialektik in der Philosophie . . . ist der Ausdruck einer Verlegenheit." Heidegger, *Grundbegriffe der Metaphysik,* p. 276; *Fundamental Concepts of Metaphysics,* p. 187. In the sentence immediately prior, Heidegger states: "It is characteristic that we repeatedly find in the history of philosophy such attempts to level off . . . [the] circularity and ambiguity of philosophical thinking through the use of dialectic, and most recently in a grand and impressive form." Heidegger in disparaging dialectics most certainly has Hegel's system in mind. However, while disclaiming any affinity to such a "dialectic," Heidegger in the mid- to late 1930s (e.g., in his *Beiträge*) does speak of the reciprocity or interplay in "the event of en-owning" (*Er-eignis*) that opens up a new epoch. He calls this the "turning" (*Kehre*) of being, whereby in his projection (*Entwurf*) that opens up a world, man is "thrown" into that world, i.e., the thrower is thrown (*werfen*). Such reciprocity that underscores the finitude of man in Heidegger may perhaps be comparable to Nishida's notion of inverse correspondence.

13. Merleau-Ponty, *Visible and the Invisible,* pp. 94–95.

14. "Tautology is the only possibility for thinking what dialectic can only veil." See Martin Heidegger, "Seminar in Zähringen, 1973," in *Vier Seminare,* p. 400; and in *Four Seminars,* p. 81. This statement comes much later (1973) than the quotation in note 12 (1929/1930).

15. The dialectic in Nishida's case is an expression of the self-forming formlessness, the abyssal nothing, that envelops and allows for the irreducible complexity of its chiasma, in excess of mere triadic or bi-nomial formulas and structures.

16. For example, see J. S. O'Leary's chastisement of Nishida in his later works for obscuring his themes in "complex dialectical language" in his foreword to Nishida, *Intuition and Reflection in Self-Consciousness,* p. ix. Here I sympathize with O'Leary, although my point is that the matter underlying Nishida's dialectical formulations in fact far exceeds those formulations in complexity. O'Leary suggests that a more strictly phenomenological approach might have served his purpose well instead. I would add that a phenomenological approach that does justice to the matter must acknowledge that excess.

17. For example, I have in mind the language of someone like Nishida's student Nishitani Keiji, or, in turn, Nishitani's student Ueda Shizuteru. These thinkers, taking off from Nishida's work, appear to provide, or at least move toward, alternative modes of conceiving, articulat-

ing, and discussing the matter of the concrete that traditional metaphysics fails to convey and of responding to the traditional metaphysical issues of the one and the many and of dualism that Nishida was struggling with. To delve into this now, however, would take me beyond the immediate concerns of this work.

18. "Emptiness" here should be taken in its Buddhist sense of being empty of "own-being" (svabhāva). What I mean is that these horizons, whether religious or cultural or ideological, brought into the midst of one another, are shown to be contingent and conditioned both historically and environmentally; i.e., they can no longer be taken to be absolute.

19. Vattimo, *End of Modernity*, p. 152.

20. Vahabzadeh, "Of Hegemonies Yet to Be Broken," p. 376.

21. On this issue of homogenization in modernity, see Taylor, *Hegel*, pp. 412–414.

22. Casey, *Getting Back into Place*, p. xv; see also pp. xii and xiv.

23. Bret Davis poignantly descries this duplicity as both "enabling and undermining cross-cultural encounter." While providing "ease of communication, it also tends to homogenize the voices that speak to one another." Hence "as we fly around the world to look-alike cities and log in to cyberspace to create virtual realities, we are uprooted and displaced in the process." See Davis, "Toward a World of Worlds," p. 206.

24. The situation is even more complicated, however, because that "pronouncement of difference" is often mediated and thus muted by the global media serving consumerist tendencies.

25. On this and the following, see Ueda, "Nishida, Nationalism, and the War in Question," pp. 102–103.

26. Ibid., p. 103.

27. In regard to the controversy concerning Nishida's supposed complicity with the militarists, I am not sure to what extent—on the basis of his writings, letters, and his biography— we can speak of his "guilt." He certainly was not a zealous supporter of expansionist imperialist policies. Here, rather than pointing an accusatory finger at him for not being more publicly defiant, I am interested in examining his ideas and looking for ingredients that we may be able to appropriate in ways viable for us today. However, I cannot simply pass over this controversy, and in much of what follows I will address the issue with references to previous studies by Ueda Shizuteru, John Maraldo, Bret Davis, Gereon Kopf, and Christopher Goto-Jones that have dealt with the subject.

28. See Goto-Jones, *Political Philosophy in Japan*, pp. 71–72.

29. This text of "Sekai no shinchitsujo no genri" ("The Fundamental Principles of a New World Order"), however, was distorted and simplified under government hands. Nishida complains about Prime Minister Tōjō Hideki's speech for failing to convey his ideas in a letter to Watsuji Tetsurō. (This was Nishida's claim in a 1943 letter in *Z*23 110, no. 3821; on the following, see also the editor's postscript to *Z*11 560–561). Nishida was invited by the Research Center on National Policy/Strategy (Kokusaku kenkyūkai 国策研究会), which had close ties to the army, to participate in discussions about the situation in East Asia. He was requested to put his talk into writing and did so after being persuaded that this could give him the opportunity to influence the content of a speech Tōjō was preparing. According to Tanabe Juri, the army officials found Nishida's draft incomprehensible and wanted it simplified. When Nishida did not respond to this request, Tanabe (together with Kanai Shōji) out of necessity rewrote the manuscript, evidently altering its tone, and distributed copies to the officials, as well as to Nishida. In Goto-Jones's reading, the newer tone resonates much more closely with the orthodoxy of the time, making it confrontational and conducive to Japanese enforcement of the "co-prosperity sphere" on other nations, in contrast to the more inclusivist and non-confrontational nature of Nishida's version (see Goto-Jones, *Political Philosophy in Japan*, pp. 22, 76, 79). This was the version Nishida

complained about as a distortion of his original work. He warns in one letter to Watsuji that the newer version could be the seed of future attacks on him and adds that he wanted instead to emphasize the global aspect of the Japanese spirit in contrast to the narrow vision of the militant nationalists. It appears that Tōjō had read Nishida's edited version "in the context of the orthodox conventions of the dominant social discourse" (see Goto-Jones, *Political Philosophy in Japan*, p. 76). In another letter (Z23 110) a few days later Nishida thus expresses his disappointment after reading about Tōjō's speech in the newspaper. He writes that not an ounce of his original idea was comprehended or included in the speech (editor's postscript in Z11 560–561). Moreover, according to Goto-Jones (pp. 108–109), even Nishida's original version (before its distortion) was written in response to the politicization of his philosophy (from his 1937 *Rekishiteki Shintai*「歴史的身体」; *The Historical Body*) by his students Nishitani Keiji and Miki Kiyoshi and his colleague Tanabe Haijme in their respective responses published throughout the late 1930s to early 1940s and in the symposium "Sekaishiteki tachiba no nihon" (「世界史的立場の日本」; "Japan from the Standpoint of World History)" that they jointly held. Nishida was thus forced to take up their politicized language. The suggestion is that this politicized language made its subsequent distortion easier. In any case, after Tōjō's speech, Nishida revised that draft in 1944, presumably to bring it more in line with the original, and this is what we have in his *Zenshū* (*Collected Works*) (Goto-Jones, *Political Philosophy in Japan*, p. 77).

30. In other words, Nishida means by "co-prosperity sphere" something quite distinct from what the Japanese army leaders had in mind when they were promoting their idea of a "Greater East Asia Co-Prosperity Sphere."

31. Ueda, "Nishida, Nationalism, and the War in Question," p. 89.

32. The term is inspired by Goethe's "primal image" (*Urbildliche*) and "primal plant" (*Urpflanze*), which does not really exist but serves as a regulative ideal, "plantness," that is empirically valid. See Goethe, *Sämtliche Werke nach Epochen seines Schaffens Bd. 12: Zur Naturwissenschaft*, pp. 98–99; and *Italian Journey*, pp. 310–311. For a discussion of Goethe's concept of the "primal plant," see Gábor, "Form as Movement in Goethe's 'The Metamorphosis of Plants.'"

33. See Goto-Jones, *Political Philosophy in Japan*, p. 73. Goto-Jones views this as another example of how Nishida was forced to use the language required by the circumstances of the day because of the activities of the Thought Police.

34. See ibid., pp. 87–88.

35. Editor's afterword to the 1966 edition of *Nishida Kitarō zenshū*, vol. 12, p. 471.

36. See Ueda, "Nishida, Nationalism, and the War in Question," pp. 90–95.

37. Bret Davis develops this in terms of cross-cultural dialogue that would bring various cultural worlds into communication with one another—a "multi-cultural conversation"—without canceling their specific perspectival differences. See Davis, "Toward a World of Worlds," pp. 216–219.

38. On this, see also, for example, ibid., pp. 220–222.

39. I agree here with Bret Davis's reading that the world-of-worlds qua place of nothing means "ethical respect for the alterity and autonomy of other cultures which should never be imperialistically reduced to the form of one's own" (ibid., p. 225).

40. The phrase *hakkō iu* (八紘為宇) originally appeared in the ancient chronicle *Nihon shoki* (『日本書紀』; *Chronicles of Japan*). From this phrase another phrase, *hakkō ichiu* (八紘一宇), was coined and was also being used by militarists, Japanists, and the radical right with similar meanings.

41. See also Davis, "Toward a World of Worlds," p. 238.

42. On this, see Kopf, "Between the Global and the Local," p. 77; and Goto-Jones, *Political Philosophy in Japan*, p. 89. On the following, see also Davis, "Toward a World of Worlds," pp. 231–232, 234, 236–237.

43. Davis," Toward a World of Worlds," p. 230; see also pp. 235, 239–240.

44. On this, and on the following as well, see Kopf, "Between the Global and the Local," p. 79.

45. John Maraldo writes that they sound like caricatures, and I agree. See Maraldo, "Problem of World Culture," pp. 192–193.

46. See Kopf, "Between the Global and the Local," p. 79.

47. See ibid., p. 82.

48. See Maraldo, "Problem of World Culture," p. 194; and Davis, "Toward a World of Worlds," p. 225.

49. See Appiah, *Cosmopolitanism*.

50. Heidegger, *Question Concerning Technology*, p. 27; see also p. 19.

51. The ecological usefulness of Nishida's philosophy has been suggested by Kosaka in *Nishida tetsugaku to gendai*, chapters 6 and 7.

52. In general, I agree with Bret Davis's conclusion on this issue of Nishida's world-of-worlds that the core enigma of how to conceive a world-of-worlds as a place of genuine dialogue is one that "we must pass through, again and again, rather than avoid," and that "the place for dialogue can itself only, and ever again, be opened up dialogically" (Davis, "Toward a World of Worlds," p. 245). Here I am extending that dialogue or multilogue to our surrounding nature.

53. By "synthesis" here I do not mean that Nishida has constructed a synthesizing theory that claims to speak for, or encompass with some universal essence, the various modes of thinking from the disparate traditions of East and West. It is not a universal theory that would resolve distinctions. And this, of course, has to do with how he understands the place of absolute nothing and its distinction from Hegel's absolute concept. At least, the eclectic nature of his thinking is undeniable in that it brings together elements drawn from a variety of sources. In responding to issues he finds in Western philosophy—e.g., dualism—he brings insights that he identifies as "Eastern" (e.g., "the form of the formless") or finds commensurate with Mahāyāna Buddhism together with the method of Western philosophy and more specifically its various terminologies and conceptual formulations, especially that of Hegelian dialectics. Yet to classify his thought as a mere synthesis of those two elements—Buddhism and Hegel would be to ignore his unique contributions that extend beyond either.

Bibliography

Works by Nishida Kitarō

Japanese Language

Nishida Kitarō tetsugaku ronshū [*Philosophical Essays*]. Vols. 1–3. Edited by Ueda Shizuteru. Tokyo: Iwanami shoten, 2000, 1989.

Nishida Kitarō zenshū [*Collected Works*]. Multiple volumes. Tokyo: Iwanami shoten, 2002– , 1978–1980, 1965–1966, 1947–1953. Pagination in this work refers to the newest edition unless otherwise noted.

English Translations

Art and Morality. Translated by David Dilworth and Valdo H. Viglielmo. Honolulu: University Press of Hawai'i, 1973.

Fundamental Problems of Philosophy: The World of Action and the Dialectical World. Translated by David Dilworth. Tokyo: Sophia University, 1970.

"Historical Body." In *Sourcebook for Modern Japanese Philosophy*, edited by David Dilworth, Valdo H. Viglielmo, and Jacinto Zavala. Westport, CT: Greenwood Press, 1998, pp. 37–53.

An Inquiry into the Good. Translated by Masao Abe and Christopher Ives. New Haven, CT: Yale University Press, 1990.

Intelligibility and the Philosophy of Nothingness: Three Philosophical Essays. Translated by Robert Schinzinger. Tokyo: Maruzen, 1958.

Intuition and Reflection in Self-Consciousness. Translated by Valdo H. Viglielmo, Takeuchi Yoshinori, and Joseph S. O'Leary. Albany: SUNY Press, 1987.

Last Writings: Nothingness and the Religious Worldview. Translated by David Dilworth. Honolulu: University of Hawai'i Press, 1987.

"The Logic of *Topos* and the Religious Worldview, Part I." Translated by Michiko Yusa. *Eastern Buddhist*, vol. 19, no. 2, Autumn 1986, pp. 1–29.

"The Logic of *Topos* and the Religious Worldview, Part II." Translated by Michiko Yusa. *Eastern Buddhist*, vol. 20, no. 1, Spring 1987, pp. 81–119.

"My Philosophical Path." Translated by Michiko Yusa. In Michiko Yusa, *Zen and Philosophy: An Intellectual Biography of Nishida Kitarō*. Honolulu: University of Hawai'i Press, 2002, pp. 301–304.

"On the National Polity." In *Sourcebook for Modern Japanese Philosophy*, edited by David Dilworth, Valdo H. Viglielmo, and Jacinto Zavala. Westport, CT: Greenwood Press, 1998, pp. 78–95.

Place and Dialectic: Two Essays by Nishida Kitarō. Translated by John W. M. Krummel and Shigenori Nagatomo. New York: Oxford University Press, 2012.

"Problems of Japanese Culture." Translated by Masao Abe. In *Sources of Japanese Tradition*, edited by Ryusaku Tsunoda, Wm. Theodore de Bary, and Donald Keene. New York: Columbia University Press, 1958, pp. 851–872.

A Study of Good. Translated by V. H. Viglielmo. Tokyo: Japanese Government, 1960.

"Towards a Philosophy of Religion with the Concept of Pre-established Harmony as Guide." Translated by David Dilworth. *Eastern Buddhist,* vol. 3, no. 1, June 1970, pp. 19–46.

"The Unsolved Issue of Consciousness." Translated (and introduction) by John Krummel. *Philosophy East and West,* vol. 62, no. 1, January 2012, pp. 44–59.

Works by Other Authors

Abe, Masao. "'Inverse Correspondence' in the Philosophy of Nishida: The Emergence of a Notion." *International Philosophical Quarterly,* vol. 32, no. 3, September 1992, pp. 325–344.

———. "The Logic of Absolute Nothingness as Expounded by Nishida Kitarō." *Eastern Buddhist,* vol. 28, no. 2, Autumn 1995, pp. 167–174.

———. "Nishida's Philosophy of 'Place.'" *International Philosophical Quarterly,* vol. 28, no. 4, December 1988, pp. 355–371.

———. *Zen and Comparative Studies.* Edited by Steven Heine. Honolulu: University of Hawai'i Press, 1997.

———. *Zen and Western Thought.* Edited by William R. LaFleur. Honolulu: University of Hawai'i Press, 1985.

Abe Shinobe. "Modern Sports and the Eastern Tradition of Physical Culture: Emphasizing Nishida's Theory of the Body." *Journal of the Philosophy of Sport,* vol. 14, 1987, pp. 44–47.

Anton, John Peter. *Aristotle's Theory of Contrariety.* London: Routledge, 1957.

Appiah, Kwame Anthony. *Cosmopolitanism.* New York: Norton, 2007.

Arisaka, Yoko. "Beyond 'East and West': Nishida's Universalism and Postcolonial Critique." In *Border Crossings: Toward a Comparative Political Theory,* edited by Fred Dallmayr. Lanham, MD: Lexington Books, 1999, pp. 236–252; and *Review of Politics,* vol. 59, no. 3, Summer 1997, pp. 541–560. Citations in the notes refer to the 1999 publication.

———. "The Nishida Enigma: 'The Principle of the New World Order' (1943)." *Monumenta Nipponica,* vol. 51, no. 1, Spring 1996, pp. 100–105.

———. "System and Existence: Nishida's Logic of Place." In *Logique du lieu et dépassement de la modernité,* edited by Augustin Berque. Brussels: Ousia, 1999, pp. 41–65.

Arisaka, Yoko, and Andrew Feenberg. "Experiential Ontology: The Origins of the Nishida Philosophy in the Doctrine of Pure Experience." *International Philosophical Quarterly,* vol. 30, no. 2, issue no. 118, June 1990, pp. 173–205.

Aristotle. *The Basic Works of Aristotle.* Edited by Richard McKeon. New York: Random House, 1941.

———. *The Philosophy of Aristotle.* Translated by J. L. Creed and A. E. Wardman. New York: Penguin Books, Mentor, n.d.

Asami Hiroshi and Sakurai Kan. *Nishida Kitarō: Sunshin no Shisō* [*Nishida Kitarō: The Thought of Sunshin*]. Kanazawa: Kanazawashi Kokusai Bunkaka, 2005.

Asanga. *The Summary of the Great Vehicle by Bodhisattva Asanga.* Translated by John P. Keenan. Berkeley, CA: Numata Center for Buddhist Translation and Research, 1992.

Aśvaghosha. *The Awakening of Faith Attributed to Aśvaghosha.* Translated by Yoshito S. Hakeda. New York: Columbia University Press, 1967.

Augustine. *Confessions.* Translated by Henry Chadwick. Oxford: Oxford University Press, 1991.

Axtell, G. S. "Comparative Dialectics: Nishida Kitarō's Logic of Place and Western Dialectical Thought." *Philosophy East and West,* vol. 41, no. 2, April 1991, pp. 163–184.

Barth, Karl. *From Rousseau to Ritschl.* London: SCM Press, 1959.

Bergson, Henri. *Creative Evolution.* Translated by Pete A. Y. Gunter. New York: Barnes and Noble, 2005.

———. *Matter and Memory.* Translated by Nancy Margaret Paul and W. Scott Palmert. Mineola, NY: Dover, 2004.

———. *Time and Free Will: An Essay on the Immediate Data of Consciousness.* New York: Harper and Row, 1960; London: George Allen and Unwin, 1910.

Berque, Augustin. "The Choretic Work of History." *Semiotica, Journal of the International Association for Semiotic Studies,* vol. 2009, Issue 175, 2009, pp. 163–176.

———. *Écoumène: Introduction à l'étude des milieux humains.* Paris: Éditions Belin, 2000.

———. *Fūdogaku josetsu—Bunka o futatabi shizen ni, shizen o futatabi bunka ni* [*Introduction to the Study of Milieu: From Culture to Nature and from Nature to Culture*]. Translated by Nakayama Gen. Tokyo: Chikuma shobō, 2002.

———. "Indigenous beyond Exoticism." *Diogenes,* vol. 50, no. 4, 2003, pp. 39–48.

———. "Landscape and Immanence." *Thesis Eleven,* no. 54, August 1998, pp. 106–116.

———. "Offspring of Watsuji's Theory of Milieu (*Fūdo*)." *GeoJournal,* vol. 60, no. 4, 2004, pp. 389–396.

———. "The Ontological Structure of Mediance as a Ground of Meaning in Architecture." In *Structure and Meaning in Human Settlements,* edited by Tony Atkin and Joseph Rykwert. Philadelphia: University of Pennsylvania Museum of Archaeology and Anthropology, 2005, pp. 97–105.

———. "Overcoming Modernity, Yesterday and Today." *Journal of East Asian Studies,* vol. 1, no. 1, 2002, pp. 89–102.

Blocker, H. Gene, and Christopher L. Starling. *Japanese Philosophy.* Albany: SUNY Press, 2001.

Botz-Bornstein, Thorsten. "*Khōra* or Idyll? The Space of the Dream." *Philosophical Forum,* vol. 33, no. 2, Summer 2002, pp. 173–194.

Boutot, Alain. *Heidegger et Platon: Le problème du nihilisme.* Paris: Presses Universitaires de France, 1987.

Brisson, Luc. *Le même el l'autre dans la structure ontologique du "Timée": Un commentaire systématique du "Timée" de Platon.* Sankt Augustin: Akademia Verlag, 1994.

Carter, Robert E. *The Nothingness beyond God: An Introduction to the Philosophy of Nishida Kitarō.* St. Paul, MN: Paragon House, 1997.

Casey, Edward S. *The Fate of Place: A Philosophical History.* Berkeley: University of California Press, 1997.

———. *Getting Back into Place: Toward a Renewed Understanding of the Place-World.* Bloomington: Indiana University Press, 1993.

———. "Smooth Spaces and Rough-Edged Places: The Hidden History of Place." *Review of Metaphysics,* vol. 51, December 1997, pp. 267–296.

Cestari, Matteo. "Between Emptiness and Absolute Nothingness: Reflections on Negation in Nishida and Buddhism." In *Frontiers of Japanese Philosophy,* vol. 7, *Classical Japanese Philosophy,* edited by James Heisig and Rein Raud. Nagoya: Nanzan Institute for Religion and Culture, 2010, pp. 320–346.

———. "The Knowing Body: Nishida's Philosophy of Active Intuition." *Eastern Buddhist,* vol. 31 no. 2, 1998, pp. 179–208.

Chan, Wing-tsit. *A Source Book in Chinese Philosophy.* Princeton, NJ: Princeton University Press, 1963.

Chang, Garma Cheng Chi (Zhenji Zhang). *The Buddhist Teaching of Totality: The Philosophy of Hwa Yen Buddhism.* University Park: Pennsylvania State University Press, 1971.

Cleary, Thomas. *Entry into the Inconceivable.* Honolulu: University of Hawai'i Press, 1983.

Cobb, John B., Jr., and Christopher Ives, eds. *The Emptying God: A Buddhist-Jewish-Christian Conversation.* Maryknoll, NY: Orbis Books, 1990.

Conze, Edward. *Buddhist Thought in India: Three Phases of Buddhist Philosophy.* Ann Arbor: University of Michigan Press, 1967, 1962.

Cook, Francis H. *Hua-yen Buddhism: The Jewel Net of Indra.* University Park: Pennsylvania State University Press, 1977.

Cornford, F. M. *Principium Sapientiae.* New York: Harper and Row, 1965.

Cresswell, M. J. "Non-contradiction and Substantial Predication." *Theoria,* vol. 69, 2003, pt. 3, pp. 166–183.

Crowell, Steven G. "Transcendental Logic and Minimal Empiricism: Lask and McDowell on the Unboundedness of the Conceptual." In *Neo-Kantianism in Contemporary Philosophy,* edited by Rudolf A. Makkreel and Sebastian Luft. Bloomington: Indiana University Press, 2010, pp. 150–174.

Davidson, Cynthia C., ed. *Anywhere.* New York: Anyone Corp., 1992.

Davis, Bret W. "Toward a World of Worlds: Nishida, the Kyoto School, and the Place of Cross Cultural Dialogue." In *Frontiers of Japanese Philosophy,* vol. 1, edited by James W. Heisig. Nagoya: Nanzan Institute for Religion and Culture, 2006, pp. 205–245.

Davis, Bret W., Brian Schroeder, and Jason M. Wirth, eds. *Japanese and Continental Philosophy: Conversations with the Kyoto School.* Bloomington: Indiana University Press, 2011.

De Bary, William Theodore. *The Buddhist Tradition in India, China and Japan.* New York: Vintage Books, Random House, 1972, 1969.

Deleuze, Gilles. *Difference and Repetition.* Translated by Paul Patton. New York: Columbia University Press, 1994.

Derrida, Jacques. "Faxitexture." In *Anywhere,* ed. Cynthia C. Davidson. New York: Anyone Corp., 1992, pp. 18–33.

———. "Khōra." In *On the Name.* Stanford, CA: Stanford University Press, 1995.

———. "Tense." In *The Path of Archaic Thinking: Unfolding the Work of John Sallis,* edited by Kenneth Maly. Albany: SUNY Press, 1995, pp. 49–74.

Descartes, René. *The Philosophical Works of Descartes.* Vol. 1. Translated by Elizabeth S. Haldane and G. R. T. Ross. Cambridge: Cambridge University Press, 1911.

Dillon, M. C. "Merleau-Ponty and the Reversibility Thesis." *Man and World,* vol. 16, no. 4, 1983, pp. 365–388.

Dilworth, David A. "The Concrete World of Action in Nishida's Later Thought." In *Japanese Phenomenology: Phenomenology as the Trans-cultural Philosophical Approach,* edited by Yoshihiro Nitta and Hirotaka Tatematsu. Dordrecht: D. Reidel, 1979, pp. 249–270.

———. "Introduction: Nishida's Critique of the Religious Consciousness." In *Last Writings: Nothingness and the Religious Worldview,* by Nishida Kitarō. Honolulu: University of Hawai'i Press, 1987, pp. 1–45.

———. "Nishida Kitarō: Nothingness as the Negative Space of Experiential Immediacy." *International Philosophical Quarterly,* vol. 13, no. 4, December 1973, pp. 463–483.

———. "Nishida's Final Essay: The Logic of Place and a Religious World-View." *Philosophy East and West,* vol. 20, no. 4, October 1970, pp. 355–367.

Dilworth, David A., Valdo H. Viglielmo, and Agustin Jacinto Zavala, eds. *Sourcebook for Modern Japanese Philosophy: Selected Documents.* Westport, CT: Greenwood Press, 1998.

Dobbins, James C. *Jōdo Shinshū: Shin Buddhism in Medieval Japan.* Bloomington: Indiana University Press, 1989.

Dōgen. *The Heart of Dōgen's "Shōbōgenzō."* Translated by Masao Abe and Norman Waddell. Albany: SUNY Press, 2002.

———. *Shōbōgenzō.* Annotated by Mizuno Yaoko. Tokyo: Iwanami, 2000, 1990.

———. *Shōbōgenzō: Zen Essays by Dōgen.* Translated by Thomas Cleary. Honolulu: University of Hawai'i Press, 1986.

———. "Shōbōgenzō Genjōkōan." Translated by Masao Abe and Norman Waddell. *Eastern Buddhist,* vol. 5, no. 2, October 1972, pp. 129–140.

Elwood, Brian D. "The Problem of the Self in the Later Nishida and in Sartre." *Philosophy East and West,* vol. 44, no. 2, April 1994, pp. 303–316.

Feenberg, Andrew. "Experience and Culture: Nishida's Path 'To the Things Themselves.'" *Philosophy East and West,* vol. 49, no. 1, 1999, pp. 28–44.

———. "The Problem of Modernity in the Philosophy of Nishida." In *Rude Awakenings: Zen, the Kyoto School, and the Question of Nationalism,* edited by James W. Heisig and John C. Maraldo. Honolulu: University of Hawai'i Press, 1994, pp. 151–173.

Fichte, Johann Gottlieb. *Fichtes Werke.* Vol. 1, *Zur theoretischen Philosophie I.* Edited by Immanuel Hermann Fichte. Berlin: Walter de Gruyter, 1971.

———. *Science of Knowledge.* Edited and translated by Peter Heath and John Lachs. Cambridge: Cambridge University Press, 1982, 1970.

Fink, Eugene. *Zur ontologischen Frühgeschichte von Raum-Zeit-Bewegung.* The Hague: Martinus Nijhoff, 1957.

Frank, Frederick, ed. *The Buddha Eye: An Anthology of the Kyoto School.* New York: Crossroad, 1991, 1982.

Fujimoto Kiyohiko. "A Study of Honen's Doctrine of Evil Persons as the Object of Salvation." http://www.jsri.jp/English/Jodoshu/conferences/AAS/fujimoto.html.

Fujita Masakatsu. "Nishida Kitarō to Hēgeru" ["Nishida Kitarō and Hegel"]. In *Nishida tetsugaku: Botsugo gojūnen kinenronbunnshū,* edited by Ueda Shizuteru. Tokyo: Sōbunsha, 1994, pp. 161–181.

———. "The Significance of Japanese Philosophy." *Journal of Japanese Philosophy,* vol. 1, no. 1, Spring 2013, pp. 5–20.

Funayama Shinichi. *Hēgeru tetsugaku to Nishida tetsugaku* [*Hegelian Philosophy and Nishidian Philosophy*]. Tokyo: Miraisha, 1984.

Gábor, Zemplén. "Form as Movement in Goethe's 'The Metamorphosis of Plants.'" http://hps.elte.hu/~zemplen/goethemorph.html.

Gadamer, Hans-Georg. *Dialogue and Dialectic: Eight Hermeneutical Studies on Plato.* Translated by P. Christopher Smith. New Haven, CT: Yale University Press, 1980.

Garfield, Jay L. *Empty Words: Buddhist Philosophy and Cross-Cultural Interpretation.* Oxford: Oxford University Press, 2002.

Gethin, Rupert. *The Foundations of Buddhism.* Oxford: Oxford University Press, 1998.

Goethe, Johann Wolfgang von. *Italian Journey.* Trans. W. H. Auden and Elizabeth Mayer. London: Penguin, 1970.

———. *Sämtliche Werke nach Epochen seines Schaffens Band 12: Zur Naturwissenschaft überhaupt, besonders zur Mophologie.* Munich: Hanser Verlag, 1989.

Goto-Jones, Christopher S. *Political Philosophy in Japan: Nishida, the Kyoto School and Co- prosperity.* London: Routledge, 2005.

Haldane, J. S. *The Philosophical Basis of Biology.* Garden City, NY: Doubleday, Doran, 1931.

Han Fei Tzu (Hanfeizi). *The Complete Works of Han Fei Tzu: A Classic of Chinese Political Science.* Vol. 2. Translated by W. K. Liao. London: Arthur Probsthain, 1959.

Harris, Ian Charles. *The Continuity of Madhyamaka and Yogācāra in Indian Mahāyāna Buddhism.* Leiden, Netherlands: E. J. Brill, 1991.

Harrison, Jane Ellen. *Themis: A Study of the Social Origins of Greek Religion.* Cambridge: Cambridge University Press, 1912.

Hegel, Georg Wilhelm Friedrich. *The Difference between Fichte's and Schelling's System of Philosophy.* Translated by H. S. Harris and Walter Cerf. Albany: SUNY Press, 1977.

———. *Differenz des Fichteschen und Schellingschen Systems der Philosophie.* In *Werke in zwanzig Bänden,* vol. 2. Frankfurt: Suhrkamp, 1970.

———. *The Encyclopaedia Logic (with the Zusätze): Part I of the "Encyclopaedia of Philosophical Sciences."* Translated by T. F. Geraets, W. A. Suchting, and H. S. Harris. Indianapolis: Hackett, 1991.

———. *Enzyklopädie der philosophischen Wissenschaften im Grundrisse.* Edited by Friedhem Nicolin and Otto Pöggeler. Hamburg: Felix Meiner, 1959, 1830.

———. *Grundlinien der Philosophie des Rechts.* Edited by J. Hoffmeister. Berlin: Nicolaischen Buchhandlung, 1833.

———. *Grundlinien der Philosophie des Rechts.* Edited by Johannes Hoffmeister. 4th ed. Hamburg: Felix Meiner, 1955.

———. *Hegel's Logic: Being Part One of the "Encyclopaedia of the Philosophical Sciences" (1830).* Translated by William Wallace. Oxford: Clarendon/Oxford University Press. 1975.

———. *Hegel's Philosophy of Mind: Being Part Three of the "Encyclopaedia of the Philosophical Sciences" (1830).* Translated by William Wallace. Oxford: Clarendon Press, 1971.

———. *Hegel's Philosophy of Right.* Translated by T. M. Knox. Oxford: Oxford University Press, 1967.

———. *Natural Law: The Scientific Ways of Treating Natural Law, Its Place in Moral Philosophy, and Its Relation to the Positive Sciences of Law.* Translated by T.M. Knox. Philadelphia: University of Pennsylvania Press, 1975.

———. *Phänomenologie des Geistes.* Hamburg: Felix Meiner, 1952.

———. *The Phenomenology of Mind.* Translated by J. B. Baillie. London: George Allen and Unwin, 1931, 1910.

———. *Phenomenology of Spirit.* Translated by A. V. Miller. Oxford: Oxford University Press, 1977.

———. *Philosophy of History.* Translated by J. Sibree. Buffalo, NY: Prometheus Books, 1991; New York: Colonial Press, 1899.

———. "Preface to the *Phenomenology.*" In *Hegel: Texts and Commentary,* edited and translated by Walter Kaufmann. Garden City, NY: Doubleday, 1966, 1965.

———. *Science of Logic.* 2 vols. Translated by W. H. Johnston and L. G. Struthers. London: George Allen and Unwin, 1961, 1929.

———. *Science of Logic.* Translated by A. V. Miller. Amherst, NY: Humanity Books, 1969.

———. *System der Sittlichkeit.* Edited by Georg Lasson. Hamburg: Felix Meiner, 1967.

———. *System of Ethical Life and First Philosophy of Spirit.* Edited and translated by H. S. Harris and T. M. Knox. Albany: SUNY Press, 1979.

———. *Werke in zwanzig Bänden.* Vol. 1, *Frühe Schriften,* Theorie–Werkausgabe. Frankfurt: Suhrkamp, 1971.

———. *Werke in zwanzig Bänden.* Vol. 2, *Jenaer Schriften, 1801–1807,* Theorie–Werkausgabe. Frankfurt: Suhrkamp, 1970.

———. *Wissenschaft der Logik.* Pt. 1. Edited by Georg Lasson. Hamburg: Felix Meiner, 1971.

———. *Wissenschaft der Logik.* Pt. 2. Edited by Georg Lasson. Hamburg: Felix Meiner, 1969.

Heidegger, Martin. *Four Seminars.* Translated by Andrew Mitchell and Francois Raffoul. Bloomington: Indiana University Press, 2003.

———. *The Fundamental Concepts of Metaphysics: World, Finitude, Solitude.* Translated by William McNeill and Nicholas Walker. Bloomington: Indiana University Press, 1995.

———. *Die Grundbegriffe der Metaphysik: Welt—Endlichkeit—Einsamkeit.* In: *Gesamtausgabe,* II. Abteilung: *Vorlesungen 1923–1944,* Band 29/30. Frankfurt: Klostermann, 1992, 1983.

———. *The Question Concerning Technology, and Other Essays.* Translated by William Lovitt. New York: Harper Torchbooks, 1977.

———. *Vier Seminare.* In *Gesamtausgabe,* I. Abteilung: *Veröffentlichte Schriften, 1910–1976,* Band 15. Frankfurt: Klostermann, 1986.

Heisig, James W. *Philosophers of Nothingness: An Essay on the Kyoto School.* Honolulu: University of Hawai'i Press, 2001.

Heisig, James W., Thomas P. Kasulis, and John C. Maraldo, eds. *Japanese Philosophy: A Sourcebook.* Honolulu: University of Hawai'i Press, 2011.

Heisig, James W., and John C. Maraldo, eds. *Rude Awakenings: Zen, the Kyoto School, and the Question of Nationalism.* Honolulu: University of Hawai'i Press, 1994.

Heller, Agnes. *A Theory of Modernity.* Oxford: Blackwell. 1999.

Hofstadter, Albert. "How to Escape from Hegel's Aesthetics!" *Graduate Faculty Philosophy Journal,* vol. 9, no. 1, Winter 1982, pp. 5–30.

Holy Bible. New International Version. East Brunswick, NJ: International Bible Society, 1984, 1973.

Holy Bible. Red Letter, Dictionary-Concordance, Revised Standard Version. Nashville: Thomas Nelson, 1972. [Quotations are from this version.]

Huang Wen-hong. "The Shift in Nishida's Logic of Place." In *Frontiers of Japanese Philosophy,* vol. 4, *Facing the Twenty First Century,* edited by Lam Wing-keung and Cheung Ching-yuen. Nagoya: Nanzan Institute for Religion and Culture, 2009, pp. 135–151.

Hubbard, Jamie, and Paul L. Swanson, eds. *Pruning the Bodhi Tree: The Storm over Critical Buddhism.* Honolulu: University of Hawai'i Press, 1997.

Huh, Woo-Sung. "The Philosophy of History in the 'Later' Nishida: A Philosophic Turn." *Philosophy East and West,* vol. 40, no. 3, July 1990, pp. 343–374.

Husserl, Edmund. *Ideas Pertaining to a Pure Phenomenology and to a Phenomenological Philosophy, First Book: General Introduction to a Pure Phenomenology.* Translated by F. Kersten. Dordrecht: Kluwer Academic, 1983.

Hyppolite, Jean. *Genesis and Structure of Hegel's "Phenomenology of Spirit."* Translated by Samuel Cherniak and John Heckman. Evanston, IL: Northwestern University Press, 1974.

———. *Logic and Existence.* Translated by Leonard Lawlor and Amit Sen. Albany: SUNY Press, 1997.

Inoue Enryō. "A View of the Cosmos." In *Japanese Philosophy: A Sourcebook,* edited by James W. Heisig, Thomas P. Kasulis, and John C. Maraldo. Honolulu: University of Hawai'i Press, 2011, pp. 623–627.

Inwood, Michael. *A Hegel Dictionary.* Oxford: Blackwell, 1992.

Irigaray, Luce. *An Ethics of Sexual Difference.* Ithaca, NY: Cornell University Press, 1984.

Isozaki Arata. "Demiourgos in Anywhere." *Anywhere,* vol. 2. Edited by Cynthia C. Davidson. New York: Anyone Corp., 1992, pp. 238–245.

———. "Ma: Japanese Time-Space." *Japanese Architect: International Edition of Shinkenchiku,* no. 262, February 1979, pp. 69–80.

Israel, Joachim. *The Language of Dialectics and the Dialectics of Language.* Atlantic Highlands, NJ: Humanities Press, 1979.

Jacinto-Zavala, Agustin. "The Relationship between the Historical Body and the Environment in Late Nishida Philosophy." *Transactions of the International Conference of Orientalists,* no. 35, 1990, pp. 44–57.

James, William. "A World of Pure Experience." In *The Writings of William James: A Comprehensive Edition,* edited by John J. McDermott. Chicago: University of Chicago Press, 1977, 1967.

———. *The Writings of William James: A Comprehensive Edition.* Edited by John J. McDermott. Chicago: University of Chicago Press, 1977, 1967.

Jammer, Max. *Concepts of Space.* Cambridge, MA: Harvard University Press, 1970.

Jonas, Hans. "The Concept of God after Auschwitz: A Jewish Voice." *The Journal of Religion,* vol. 67, no. 1, 1987, pp. 1–13.

Kazashi, Nobuo. "Bodily Logos: James, Merleau-Ponty, and Nishida." In *Merleau Ponty: Interiority and Exteriority, Psychic Life and the World,* edited by Dorothea Olkowski and James Moreley. Albany: SUNY Press, 1999, pp. 107–120.

Keenan, John P. "Yogācāra." In *Buddhist Spirituality: Indian, Southeast Asian, Tibetan, and Early Chinese,* edited by Takeuchi Yoshinori. New York: Crossroad, 1997, pp. 203–212.

Kierkegaard, Søren. *Concluding Unscientific Postscript.* Translated by David F. Swenson. Princeton, NJ: Princeton University Press, 1941.

———. *Philosophical Fragments; or, A Fragment of Philosophy by Johannes Climacus.* Translated by David F. Swenson. Princeton, NJ: Princeton University Press, 1962.

Kim, Ha Tai. "The Logic of the Illogical: Zen and Hegel." *Philosophy East and West,* vol. 5, no. 1, April 1955, pp. 19–29.

———. "Nishida and Royce." *Philosophy East and West,* vol. 1, no. 4, January 1952, pp. 18–29.

King, Richard. "Early Yogācāra and Its Relationship with the Madhyamaka School." *Philosophy East and West,* vol. 65, no. 9, 1994, pp. 659–683.

Kirk, G. S., J. E. Raven, and M. Schofield, eds. *The Presocratic Philosophers.* Cambridge: Cambridge University Press, 1983, 1957.

Kisiel, Theodore. "Why Students of Heidegger Will Have to Read Emil Lask." *Man and World,* vol. 28, no. 3, 1995, pp. 197–240.

Kopf, Gereon. "Between Foundationalism and Relativism: Locating Nishida's 'Logic of Basho' on the Ideological Landscape." *Nanzan Bulletin,* no. 27, 2003, pp. 24–45.

———. "Between Identity and Difference: Three Ways of Reading Nishida's Non-Dualism." *Japanese Journal of Religious Studies,* vol. 31, no. 1, 2004, pp. 73–103.

———. "Between the Global and the Local: Applying the Logic of the One and the Many to a Global Age." In *Frontiers in Japanese Philosophy,* vol. 4, *Facing the Twenty First Century,* edited by Lam Wing-Keung and Cheung Ching-yuen. Nagoya: Nanzan Institute for Religion and Culture, 2009, pp. 76–89.

———. "Critical Comments on Nishida's Use of Chinese Buddhism." *Journal of Chinese Philosophy,* vol. 32, no. 2, June 2005, pp. 313–329.

———. "Nationalism, Globalism, and Cosmopolitanism." In *Frontiers of Japanese Philosophy,* vol. 6, *Confluences and Cross-Currents,* edited by Raquel Bouso García and James W. Heisig. Nagoya: Nanzan Institute for Religion and Culture, 2009, pp. 170–189.

———. "On the Brink of Postmodernity: Recent Japanese-Language Publications on the Philosophy of Nishida Kitarō." *Japanese Journal of Religious Studies,* vol. 30, nos. 1–2, 2003, pp. 133–156.

———. "Temporality and Personal Identity in the Thought of Nishdia Kitarō." *Philosophy East and West,* vol. 52, no. 2, April 2002, pp. 224–245.

Kosaka Kunitsugu. *Nishida Kitarō no shisō* [*The Thought of Nishida Kitarō*]. Tokyo: Kōdansha, 2003, 2002.

———. *Nishida Kitarō o meguru tetsugakusha gunzō: Kindai nihon tetsugaku to shūkyō* [*Portraits of Philosophers Surrounding Nishida Kitarō: Modern Japanese Philosophy and Religion*]. Kyoto: Mineruva shobō, 1997.

———. *Nishida tetsugaku to gendai: Rekishi, shūkyō, shizen o yomitoku* [*Nishida Philosophy and Today: Reading History, Religion, and Nature*]. Kyoto: Mineruva shobō, 2001.

Kozyra, Agniestika. "Paradokkusu ronri no nihirizumu: Nishida to Haidegā" ["The Nihilism of Paradox Logic: Nishida and Heidegger"]. *Bulletin of the International*

Research Center for Japanese Studies, no. 33, October 2006. Kyoto: Kokusai Nihon Bunka Kenkyū Center, pp. 93–149.

Krummel, John. "*Basho*, World, and Dialectics: An Introduction to the Philosophy of Nishida Kitarō." In *Place and Dialectic: Two Essays by Nishida Kitarō*, translated by John W. M. Krummel and Shigenori Nagatomo. New York: Oxford University Press, 2012, pp. 3–48.

———. "Embodied Implacement in Kūkai and Nishida." *Philosophy East and West*, vol. 65, no. 3, July 2015, forthcoming.

———. "The Originary *Wherein*: Heidegger and Nishida on 'the Sacred' and 'the Religious.'" *Research in Phenomenology*, vol. 40, no. 3, September 2010, pp. 378–407.

———. "'The Place of Nothing' in Nishida as *Chiasma* and *Chōra*." *Diaphany*, vol. 1, no. 1, 2015, forthcoming.

———. "Transcendent or Immanent? Significance and History of *Li* in Confucianism." *Journal of Chinese Philosophy*, vol. 37, no. 3, September 2010, pp. 417–437.

Kuchner, Harold. *When Bad Things Happen to Good People*. New York: Anchor, 2004.

Küng, Hans. *Does God Exist? An Answer for Today*. Translated by Edward Quinn. Garden City, NY: Doubleday, 1980.

Lask, Emil. *Sämtliche Werke*. Vol. 2. Jena: Dietrich Scheglmann, 2003.

Lawler, James. "Hegel on Logical and Dialectical Contradictions, and Misinterpretations from Bertrand Russell to Lucio Colletti." In *Dialectical Contradictions: Contemporary Marxist Discussions*, edited by Erwin Marquit, Philip Moran, and Willis H. Truitt. Minneapolis: Marxist Educational Press, 1982.

Lawlor, Leonard. "Essence and Language: The Rupture in Merleau-Ponty's Philosophy." In *Essays in Celebration of the Founding of the Organization of Phenomenological Organizations*, edited by Chan-Fai Cheung, Ivan Chvatik, Ion Copoeru, Lester Embree, Julia Iribarne, and Hans Rainer Sepp. www.o-p-o.net, 2003.

Lefebvre, Henri. *The Production of Space*. Translated by Donald Nicholson-Smith. Oxford: Blackwell, 1991, 1974.

Leibniz, Gottfried Wilhelm von. *Discourse on Metaphysics, and Other Essays*. Edited by Daniel Garber and Roger Ariew. Indianapolis: Hackett, 1991.

———. *Discourse on Metaphysics, Correspondence with Arnauld, and Monadology*. Translated by George R. Montgomery. LaSalle, IL: Open Court, 1937.

———. *The Monadology, and Other Philosophical Writings*. Translated by Paul Schrecker and Anne Martin Schrecker. Indianapolis: Bobbs-Merrill, 1965.

———. *The Shorter Leibniz Texts: A Collection of New Translations*. Edited by Lloyd Strickland. London: Continuum, 2006.

Lotze, Hermann. *Logic in Three Books: Of Thought, of Investigation, and of Knowledge*. Vol. 2. Translated and edited by Bernard Bosanquet. Oxford: Clarendon Press, 1888.

———. "Philosophy in the Last Forty Years: First Article." In *Kleine Schriften*, vol. 3, pt. 2. Leipzig: S. Hirzel, 1891, pp. 451–479.

Loy, David. *Nonduality: A Study in Comparative Philosophy*. Amherst, NY: Humanity Books, 1998; New Haven, CT: Yale University Press, 1988.

Luft, Sebastian. "Reconstruction and Reduction: Natorp and Husserl on Method and the Question of Subjectivity." In *Neo-Kantianism in Contemporary Philosophy*, edited by Rudolf A. Makkreel and Sebastian Luft. Bloomington: Indiana University Press, 2010, pp. 59–91.

Lukasiewicz, J. "Aristotle on the Law of Contradiction." In *Articles on Aristotle,* vol. 3, *Metaphysics,* edited by Jonathan Barnes, Malcolm Schofield, and Richard Sorabji. New York: St. Martin's Press, 1960, pp. 50–62.

Luria, Isaac. *Kabbalah: A Study of the Ten Luminous Emanations.* Vol. 2. Jerusalem: Research Centre of Kabbalah, 2004.

Makkreel, Rudolf A., and Sebastian Luft, eds. *Neo-Kantianism in Contemporary Philosophy.* Bloomington: Indiana University Press, 2010.

Maly, Kenneth, ed. *Archaic Thinking: Unfolding the Work of John Sallis.* Albany: SUNY Press, 1995.

Maraldo, John C. "The Absolute Present: Chasm or Chiasm of History in Nishida's Philosophy?" In *Nishida tetsugaku,* edited by Ueda Shizuteru. Tokyo: Sōbunsha, 1994, pp. 1–17 (from back flap).

———. "Nishida and the Individualization of Religion." *Zen Buddhism Today: Annual Report of the Kyoto Zen Symposium,* November 1988, manuscript, pp. 70–87.

———. "The Problem of World Culture: Towards an Appropriation of Nishida's Philosophy of Nation and Culture." *Eastern Buddhist,* vol. 28, no. 2, Autumn 1995, pp. 183–197.

———. "The War over the Kyoto School." *Monumenta Nipponica,* vol. 61, no. 3, Autumn 2006, pp. 375–406.

Marquit, Erwin, Philip Moran, and Willis H. Truitt, eds. *Dialectical Contradictions: Contemporary Marxist Discussions.* Minneapolis: Marxist Educational Press, 1982.

Matsumoto Masao. "The Absolute, Relatives and Nothingness." *Revue Internationale de Philosophie,* nos. 107–108, fasc. 1–2, 1974, pp. 69–81.

McCagney, Nancy. *Nāgārjuna and the Philosophy of Openness.* Lanham, MD: Rowman and Littlefield, 1997.

Merleau-Ponty, Maurice. *The Primacy of Perception.* Edited by James Edie. Evanston, IL: Northwestern University Press, 1964.

———. *The Visible and the Invisible.* Translated by Alphonso Lingis. Evanston, IL: Northwestern University Press, 1968.

Moore, Charles A., ed. *Essays in East-West Philosophy: An Attempt at World Philosophical Synthesis.* Honolulu: University of Hawai'i Press, 1951.

Mutai Risaku. *Basho no ronrigaku* [*The Logic of Place*]. Tokyo: Kobushi shobō, 1996.

———. *Shisaku to kansatsu* [*Thought and Observation*]. Tokyo: Keisō shobō, 1968.

Nagao, Gadjin M. *Mādhyamika and Yogācāra: A Study of Mahāyāna Philosophies.* Translated by Leslie S. Kawamura. Albany: SUNY Press, 1991.

Nāgārjuna. *The Fundamental Wisdom of the Middle Way: Nāgārjuna's "Mūlamadhyamakakārikā.* Translated by Jay L. Garfield. Oxford: Oxford University Press, 1995.

———. *Nāgārjuna, the Philosophy of the Middle Way: Mūlamadhyamakakārikā.* Translated by David J. Kalupahana. Albany: SUNY Press, 1986.

Nakamura, Hajime. "Mahāyāna Buddhism." In *Buddhism and Asian History: Religion, History, and Culture,* edited by Joseph M. Kitagawa and Mark D. Cummings. New York: Macmillan, 1987, pp. 215–239.

Nakamura Yūjirō. "Chōetsu—'Zettaimujunteki jikodōitsu'" ["Transcendence: 'Absolutely Contradictory Self-identity'"]. In *Nishida Kitarō.* Tokyo: Midorigawa, 1983, pp. 195–232; and in *Nishida Kitarō I.* Tokyo: Iwanami, 2001, pp. 159–200.

———. *Nishida Kitarō.* Tokyo: Midorigawa, 1983.

———. *Nishida Kitarō I*. Tokyo: Iwanami, 2001.

———. *Nishida Kitarō II*. Tokyo: Iwanami, 2001.

———. *Nishida Kitarō no datsukōchiku* [*The Deconstruction of Nishida Kitarō*]. Tokyo: Iwanami, 1987.

———. "Nishida Kitarō no shūkyōron to rekishiron" ["Nishida Kitarō's Theory of Religion and Theory of History"]. In *Nishida Kitarō no datsukōchiku* [*The Deconstruction of Nishida Kitarō*]. Tokyo: Iwanami, 1987, pp. 217–258; and in *Nishida Kitarō II*. Tokyo: Iwanami, 2001, pp. 199–244.

Nancy, Jean-Luc. *The Inoperative Community*. Minneapolis: University of Minnesota Press, 1991.

Narski, Igor S. "A Commentary on Hegel's Interpretation of 'Contradiction.'" In *Dialectical Contradictions: Contemporary Marxist Discussions*, edited by Erwin Marquit, Philip Moran, and Willis H. Truitt. Minneapolis: Marxist Educational Press, 1982.

Natorp, Paul. *Allgemeine Psychologie nach kritischer Methode: Erstes Buch: Objekt und Methode der Psychologie*. Amsterdam: E. J. Bonset, 1965; Tübingen: Mohr/Siebeck, 1912.

Nicholas of Cusa. *Nicholas of Cusa: Selected Spiritual Writings*. Translated by H. Lawrence Bond. New York: Paulist Press, 1997.

Nīgata Nobukazu. *Mu no hikakuteki shisō—Nōvarisu, Hēgeru, Heidegā kara Nishida e* [*The Comparative Thought of Nothing: From Novalis, Hegel, and Heidegger to Nishida*]. Kyoto: Mineruva shobō, 1998.

Nishitani Keiji. *Nishida Kitarō*. Translated by Yamamoto Seisaku and James W. Heisig. Berkeley: University of California Press, 1991.

Nitta Yoshihiro. "Nishida tetsugaku ni okeru 'tetsugaku no ronri'" ["The 'Logic of Philosophy' in Nishidian Philosophy"]. In *Nishida tetsugaku: Botsugo gojyusshūnen ronbunshū* [*Essays on Nishidian Philosophy Commemorating Fifty Years since the Death of Nishida*], edited by Ueda Shizuteru. Tokyo: Sōbunsha, 1994, pp. 29–49.

Odin, Steve. "The Epochal Theory of Time in Whitehead and Japanese Buddhism: An East-West Study of Whitehead, Dōgen, and Nishida." *Process Studies*, vol. 23, no. 2, Summer 1994, pp. 119–133.

Ogawa, Tadashi. "The Kyoto School of Philosophy and Phenomenology." In *Japanese Phenomenology: Phenomenology as the Trans-cultural Philosophical Approach*, edited by Yoshihiro Nitta and Hirotaka Tatematsu. Analecta Husserliana, vol. 8. Dordrecht: D. Reidel, 1978/1979, pp. 207–221.

Oh, Kang-Nam. "*Dharmadhātu*: An Introduction to Hua-yen Buddhism." *Eastern Buddhist*, vol. 12, no. 2, October 1979, pp. 72–91.

Olson, Carl. *Zen and the Art of Postmodern Philosophy: Two Paths of Liberation from the Representational Mode of Thinking*. Albany: SUNY Press, 2000.

Ōmine Akira. "Gyakutaiō to myōgō—Nishida tetsugaku to Jōdo shinshū" ["Inverse Correspondence and *Myōgō*: Nishidian Philosophy and the True Pure Land School"]. In *Nishida tetsugaku: Botsugo gojyusshūnen ronbunshū* [*Essays on Nishidian Philosophy Commemorating Fifty Years since the Death of Nishida*], edited by Ueda Shizuteru. Tokyo: Sōbunsha, 1994, pp. 417–439.

Park, Jin Y., and Gereon Kopf, eds. *Merleau-Ponty and Buddhism*. Lanham, MD: Lexington Books, 2009.

Parmenides. *Parmenides of Elea*. Translated by David Gallop. Toronto: University of
  Toronto Press, 1984.
Pascal, Blaise, *Pensées*. Translated by A. J. Krailsheimer. London: Penguin, 1995, 1966.
Pinkard, Terry. *Hegel: A Biography*. Cambridge: Cambridge University Press, 2000.
Piovesana, Gino K. "Contemporary Japanese Philosophy." In *Asian Philosophy Today*,
  edited by Dale Riepe. New York: Gordon and Breach, 1981, pp. 223–291.
———. *Recent Japanese Philosophical Thought, 1862–1962: A Survey*. Tokyo: Enderle
  Bookstore, 1968.
Plato. *Complete Works*. Edited by John M. Cooper. Indianapolis: Hackett, 1997.
Plotinus. *The Enneads*. Translated by John Dillon. London: Penguin, 1991.
Plutarch. *Plutarch über die Seelenschöpfung im Timaeus*. Edited by Berthold Müller.
  Breslau: Druck von Grass, Barth und Comp., 1873.
Pradeau, Jean-François. "Être quelque part, occuper une place: *Topos* et *chōra* dans le
  Timée" [Being Somewhere and Occupying a Place: *Topos* and *Chōra* in the
  Timaeus]. *Les études philosophiques*, vol. 3, 1995, pp. 375–400.
Putney, David. "Identity and the Unity of Experience: A Critique of Nishida's Theory
  of Self." *Asian Philosophy*, vol. 1, no. 2, 1991, pp. 141–60. Also available online at
  http://sino-sv3.sino.uni-heidelberg.de/FULLTEXT/JR-ADM/putney.htm.
Raud, Rein. "'Place' and 'Being-Time': Spatiotemporal Concepts in the Thought of
  Nishida Kitarō and Dōgen Kigen." *Philosophy East and West*, vol. 54, no. 1,
  January 2004, pp. 29–51.
Reck, Andrew J. "Aristotle's Concept of Substance in the Logical Writings." *Southwest-
  ern Journal of Philosophy*, vol. 3, Spring 1972, pp. 7–15.
Royce, Josiah. *The World and the Individual*. Vols. 1 and 2. New York: Dover, 1959.
———. *The World and the Individual, Second Series: Nature, Man, and the Moral Order*.
  New York: Macmillan Co., 1904.
Sallis, John. *Chorology: On Beginning in Plato's "Timaeus."* Bloomington: Indiana
  University Press, 1999.
Sambursky, Shmuel. *The Concept of Place in Late Neoplatonism* Jerusalem: Israel
  Academy of Sciences and Humanities, 1982.
Schopenhauer, Arthur. *The World as Will and Representation*. Translated by E. F. J.
  Payne. New York: Dover, 1969, 1958.
Schultz, Lucy. "Nishida Kitarō, G. W. F. Hegel, and the Pursuit of the Concrete: A Dialectic
  of Dialectics." *Philosophy East and West*, vol. 62, no. 3, July 2012, pp. 319–338.
Schürmann, Reiner. *Broken Hegemonies*. Bloomington: Indiana University Press, 2003.
———. *Heidegger on Being and Acting: From Principles to Anarchy*. Bloomington:
  Indiana University Press, 1987.
Shinran. *The Collected Works of Shinran*. Vol. 1, *The Writings*. Kyoto: Jōdo Shinshū
  Hongwanji-ha, 1997.
Spinoza, Benedict de. *On the Improvement of the Understanding; The Ethics; Correspon-
  dence*. Translated by R. H. M. Elwes. New York: Dover, 1955, 1883.
Stambaugh, Joan. *Impermanence is Buddha-Nature: Dōgen's Understanding of Temporal-
  ity*. Honolulu: University of Hawai'i Press, 1990.
Stevens, Bernard. "Self in Space: Nishida Philosophy and Phenomenology of Maurice
  Merleau Ponty." In *Merleau-Ponty and Buddhism*, edited by Jin Y. Park and
  Gereon Kopf. Lanham, MD: Lexington Books, 2009, pp. 133–140.

Suares, Peter. *The Kyoto School's Takeover of Hegel: Nishida, Nishitani, and Tanabe Remake the Philosophy of Spirit.* Lanham, MD: Lexington Books, 2011.

Sueki Takehiro. *Nishida Kitarō: Sono tetsugaku taikei [Nishida Kitarō and His System of Philosophy].* Vol. 1. Tokyo: Shunshūsha, 1983.

Suzuki, Daisetz Teitarō. *Collected Writings on Shin Buddhism.* Kyoto: Shinshū Ōtaniha, 1973.

———. "How to Read Nishida." In *A Study of Good,* by Nishida Kitarō. Translated by V. H. Viglielmo. Tokyo: Japanese Government, 1960, pp. iii–vi.

———. *Kongōkyō no Zen [The Zen of the Diamond Sūtra].* In *Suzuki Daisetsu zen senshū* vol. 4. Tokyo: Shunshūsha, 2001, 1991, pp. 1–117.

———. *Kongō-kyō no Zen [The Zen of the Diamond Sūtra].* In *Suzuki Daisetsu zenshū [Collected Works],* vol. 5. Tokyo: Iwanami, 2000, pp. 363–455.

———. "Reason and Intuition in Buddhist Philosophy." In *Essays in East-West Philosophy: An Attempt at World Philosophical Synthesis,* edited by Charles A. Moore. Honolulu: University of Hawai'i Press, 1951, pp. 17–48.

———. *Studies in Zen.* Edited by Christmas Humphreys. New York: Dell, 1955.

Swanson, Paul L. *The Foundations of T'ien-T'ai Philosophy: The Flowering of the Two Truths Theory in Chinese Buddhism.* Berkeley, CA: Asian Humanities Press, 1989.

Tachikawa, Musashi. "The Tetralemma in Chinese *Hua-Yen* School: In Comparison with That of the Madhyamaka-Kārika." In *Kalyāṇa-mitta: Professor Hajime Nakamura Felicitation Volume,* edited by V. N. Jha. Delhi: Sri Satguru, Indian Books Centre, 1991, pp. 87–100.

Takakusu Junjiro. *The Essentials of Buddhist Philosophy.* Westport, CT: Greenwood Press, 1956.

Takakusu Junjiro and Watanabe Kaigyoku, eds. *Taishō shinshū daizōkyō,* vol. 45. Tokyo: Taishō shinshū daizōkyō kankōkai, 1968.

Takeda Hiromichi. "Brief Note on Nishida's Doctrine of Universals." *Monumenta Nipponica,* vol. 23, nos. 3–4, 1968, pp. 497–502.

Takemura Makio. *Nishida Kitarō to Bukkyō—Zen to Shinshū no kontei o kiwameru [Nishida Kitarō and Buddhism: Mastering the Roots of Zen and Shinshū].* Tokyo: Daitō shuppan, 2002.

Takeuchi Yoshinori, ed. *Buddhist Spirituality: Indian, Southeast Asian, Tibetan, and Early Chinese.* New York: Crossroad, 1997.

———. "The Philosophy of Nishida." In *The Buddha Eye: An Anthology of the Kyoto School,* edited by Frederick Franck. New York: Crossroad, 1991, 1982, pp. 179–202.

Tanabe Hajime. *Tanabe Hajime zenshū yon maki [Tanabe Hajime Collected Works vol. 4].* Tokyo: Chikuma shobō, 1963.

Taylor, Charles. *Hegel.* New York: Cambridge University Press, 1975.

Thurman, Robert A. F. "Voidness and Totalities: Mādhyamika and Hua Yen." In *Studies in History of Buddhism,* edited by A. K. Narain. Delhi: B. R. Pub. Corp, 1980.

Tucker, John Allen. "Nāgārjuna's Influence on Early *Hua-yen* and *Ch'an* Thought." *Chinese Culture: A Quarterly Review,* vol. 25, no. 2, June 1984, pp. 43–61.

Ueda Shizuteru. "Nishida, Nationalism, and the War in Question." In *Rude Awakenings: Zen, the Kyoto School, and the Question of Nationalism,* edited by James W. Heisig and John C. Maraldo. Honolulu: University of Hawai'i Press, 1994, pp. 77–106.

———, ed. *Nishida tetsugaku: Botsugo gojyusshūnen ronbunshū* [*Essays on Nishidian Philosophy Commemorating Fifty Years since the Death of Nishida*]. Tokyo: Sōbunsha, 1994.

———, ed. *Nishida tetsugaku e no toi* [*Questioning Nishidian Philosophy*]. Tokyo: Iwanami shoten, 1991, 1990.

———. "Pure Experience, Self-Awareness, 'Basho.'" *Etudes phénoménologiques*, vol. 18, 1993, pp. 63–86.

Unno, Taitetsu. "San-lun, T'ien-T'ai, and Hua-yen." In *Buddhist Spirituality: Indian, Southeast Asian, Tibetan, and Early Chinese,* edited by Takeuchi Yoshinori. New York: Crossroad, 1997, pp. 343–365.

Vahabzadeh, Peyman. "Of Hegemonies Yet to Be Broken: Rhetoric and Philosophy in the Age of Accomplished Metaphysics." *European Legacy: Toward New Paradigms,* vol. 10, no. 4, July 2005, pp. 375–388.

Vasubandhu. *Seven Works of Vasubandhu: The Buddhist Psychological Doctor.* Translated and edited by Stefan Anacker. Delhi: Motilal Banarsidass, n.d.

Vattimo, Gianni. *The End of Modernity: Nihilism and Hermeneutics in Postmodern Culture.* Translated by Jon R. Snyder. Baltimore: Johns Hopkins University Press, 1985.

Verdú, Alfonso. *Dialectical Aspects in Buddhist Thought: Studies in Sino-Japanese Mahāyāna Idealism.* Lawrence: Center for East Asian Studies, University of Kansas, 1974.

———. *The Philosophy of Buddhism: A "Totalistic" Synthesis.* The Hague: Martinus Nijhoff, 1981.

Waldenfels, Hans. "Absolute Nothingness: Preliminary Considerations on a Central Notion in the Philosophy of Nishida Kitarō and the Kyoto School." *Monumenta Nipponica,* vol. 21, nos. 3–4, 1966, pp. 354–391.

Wargo, James J. J. *The Logic of Nothingness: A Study of Nishida Kitarō.* Honolulu: University of Hawai'i Press, 2005.

Wilkinson, Robert. *Nishida and Western Philosophy.* Burlington, VT: Ashgate, 2009.

Yuasa Yasuo. *The Body: Toward an Eastern Mind-Body Theory.* Translated by Shigenori Nagatomo and Thomas Kasulis. Albany: SUNY Press, 1987.

Yusa, Michiko. "Contemporary Buddhist Philosophy." In *A Companion to World Philosophies,* edited by Eliot Deutsch and Ron Bontekoe. Oxford: Blackwell, 1999, 1997, pp. 564–572.

———. "From *Topos* to Environment: A Conversation with Nishida Kitarō." In *The Future of Religion: Postmodern Perspectives,* edited by Christopher Lamb and Dan Cohn-Sherbok. London: Middlesex University Press, 1999, pp. 112–127.

———. "The Religious Worldview of Nishida Kitarō." *Eastern Buddhist,* vol. 20, no. 2, Autumn 1987, pp. 63–76.

———. *Zen and Philosophy: An Intellectual Biography of Nishida Kitarō.* Honolulu: University of Hawai'i Press, 2002.

Zimmermann, Maren. "Nishida's 'Self-Identity of Absolute Contradiction' and Hegel: Absolute Negation and Dialectics." In *Frontiers of Japanese Philosophy,* vol. 1, edited by James W. Heisig. Nagoya: Nanzan Institute for Religion and Culture, 2006, pp. 184–204.

Index

The index is limited to the appearance of words or names in the text and notes, and excludes their appearance in bibliographical references or the lexicon.

Abe, Masao, 187, 244n31, 245n2, 252n17, 255n12, 255n15, 258n55

absolute (*zettai*), 31, 42, 124–136, 151–155, 159–163, 171–179, 181–185, 187–188, 204–207, 262n40; dethronement of, 143; discontinuity, 81; essence, 16; and finite, 2, 135, 136, 137, 177, 181, 184, 187, 194; and God, 119, 120, 125, 252n11; in Hegel, 34, 145, 150, 255n25, 152; homogeneity, 250n17; horizon, 265n18; idea as, 27; idea of, 36; independence, 81, 97; and infinite, 257n23; infinite force, 151; irreducibility, 247n14; locus, 113; metaphysical, 145; in Nicholas of Cusa, 252n8; nothing as, 25; ontological, 143; and relative, 39, 41, 125, 126, 127, 128, 129, 133, 134, 172, 176, 196, 197, 198, 241n18, 244n28, 245n41, 262n40; in Royce, 246n12; rupture, 103; and the sacred, 125; and self, 125; self-conception, 145; self-limitation of, 35; standpoint of, 36; substantiality, 29, 99, 174; title of, 224

absolute alterity, 185, 187

absolute cognition, 35

absolute concept, 101, 148, 198; in Hegel, 46, 146, 150, 157, 226, 267n53; qua predicate, 192; substance as, 33; of the whole, 33

absolute contradiction (or absolutely contradictory), 106, 110, 125, 127, 179

absolute conversion, 188

absolute death, 77

absolute dialectic (*zettai benshōhō*), 98–99, 159, 162–163, 175, 177, 211, 213–215; and chiasma, 193, 207; as chiasmalogy, 201; as chiasmatic chorology, 191, 226; and chōra, 207; concept of, 60; as dialectic of place, 254n3; and Hegel's dialectic, 211; position of, 152; reciprocity of, 148; source of, 125; system of, 144; thought of, 7; world of, 7

absolute freedom, 97, 184–185

absolute I, 61

absolute idea, 35, 46, 67, 143, 149, 163, 243n16, 245n41

absolute idealism, 36, 59, 150

absolute identity, 32, 109

absolute love (*zettai ai*), 129

absolute movement, 177

absolute negation (*zettai hitei*), 80, 91, 99–101, 111, 126–128, 130–131, 153–154, 162, 171–173, 226; affirmation of, 108, 185; of God, 177; logic of, 210; as structure of basho, 261n20

absolute nothing (*zettai mu*), 2–4, 65–74, 110–117, 125–130, 171–173, 177–179, 226, 262n40; and absolute dialectic, 162; and absolute negation, 101; as basho, 197, 204; and chiasma, 193; concept of, 37, 47; and contradictory self-identity, 120; encompassing opposites, 192; and environment, 99; formlessness of, 97; as ground, 25–26; logic of, 210; and Mahāyāna, 167; non-substantiality as, 190; notion of, 249n10; and place, 61, 197, 205; as place, 60, 78, 213, 225; qua being, 99; self-determination of, 91, 94, and self-negation, 192; universal as, 181. *See also* place of absolute nothing

absolute one, 126, 130, 135, 163, 178

absolute opposites (or absolute opposition), 109, 110

absolute other (*zettai ta*), 81, 115

absolute other-power, 188

absolute paradox, 177, 253n23

absolute place, 198

absolute present (*zettai genzai*), 91, 114, 124, 134, 135–136, 182–184, 188, 222, 263n51

absolute principle, 160, 199, 251n2

absolute rest, 177

absolute spirit (*absoluter Geist*), 143, 150, 152–155, 161, 191

absolute subject, 153, 163

absolute substance, 94, 163, 174, 198

absolute truth, 38

absolute unity, 34

absolute will (*zettai ishi*), 7–8, 23, 28, 30, 51–53, 56–58, 60–61, 133

non-dualism, 2, 5, 13–14, 56, 59, 76; Buddhist, 168, 264n4; concrete, 83; dialectical, 14, 223; Mahāyāna, 3, 29–30, 36–37, 39, 42, 44–45, 47, 52, 91, 164, 167–168, 176, 178, 189, 191, 207, 243n16; Nishida's, 51, 53, 172, 199, 223. *See also* non-duality

non-duality: of being and sense, 21; between saṃsāra and nirvāṇa, 130, 179, 184, 253n19; between thing-events and emptiness, 41;concrete, 87, 117; of the concrete, 59, 80; and emptiness, 37, 42; of individual and universal, 171; of inner and outer, 80; Mahāyāna, 41, 141, 168; of opposites, 47; pre-dichotomized, 45; reciprocal, 133; self-seeing in, 76; in soku-hi, 125; of subject and predicate, 76. *See also* non-dualism

non-obstruction (*muge*), 41–42, 46, 93, 167, 170, 179–182, 189. See also *lishi wuai*; *shishi wuai*

non-substantiality (*mukitei*), 72, 179, 213; of being, 78; of concrete reality, 100; and dialectic, 99; of dialectical universal, 94, 99, 111; of the field, 112; of God, 128, 130; of the ground of knowledge and being, 71; immeasurable depth of, 135; impermanence as, 130; of the nothing, 172; the nothing as, 113, 115, 190; of opposites, 173; of the place of nothing, 181; of predicate, 72; of the present, 115; of the real, 99, 125; at the root of existence, 78; of the self, 107, 130; of substance, 111; temporal, 114; of time, 115; of the universal, 94, 97, 99, 181; of the world, 163

nothing (*mu*), 52, 67–75, 110–113, 119–121, 151–155, 170–176, 193, 203–205; and the absolute, 126; the absolute as, 161, 196, 262n40; abyssal, 130, 153, 201, 264n15; amorphous, 203; awareness of, 210; and being/s, 2, 25, 39, 40, 63, 77, 94, 99, 126, 130, 133, 152, 160, 178, 179, 197, 198, 214, 244n28; the beyond as, 201; in Buddhism, 30, 37, 167; Buddhist, 171; concrete reality as, 63; and concrete universal, 65; and contradictory self-identity, 105; culture of, 223; in Daoism, 37; dark, 131; and death, 104; desubstantializing, 128; dialectic of, 152, 163; dialectics and, 142, 146, 164; Eastern, 175; eternal, 113; fecund, 192; field of, 70, 255n22; field of consciousness as, 25; formless, 206; foundational, 83; as giving space, 218; as horizon, 201; intuition of, 210; kōan of, 165; literal, 26; logic of, 209; in Mahāyāna, 36, 37, 142; medium of, 104; and monism, 198; non-differentiated, 74; non-substantial, 112, 172; as one and many, 63; originary, 72; and place, 64, 246n3; as place, 172, 192, 219; place delimited by, 58, 64, 102,

104, 157, 161, 200; place encompassed by, 200; place environed by, 221; predicate as, 26; primal, 219; pure, 186; of reality, 162; and the self, 130–131; self-awareness of, 258n48; self-determination of, 75, 112, 160, 172; self-mirroring of, 76; self-negating, 74, 126, 204; self-negation of, 74, 172; self-realization of, 111; as suchness, 244n31; unconceptualizable, 145; undelimited, 65, 115, 134, 214; as undelimitable nothing, 201; undeterminable, 78; universal, 68; universal as, 63, 99, 101; universal delimited by, 101; universal of, 111, 112, 195, 255n10; as the unlimited sphere, 195; utter, 39–40, 43–44, 192, 198; will as, 58; world-denying, 44; world qua, 108; in Zen, 37, 45, 167. *See also* absolute nothing; *Nichts*; oppositional nothing; place of absolute nothing; place of nothing; place of oppositional nothing; place of relative nothing; place of true nothing; true nothing

object logic (*taishō ronri*), 15, 18, 66, 143, 159, 177, 214; of Aristotle, 21, 24; of Aristotelian logic, 109; of Hegel, 66, 148, 159, 175; of Kant, 21

one is many, 99, 148, 169, 175. See also *ichi soku ta*

ontology, 224; in Aristotle, 200; in Plato, 17

oppositional nothing (*tairitsuteki mu*), 25, 65, 70, 74, 201. *See also* place of oppositional nothing; relative nothing

ordinary mind (*byōjōshin*), 184, 254n30

Ortzeit, 115. *See also* place-time

other-power (*tariki*), 132, 170, 173, 187–188, 253n18, 253n22, 258n46, 258n58

ought, the (*tōi*), 57, 115, 246n14. See also *Sollen*

ousia, 15–16, 22, 106, 200, 262n42, 263n45; logic of, 199

paradox (*mujun*), 92, 97, 113, 115, 127, 173, 198, 208, 241n2; of absolute self-contradiction, 127; of absolute-self correlation, 133; of the concrete, 127; of concrete reality, 213; as contradiction, 211–212; of contradictory self-identity, 125; existence as, 163, 186; of God, 129, 253n23; in Kierkegaard, 187, 253n23; logic of, 125, 144, 175–176, 211; in Merleau-Ponty, 193; in Paul, 186; of a philosophical system, 213; in the *Prajñāpāramitā sūtras*, 178; relationships of, 82; thought patterns of, 43; as trans-logical, 212; unity of, 47, 187; in Zen, 191–192. *See also* absolute paradox; contradiction

paramārtha, 38, 178

Rahner, Karl, 252n17

relative nothing (*sōtai mu*), 70, 25, 74, 201. *See also* oppositional nothing; place of relative nothing

religion (*shūkyō*), 9, 119, 128–134; Abrahamic, 183; and contradiction, 165; and contradictory self-identity, 125, 169; dialectic of, 52, 119, 120, 141, 176, 185; of Eastern nothing, 175; as the end of philosophy, 165; and globalism, 225; God or, 119, 125, 154; grace-oriented, 185; and ground of reality, 120; and inverse correspondence, 186–187; of other-power, 253n22; Persian, 183; phenomenon of, 124; philosophy of, 168, 176, 254n28; self-awareness in, 173; of self-power, 253n22; standpoint of, 136

religious consciousness (*shūkyōteki ishiki*), 170

reverse determination (*gyaku gentei*), 83; of the chiasma, 195, 249n3; and the dialectical universal, 93, 252n13; of the environment, 97; and self-negation, 127; of the universal, 96–97, 111–112, 114, 128, 161, 181–183, 194; and the universal's self-negation, 100, 112; of the world, 98. *See also* counter-determination

Rickert, Heinrich, 20, 56, 57

Rinzairoku (*Linji yū lū*), 165, 168

Royce, Josiah, 56, 246n12, 248n2

rūpa, 37, 173, 243n18

Sache, 141, 149, 191, 213

Sallis, John, 3, 206, 262n38, 262n42, 263n49

saṃsāra: bondage to, 38; and nirvāṇa, 2, 38–40, 44, 130, 173, 178–179, 184, 187, 211, 253n19; and paratantra, 40; transcendence of, 44

saṃvṛti, 38, 178

San-lun, 127, 179

satori, 131. *See also* enlightenment

Schelling, Friedrich, 31, 154, 155

Schopenhauer, Arthur, 54, 57

Schürmann, Reiner, 67, 247n13

self-awareness (*jikaku*), 7–8, 28, 51–53, 56–62, 80, 128, 134, 173, 205, 239n6; of the absolute, 155; of absolute nothing, 113, 170; of the acting self, 90; and angst, 130; authentic, 136; and basho, 23; and the body, 89; and concrete whole, 23; creative act of, 122; deepening of, 73; determining act of, 66; and dialectics, 90; as finite, 184; of finitude, 132, 210; and God, 119; of the individual, 128, 132; of inner contradiction, 130; interiority of, 109; of life, 78; and life and death, 77, 119, 123; mirroring the absolute, 136; and the nothing, 72, 171, 201,

214, 258n48; of one amid many, 214; and the other, 81, 119; psychologism of, 23; of reality, 1; religious, 132, 135–136, 173; self-contradiction of, 74; self-mirroring, 23, 64, 69; self-seeing, 214; of sin, 188, 212; of singularity, 196; system of, 205; theory of place and, 27; true, 175; via acting-intuition, 88; via self-negation, 108; vision of, 177; and the world, 83, 86, 88, 92, 109, 111, 121, 123; of the world, 88, 90, 121, 123, 132

self-contradiction (*jiko mujun*), 60, 73, 175, 177; of the absolute, 126, 130, 135; according to Nāgārjuna, 38; dialectic of, 3, 189, 211; of dialectical universal, 106; existential awareness of, 173, 185; existential sense of, 212; in generation-and-extinction, 210; in Hegel, 153; of human existence, 77–78, 130, 253n21; of the individual, 161, 175; of life, 128; in life and death, 119; of microcosm and macrocosm, 128; of the ordinary, 136; paradox of, 127; of place, 73; place of, 15; primal source of, 219; of the self, 74, 130; and self-determination, 105; vis-à-vis death, 128, 144; of the will, 58, 64; of the world, 106, 108. *See also* absolute contradiction; contradiction

self-identity of opposites (*sōhansurumono no jikodōitsu*), 105

self-negation (*jiko hitei*), 1–4, 42–44, 70–74, 99–106, 111–117, 119, 126–137, 185–189, 219–224; of the absolute, 128–131, 134, 171–173, 177, 184, 262n40; of the absolute present, 135; affirmation in, 192; of chōra, 206; contradictory, 134; creative, 171; in the creative act, 123; dialectic of, 37, 91, 211, 226; dialectical ethics of, 253n24; divine, 132; divine incarnation as, 253n23; of divine love, 177; of each moment, 157, 183; exhaustive, 198; existential, 186; global, 220; of God, 129, 130, 135, 154, 187, 253n21; in Hegel, 153; of the holistic one, 123; of the individual, 123, 132, 135, 192; inter-dimensional, 198; in Judaism, 253n24; of man, 172; in the matrix, 198; mutual, 39, 52, 72, 82, 100–102, 106, 110, 111, 116, 117, 121, 123–125, 129, 131–134, 145, 159, 162, 167, 172, 177–179, 186, 187, 192, 195, 197, 198, 207, 215, 219–221; and nihilism, 192; of nothing, 74, 172; in Paul, 173; of place, 192, 198; as positive, 192; in Pure Land Buddhism, 253n18; in the realm of interrelations, 182; of the self, 132, 172; and self-affirmation, 192; self-awareness via, 108, 177; self-determination in, 76; self-expression in, 124; self-identity in, 173; spirit of, 221; of the universal, 100, 151, 162; vis-à-vis

dynamism of, 54, 80, 86–88, 109; and element, 198; entire, 62; environing, 58, 225; epistemological dimension of, 63; establishment, 185; of everyday existence, 184; of experience, 27; expression of, 120, 121; of expression, 63–64, 120; exterior, 81; formation/s of, 84, 87, 88, 194, 196, 222; formativity of, 90; generation and extinction in, 258n58; global, 6, 9, 141, 218, 219, 224; and globalism, 265n23; God's relation with, 129, 177; of the grammatical subject, 74, 93; in Hegel, 144, 160; Hegelian approach to, 46; in Heidegger, 264n12; of historical actuality (*rekishiteki genjitsu no sekai*), 84; of historical reality, 108; historical unfolding of, 82; history of, 36, 44, 152, 156, 196, 206, 210, 211, 219; holism of, 106; as horizon, 201; horizonal, 218; implacement in, 201, 225; of implacement, 84; implacement in the open, 261n29; and individual, 29, 177, 180, 244n28; individuals of, 128, 160; of individual/s, 4, 100, 101, 105, 161, 172, 181; of interaction, 30, 78, 84, 85, 87, 194; interaction with, 26, 172; interactive, 105; of interactivity, 109, 151; interactivity in, 4, 26, 83, 120; of interdetermination, 40, 161–162; interrelationality of, 182; in James, 245n9, 248n8; and language, 18; of life, 85, 120; lived, 26; logos-structure of, 108; of many, 116, 126; of matter, 83; -matrix, 116, 117, 179, 250n16; matrix of, 198, 201; meaning of, 58; of meanings, 205; in Merleau-Ponty, 259–260n8; of mind, 62; mind-related, 39; and the moment, 117, movement-in-stillness of, 115; multicultural, 218; natural, 69; non-substantiality of, 163; objective, 34; of objects, 20, 25, 54, 57, 62, 70, 74, 194; in Parmenides, 17; and particular, 180; particular (*tokushteki sekai*), 219, 221; of the personal self, 116; phenomenal, 25, 44; philosophy, 4, 6, 169, 189, 190, 226; as place, 201, 261n28; as place, 64, 84, 86, 129, 137, 192, 223; place of, 110, 134, 192, 205; in Plato, 202; *poiēsis* of, 86, 87, 90, 93; and the present, 116; qua dialectical universal, 41, 95, 198; qua uni-

versal, 41, 106, 110; of reality, 63; realization of, 160; redemption of, 129; of relative beings, 42; in Royce, 248n2; and self, 58, 60, 62, 198; self-awareness of, 88, 132; self-contradictory, 107, 145; of self-determination, 161–162; self-creation of, 96, 194; self-creative, 94, 135; self-creativity of, 86, 112, 161; self-determination of, 82, 88, 92, 93, 96, 97, 121, 123, 128, 137, 148, 161, 181, 257n28; self-expression of, 107, 120, 122, 123; self-expressive, 90, 121, 136; self-formation of, 80, 88, 89, 98, 121, 124, 180, 192, 197, 202; of self-formations, 85; self-mirroring of, 121; and self-negation, 162; sense-, 67; social, 82, 83, 104, 145, 190; soul of, 34; source of, 130; spatial, 117; spatiality of, 116, 198, 251n19; spatiotemporal, 28, 107; subjectivity of, 155; substance of, 94; of substances, 17–19; substantialist view of, 14; surrounding, 83, 88; of things, 44, 62, 192; of things-in-themselves, 31; of transience, 126; unfolding of, 144–145, 201; universal of, 93; volitional dimension of, 63; Western, 189; and will, 58; world-historical (*sekaishiteki sekai*), 220; in Yogācāra, 39. *See also* dialectical world; historical world; life-world; sociohistorical world

worldism (*sekaishugi*), 122, 220

world-of-worlds (*sekaiteki sekai*), 218–223, 225, 266n39, 267n52. *See also* multi-world

wu, 167. *See also Nichts*; nothing

Yogācāra, 37, 39, 40, 44, 46

zazen, 170, 182

Zen, 2, 37, 42–45, 129–132, 134–136, 165–170, 182–185, 208, 256n6; discourse, 191; and Dōgen, 172–173, 189; and Hegel, 29–30, 226; form of meditation, 36, 142, 217; and Linji, 189; and Myōchō, 177; Nishida's practice of, 188; and the nothing in, 37; prāxis, 4; as religion of self-power, 253n22; and Suzuki, 36, 175; thought, 189. *See also* Chan, *zazen*

Zhiyi, 40

JOHN W. M. KRUMMEL received his PhD in philosophy from the New School for Social Research in 1999 and his PhD in religion from Temple University in 2008. His dissertation at the New School was on Heidegger and Kant, and his dissertation at Temple University was on the dialectic of Nishida. His writings on various topics (many on Heidegger, Nishida, Schürmann, and Buddhist philosophy but also on other topics) have been, or will be, published in *Auslegung, PoMo Magazine, Dao, International Philosophical Quarterly, Existentia, Philosophy Today, Vera Lex, Journal of Chinese Philosophy, Research in Phenomenology, Philosophy East and West,* and *H-Net,* as well as in several books as chapters. He is the co-translator of, and author of the introduction for, *Place and Dialectic: Two Essays by Nishida Kitarō* (New York: Oxford University Press, 2011). His other translations of philosophical works from both German and Japanese into English have appeared in books and journals. He is assistant editor of the *Journal of Japanese Philosophy* (SUNY Press) and co-editor of *Social Imaginaries* (Zeta Books). His scholarly interests include Continental philosophy, phenomenology, Heidegger, Schürmann, Kant, Nietzsche, Castoriadis, Buddhism, Dōgen, Kūkai, Japanese and Kyoto school philosophy, Nishida, Nishitani, Dostoevsky, Mishima, comparative philosophy and religion, nihilism, the social imaginary, the philosophy of religion, anarchism, and mysticism, among others. He was born and raised in Tokyo, Japan, in a bilingual family. He is currently an associate professor in the Department of Religious Studies at Hobart and William Smith Colleges in Geneva, New York.

CPSIA information can be obtained at www.ICGtesting.com
Printed in the USA
BVOW02*0317200815

414224BV00009B/44/P